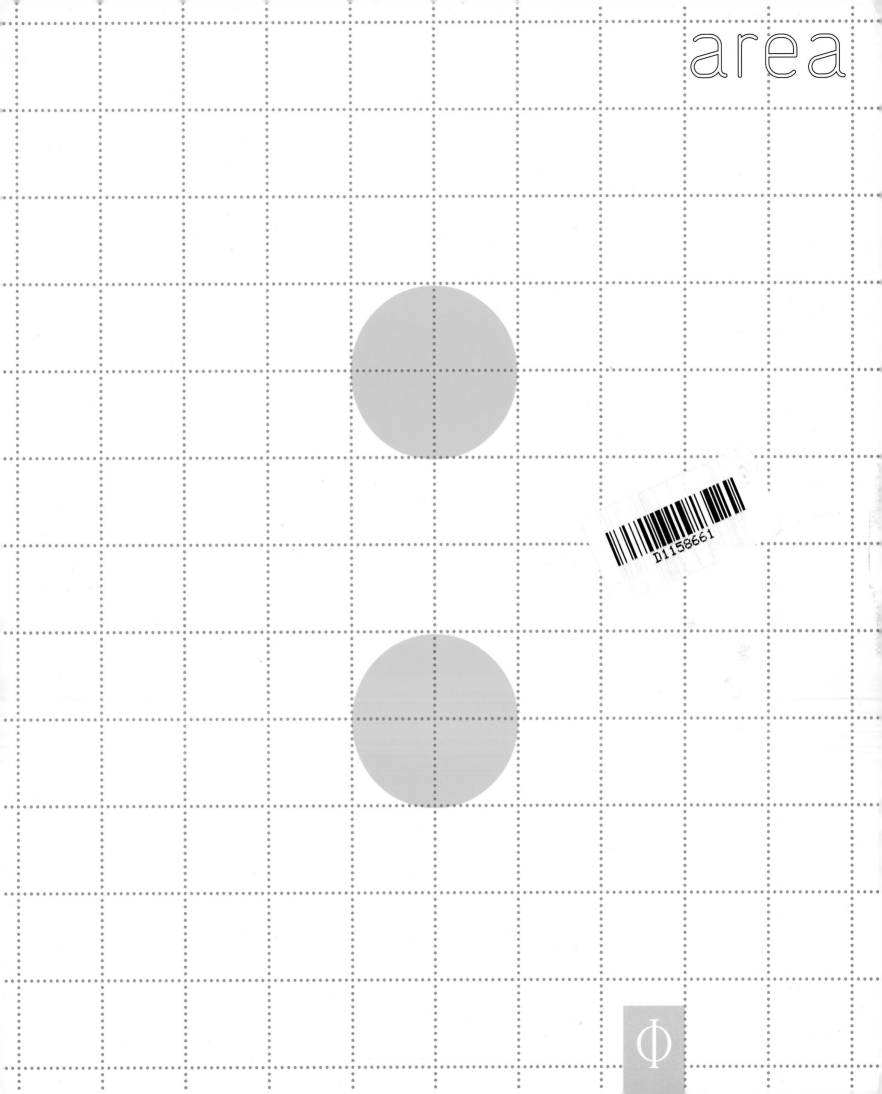

area

contents

100 graphic designers

010 curators

010 design classics

Phaidon Press Limited

Regent's Wharf

All Saints Street

London N1 9PA

Phaidon Press Inc.

180 Varick Street

New York, NY 10014

www.phaidon.com

First published 2003

Reprinted in paperback (twice) 2005, 2006, 2007

© 2003 Phaidon Press Limited

Images © the graphic designers unless otherwise stated

ISBN 978 0 7148 4515 9

A CIP catalogue record of this book is available from the British Library.

Editor: Valérie Vago-Laurer

Project Editor: Patrick Busse

Editorial Assistant: Jesse Donaldson

Designer: Julia Hasting

Production Manager: Karen Farquhar

Printed in China

Acknowledgements

Special thanks are due to the 100 designers and the ten curators: Anthon Beeke, Nick
Bell, Ken Cato, Shigeo Fukuda, Fernando Gutiérrez, Werner Jeker, Uwe Loesch, Stefan
Sagmeister, Serge Serov, Omar Vulpinari. Special thanks are also extended to Sacha
Happee of Studio Anthon Beeke and Elise Bufton of Cato Partners for their invaluable
contributions. Thank you to Elisabeth Johnson for copyediting and Heidi Bek, Fay
Maruyama, Studio Anthon Beeke, and Alex Padalka for translation. Werner Jeker would
like to thank Elisabeth Schwarzenbeck of Les Ateliers du Nord for her assistance in the
writing of his texts.

The publisher would also like to thank the following for their assistance in providing the
images for various graphic designers and the design classics: *Eye, The International
Review of Graphic Design*, London's Transport Museum, Niklaus Troxler, Alain Weill,
Elisabeth Schwarzenbeck, and Anne-Claude Lelieur of the Bibliothèque Forney, Paris.
Thanks also to Nico Schweizer of Mediadub.com for providing *area*'s typeface Typ 1441.

area is an exhibition in a book dedicated to 100 of the most significant new graphic designers today. It brings together the curatorial input of ten distinguished design leaders from around the world, each asked to select their ten favorite "rising stars"— graphic designers who have emerged and broken new ground over the last five years. The curators are internationally respected teachers, practitioners, and art directors recognized not only for their own work, but also for their active involvement in the current scene. Their choices are organized in an A to Z order with each designer's work represented in four pages, along with an introductory text written by the selecting curator.

area's roster of 100 designers is characterized not by one theme but rather by its diversity. From the rebirth of the elegant, detail-driven Swiss school to an embrace of a more playful, unstructured, and, at times, even vulgar aesthetic; from the glorification of a technology-driven process to the re-emergence of the heroic amateur and the "home-made"; from the development of a truly international, interconnected, and inter-disciplinary medium to the rise of regional styles, it documents the trends shaping today's graphic-design culture.

Like all the graphic work featured in this book, *area* is defined by its choices. The curators were limited to a selection of ten and a representative sampling of works from each designer's portfolio. For coherency, Web design and motion graphics were excluded from this study. Yet it is precisely these focused parameters that make it possible to distinguish the key players and ideas in this rich and prolific field.

In addition to their choice of ten designers, all of the curators were asked to pick a "classic"—a piece of graphic design from any era that is of particular significance to them. The curators' choices—and their candid and often humorous texts explaining those choices—are not just indicators of their individual points of view, but also forays into many layers of graphic-design history.

preface

area

Anthon Beeke

is known as the ultimate provocateur, the *enfant terrible* of Dutch graphic design. Largely self-trained, he overturned conventions and created sensational images, relentlessly exposing the human body. He was a partner of the legendary Amsterdam design firm Total Design before creating his own design agency, Studio Anthon Beeke in 1989. He is chief lecturer in the department of People and Information at the Design Academy in Eindhoven, the Netherlands.

Nick Bell

is director of UNA (London) designers, known as Nick Bell Design until 1998 when his practice became associated with UNA in Amsterdam. In 1997 he became the art director of *Eye, The International Review of Graphic Design*, for which he has won numerous design awards. Bell has lectured widely in the United States and Europe. His clients include The British Council, Tate Britain, The Barbican Centre, and The Royal Mail.

Ken Cato

is chairman of Cato Partners, established in Melbourne, Australia in 1970. With eight offices worldwide, it has become the largest design company in the Southern Hemisphere. Cato's work encompasses all facets of design, ranging from graphic and product design, to fashion, to interior and environmental design. An indefatigable advocate of the cause of graphic design worldwide, Cato was president of AGI from 1997 to 2001, and in 1991 created AGIdeas, which has become the world's biggest student graphic design conference.

Shigeo Fukuda

is one of the world's leading contemporary visual artists. With graphic design as his base, he is active in a variety of genres including sculpture and environmental and monument design. Fukuda's playful designs, which are humorous while displaying a sense of irony, have won him international acclaim. Based in Tokyo, Fukuda is a visiting professor at Tokyo National University of Fine Arts and Music, and is currently chairman of the Japan Graphic Designers Association.

Fernando Gutiérrez

is a partner of the international design firm Pentagram, and since 2000 the creative director of *Colors*, the global magazine created for Benetton by Tibor Kalman and Oliviero Toscani. Based in London, Gutiérrez has kept close ties to his homeland, Spain. He is the art director of *Matador*, an annual Spanish literary and photography journal, and frequently works for the national daily newspaper *El Pais*. He is consultant creative director for the Museo Nacional del Prado in Madrid.

Werner Jeker

who founded the Ateliers du Nord in 1984, is one of the most renowned Swiss graphic designers. Based in Lausanne, he works regularly with local cultural institutions and has clients worldwide. He has also worked as an architect and recently designed the "Pavillon Signalschmerz" for the Swiss Expo.02, an acclaimed success. He has taught at the most prestigious design schools and is currently chair of the Visual Communications department at the Hochschule für Gestaltung, Kunst, und Konservierung (HGKK) in Bern.

Uwe Loesch

is acknowledged as one of the world's most important poster designers. In the past twenty years he has won nearly all the existing international poster design awards, and his work is represented in the permanent collections of the world's major museums. Since 1990 a professor of Communication Design at the University of Wuppertal, Germany, Loesch is an eminent teacher, whose work is frequently emulated and who has influenced generations of young designers.

Stefan Sagmeister

was born in Vienna and first moved to New York City in 1987. In 1993 he formed his own company, Sagmeister Inc., focusing on the music industry. He has designed graphics and packaging for the Rolling Stones, David Byrne, Lou Reed, Aerosmith, and Pat Metheny and his work has received four Grammy nominations as well as many international design awards. Sagmeister, who is a frequent lecturer and participant in international graphic design juries, has become an advocate for change in the design world.

Serge Serov

is the foremost spokesperson of graphic design in Russia and Eastern Europe. He is the founding president of the Golden Bee Moscow International Biennale of Graphic Design and since 1998 heads the Graphic Design School of the College of Applied Arts in Moscow. Serov also works as an editor and has curated a number of graphic design exhibitions.

Omar Vulpinari

heads the department of Visual Communication Design at Fabrica in Treviso, Italy, the research and development center for communication created by Luciano Benetton and Oliviero Toscani. He has been a consultant to, among others, the United Nations, Witness, Coca Cola, Nikon, Fuji, Porsche, *The New Yorker* magazine, and MTV. He is a member of the International Society of Typographic Designers.

010 curators

100 graphic designers

In 1972, on a voyage to the distant kingdom of Afghanistan, I passed through Iran and discovered Persia, this fairy-tale land that a long time ago gave the world such grandiose poets as Ferdowsi, Jalal ad-Din ar-Rumi, and Hafez. Iran still has a notable book culture and to this day cultivates the special tradition of calligraphy. ••Thirty years later an invitation by Morteza Momayez allowed me to travel back to Iran. In Tehran he presented me to Majid Abassi, who promptly showed me his work on an old IBM computer in Reza Abedini's studio. I was impressed. ••Abassi works with minimal graphic and typographic means and has perfected the art of forming a relationship between Persian and Latin writing. This allows him to combine his own tradition with new, mostly Western forms of expression and to create something unique. ••Abassi has designed many book covers and posters. Especially with the book covers, he handles image and text with a great deal of craftsmanship. Some of these designs are full of poetry, others full of wit, like the photomontage of a glass eye under a magnifying glass for a detective novel. One of his posters (poster for exhibition of photographs by Sadeq Hedayat) has become so popular that it is becoming an icon of Iranian graphic design. This comes as no surprise, as posters are surely his secret passion, for they provide him with the space to realize his large-scale ideas. ••Abassi was born in Tehran in 1965 and graduated from the fine-arts department of the University of Tehran in 1996. He has received numerous awards at national and international competitions, and over the last few years his work has been represented at all the major poster biennials. ••Uwe Loesch••

1   Book cover, *Iranian Folk Culture* / Cheshmeh Publications / Iran / 1999
2   Book cover, *The Coolness of the Journey's Dawn* / Khojasteh Publications / Iran / 2001
3   Book cover, *Ahmad Shamlou's Poems* / Cheshmeh Publications / Iran / 2001
4   Book cover, *Eye to Eye* / Did Publications / Iran / 2002
5   Book cover, *My Favorite Stories*, Vol. 1 / Cheshmeh Publications / Iran / 2001
6   Book cover, *Jeux de Massacre* / Did Publications / Iran / 2000
7   Poster for the Persian typography exhibition inspired by the novel *Blind Owl* / The 5th Color / Iran / 2002
8   Poster for the book *Graphic Design Iran 1* / Iranian Graphic Designers Society (IGDS) / Iran / 2002
9   Logo / Kajé Construction Company / Iran / 1997
10 Logo / Borzoyeh Medical Publications / Iran / 1994
11 Logo / Doran Publishing / Iran / 1998
12 Logo for Bouda Bana building in Tehran / Tazdgol Company / Iran / 2003
13 Logo / Mehr Publishing / Iran / 2002

Majid Abbasi

Tehran

...منتشر شد!

Majid Abbasi

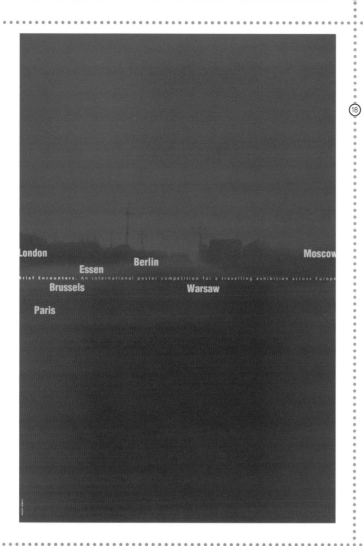

London   Berlin   Moscow

Essen

Brief Encounters. An international poster competition for a travelling exhibition across Europe

Brussels   Warsaw

Paris

An Exhibition of the Photographs (original prints) of Sadeq Hedayat

اثر ویلیام شکسپیر

هاملت

کارگردان : حسینعلی طباطبایی

حمید زارع ، مهتاب نصیرپور ، فریبا شفیعی ، کیومرث فرباخی

تهران . تالار شهر ۱۹ دی الی ۲۵ اسفند ۱۳۷۸

I met the Iranian designer Reza Abedini at the June 2002 biennial in Brno. He was a relatively young man dressed in white with an acute, burning stare. In Tehran, he organizes the biennial of Iranian graphic designers, which he is now planning to make international. He gave me a catalogue of his work, which seemed a bit too small. I flipped through it, and I can't say I liked it much. ●● My conception of the three paradigms of graphic design looks something like this: In classical typography, illustration is entirely dictated by text. The range of font in the text sets the standard for the tonal range of the images. They must not contain lines wider than the largest or nar- rower than the smallest font used: a strong, healthy family, the patri- archy of text. In modern typography, image and text become inde- pendent, equal, strong partners. Image is the liberated woman of modernism. She may become the illustration for the text; or she can do without text, creating an independent "visual row," or even become the "visual text" herself. With the postmodern paradigm now beginning to reveal itself, we approach the domination of image, trapping, enveloping, and swallowing the text. ●● At the Brno biennial, which showcases the freshest ideas from around the world, even poster slogans now dissolved amid the gentle grids of the image. ●● In the works of Reza Abedini I also find the precise embod- iment of my conception of stylistic processes in typography world- wide. Abedini's text is almost always not next to the image, but inside it. Dark font on light images, light font on dark images. He leaves tons of free space around for the text. But this is no longer empty whiteness or the blackness of the modernist cosmos; this is a living environment of the image that fills all of the surrounding space with itself—an alloy of image and text. ●● It was only on revisiting his work that I fully appreciated Abedini's design. On closer look, I see him as a unifying phenomenon, joining national color with international quality, regionalism with globalism, Iran's traditional Farsi writing with the most modern European typography. What's more, this powerful synthesis comes to him with ease and noncha- lance. ●● Serge Serov ●●

1   Book cover, *Raporthaye Yomyeh* / Rozaneh Publishing / Iran / 1999
2   Book cover, *Shere Tanze Emroz Iran* / Rozaneh Publishing / Iran / 1999
3   Poster for Polish Film Week / Tehran Museum of Contemporary Art / Iran / 2000
4   Book cover, *Resale Se Asl* / Rozaneh Publishing / Iran / 1998
5   Poster for personal theatrical project focussing on dance, light, and graphic
    design / Iran / 2000
6   Book cover, *Resale Delgosha* poetry selection / Rozaneh Publishing / Iran / 2000
7   Poster for lecture on the Iranian poet Mowlana / Marc Bloch University /
    France / 1999

Reza Abedini

Tehran

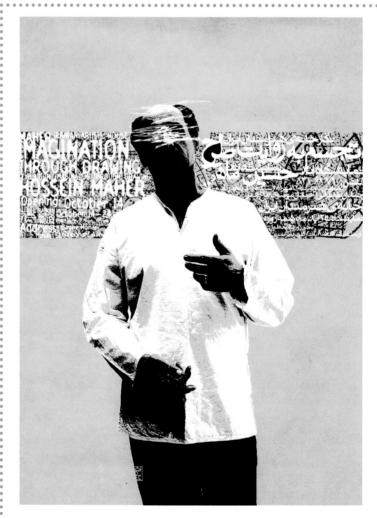

8   Poster for exhibition of photographs by Jamshid Bayrami / Sayhoon Art Gallery / Iran / 2000
9   Poster for Reza Abedini solo exhibition / Hafiz Cultural Complex / Iran / 2001
10 Poster for *Imagination Through Drawing* exhibition / Iranian Artists House Gallery / Iran / 2002
11 Poster for 7th Biennial of Iranian Graphic Designers / Iranian Graphic Designers Society (IGDS) and
    Tehran Museum of Contemporary Art / Iran / 2002
12 Poster for International Conference on the Philosophy of Art / Tehran Museum of Contemporary Art /
    Iran / 2001
13 Poster for International Conference on Post-Modernism and Contemporary Art / Tehran Museum of
    Contemporary Art / Iran / 2001
14 Poster for The Second International Biennal, Painting of the Islamic World / Tehran Museum of
    Contemporary Art / Iran / 2002

Reza Abedini

11

12

13

14

I have known Sebastian Campos—a.k.a. Aficionado—for six or seven years, since he was a design student in Barcelona. His approach to work was always considered; he has always had a very specific way of doing things. Since then he has moved to London and established a fine reputation for himself, initially as a partner of the the design trio Praline. He has remained true to his own unique way of working, but living in London seems to have sharpened him up somewhat.**Recent projects include an identity, packaging, and promotional program for the English punk band Ikara Colt. He describes the project as "an oblique attempt to update and expand 'punk' clichés," which is exactly what he did, with a visual language that expresses the punky, art-rock dynamic of the band. Typography plays an important role, with clear sans-serif type and ordered grids. However, it's the cut-and-paste aesthetic of original punk graphics that is updated to great effect here. Each band member was given a disposable camera to take "on tour" photographs, which were edited by the band and placed in the inner sleeve of the CD as stickers. The front cover and gatefold interior have blank squares with generic captions, leaving the fans to choose their own story. It is a great idea that actively involves both the band and their fanbase.**The catalogue/poster/invitation Aficionado created with Praline for the exhibition *My Generation: 24 Hours of Video Art* recalls the moving type of video and film credits: The type has been layered and overprinted to create a sense of animation. Everything was designed in modules, so that each plate produced nine flyers/invitations, two posters, and one catalogue (with copy printed on the reverse). This ingenious solution put all the budget into one piece of print, and the results speak for themselves.**In September 2000, Praline gave a talk that dealt with the theme of "wayfinding" in their work. The poster designed to promote the event employs an arrow-shaped Post-it note, found among their office supplies, and a great bit of copy: "(t)here." Here and there. It is a very direct piece of communication, a problem solved with characteristic logic and clarity. Quiet and unassuming, it does everything it needs to do and nothing more.**Fernando Gutiérrez**

1-2 Front and back of unfoldable leaflet/poster for the presentation of the Interactive Surfaces project / Royal College of Art and Harper Mackey Architects / United Kingdom / 2002
3 Invitation to talk by Rebecca Brown and Mike Heath (with Matthew Savidge) / Central Saint Martins College of Art and Design / United Kingdom / 2000
4 Souvenir for talk by Praline at Harper Mackay Architects (with Regine Stefan and David Tanguy) / United Kingdom / 2000
5 Poster for *Graphic Britain* exhibition at Magma Bookshop / United Kingdom / 2002
6 Poster for *Transmission02: Utopia* exhibition and publication (with Regine Stefan and David Tanguy) / :phunk / Singapore / 2001

Aficionado

London

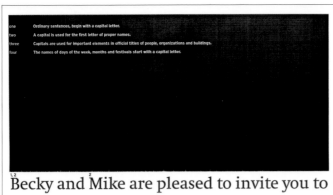

one   Ordinary sentences, begin with a capital letter.
two   A capital is used for the first letter of proper names.
three   Capitals are used for important elements in official titles of people, organizations and buildings.
four   The names of days of the week, months and festivals start with a capital letter.

Becky and Mike are pleased to invite you to attend a casual gathering[comma] in which they will reveal the conceptual framework that underlies their professional practice[full stop]

comma — indicates a short pause or slight interruption

full stop — Used at the end of sentences that express complete statements

Friday 3rd of March[comma] 12 pm[full stop]

Room 410[semicolon] Graphics[comma] 3rd year studio[full stop]

comma — Indicates a short pause or slight interruption

full stop — Used at the end of sentences that express complete statements

semicolon — A stronger more definite break in a sentence than a comma, less than a full stop

---

Próliné

P: 55 Tompion House, Percival St, London, ec1v 0hx
T: +44 20 7689 1372   F: +44 490 2167
E: prolinefamily@hotmail.com

Sebastián Campos   M: 07880 638 951
Regine Stefan   M: 07818 072 788
David Tanguy   M: 07799 842 997

(t)here

Poster
Elementary Edutainment

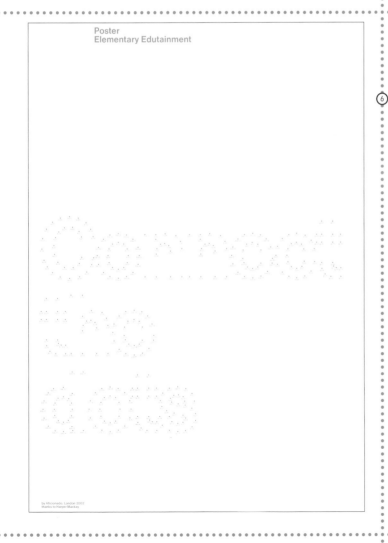

By Aficionado, London 2002
Thanks to Harper Mackay

Somehow

Something

Someone

Sometime

Somewhere

(Not a means to an end) a poster conceived/designed by Próliné, London 2001

ikara colt

extendedplay
basic instructions ep

longplay
chat and business

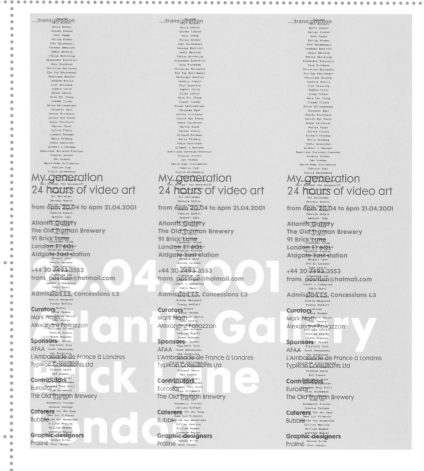

7-8 CD packaging, *Chat and Business*, by Ikara Colt / Fantastic Plastic Records / United Kingdom / 2001 /
Inner sleeve contains adhesive photographs by the band that can be used to personalize the generic
cover.

9 Poster for two recordings by Ikara Colt / Fantastic Plastic Records / United Kingdom / 2002

10 Cover, *My Generation, 24 Hours of Video Art* exhibition catalogue (with Regine Stefan and David Tanguy) /
Atlantis Gallery / United Kingdom / 2001 / Catalogue designed as part of a module that allows each print
plate to produce nine invitations, two posters, and one catalogue.

11-14 Book design for *The Mobile Effect* by Sadie Plant / Milk Projects and Motorola / United
Kingdom / 2001

15-18 Cover and spreads, first issue of *Graphic* magazine, Spring 2003 (with Sam Baker and Inca Starzinsky) / BIS
Publishers / United Kingdom and The Netherlands / 2003

Aficionado

Photography: Dr Soda-Point (except pp 4, 6, 11–13 Grieu Jones)

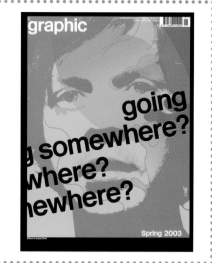

graphic
going somewhere? somewhere? where? mewhere?
Spring 2003

on
page 30

(♂ & ♀ ?)

mobile minds

According to the *Oxford English Dictionary*, one of the earliest uses of the word 'mobile' was in association with the Latin phrase *mobile vulgus*, the excitable crowd. Today's mobile lives up to these origins: the mobile introduces new senses of speed and connectivity to social life, establishing new kinds of relationships between individuals and with the urban crowd. In this respect, the mobile can facilitate the emergence of a new private world, a virtual community which can be pulled together in a matter of moments.

Loose arrangements can be made in the knowledge that they can be firmed up at a later stage: people can be forewarned about late or early arrivals; arrangements to meet can be progressively refined. But this kind of flexibility – we can call it approximeeting – can also engender a new sense of insecurity. Everything is virtual until the parties, the places and the moments come together to make it real. In this context the person without a phone becomes something of a liability.

This psychological mobility makes 'Where are you?' far more than a practical question. 'Where are you?' is an attempt to locate and contextualise what would otherwise be a displaced voice, and also a recognition of the fact that mobile users operate in a dislocated, slightly schizophrenic world.

Breathless
written by Marc-A Valli

Breathless
written by Marc-A Valli

'Daring!'
'Vivid!'
'Explicit!!!'
'An intellectual tour-de-force!!!!'
'Breathtaking!!!!!'

Breathless
written by Marc-A Valli

Breathless
written by Marc-A Valli

Breathless

Marc-A Valli
is Swiss-Brazilian but lives and works in London

Many people feel irritated and disconcerted by this new electronic soundtrack. All ringing phones are disruptive, even arresting. As Marshall McLuhan observed in *Understanding Media*, an incoming call provokes a sense of expectation, even urgency, which is why usually feel compelled to answer a ringing phone, even when they know the call is not for them. Like a crying bird, a ringing phone demands a response. Public uses of the mobile spread this tension to all those within earshot, while leaving them powerless to intervene: only the person to whom the call is made is in a position to respond.

Mobile calls can come at any time, at any place, and in the company of any number of onlookers and eavesdroppers. The etiquette of handling such interventions has become a matter of some debate, and in many parts of the world, the ability to handle them – on the part of the recipient and all those within earshot – has become an important social skill. A ringing mobile will often take precedence over the social interactions it disrupts: the need or desire to answer a call often outweighs the importance of maintaining the flow of face-to-face conversation. This is why even a silent mobile can make its presence felt as though it were an addition to a social group, and why many people feel that just the knowledge that a call might intervene tends to divert attention from those present at the time. The mobile tends to siphon concentration, demanding attention even when it is not in use; for many couples, its presence can be as powerful and distracting as that of a third person. Some contributors to this research suggested that the mobile functions as a *gooseberry phone* – an unwanted addition to the pair. In the UK, a few people admitted to making *gooseberry calls* to friends out on dates in order to get a progress report.

The receipt of a public call tends to be met by one of three responses. These are flight, in which users immediately move to absent themselves from their social situation; suspension, in which recipients stay put, but stop whatever they are doing for the duration of a call and effectively cut themselves off from their environment; and persistence, in which users stay put and engaged with the actual world, as far as possible carrying on with whatever they were doing before they mobile or took the call.

All these responses run some risk that people who are present at the time will feel abandoned by the person who has answered the mobile, and in so doing has opted to be answerable to the device rather than to them. Several American contributors to this research drew attention to the disempowering effects of situations in which they felt as though they were being dropped and picked up by their companions without any chance to negotiate the terms. As well as regarding the mobile monologues of passing strangers as inappropriate and unwelcome impositions on their personal space, they expected calls to be deferred or at least taken out of earshot when in the company of friends.

Observers tend to be more tolerant of users where mobile use is long-standing and high. Users also tend to be more considerate, more sensitive to their surroundings than their counterparts in countries where the mobile is less integrated into the conduct of everyday life. Users in more mobile countries are also more likely to use their devices for purposes other than telephony, and much of this use is inoffensive and discreet.

This also accounts for the profound sense of melancholy associated with overlowered calls, especially when, as is often the case or the scale of mass crashes, car accidents, or natural disasters, mobile phones keep ringing long after those to answer them.

Peter Lewis, *Wireless Etiquette: A Guide to the Changing World of Internet Communications*, Compactor Communications, 1999

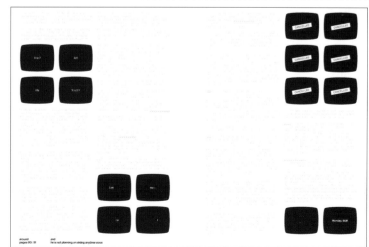

and
he is not planning on asking anyone soon

The posters from Kum Nam Baik's "Recollection" series are filled with countless dots created by brushwork reminiscent of snowflakes in a cold Korean winter gust or petals dancing in the wind of a spring thunderstorm. Using the technique of pointillism, Baik seems to push the underlying meaning of the letters and words deep into the backdrop of the picture. Are they expressions of anger or pain, or of joy? In this group of works we can find the origin of Baik's sensitivities, and within its creative process we can even sense the presence of his hopes and aspirations.••One can find the same spirit in his posters that contain more concrete visual messages. Among the works of his private exhibition titled *The Style of Korea* one can find deeply felt songs in praise of human creativity through the still, round-shaped motifs—the Korean coins, the wheels, the oval-shaped bamboo basket, the round tiles, and the round pile of hot red peppers.••In the posters for the exhibition of Korean Buddha statues, Baik's wisdom becomes apparent, for he goes beyond the traditional worshiping of the Buddha from a frontal view, and, by also showing the Buddha in profile, focuses on the beauty of the sculpture itself.••In one of the posters from the "My favorite Seoul" series, there is a colorful Korean pastry with the face of a fish floating in the sky above the Seoul Tower, a nostalgic symbol of gentle, heartwarming East Asian humor.••The name "Baik" means "white." The Asian design world of the present day tends to be swallowed into the whirl of the volatile economic realities and the culture of the information age. It is my wish that amid all this turmoil Baik will remain a precious white bastion, reminding us of the importance of true creativity.••Shigeo Fukuda••

Kum Nam Baik

Seoul

1–2 Posters for *Exhibition of Korean Buddhism* [sic] *Sculpture* / National Museum of Korea / 2002
3–4 Posters for museum opening / Haein-sa Museum / Korea / 2002
5–6 Posters for museum opening / Gahoe Museum / Korea / 2002

Kum Nam Baik

7–8 Self-commissioned poster series "Letter" / Korea / 1984
9–10 Self-commissioned poster series "Recollection" / Korea / 2002
11–19 Self-commissioned poster series "The Style of Korea" / Korea / 2002

The style of Korea

The style of Korea

The style of Korea

The style of Korea

The style of Korea

The style of Korea

14 15 16

The style of Korea

The style of Korea

The style of Korea

17 18 19

23

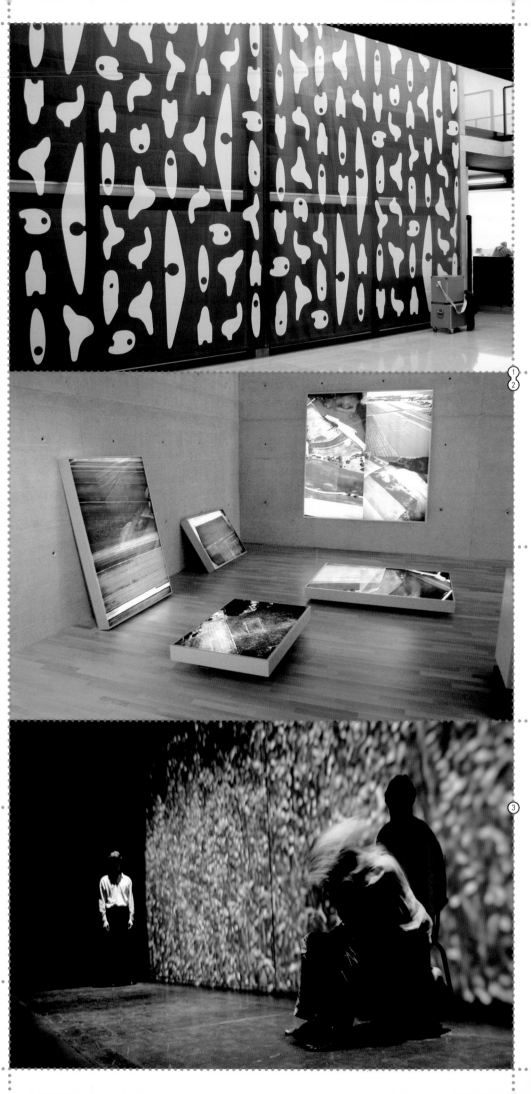

Newut is the name of one of André Baldinger's font designs. It sounds like "*die neue Wut*" (the new rage). Yet this Newut is quite tame, no sign of rage at all. Here somebody has cultivated a rage, abstracted it, safeguarded its essence, and divided it into spatial forms with a clear perception. Baldinger deliberately strips away everything that is inessential and dismisses it. As independent, self-reliant entities, what remains forms his true illustrative starting point. The resulting unobtrusive complexity makes for a linear thinker, who never wants to be didactic with his work. The Newut font cannot deny an affinity to the Nordic. The German characteristic is very much anchored in it, as becomes apparent in the lowercase application of capital letters. Maybe it represents the first steps toward the German adoption of the lowercase for nouns.●●Baldinger likes to expand toward the plane, measure far across spaces, and sit down in these typographical worlds. Three-dimensionality tempts him, and his answers are convincing, because he transports and transposes in an illustrative language that speaks of respect. He is a democrat of forms.●●Turning the world by 90 degrees makes him a "mover of perspectives" in the positive sense, not a magician, but an observer who likes to retell a story. Although, or because, he orients himself with the help of grids, real and metaphoric, the observer feels further planes lurking behind. It is as if a book became transparent and the complete contents could enjoy visual equality.●● Baldinger is distinct, his path seems logical and straightforward. As a typographer he comes from the two-dimensional, further along he turned to three-dimensional exhibition and interior design, and now, in his stage designs, he is adds the element of movement. Precisely because he is a linear thinker and his illustrative deductions are of interest, his work will gain in importance; he is a man of quiet persistence. Yet at times he allows himself to submerge the world in outrageous colors.●●Werner Jeker●●

1–2 Entrance wall and light boxes as part of visual conception for the permanent exhibition (with Anne Crausaz and François Rappo) / Musée Latenium, Neuchatel / Switzerland / 2001

3 Stage design for play *Le Triptique de tiberiade*, by Jose Saramago (with Rodolphe Aute) / Le crochet a nuages / Switzerland / 2002

4 Poster for promotion of the Newut typeface / amb+ / Switzerland / 2000

5 Poster for play *La vie est un songe*, by Pedro Calderón de la Barca / Le crochet a nuages / Switzerland / 1996

6 Poster for play *Le Triptique de tiberiade*, by Jose Saramago / Le crochet a nuages / Switzerland / 2002

7 Poster for play *Tandis que j'agonise*, by William Faulkner / Le crochet a nuages / Switzerland / 2000

André Baldinger

Paris/Lausanne

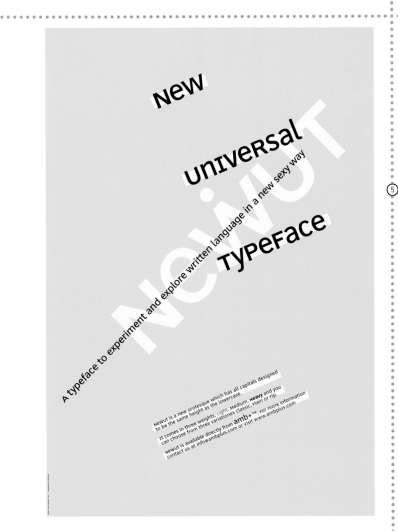

New

universal

Typeface

New∪t

A typeface to experiment and explore written language in a new sexy way

Newut is a new grotesque which has all capitals designed to be the same height as the lowercase.
It comes in three weights, Light, medium, Heavy and you can choose from three variationes classic, plain or rip.
Newut is available directly from amb+™. For more information contact us at info@ambplus.com or visit www.ambplus.com

calderón

La vie est un songe

9.Juin – 22.Juin

arche du pont bessières

LE TRIPTYQUE DE TIBERIADE DE JOSE SARAMAGO

THEATRE PAR LE CROCHET A NUAGES

GRANGE DE DORIGNY DU 3 AU 15 DECEMBRE

LOCATION 021 318 71 71 OU 021 692 21 12

AVEC LE SOUTIEN DE LA VILLE DE LAUSANNE — LA FONDATION NESTLE POUR L'ART — LA LOTERIE ROMANDE

10 JUIN WILLIAM FAUEKNER
– 14 JUIN
à 21H00 TANDIS QUE J'AGONISE

ADAPTATION POUR LE THEATRE: LE CROCHET A NUAGES
AVEC LE SOUTIEN DE LA VILLE DE LAUSANNE, LA LOTERIE ROMANDE, LA FONDATION NESTLE POUR L'ART
TIR GROUPE-ANCIENNE ECOLE DE CHIMIE (PLACE DU TUNNEL, LAUSANNE)
LOCATION: 021-323 08 59, LIBRAIRIE DES ECRIVAINS, GRAND ST-JEAN 5, 1003 LAUSANNE

all signes of amb+ B-Dot shown in Light

Aa Bb Cc Dd Ee Ff Gg Hh Ii Jj Kk Ll Mm Nn Oo Pp Qq Rr Ss Tt Uu Vv
Ww Xx Yy Zz 1234567890¬%%.·,;;---·.'',""„<>«»*/?!SÏ()[]{}
†‡§¶¤¥£ƒ¢$flfiβæÆœŒøØ&áâàäãåçéêèëíîìïñóôòöõúûùüÿÀÂÁ
ÃÀÇÉÊÈËÍÎÌÏÑÓÔÒÖÕÚÛÙÜŸ©®™ə≡…#ªº+−=≠±μ|¢>

(10)

amb+ B-Dot Light, Regular, Bold, Black

The quick brown fox jumps over the lazy dog 1234567890 ©®™ə≡
The quick brown fox jumps over the lazy dog 1234567890 ©®™ə≡
The quick brown fox jumps over the lazy dog 1234567890 ©®™ə≡
The quick brown fox jumps over the lazy dog 1234567890 ©®™ə≡

amb+ B-Dot special

The quick brown fox jumps over the lazy dog 1234567890 ©®™ə≡

aaalso…………B-Dot

André Baldinger

8-9 Lettering on roof of the railway station Interface Flon / Tschumi/Merlini/Ventura Architects / Switzerland / 2000
10 Type sample for the B-Dot typeface / amb+ / Switzerland / 2000
11-12 Cover page and spread, cultural newspaper *Rote Fabrik Zeitung* no. 157 / IG Rote Fabrik / Switzerland / 1999
13 Cover and spreads, *Toit du Monde* / Sigismond de Vajay and Lars Mueller Publishers / Switzerland / 2002

Jop van Bennekom is a pure avant-gardist, an artist who uses the medium of a "magazine" as his canvas. His own publication, *Re-Magazine*, is actually visual art. It is the communications instrument of a small group of kindred spirits, but the communication is channeled through bookstores. Another magazine, which he generates with other partners, is the gay zine *Butt*, a demonstrative expression of his own homosexuality. But here too he uses the publication to comment on—or rather to pay homage to—the kind of design amateurism that characterizes such zines: fast, artless typography, improper fonts for headlines. Still, the details show that van Bennekom knows what he's doing; he's just not that interested in the craft. He is an anti-designer. He is a writer, editor, what have you, but he always gets a bit grouchy when you call him a "graphic designer." "Magazine maker" would be more appropriate. Or "artist."**Van Bennekom's design for the architecture magazine *Forum*, on the other hand, is the complete opposite of the deliberate amateurism of his other publications. He uses carefully balanced texts and images with very readable typography. But here also, he is looking for the edges of what still communicates and what doesn't. All of his work demonstrates he is a good designer who probably thinks that's not enough. In an Andy Warhol–like fashion, working with a loose group of like minds, he experiments with the medium of magazines, with communication, with editorial formats.**I find it hard to define van Bennekom's work, but I love the research it confronts you with: a *Fluxus*-like approach to "performing" a magazine. *Re-Magazine* is a performance about the medium of magazines. Seeing it in the light of my own background with *Fluxus*, I can't help finding that fascinating.**Anthon Beeke**

droog

droog

droog

droog

droog

droog

droog

droog

droog

droog invitation

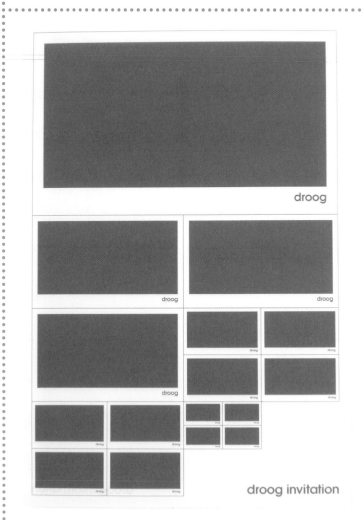

1 Invitation for presentation of Droog design at the Salone del Mobile, Milan / Droog Design / Netherlands / 2001 / The invitation also introduced Droog's new house style "droog non id."
2 Invitation for spring/summer collection fashion show / So by Alexander van Slobbe / Netherlands / 2000
3–6 Cover and spreads, *BUTT* magazine no. 3 / Netherlands / 2002 / *BUTT* is a self-published, interview-based gay magazine.
7–8 Cover and spread, *BUTT* magazine no. 5 / Netherlands / 2002
9–10 Spreads, *BUTT* magazine no. 4 / Netherlands / 2002

Jop van Bennekom

Amsterdam

Page 31/

SURFACE

A Re-Make Of a Fashion Magazine   The Summer of 1998   Abstraction Rules!

The Summer of.
Nineteen Ninety-Eight

SurFace: a Re-Make of
a Fashion Magazine

A girl lies in the swimming pool. With her hands she just holds her head above water. The blue sky reflects in the water and beams light spots on her black swimsuit.

**10.
Niet Parkeren**
/Not Parking?

Storage

Jop van Bennekom

IT'S SPRING
TWO THOUSAND SEVEN

(2007)

NEW IRAQ

A MONTHLY PICTORIAL MAGAZINE ISSUED BY THE MINISTRY OF GUIDANCE

FreeStylin'
Looking at forms
of boredom.
Creating clouds
of text.

'Like'...

PART I

WE THOUGHT:
AN INCOMPLETE ARCHEOLOGY OF THE
HISTORY OF THE FUTURE

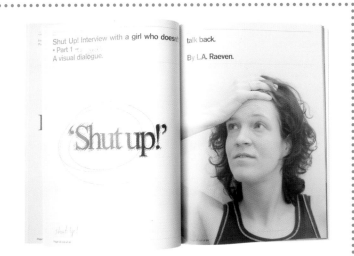

Shut Up! Interview with a girl who doesn't talk back.
• Part 1
A visual dialogue.

By L.A. Raeven.

'Shut up!'

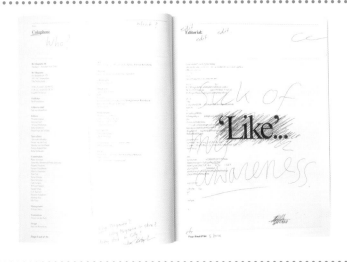

Before Andrew Blauvelt attended Cranbrook Academy of Art, he studied photography and typography. These studies were oriented toward the theoretical, with aspects of semiotics, structuralism, poststructuralism, and postmodernism. At Cranbrook he applied these ideas to design. "This theoretical aspect became the central component of my teaching, writing, and approach to design," he says. "Over the years, the theoretical has broadened to include aspects of sociology and cultural anthropology: more human, less abstract." ● ●Blauvelt takes design very seriously. He believes that "designers must be open to the entire culture and to history, not to mimic the past or other ideas but to see how design might be changed if it were open to such ways of thinking. I'm more interested in what you might call the history of ideas or a culture of ideas than in designs from the past." At the Walker Art Center in Minneapolis he directs more than one hundred cultural projects a year and thinks deeply and broadly about what is produced. ● ●In examining projects like *The Indexical Archive*, *365: A Year to View*, and the Design Internship poster, it seems that Blauvelt is focused on transforming overlooked data into fresh, beautiful, informational visual art. "These projects and others come out of a desire to approach design conceptually and systematically. It establishes the parameters, or the rules of the game, and lets the design happen out of these conditions and limitations," he notes. "This was an approach that I had been interested in for many years—which had developed out of a comment I once wrote, 'Why is so much information design so boring?' I was also interested in not being defined by my studies at Cranbrook, which so many people associate with formal excess and visual complexity. It was simply too fashionable to be producing this kind of work." He continues: "I find data and information can be beautiful, especially when it is given visual form: It becomes intelligible in this process. Information is rhetorical, not neutral. It tells a story. For *The Indexical Archive* the story it tells is about a design competition and the many ways in which you can see it; for *365: A Year to View*, it tells of everything the Walker does in one year, it is literal not metaphoric; in the Design Internship poster it shows duration and accumulation, gives an indication of the work produced by the interns. I advocate a simple approach to graphic design but with a complexity of content and information." ● ●Omar Vulpinari ● ●

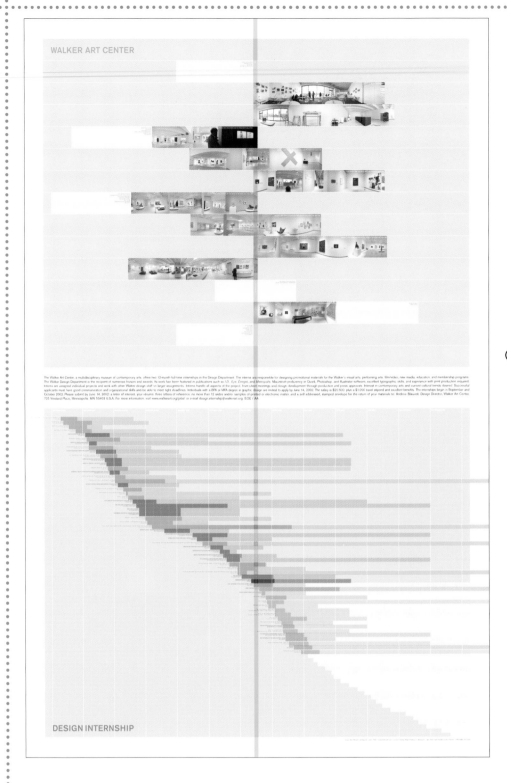

Andrew Blauvelt

Minneapolis, Minnesota

1   Poster advertising design internship program (with Alex DeArmond and Alejandro Quinto) / Walker Art Center / USA / 2002
2–4 Cover and spreads, exhibition catalogue *Painting at the Edge of the World* (with Santiago Piedrafita) / Walker Art Center / USA / 2001
5–7 Cover and spreads, exhibition catalogue *Let's Entertain: Life's Guilty Pleasures* (with Santiago Piedrafita) / Walker Art Center / USA / 2000

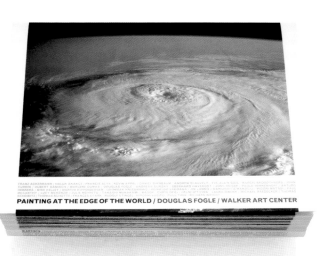

PAINTING AT THE EDGE OF THE WORLD / DOUGLAS FOGLE / WALKER ART CENTER

LET'S
ENTERTAIN:
LIFE'S
GUILTY
PLEASURES

LET'S
ENTERTAIN:
LIFE'S
GUILTY
PLEASURES

Painting: The Task of Mourning
Yve-Alain Bois
1986

March 27, 1999—Bellagio Casino and Art Gallery, Las Vegas. Olukemi Ilesanmi and Philippe Vergne continue their conversation. As we meet them, they are sitting on a bench in front of the casino, watching the "dancing waters" with 125 other visitors.

PAINTING AT THE EDGE OF THE WORLD
298

Julie Mehretu

Born 1970 Ethiopia; lives and works in New York City

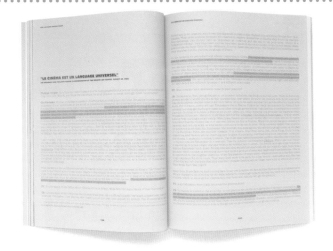

8–10 Cover and spreads, exhibition catalogue *Zero to Infinity: Arte Povera 1962–1972* (with Linda Byrne) / Walker Art Center and Tate Modern / USA and United Kingdom / 2001

11–14 Cover and spreads, exhibition catalogue *How Latitudes Become Forms: Art in a Global Age* (with Chad Kloepfer) / Walker Art Center / USA / 2001

15 "Walk Around Time: Mapping the Artists of the Permanent Collection" gallery guide and poster (with Alejandro Quinto) / Walker Art Center / USA / 2002

16 Spread from *The Indexical Archive*, a publication accompanying the American Center for Design's 21st Annual 100 Show of Excellence (with Santiago Piedrafita) / American Center for Design / USA / 2000

Andrew Blauvelt

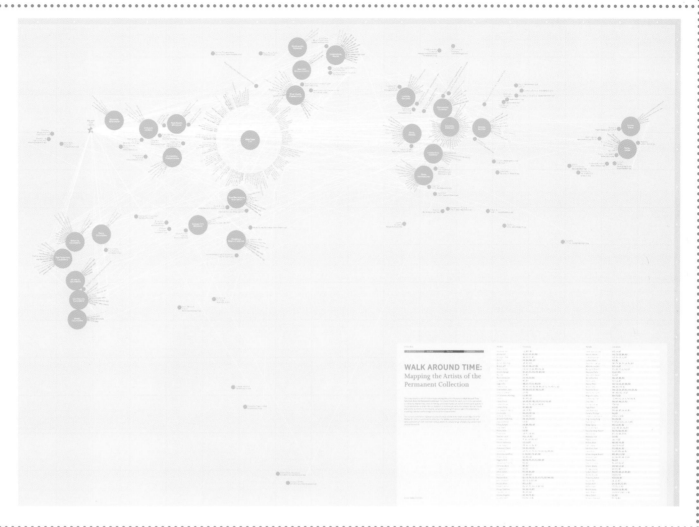

WALK AROUND TIME:
Mapping the Artists of the
Permanent Collection

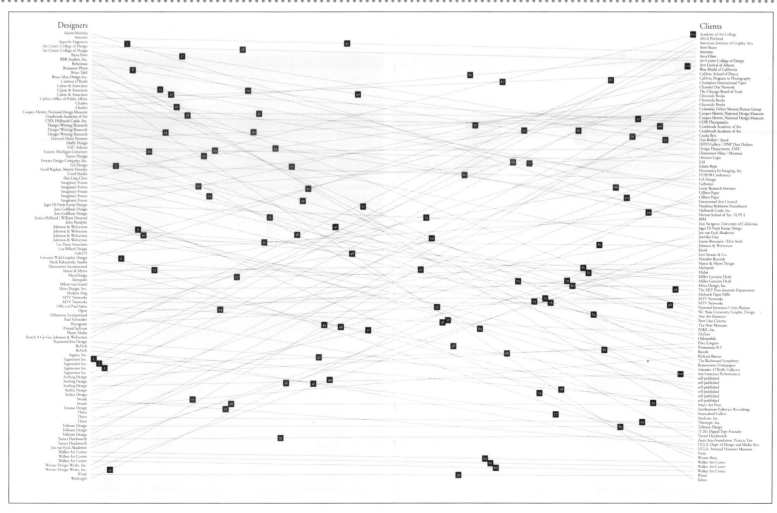

Designers

Clients

Blue Source is a classic, high-quality studio specializing in design for the music industry. While they work for a number of companies and brands outside the music industry, music and its audience are at the core of the studio's identity.●●They are art directors of the highest league (just look at those photographs for Kosheen), original illustrators (check out the images for the self-commissioned film *Hair*), film directors (ditto), competent typographers (see the Union Brand identity and the typography of the Levi's Silver Tab campaign), but most of all just designers who after a decade in the business still seem to have a lot of fun: Their depiction of a wide-eyed couple, Macintosh Power Book in hand, gazing into the future and petting a goat is one of the more original portraits produced in design.●●Blue Source calls their work "media neutral," meaning that they develop ideas in response to each project's unique needs. The idea comes first and is then developed trough the appropriate communications channel.●●The visual series they develop for bands—such as the deconstructed 3-D portraits for Coldplay, the fashion-porn paintings for Dirty Vegas, the strangely inanimate objects for Faultline, the modern psychedelia for the Chemical Brothers, the hyperrealistic photography for Birth, or the architectural landscapes for Travis—have the feel of all-encompassing campaigns. They define the look and feel of a band in a way rarely seen since the heyday of the 12-inch album cover.●●Stefan Sagmeister●●

1   Vinyl/CD cover, *A Rush of Blood to the Head*, by Coldplay (photography Sølve Sundsbø) / Parlophone Records / United Kingdom / 2002
2   Vinyl/CD cover, *The Invisible Band*, by Travis (photography Stefan Ruiz) / Independiente / United Kingdom / 2002
3   Vinyl/CD cover, *Star Guitar*, by The Chemical Brothers (artwork Kate Gibb) / Virgin Records / United Kingdom / 2002
4   Vinyl/CD cover, *Resist*, by Kosheen (photography Patrice Hanicotte) / Arista BMG Records / United Kingdom / 2001
5   Vinyl/CD cover, *On My Mind*, by Futureshock (photography Dan Holdsworth) / Parlophone Records / United Kingdom / 2003
6   De-bossed promotional record sleeve with information sticker, *Phantom Theory*, by Futureshock / Parlophone Records / United Kingdom / 2003
7   Vinyl/CD cover, *Phantom Theory*, by Futureshock (photography Dan Holdsworth) / Parlophone Records / United Kingdom / 2003
8   Print advertising campaign for the shoe Star Racer (illustration Kam Tang) / Adidas / Netherlands / 2001
9   Print advertising campaign for the shoe Water Moccasin (artwork James Dimmock) / Adidas / Netherlands / 2001

Blue Source

London

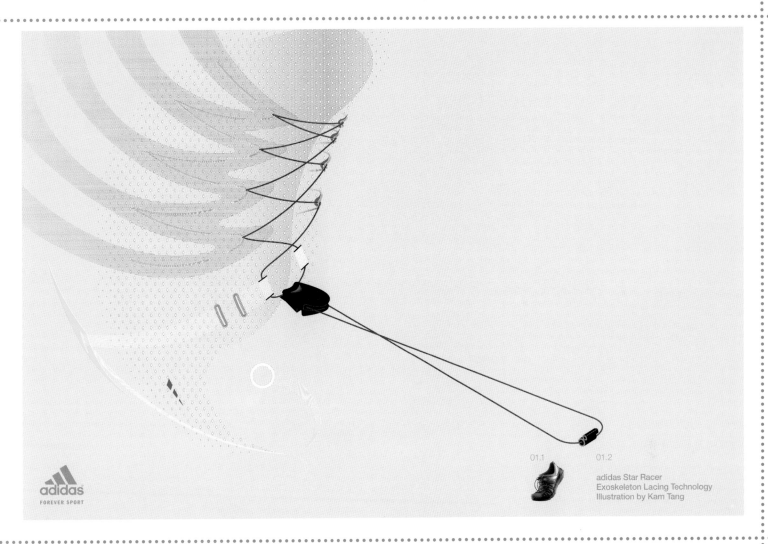

01.1   01.2

adidas Star Racer
Exoskeleton Lacing Technology
Illustration by Kam Tang

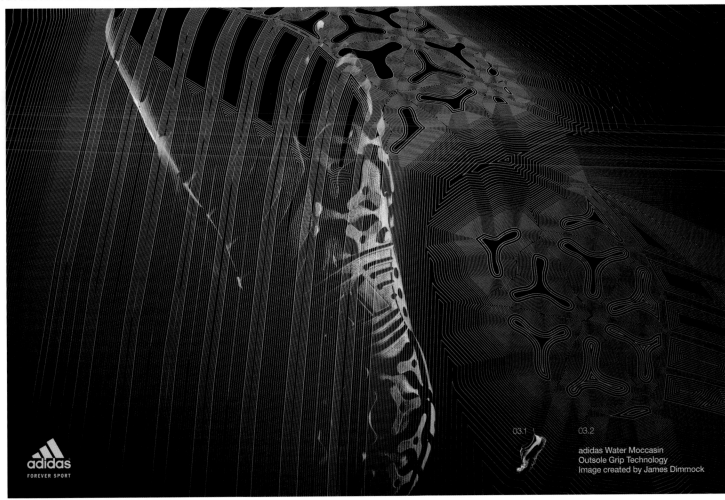

03.1   03.2

adidas Water Moccasin
Outsole Grip Technology
Image created by James Dimmock

Blue Source

10   Clockwise from top left: Vinyl/CD covers, "Days Go By" single, "Ghosts" single, and self-titled LP by Dirty
      Vegas (artwork Richard Phillips) / Parlophone Records / USA and United Kingdom / 2003
11–12 Visual identities for music channel The Amp / BSkyB Broadcasting / United Kingdom / 2003
13   Cover illustration, *Gas Book 08–Blue Source* / DesignEXchange / Japan / 2002

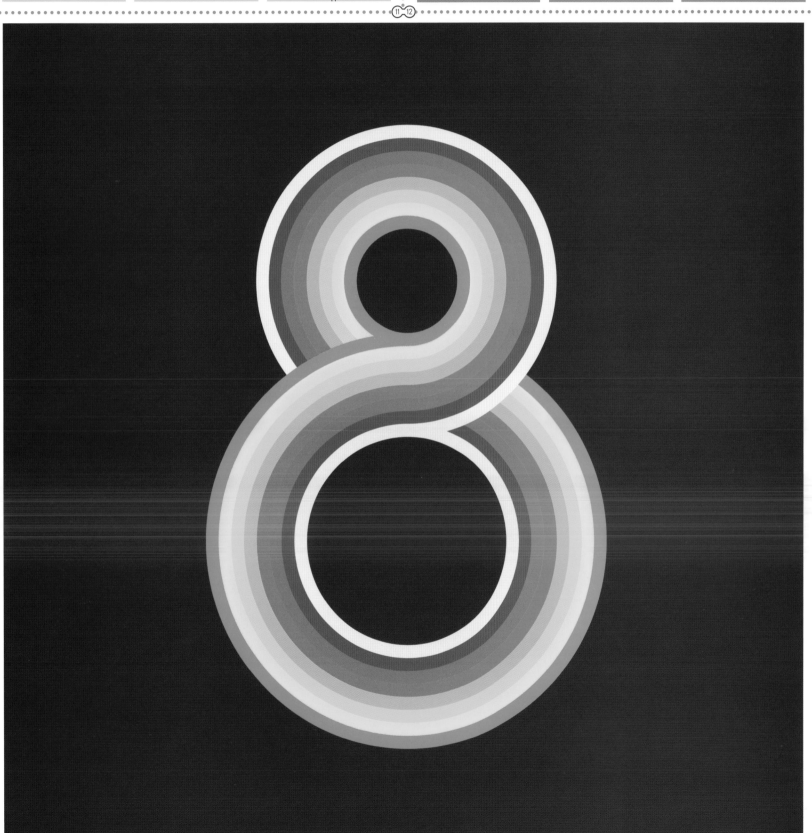

Life is mundane, frequently banal, but it also never fails to surprise or shock. So if your business is communication, your worth can be measured according to how well you can respond to special circumstances with the same tools you've deemed necessary under normal conditions. *The New York Times* has passed this test. The way in which the paper responded to the extraordinary events of 11 September 2001 was exemplary. Particularly impressive was the calm manner in which the paper communicated the numbing enormity of the event and the magnitude of the loss by simply putting into action the basic, sober principles of their trade: "clarity, balance, and modulation." There are aspects of the paper's typography that many would take issue with—the centered headlines in quirky fonts, the old-fashioned use of rules—but somehow since all visual aspects of the paper are in synthesis with the content, those details don't seem to matter. The experience of the whole is such a nourishing one it is possible to forgive the idiosyncrasies—some would say it's those that give the paper its personality. **One would think a product that is issued every day would depend on a heavy manual of rigid guidelines to standardize the design, but according to assistant managing editor and design director Tom Bodkin, nothing could be further from the truth. Speaking over a year before September 11, he said, "Surprising to some, we don't have a design stylebook. We have guidelines for typography and color palette, but little on paper in any organized form. That is deliberate. What we want is the exercise of individual interpretation and creativity in addressing the ever-changing demands of a newspaper page." **One doesn't normally expect to see great graphic design emerging from large companies. The quality of *The New York Times*' design is all the more remarkable for the fact that more than one hundred people are under Bodkin's charge. How Bodkin gets all of his team and other departments working together so efficiently cannot be put down merely to practiced tradition. The way he describes his job provides a clue: "I help artists think like editors and editors think like artists, making sure artists never lose sight of content and instructing editors on the importance of form." **Nick Bell**

1   Front page, *The New York Times*, 12 September 2001 / The New York Times / USA / 2001
2   Page from "The Year in Pictures" section, *The New York Times*, 31 December 2001
3   Page from *The New York Times*, 16 September 2001
4   Page from *The New York Times*, 13 September 2001
5   Front page, "A Nation Challenged" special section, *The New York Times*, 18 September 2001
6   Front page, "A Nation Challenged" special section, *The New York Times*, 23 September 2001
7, 9 Spreads from "The Year in Pictures" section, *The New York Times*, 31 December 2001
8   Spread from *The New York Times*, 13 September 2001

Tom Bodkin

New York

Tom Bodkin

A NATION CHALLENGED: Portraits of Grief

Pictures of the World Trade Center disaster whose identities have appeared in Portraits of Grief.

THE PORTRAITS

Closing a Scrapbook Full of Life and Sorrow

By JANNY SCOTT

It began as an imperfect answer to a journalistic problem, the absence of a defining list of the dead in the days after the World Trade Center was attacked. But it evolved improbably in the weeks and months after Sept. 11 into a sort of national shrine.

THE VICTIMS

The Chaplain's Embrace, the Sergeant's Songs, and More Than One Parent's Devotion

Here are glimpses of some of the victims of the Sept. 11 attack on the World Trade Center.

MYCHAL JUDGE
Where He Was Needed

LUKE NEE
Bronx in His Blood

GEORGE LLANES
A Poet of Bensonhurst

LINDA OLIVA
Taking Charge With a Smile

THOMAS J. KENNEDY
Last Wishes, First Steps

CATHERINE A. NARDELLA
Someone to Lean On

MARY ALICE WAHLSTROM
Unstoppable 78

At Pier 94 in Manhattan, where an assistance center has been helping the families of World Trade Center victims.

KATHLEEN HUNT-CASEY
A Friend, a Sister

SEAN LYNCH
Red Sox and Best Friends

FRANK V. MOCCIA SR.
Laughter, Win or Lose

JACK CHARLES ARON
A Salt Baron's True Riches

VICTOR J. SARACINI
Making Moments Count

Portraits of Grief continues on the next page.

THE MISSING

Snapshots of Their Lives, Told With the Pain of Those Who Loved Them

Honoring the Rescuers

A NATION CHALLENGED: Those Who Answered the Call

Günter Karl Bose has an autodidactic approach to graphic design. He never attended one of those universities or academies with a department of graphic design—those institutions that succeeded the Bauhaus and now proliferate around the world. Bose studied something decent: German philology, art history, and political science in the beautiful city of Freiburg, located at the edge of the Black Forest. Perfectly armed with a knowledge of the origins of language, especially German and its early literature, Bose settled down in West Berlin, a sort of no-man's-land in the divided Germany of the time. ● ● Bose is a refined man of culture but at the same time a secretive fighter for the cause, a man of convictions, a "zoon politicon." Tellingly, he didn't try to impose his ideas and visions on others, but instead preferred to found his own publishing house. Under the imprint of Brinckmann & Bose he releases titles dedicated to philosophy and literature, as well as film, art, and typography. In the process he has discovered a particular passion for the subtle typographic elements that express an intellectual culture, something not revealed in the decorative surface of an interface, but rather rooted in Marshall McLuhan's *The Gutenberg Galaxy*. ● ●In 1987 Bose republished Jan Tschichold's famous book *The New Typography*, which had first appeared in 1928; in 1991 this was followed by Tschichold's *Writings 1925–1974*. Two years later Bose became a professor at Leipzig's historic university of applied arts. In 2000 he not only opened his lmn-studio in Berlin, but also was made a member of the Alliance Graphique Internationale (AGI). ● ●Simultaneously with his work as a publisher and teacher he has designed a number of books and posters for the Deutsche Oper Berlin, the Oper Leipzig, Musica Viva (of the Bavarian Radio), and the Literaturhaus Berlin. These works are unique in their conceptual grasp and sensitive typographic translation of the subject matter. They are not superficially loud or catchy when the task is to announce a concert or an opera. ● ●Bose's approach is quiet, yet his typographic experiments are unmistakable. They are manifestos of cultural experience. In his work, ubiquitous, almost invisible elements are staged in a new and surprisingly contemporary way. ● ●Uwe Loesch ● ●

1   Musica Viva concert poster / Musica Viva / Germany / 1997
2   Poster for *Industriegebiet der Intelligenz* exhibition on cultural life in West Berlin during the 1920s and 1930s / Literaturhaus Berlin / 1988
3   Poster for *Protest! Literatur um 1968* exhibition on the literature influenced by the student uprisings of 1968 / Literaturhaus Berlin / 1999
4   Poster announcing change and reform efforts at the Academy of Visual Arts, Leipzig / Hochschule für Grafik und Buchkunst, Leipzig / Germany / 1999
5-6 Posters for premieres of the operas *Jenufa*, by Leos Janácek and *Semiramide*, by Gioacchino Rossini / Deutsche Oper Berlin / 2002-2003

Günter Karl Bose

Berlin

MACH MIR EINE SCHULE

DESSINE MOI UNE ECOLE

DESIGN ME A SCHOOL

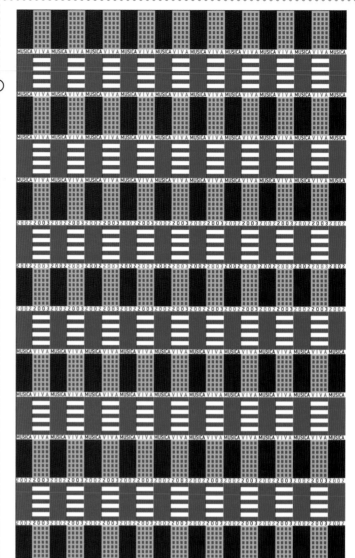

7   Poster for lecture series at the Academy of Visual Arts, Leipzig / Institut für Buchkunst, Hochschule für
     Grafik und Buchkunst, Leipzig / Germany / 1998
8   Cover, Musica Viva concert program for the season 2002-2003 / Musica Viva / Germany / 2002
9   Poster for Musica Viva concert dedicated to compositions by John Cage / Musica Viva / Germany / 2002
10 Poster for Musica Viva concert dedicated to the works of various contemporary composers / Musica Viva /
     Germany / 2002
11 Poster for premiere of the opera *Dmitri oder Der Künstler und die Macht*, by Luca Lombardi /
     Oper Leipzig / 2000
12 Poster for premiere of Musica Viva concert "Voiceless Voice in Hiroshima," by Toshio Hosokawa / Musica
     Viva / Germany / 2001

Günter Karl Bose

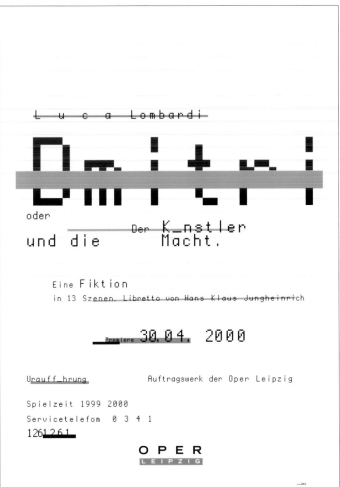

The feeling of a bag filled with soft feathers slowly sinking toward the bottom of the soul. A full, dark sound developing. The CD cover resonates in my eyes and in my mind. Munich's ECM Records has been using Mayo Bucher's strong paintings for selected new CD covers for several years now.**Someone wrote that Bucher's images stand "at the end point of reduction," at the "threshold to self-dissolution." I believe that in reduction he has found a stillness that allows me to pause and breathe deeply. There might be something quietly holy, a tinge of the other, in Bucher's work.**Central to his opus is the conceptual relationship he explores at the intersection of painting, graphic design, architecture, and music. Bucher has the courage to wander about where others burn their fingers, even their faces. For him visual arts, which he studied, are the entrance to graphic design. As a discoverer and creator of images he concentrates everything around and in him. He masters the visual language completely, he doesn't make any spelling mistakes, his sentences are always intelligible. Bucher speaks perfect Visual. Therefore no fissure opens between his graphic work and his two- and three-dimensional artistic works. He bridges obvious critical spots with words. His letters force their shape on me before I am able to grasp their meaning. Forms turn to letters turn to words turn to forms. Bucher is a language talent, because he knows how to delineate and enrich the delineated—and he leaves me alone. Perhaps it is the strength mentioned at the beginning that makes me stand there, the deliberate, space-taking vacuum, this one full, dark sound surrounding his work. He does it on purpose. Bucher is an artist, and he has given me as a present a piece of the universe.**Werner Jeker**

①

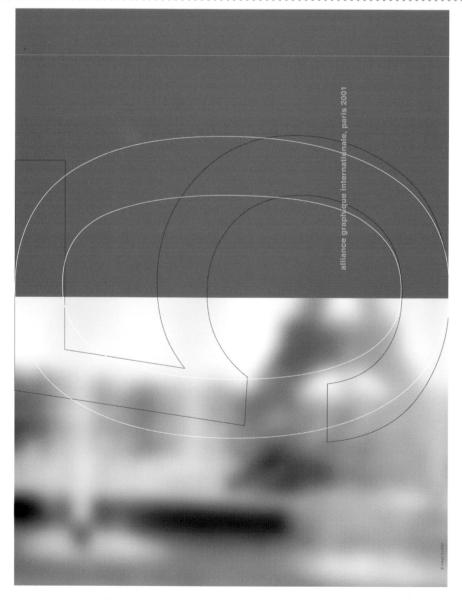

②

1 Self-commissioned piece "Figures 1 to 9" / Switzerland / 2001
2 Poster for fiftieth anniversary of the Alliance Graphique Internationale (AGI) / France / 2001
3 Facade concept in collaboration with Lussi & Halter Architects for a building in Emmenbrücke / Migros Genossenschaftsbund / Switzerland / 2002
4 Entrance-hall mural and light installation in collaboration with Burkhalter & Sumi Architects for Sulzer headquarters in Winterthur / Switzerland / 2003
5 Project study for a facade concept in collaboration with DGJ Architects / Museum Deutsche Bücherei, Leipzig / Germany / 2002

Mayo Bucher

Zurich

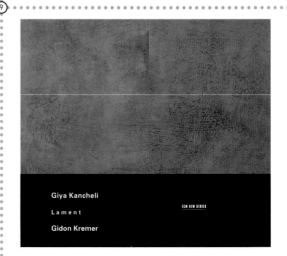

6-9 Cover and section dividers for publication accompanying a McKinsey international corporate conference
(with Mifflin-Schmid Designers, Zurich) / Switzerland / 1999
10 CD cover, Keith Jarret at La Scala / ECM / Germany / 1995
11 CD cover, *Dolorosa*, pieces by Shostakovich, Vasks, and Schnittke / ECM / Germany / 1997
12 CD cover, *Trio Sonatas*, by Jan Dismas Zelenka / ECM / Germany / 1999
13 CD cover, *Lament*, by Giya Kancheli / ECM / Germany / 2000
14 Poster for *Mayo Bucher: OPEN SIGN in progress* exhibition / Academy of Visual Arts, Leipzig / Germany / 2002
15–16 "EINSZWEIDREIVIER" and "ZEROZERO" floor installations for *Mayo Bucher: OPEN SIGN in progress* exhibition /
Academy of Visual Arts, Leipzig / Germany / 2002

Mayo Bucher

MAYO BUCHER

Galerie der Hochschule für Grafik und Buchkunst
Academy of Visual Arts, Leipzig

Ausstellung "OPEN SIGN in progress" 11. 11. 02 – 8. 12. 02
Eröffnung: 25. November 2002, 18:00

Cello – Konzert mit Thomas Demenga (Bach, Demenga, Zimmermann)
Poetry – Improvisation "1234" von Mayo Bucher und Thomas Demenga

Zur Ausstellung Mayo Bucher OPEN SIGN ist die gleichnamige Monografie im Verlag Lars Müller Publishers / ECM erschienen

Das Buch ist Resultat einer Zusammenarbeit der HGB, Leipzig mit der University of Brighton

Als integrierter Bestandteil sind Arbeiten aus dem Workshop "visuelle partitur" von Mayo Bucher mit Studenten der HGB ausgestellt.

Mit freundlicher Unterstützung von PRO HELVETIA

Some people are literally fated to be famous. Vladimir Chaika's last name in Russian means "seagull," an unimpeded sea bird, a symbol of freedom. And his ascent in the profession was bright and swift. ●● Chaika dreamed of being a well-known designer while he was still a student at Strogonov University, and he became famous in Russia very early, in the mid-1980s. He became a bridge between the old Soviet school of graphic design and the new professional generation. For the new generation of designers he became a symbol of design itself. One can say, with a little exaggeration, that he bore this new generation, having shown the path to glory and fame to his only slightly younger comrades, who strove to imitate him in every way, right up to his hairstyle and dress. ●●I had a moniker for this generation of young designers, who appeared in Russia in the late 1980s: "Chaika's younger brothers." Alexander Gelman, now a famous New York designer, as well as Andrey Logvin and Yuri Surkov were all part of this circle. This was still in the 1980s, in what was, for Russia, the precomputer era. ●●In 1990, Chaika spent half a year in New York, in the studio of Massimo Vignelli, who became his idol. Chaika became a fan of Swiss minimalism and decided to become more Swiss than the Swiss themselves. In the mid-1990s Chaika gained wide international popularity. Many top designers who know him personally adore him for his charm and cheerfulness. ●●I most value the work Chaika himself calls "HE-story," history of "him," a character made up of four little lines, short strokes, suggesting the outline of a face. He started drawing these lines, or finding them in the surrounding environment and photographing them, and turning them into posters or magazine covers in the late 1980s. In the past fifteen years one could come across these well-known strokes in different and sometimes the most unexpected of places throughout Russia and eventually the whole world. ●●Who is this mysterious "HE"? Chaika's personal symbol? His mantra? A way of comprehending reality? A game? An omnipresent guardian angel? Or the soul of all things? I don't know. But if you see these lines somewhere high in the Himalayas or in unpopulated Mongolia, know this: Chaika was here, designer from Moscow. ●●Serge Serov ●●

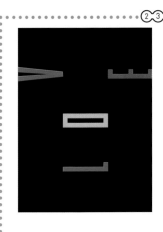

1   Posters from self-commissioned "HE-story" series: He Sees Nothing, He Senses Nothing, He Tells Nothing; He Sees, He Senses, He Tells / Russia / 1995
2-4 Kiss, Smile of EUROpe, and Love, from "HE-story" poster series / Russia / 2000-2002
5   Four Seasons, from "HE-story" poster series / Russia / 1996
6   He Is Here, from "HE-story" poster series / Russia / 1995
7   Poster dedicated to memory of Ikko Tanaka, from "HE-story" series / Russia / 2002
8   "HE," personal symbol of Vladimir Chaika / Russia / 1988

Vladimir Chaika

Moscow

He is here

Ikko Tanaka 1930-2002

9   Self-commissioned Radioactive Mother of God poster dedicated to the victims of the Chernobyl radiation
    disaster / Russia / 1996
10 Poster for Alternative Music Festival in Moscow / Alternative Festival Organization / Russia / 1998
11 Dialogue of Other Worlds poster for Moscow International Festival of Visual Anthropology / Russia / 2002
12 Logo and pictograms for first World Youth Games held in Moscow / World Youth Games Organizational
    Committee / Russia / 1997
13-14 Logo and logo application / Oriol Avia Airlines / Russia / 1991
15 Logo / International Cultural Collaboration Art-Ark / Russia / 1991
16 Logo for *Go* graphic-design magazine / Go / Russia / 1992

Vladimir Chaika

**Первые Всемирные
Юношеские Игры
Москва 1998**

Marcel Hermans is a former student of mine, from the Rietveld Academy in Amsterdam, and he worked for about three years in my studio. Then he took off to the United States, with his Swiss girl-friend, Cornelia Blatter, and now they live between Amsterdam and New York. Their shared firm is COMA. Blatter, originally an artist, brought in her own background. I think COMA's work is thoroughly Swiss-Dutch, fiercely analytical and organized and at the same time adventurous and experimental. They work mainly for museums and publishers, and they art-direct the Dutch design magazine *Frame*.
••COMA continually thinks of new ways to formally organize the material they present in order to arrive at its essence. They make gorgeous catalogues in which they employ any typographic and visual means necessary to structure the work. With Swiss precision and Dutch playfulness, they unravel the artist's work and use it to make their own visual statement. Their choice of work is, in a sense, uncompromising: they stick to their own points of departure. They can work for clients around the world by virtue of the Internet, which makes it easier to exchange high-quality artwork and comps.••For each issue of *Frame* magazine, they choose a different typographic approach, giving each issue its own character. They redefine their position vis-à-vis the publication according to the contents at hand. Matching type and art is often complicated with a magazine: a pot-pourri of visual material lands on your desk, and you have to massage that into a coherent whole. COMA does that by devising a new—strong and inventive—mold for each issue. Clear, transparent, and imaginative within a rigidly researched concept. Their choice of scrutinizing a design to arrive at a personal statement, an individual interpretation, is very close to my own view on design.••Anthon Beeke••

1-4 Cover and spreads, *Greg Lynn and Hani Rashid: Architectural Laboratories* / NAi Publishers / Netherlands / 2002 / The book showcases projects from a four-week workshop for architectural discourse at the 2000 Venice Biennale.
5-8 Cover and spreads, *Peter Halley–Maintain Speed* / Distributed Art Publishers (D.A.P.) / USA / 2000
9-12 Cover and spreads, *The Hugo Boss Prize 2002* / Solomon R. Guggenheim Museum New York / USA / 2002 / Publication accompanying Guggenheim Museum's fourth biennial Hugo Boss prize competition for contemporary art.

COMA

New York/Amsterdam

5
6
7
8

9
10
11
12

every encounter has a color.
iridescent white for kate, sneeuwwit voor valentine, bleach blond for andrea, parelwit voor renny, amber white for beth, almond for craig, titanium white for duane, chroom voor rem, edelweiss for sandra, zilver voor sonja, ivory white for suzanne, champagne voor teo, blanc de titane pour jean-babtist, ivoor voor fieke, kanariegeel voor cisca, reichbleichgold für gaby, bri... yellow for hana, gold für hebi, lichtend zonnegeel voor jantje, safraangeel voor jeannine, oxidgelb für jens, ochre for kim, goudgeel voor krijn, zonnebloemg... ...ns geel voor maartje, vanille geel voor madeleine, mosterdgeel voor misha, goldocker für patricia, naples yellow hue for penny, rotgold für rolf, ...yellow for sally, goldgelb für trudi, ocker für werner, satijngoud voor wout, kadmiumoranje voor frits, dessert orange for will, tang... ...angerine for judith, cognac voor sebastiaan, fluorescent orange for laurie, blueish orange or pink green for burkhard, fluori... ...nrood voor ernestine, eggplant for grant, plumred for leslie, kanarierood voor marijn, scarf red for bernard, ker... ...rmiljoenrood voor jurgen, rouche de pompéi pour fabienne, krapprot für andrea, kardinaalrood voor fr... ...ina, carravagiorood voor marten, hamburger steinrot für hadi, steenrood voor jan, aard... ...y, himbeerrot für susanne, carravagio red for julia, crimson for kristin, rosso por w... ...iek, bloedrood voor lucette, karminrot für maria, carmine red for april, karmijnro... ...urple red for paola, erdbeerrot für szilvia, wine red for susanna, magenta voor maa... ...ed for margit, indian red for uschi, akari red for douglas, mauve for christopher ... ...chsia for vito, aubergine for john, roze voor eef, 87% magenta voor freek, mang... ...ink carnation for kayhan, vivid lavender for jessica, flamingoroze voor katja... ...e voor rick, light peach for theodora, old rose for fred, horizon blue for claris... ...jesblauw voor margriet, eisblau für dominik, kobaltblau für joerg, glanzend... ...or barbara, zilverblauw voor bert, denimblauw voor carl, ocean blue for deenie... ...voor ineke, hemelblauw voor floris, pale blue for gabriel, navy blue fo... ...canary blue for helga, prussian blue for katura, schimmerndes schme... ...pruisischblauw voor jaap, bleu de céruléum pour jacques, mitternach... ...tblue for joseph, indigo for mark, bertblauw voor karin, salvia blue... ...für bice, delfsblauw voor frederieke, alpineblauw voor maya, turqu... ...eladon for avo, maagdenpalmblauw voor barbera, kobaltblauw voor ... ...oor rutger, azure blue for jodi, steel blue for sarah, ultramarinblau fü... ...awrence, light blue for steve, dunkelblau for anke, staalblauw voor su... ...een for rogen, woudgroen voor ernst, jungle green for ayumi, pine green fo... ...r hans-ulrich, brilliant green for ed, lettuce green for greg, mint green for... ...n feurig für markus, venetian green for michael, mistletoe green for peter, cana... ...e green for kristjan, waldgrün für jacqueline, lime green for jennifer, calypso g... ...rown for martin, gebrande sienna voor christine, oxidbraun für marco, reebruin v... ...or auke, olivbraun für kai, sandalwood for linda, pms 877 for jason, antraciet vo... ...e gray for christoph, grüngrau für gereon, luminous silver for frank, donkergroen voor bas, hellgrau für stefan, lampzwart voor... ...ayhan, jet black for tom, perlschwarz für christoph, eisenoxidschwarz für michael, ijzeroxidezwart voor donald, parelzwart voor anthon... ...k for bruce, luminous black for jennifer, shiny black for susan and all colors of the rainbow for judith. every encounter has a color.
coma, cornelia blatter & marcel hermans

13 Self-commissioned project "Every Encounter Has A Color" / Netherlands and USA / 2001 / The project comprises ten color cards, a folded envelope, and an essay by Anna Blume. The inside of the envelope lists the names of all the people COMA encountered in 2001. Each person was given a color name in the language of the encounter. The color name, cards, and essay served as a present for friends and clients.
14–16 Self-commissioned project "Describe Something Sweet" / Netherlands and USA / 1998 / People of different ages, nationalities, and professions were asked to "describe something sweet." Each response was told on sugar-cube wrappers in the handwriting of the person asked.
17–18 Cover and spread, *Index* magazine, April–May 2000 / Peter Halley / USA / 2000
19–20 Cover and spread, *Frame* magazine, January–February 2003 / Frame / Netherlands / 2003
21–24 Cover and spreads, *Nanoarchitecture–a New Species of Architecture–John M. Johansen* / Princeton Architectural Press / USA / 2002

COMA

index

BIJOU

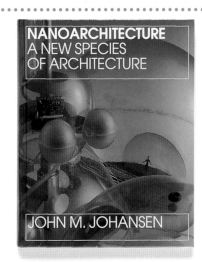

NANOARCHITECTURE
A NEW SPECIES
OF ARCHITECTURE

JOHN M. JOHANSEN

BIJOU PHILLIPS
the veritable
holy terror
of page

6

For anyone with even a casual relationship with the delicious Page Six, *The New York Post's* gossip column, "Bijou" should already be somewhat of a household word. In fact, Bijou Phillips, who will turn twenty in the year 2000, has been the veritable holy terror of Page Six for the past four or five years now. She's today's Tuesday, the new Drew, a wild child who, through fate and circumstance, was somehow allowed to partake of New York's nebulous nightlife at an age traditionally more suited to playing with dolls — that is, of the non-pharmaceutical variety.

with Bruce LaBruce
photographed by Terry Richardson

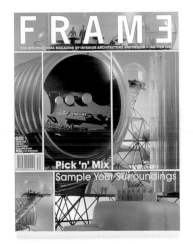

FRAM∃
THE INTERNATIONAL MAGAZINE OF INTERIOR ARCHITECTURE AND DESIGN > JAN/FEB 2002

Pick 'n' Mix
Sample Your Surroundings

textiles

CROSSING
BORDERS

Graduation projects by Dutch design students indicate that textile and product designers are pushing the envelope of their profession as never before. A selection from the rich harvest of new designs discovered at academies in Arnhem, Eindhoven, The Hague and Maastricht not only reveals the specific properties of various textiles, but also shows the degree to which textile design touches on other disciplines. Young designers are crossing borders, giving 'old' a new coat and dressing 'new' in old clothes. They are aiming tactility, for

instance, at target groups marked by a highly developed sense of touch, such as blind people and small children. Materials cleverly couched in a new context pull the wool over our eyes, making us chuckle. Patterns used in a new construction take on a different meaning and an extra dimension. The students whose projects are featured here approached the challenge of reconciling extremes and contrasts with eyes wide open. A series of photographs paints a picture of their experiments, their statements of social involvement and their prototypes for series production, while summarising the creative content of a new generation of designers.

I can't help it. Whenever I read the name Das Haus Rüegger und Albisetti (The House of Rüegger and Albisetti), I begin to imagine this house. Judith Rüegger and Anna Albisetti hereby suggest a kind of home, something intimate, for the house defines personality, manifests a style. Its site is of no importance, since their house materializes as their work, which is printed material. The two women live and work in their house. They maintain it in optimal condition. No project leaves the house through the back door, in shame. One of the women might very well work alone on occasion, but if a project is large enough for both of them, they work together, sometimes with one of them starting and the other finishing the project. This sounds symbiotic, like an intact world, like cowbells and chocolate, because the strategy is of utmost simplicity.●● Rüegger and Albisetti have known each other since their first days of training as graphic artists. Both follow the tradition of the craft, which the Schule für Gestaltung (School for Graphic Design) in Biel, Switzerland, so rapturously awakens in its students. Biel has a reputation for offering an easygoing education with an unusually strong emphasis on drawing for our time. This foundation may have generated the playful, sketchy, and collagelike element that forms the basis of Rüegger and Albisetti's work. The design process remains visible in all of their creations, they are among the few designers who are really apt at using the computer as a tool.●● Back to the "House of Symbiosis." They take their clients seriously. They become absorbed in the client's expectations. The layering of their streams of thought, allowing ideas to live next to one another, the juxtaposition of expectation, color, material, are mastered by Das Haus Rüegger und Albisetti with an enviable lightness. I would like to be a guest in such a house.●●Werner Jeker●●

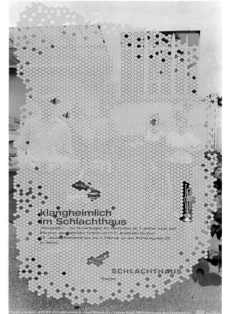

1–2   Posters for Ja'salâm! festival celebrating contemporary Arab culture in Bern /
       Pro Helvetia / Switzerland / 2002
3   Cover, Ja'salâm! festival program / 2002
4–6   Poster series *Gruppenbild* (Group Picture) announcing the theatrical program for
       the season 2000–2001 (3 of 6) / Schlachthaus Theater Bern / Switzerland /
       2000–2001 / The series is based on a photograph incorporating elements of all
       plays to be shown during the season. The individual posters are created by covering different areas of the surface. The season finale-poster reveals the photograph
       in its entirety.
7–10   Poster series *Kürzest Dialoge* (Shortest Dialogues) advertising the Schlachthaus
       Theater Bern (4 of 7) / 1998–1999

Das Haus Rüegger + Albisetti

Bern

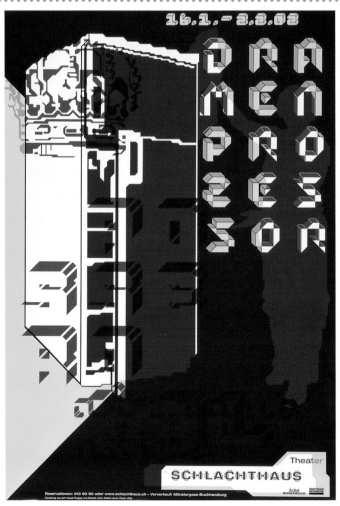

11-13 Poster series *Aus 1 mach 3* (One Becomes Three) for play *Posse Royal*, by Matto Kämpf, and theater productions *Afrique noire* and *Dramenprozessor* / Schlachthaus Theater Bern / Switzerland / 2001-2002
14-16 Poster series *Theater ist einmalig* (Theater Is Unique) advertising the Schlachthaus Theater Bern (3 of 4) / 1998-1999
17 Poster celebrating the fifth anniversary of the Schlachthaus Theater Bern / 2003

Das Haus Rüegger + Albisetti

When Richard van der Laak entered our studio as an apprentice, he made a point of not being intimidated—he more or less took over the entire studio, not forgetting to bring his dog along. I soon noticed his remarkable ability to see things in perspective, a trait that also characterizes the work he and his partners at De Designpolitie produce. I think the name is an allusion to the battle over illegal software and fonts on the Internet—a bit ironic with a laddish bravado that has become second nature to them. They are rather original with a high visual intelligence, supported by a thorough knowledge of visual culture. They are typical representatives of a young rank of image mavericks, a generation that, perhaps unwittingly, has been trained by Dick Bruna. Bruna's priceless gift to visual culture has been to demonstrate to very young kids that images are "readable." This visual language, which the partners at De Designpolitie must have been familiar with at a tender age, made quite an impression. Like Bruna, De Designpolitie knows how to make an intelligent visual statement with the sparsest of means. They are also a bit Swiss, in their tight typography and the rigorous organization of their images. In the circles for the 1997 annual report for the Raad van Cultuur (Dutch State Council for Culture), for instance, they evoke info-architecture in their interpretation of the council's work and context. Precise and cheerful, they are still not easy to intimidate.••Anthon Beeke••

1-4   Invitations/murals for various events and exhibitions at W139 art gallery in Amsterdam / W139 / Netherlands / 2002 / The invitations were first manually painted on blank walls in Amsterdam, then photographed and printed.
5-6   Posters for Springdance art and dance festival / Springdance Festival 1998 / Netherlands / 1998
7-8   Poster and cover for annual report of the Dutch State Council for Culture / Raad van Cultuur / Netherlands / 1998 / The poster folds around the book to serve as a dustjacket.

De Designpolitie

Amsterdam

SPRINGDANCE
13-25 APRIL 1999 UTRECHT

SPRINGDANCE
13-25 APRIL 1999 UTRECHT

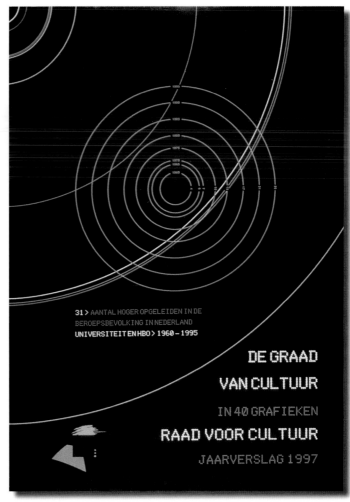

31 > AANTAL HOGER OPGELEIDEN IN DE
BEROEPSBEVOLKING IN NEDERLAND
UNIVERSITEIT EN HBO > 1960 – 1995

DE GRAAD

VAN CULTUUR

IN 40 GRAFIEKEN

RAAD VOOR CULTUUR

JAARVERSLAG 1997

kaarten: 17,50 (try out: 10,-) telefonisch reserveren vanaf 24 mei t/m 9 juni (maandag t/m donderdag tussen 10.00 uur en 12.00 uur) tel. 030-520334

De Designpolitie

Opleidingengids
2003-2004

Opleidingengids 2003-2004

Hogeschool voor
de Kunsten Utrecht

Utrecht School
of the Arts

Delaware means Masato Samata, Aya Honda, Morihiro Tajiri, and Yoshiki Watanabe. Delaware comes from Japan, from rock 'n' roll, personal computers, mobile phones, and bitmaps. Delaware takes inspiration from Western-world artists like James Brown, the Beatles, Kraftwerk, Stanley Kubrick, and Roy Lichtenstein but most of all from the Japanese artist Hajime Tachibana, former member of the Plastics.●●Very few artists have fused graphic design, music, performance, and life as originally and organically as these four Japanese, who have worked mainly on CDs, magazines, T-shirts, commercials, websites, and live performances since 1993. Truly extraordinary is the total elimination of boundaries between the disciplines they endeavor in. Sound, surface, and action create one strong and vital communication experience whose only stated goals are fun, inner peace, and the search for the "future feeling." No self-indulgence in torturing social or philosophical theories here, just self-conscious day-to-day "rockin' the house" blended with introspective dialogue. This might risk superficiality, but most of the work goes deep. Pieces like Dokuro, Umbrella, Nice to Meet You, We Are Alone, Check Yourself, You Will be Soon Born—You Will be Soon Dead, and Walking in the Forest convey both intimate and social expressions of contemporary uncertainty, solitude, and concern. Other images might make us wonder what they are all about, but when the visual treat is so astounding, should we care?●●However indivisible this mix is, Delaware's graphic-design output is outstanding. Masato Samata, the only member who doesn't play an instrument, is the graphics wizard behind the curtain conceiving their trendsetting style. He is a source of true renewal in the world where change often comes only from software updates. Delaware's iconic dimensions are developed through an instinctive and often accidental mix of cultures, music, computers, internet, and cellphones. Delaware is content and form for the future of today.●●Omar Vulpinari●●

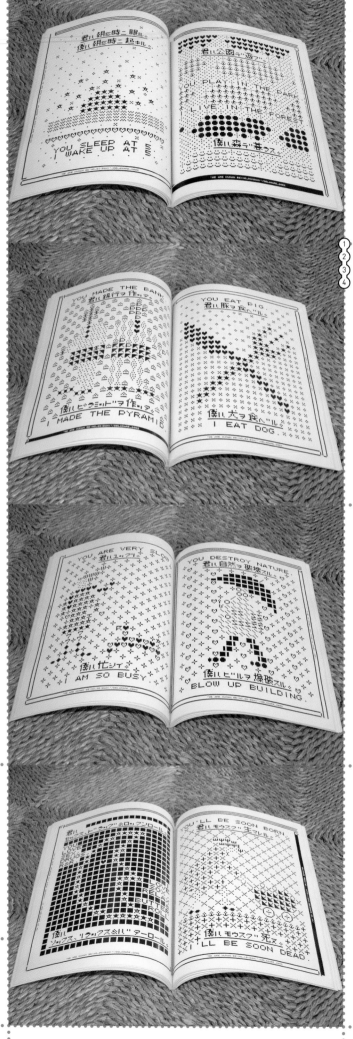

1–4   Spreads from *Textfield Magazine* 1.01 / Textfield Magazine / USA / 2003
5   Skull poster created for *I love to meet you–New graphic design* exhibition held at
       Palazzo Fortuny in Venice / Italy / 2002
6   Delaware design for the Pitti Uomo men's-fashion trade fair in Florence / Italy / 2003

Delaware

Tokyo

7   Have a Break design (unreleased) / Japan / 2003
8   We are Alone cross-stitched design for *Buzz Club: News from Japan* exhibition
    held at P.S. 1 Contemporary Art Center, New York / USA / 2001
9   Nice to Meet You poster for *JaPan Graphics* exhibition held at RAS gallery and FAD
    Capella dels Angels, Barcelona / Spain / 2002
10 You'll be Soon Born–You'll be Soon Dead design for "My Favorite Conference"
    organized by *IdN Magazine* in Hong Kong / IdN Magazine / Hong Kong / 2002
11 Work Shoes design (unreleased) / Japan / 2003
12–14 Dokuro, Umbrella, and Cool Cat projection and mural designs for Pitti Uomo
    men's-fashion trade fair in Florence / Italy / 2003
15–17 Views of Stairway to Heaven mural design at Pitti Uomo men's-fashion trade fair in
    Florence / Italy / 2003

Delaware

Chris Dixon has been working in editorial design since the mid-1990s and has created quite a name for himself. He is perhaps best known for his work on *Adbusters* magazine, which he redesigned in 1996 (and where he subsequently stayed for a further four years as art director). *Adbusters*' new look had a considerable impact on the world of editorial design and is regarded as one of the most ground-breaking publications in recent years. ••*Adbusters* requires a visual language that immediately grabs the attention of its target audience. It deals with issues of consumerism, the environment, and the mass media, with a subversive edge. As an international publication, it also demands universal appeal. Dixon's striking solution was incredibly successful: Not only did it look great—with consistently inventive covers and spreads, great image-sourcing and picture editing—it also communicated its message with impact and clarity. ••*Adbusters* provided Dixon with relative freedom and a chance to flex his muscles as an editorial designer with a seemingly endless number of ideas that always seemed appropriate to the content. He made the magazine more accessible, in a manner that retained its integrity. Circulation rose from 25,000 to 95,000 during his tenure as art director, and in terms of design, the results speak for themselves. ••Dixon's success at *Adbusters* led to other equally challenging projects, such as *rd*, a concept magazine developed for Microsoft's research and development division. Microsoft has not yet decided to go with it, which is a shame, as Dixon's initial concepts suggest a dynamism rarely found in corporate magazines. His work for *The New York Times Magazine* revealed his willingness to explore more classical forms. The spreads and covers he created for the magazine recall editorial design of the 1940s and '50s, albeit with a redefined sense of elegance and sophistication that is entirely relevant and contemporary. ••He recently designed and art directed a special anniversary magazine for the American edition of the *Financial Times*, created to suggest the *FT*'s growing popularity in the U.S. The design had to be simple and sophisticated in order to reflect the personality of the paper and the *FT* brand. Dixon succeeded: The magazine feels professional, confident, and authoritative. His versatility and prowess as a designer becomes more apparent with each project. ••Fernando Gutiérrez••

1-2 Front and back of poster launching the First Things First 2000 manifesto / The Media Foundation / Canada / 2000
3-4 Prototype covers, *rd* magazine / RD, Microsoft / USA / 2002
5-6 Covers, *Whiplash and Other Useful Illnesses*, by Andrew Malleson, and *Detemining Boundaries*, by Suzanne Lalonde / McGill-Queens Press / Canada / 2002

Chris Dixon

New York

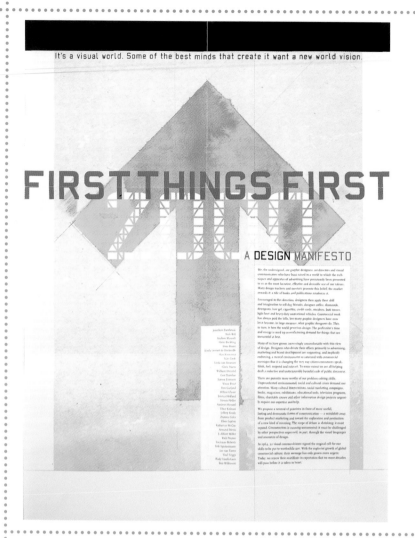

It's a visual world. Some of the best minds that create it want a new world vision.

FIRST THINGS FIRST 2000

A DESIGN MANIFESTO

FIRST THINGS FIRST 1964-2000

DESIGN ANARCHY

FIRST THINGS FIRST 2000
A DESIGN MANIFESTO

www.adbusters.org

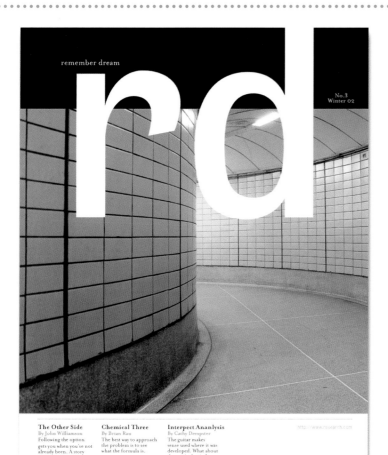

remember dream

rd

No.3
Winter 02

The Other Side
By John Williamson
Following the option gets you when you've not already been. A story about good lawyers.

Chemical Three
By Brian Rau
The best way to approach the problem is to see what the formula is.

Interpect Ananlysis
By Cathy Dempster
The guitar makes sense used where it was developed. What about the music that is done without sound?

http://www.research.com

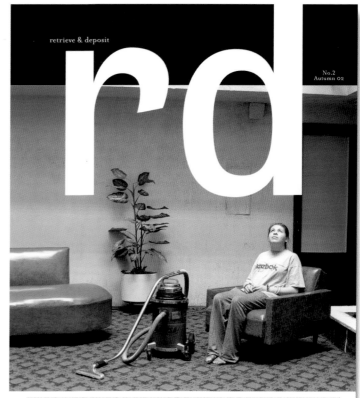

retrieve & deposit

rd

No.2
Autumn 02

Running Off Water
By John Williamson
Following the option gets you when you've not already been. A story about good lawyers who know science now.

Music Analogy
By Brian Rau
The best way to approach the problem is to see what the formula is.

Dominant Gene
By Cathy Dempster
The guitar makes sense used where it was developed. What about the music that is done?

http://www.research.com

ERROR

ERROR

ERROR

ERROR

ERROR

ERROR

ERROR

ERROR

ERROR

ERROR

ERROR

ERROR

ERROR

ERROR

ERROR

ERROR

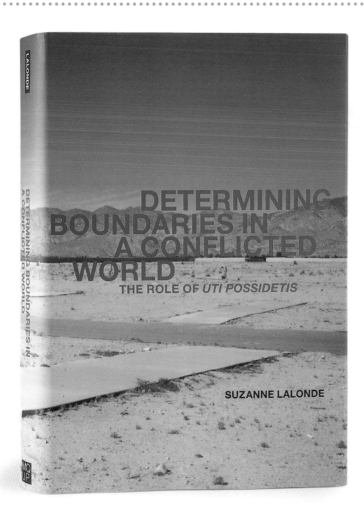

LALONDE

DETERMINING BOUNDARIES IN A CONFLICTED WORLD

THE ROLE OF *UTI POSSIDETIS*

SUZANNE LALONDE

MQUP

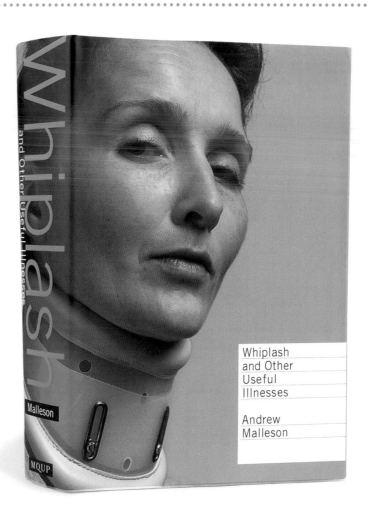

Whiplash
and Other Useful Illnesses

Whiplash
and Other
Useful
Illnesses

Andrew
Malleson

Malleson

MQUP

Chris Dixon

The View From the Bridge

In Kosovo, in the city of Mitrovica, the Ibar River maintains a fragile peace — keeping Serbs and Albanians from each other's throats.

Photographs by Paolo Pellegrin Text by Guy Lawson

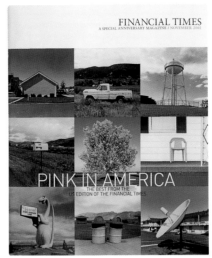

PINK IN AMERICA
THE BEST FROM THE
US EDITION OF THE FINANCIAL TIMES

Insert a Single
Spider Gene
into a Female Goat.
Milk Regularly.

Got Silk.

By Lawrence Osborne

Photographs by Mackenzie Stroh

ON THE WORLD

PLEASE HOLD MOSCOW... KIM JONG IL IS ON THE LINE

NORTH KOREA'S DICTATOR CROSSES RUSSIA IN AN ARMOUR-PLATED TRAIN, BUT LEAVES HIS REVOLUTION BEHIND

BY ROBERT COTTRELL ILLUSTRATION BY LARA TOMLIN

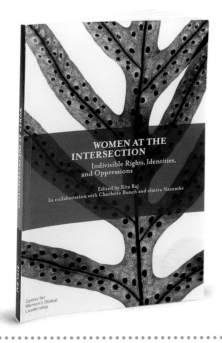

WOMEN AT THE INTERSECTION
Indivisible Rights, Identities, and Oppressions

Edited by Rita Raj
In collaboration with Charlotte Bunch and elmira Nazombe

Center for
Women's Global
Leadership

THE SUPERIORITY COMPLEX

Philip Stephens
UK Editor and
Senior Columnist

For Daniel Eatock, personal work is as important as commercial work. Each one informs the other, and with architect Sam Solhaug, Eatock has set up Foundation 33, a studio that caters specifically to that process.••If you venture into the bathroom at Foundation 33, you'll find the Big Brother Mandate, created as a guide to their working process. It says a lot about their approach to design: "DON'T DESIGN, start: crude and radical, finish: considered and radical."••There is certainly a radical quality to Eatock's work, a subversive edge communicated with the utilitarian, everyday veneer of his visual vocabulary that provides an antidote to ostentation. On the surface, it is a disciplined language, with a deadpan delivery that, when you consider the content, is very tongue-in-cheek. It constantly challenges our expectations.••Foundation 33 are doing exactly that with the billboards they are creating for British television's Channel Four, utilizing a powerful communications medium to maximum effect. For the TV drama series *Shackleton*, the warning "Danger: Ice" appears in heavy white text on a red ground: very clear, very direct. A site-specific version of the billboard (on Cromwell Road in west London) featured actual blocks of ice in front of the poster, a potent stop-and-stare solution. Challenging our expectations.••The World's Largest Signed and Numbered Limited Edition Artwork—created in 2002 for Channel Four's *The Art Show*—had an edition of a million and ran with the tagline: "This artwork is exclusive for a milion people. *The Art Show* is inclusive for everybody." Inclusive for everybody. Like E-mail, a postcard that allows people to send e-mails without a computer, or Peace Chart, a pie chart of world religions designed to resemble the CND logo. Both subversive in their own way, both simple and direct. Eatock's calling card is a sticker of used chewing gum, which he leaves under tables wherever he goes.••Eatock and Solhaug first collaborated on a series of plywood furniture, designed and manufactured so that every piece of wood was an integral component of the finished piece. Just like Foundation 33's graphic oeuvre: no waste, no trimmings. Considered and radical.••Fernando Gutiérrez••

1   Pricing Labels wrapping paper / Foundation 33 / United Kingdom / 2003
2   Used chewing-gum sticker / Foundation 33 / United Kingdom / 2003
3   Utilitarian Greeting Cards / Foundation 33 / Untited Kingdom / 2003 / The sender must appropriate each card for its recipient.
4-5 Sun Light and Aerial View postcards (photography by Daniel Eatock) / Foundation 33 / United Kingdom / 2003
6-7 The World's Largest Signed and Numbered Limited Edition Artwork hosted by Whitechapel Art Gallery, London / Channel Four Television / United Kingdom / 2002 / Project announcing Channel Four's program *The Art Show* on contemporary art, design, and culture, in which one million "artworks" were distributed for free. The project was carefully recorded and is in the process of being submitted to the Guinness World Records.

Daniel Eatock/Foundation 33

London

Occasion Card

Before giving card, tick the box relevant to the occasion being celebrated.

- Birthday
- Valentine
- Mother's Day
- Easter
- Father's Day
- Christmas
- New Year
- Anniversary
- Good luck
- Congratulations
- Well done
- Other*

*Please specify
....

Greeting Card

Using a red pen delete all descriptions that are not relevant to card's recipient.

Mum	Cousin	Enemy
Dad	Nephew	Stranger
Daughter	Niece	Teacher
Son	Twin	Boss
Sister	Girlfriend	Neighbour
Brother	Boyfriend	Other*
Grandma	Wife	
Grandad	Husband	
Aunt	Friend	
Uncle	Lover	

*Please specify
....

Birthday Card

Before giving card, tick box or specify which birthday is being celebrated.

- First
- Eighteenth
- Twenty-first
- Fortieth
- Fiftieth
- Sixtieth
- Hundredth
- Other*

*Please specify
....

Late Card

Write an excuse or apology in no more than fifty words to explain why this card is late.

_____
_____
_____
_____
_____
_____
_____
_____

Sign and date

The world's largest signed and numbered limited edition artwork

The world's largest signed and numbered limited edition artwork

Authorised signatory

Your number is

94000

/ One million

Daniel Eatock, Sam Solhaug, Hanna Werning, Lyn Winter, Flavia Müller Medeiros, Mark Hopkins, Soo Hong, Milos Covic, Naoko Sato, Kirsty Carter

8   Billboard announcing Channel Four coverage of the World Rally Championship 2002 / Channel Four Television / United Kingdom / 2001

9   Billboard announcing live broadcast of Turner Prize award ceremony from Tate Britain / Channel Four Television / United Kingdom / 2001

10   Billboard for reality TV show *Big Brother* / Channel Four Television / United Kingdom / 2001–2002

11   Update of previous year's billboard campaign for *Big Brother* / Channel Four Television / United Kingdom / 2002

12   Billboard announcing MOBO (Music of Black Origin) awards / Channel Four Television / United Kingdom / 2001

13   Untitled Beatles poster / Foundation 33 / United Kingdom / 2000 / Poster is made up of all the lyrics of every Beatles song.

Daniel Eatock/Foundation 33

Printed on 6 December 2000 / Concept & Design Daniel Eatock MR (RCA) / Published by Foundation 33 in an edition of 1000 copies

Eboy is a design squad of four crew-cut look-alike fun-lovers who from their bases in Berlin and New York are spreading digital art worldwide. **E-dudes, e-chicks, e-robots, and e-guns. E-cars, e-games, e-superstars, and e-dreams: a true boy's world that every man would want to play in, as the Eboy partners state. Images of contemporary urban youth culture that recall both ancient Byzantine mosaics and vernacular patchwork. Constructed often, like in their imaginary "eCities" project, by all four minds and eight hands of the members. Icons born for a digital, internet-connected realm but intensely speculating about today's life patterns. **Steffen Sauerteig, Svend Smital, Peter Stemmler, and Kai Vermehr draw inspiration from the society they live in, the schools where they studied, the streets they played on, and the beaches where they went on girl hunts. Very often the four artists are among the actors of their fantasy scenarios—an attentive viewer can spot the Eboys themselves protesting, shooting, driving, and fighting on the streets and rooftops of their life-bubbling landscapes. **Consumerism, MTV, supermarkets, street fashion, entertainment, sex, and violence give life to Photoshop pixel nightmares and Bézier curve dreams. A micro-to-macro investigation into environments populated by Lego- and Playskool-inspired characters exaggerate juvenile itches and desires. Pixels become subversive, beautiful, powerful, and easy to handle, while vector lines assume a seductive, intimate, and nasty allure. Eboy searches for unfettered human essentials where technology is seen as evolution, not danger. Their cities, robots, and weapons are often dark and scary because pain and fear are also part of the human spectrum. **Research with humor and irony is the main engine of the group. Most commissions come from clients who come across Eboy's experimental, fun-driven projects on their website. Here visitors can become the authors of unseen creatures. The firm's Peecol modular system enables anyone to build body-part typefaces and schizophrenic virtual characters—a bit of help to rediscover the little e-boy/e-girl inside all of us. **Omar Vulpinari**

1   Poster for exhibition celebrating the inauguration of luxury apartment
    building in Singapore / Brazen Communications / Singapore / 2002
2   Cover illustration for *IdN Magazine* (not realized) / IdN Magazine / Hong
    Kong / 2002
3   Picture for Eboy exhibition at J-10 clothing store / Hong Kong / 2002
4   Detail of illustration for *Arena* magazine (not realized) / Arena / United
    Kingdom / 2001
5   Self-commissioned In Memory camouflage graffiti / Germany / 2001
6   Illustration for energy company / Harpen AG / Germany / 2001

Eboy

Berlin/New York

③

④

⑤

⑥

⑦

⑧

⑨

⑩

7   Illustration for *Electronic Gaming Monthly* magazine / Electronic Gaming Monthly / USA / 2002
8   Spread illustration for *The Face* magazine / The Face / United Kingdom / 2002
9   Self-commissioned Venice poster from "eCities" project / Germany / 2002
10 Spread illustration for *Mass Appeal Magazine* / Mass Appeal Magazine / USA / 2002
11 Adidas print advertisement / Leagas Delaney / United Kingdom / 2001
12 Pixel portraits of the four Eboys / Germany / 2002
13 Contribution to book *Disruptive Pattern Material* / Maharishi / United Kingdom / 2002
14 Print advertisement for gamer website powerplay.de / D-office / Germany / 2000

⑪

Eboy

A billboard ad has only to hook you momentarily. It has worked if you have noticed it. No scrutiny necessary, as blanket coverage will ensure that a thousand fleeting interruptions in your day laminate into an awareness that perhaps you'd rather not have. Whereas a piece of graphic design like, say, a company brochure or a book has to hold your attention long enough to remain in your hands in order to function. It has to bear scrutiny, deliver on the promises its form makes. ●●The self-deprecating design work of writer and publisher Dave Eggers taunts you with the prospect of boredom. For issue 3 of the cult literary journal *McSweeney's*, an obsessively meticulous yet clumsily assembled wheel of words and phrases is squeezed onto the cover and crowded by tiny, crude line drawings and minuscule marginalia. Words he has set in the wheel mock his own publishing effort: "Form as decoy," "All this: Cryptic, intriguing . . . or just kind of stupid?," "Yes, but remember we did not promise," "Come winter, much of this will make sense." Anyone who had already read issue 2 would have been familiar with Eggers's humor. That cover tempts readers with a conservatively centered list of announcements set in Garamond caps and italics that includes: "Welcoming: all comers, provided they're not going anywhere." Beside that, another wheel of letters tempers expectations once you can make out that they spell "sorry already." ●●Designers more in awe than Eggers of inherited laws about what makes typography and layout tasteful will view his distinctive design work as compromised by its content. Form and content seem out of kilter. Yet it seems the more compromised his design is by verbiage, the more the content seems to promise. Eggers's use of writing as form-making gives him a completely different perspective on design. In *McSweeney's* no. 2 he asks, "And how often are formal innovations masking one's insecurity with the text?" His cover design for his second novel, *You Shall Know Our Velocity*, shows no such fear as that is where the text starts; the first paragraph unadorned, set justified to fill the space. While not a match for his first book, *A Heartbreaking Work of Staggering Genius*, it is nonetheless one that will remain in your hands for quite a while. ●●Nick Bell●●

1–3   Cover with bellyband and spreads, *The New Sins*, by David Byrne / McSweeney's Publishing / USA / 2001
4   Cover, *McSweeney's* no.9 / McSweeney's Publishing / USA / 2002
5   Cover, *McSweeney's* no.3, "Timothy McSweeney's Windfall Republic" / McSweeney's Publishing / USA / 1999
6   Spread, *McSweeney's* no.3
7   Page from "A Note About the Type," *McSweeney's* no.3

Dave Eggers

San Francisco

8 Cover, *You Shall Know Our Velocity*, by Dave Eggers / McSweeney's Publishing / USA / 2002
9–11 Spreads from *You Shall Know Our Velocity* / The blank spread appears in the middle of the sentence "…and the pause between when we became airborne [blank spread] and WHACK when we landed…"
12 Vinyl cover, *The Only Blip Hop Record You Will Ever Need* vol. 1 (with Danielle Spencer) / Luka Bop Inc. / USA / 2002
13 Back cover, *A Heartbreaking Work of Staggering Genius*, by Dave Eggers / Vintage Books / USA / 2000
14 Cover, *Timothy McSweeney's Blues–Jazz Odyssey* / McSweeney's Publishing / USA / 1999
15–16 Cover and inside booklets, *McSweeney's no.7* (booklets with Elizabeth Kairys) / McSweeney's Publishing / USA / 2001

Dave Eggers

If you are the type of person who judges people on appearances, then you may well be misled by your first impressions of Jonathan Ellery. An ex–Rugby Union player with a fondness for sharply tailored suits, he can appear to be quite an imposing character. In reality he is a sensitive, refined type, with a very good eye and a keen understanding of aesthetics, qualities that have enabled him to develop an accomplished and well-rounded body of work. ● ● When we discussed how best to present his work, we decided upon a selection of recent posters. Posters are arguably the most direct medium of communication available to graphic designers, and even though most (if not all) of Ellery's posters belong to wider promotional print programs, the direct simplicity required for poster design is apparent throughout his portfolio. ● ● Ellery's work is characterized by its distinctive Britishness. The image of Tower Bridge on the cover of the book *Browns: A Walk Through Books* (2003), which contains examples of the studio's publishing design, is indicative of this British spirit that frequently informs Ellery's vocabulary. It hints at the heritage of London and stereotypical notions of Britain, while the context suggests something more modern. ● ● When Ellery's work references the past, it does so in a way that feels contemporary, and always in a manner appropriate to the project. In 2001 Ellery designed the book *Coney Island*—featuring the photography of Bruce Gilden—with a typographical language that recalls letterpress posters and ads for carnivals, circuses, and theaters from the early twentieth century. Back then, New York's Coney Island would have been awash with such examples. Elsewhere, he references the tradition of postcards with loose, scratchy, handwritten lettering. ● ● Above all, Ellery's work is about solving problems, with an approach that is driven by communication and simplicity of expression. It sounds simple enough, and that is the point. That is what graphic design is all about. ● ● Fernando Gutiérrez ● ●

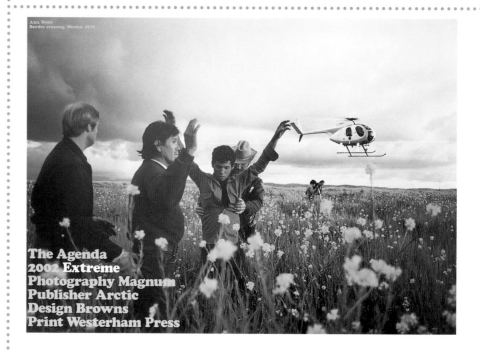

The Agenda 2003
70 Magnum Photographers
Published by Arctic Papers
Design by Browns/London
Available October 2002
www.arcticpapers.com
Price £15.00 €20.00 $20.00

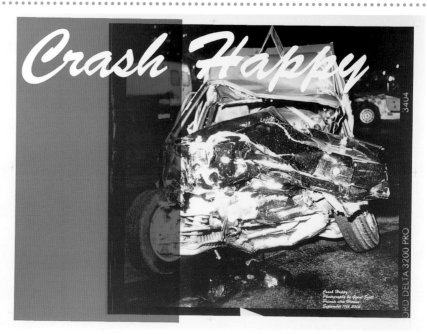

1   Poster promoting Love and Peace agenda 2003 / Artic Papers - Trebruk / United Kingdom / 2002
2   Poster promoting Extreme agenda 2002 / Arctic Papers - Trebruk / United Kingdom / 2001
3   Poster for Grant Scott photography exhibition *Crash Happy* / Grant Scott / United Kingdom / 2002
4   Poster for D&AD–Nesta Product Design and Innovation Student Awards / D&AD and Nesta / United Kingdom / 2003
5   Poster for seminar at Falmouth College of Arts / Falmouth College of Art / United Kingdom / 1999
6   Poster for international "Pure Football. Pure Hope." campaign (1 of 10) / FIFA and UNICEF / 1999
7   Poster for D&AD–Nesta Product Design and Innovation Student Awards / D&AD and Nesta / United Kingdom / 2002

Jonathan Ellery

London

"We voted him in as captain, and then...
we're always the last four to be chosen."
Angelo (age 6), Rio

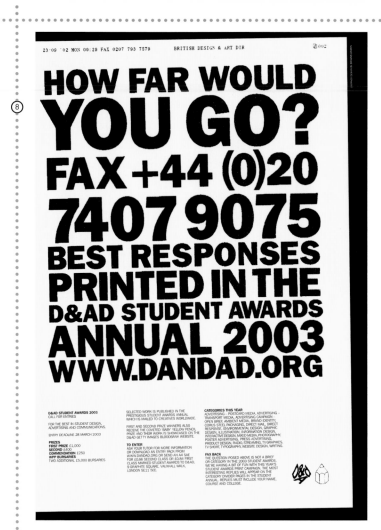

8   Poster promoting *Pandora's Box*, by Susan Meiselas (1 of 3) / Trebruk / United Kingdom / 2001
9   Call for Entries poster for 2003 D&AD Student Awards / D&AD / United Kingdom / 2002
10   Poster promoting *Go*, by Bruce Gilden / Arctic Paper and Trebruk / United Kingdom / 2000
11–12 Posters promoting *Coney Island*, by Bruce Gilden (2 of 5) / Arctic Paper and Trebruk / United Kingdom / 2001
13   Poster promoting European Clichés agenda 2000 (1 of 5) / Munkedals–Trebruk / United Kingdom / 2000
14   Briefing Day poster for 2001 D&AD Student Awards / D&AD / United Kingdom / 2000

Jonathan Ellery

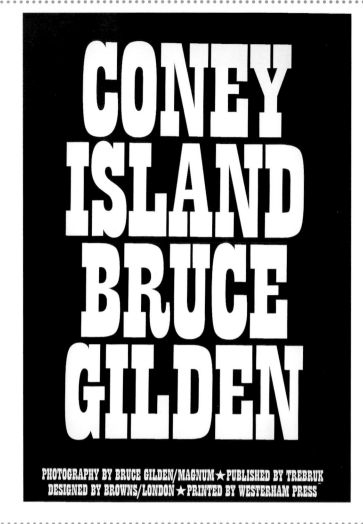

CONEY ISLAND BRUCE GILDEN

PHOTOGRAPHY BY BRUCE GILDEN/MAGNUM ★ PUBLISHED BY TREBRUK
DESIGNED BY BROWNS/LONDON ★ PRINTED BY WESTERHAM PRESS

⑬

European clichés 2000
Munken Agenda, photography by Martin Parr/Magnum
Available at www.munkedals.se

⑭

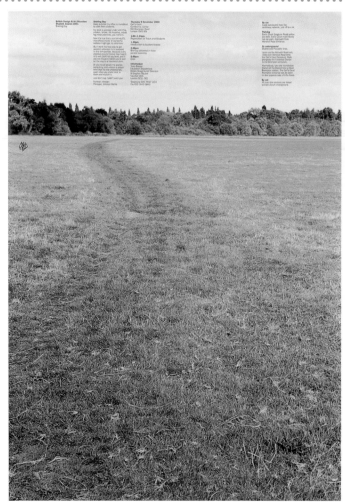

Experimental Jetset have a recurring nightmare, and it goes something like this: Your entire experience is fed to you by an image-based consumer culture that is second-guessing where you would like to go today. Marketing—it's everywhere, and it keeps EJ awake at night.••EJ live with the vain hope that it is possible to design objects that are autonomous, free in their internal logic from the recommendations of the focus group, and immune to predictions of the trend forecaster. EJ want to be taken seriously. With Maureen Mooren and Daniel van der Velden they share the same desire to engage with individuals before groups. They wish to rescue communication design from mere representation. For them, the material, physical, tactility of design-as-object will prevent design from slipping into the swamp of mass information, where the primary motive of design is to imitate audience values. EJ want to stop you in your tracks with objects that exist only in relation to themselves and are not representations of the idea, that you may have in your head, of wanting to come across objects that exist only in relation to themselves.••EJ use the visual language associated with modernism. They can't help it, it's their inheritance. Helvetica has become a signature for them, meant not as a sign of their admiration of modernist typography, but as their way of using neutrality to avoid metaphor—the use of visual effects that make associations with something other than the design object itself; for instance, the use of a rounded, friendly typeface because research has indicated that your audience is put off by things that look serious.••The EJ manifesto is "to create designs that function as a part of reality instead of as a representation of reality." But then, on seeing the December stamps EJ designed for the Dutch PTT, I thought, illustration—representation surely! The portrayal of generic people enjoying a kind of generic landscape looked not so far away from pictures one might find in one of the gargantuan stock-photo catalogues. But then I had to hand it to them: The December snow draws attention to the whiteness of the paper—it is the paper (materiality)—and the happy people are reduced to silhouettes in microns of metallic gold ink (materiality again).••Nick Bell••

1-2   Cover and spread, *Wij Bouwen Nieuwe Zinnen* (We Build New Sentences) quadrennial for exhibition space W139 / W139 / Netherlands / 2002
3-6   Cover and spreads, *Elysian Fields* exhibition catalogue / Centre Georges Pompidou and Purple Institute / France / 2000
7-9   Catalogue and intsallation, *Kelly 1:1–A cover version by Experimental Jetset* solo exhibition / Casco Projects and Editions / Netherlands / 2002 / An actual size reproduction of Elsworth Kelly's painting *Blue, Green, Yellow, Orange, Red* mapped in sheets of A4 paper. The dismantled and bound artwork itself makes up the exhibition catalogue.

Experimental Jetset

Amsterdam

3
4
5
6

Kelly 1:1
A cover version by
Experimental Jetset

Casco Editions

An interpretation of
Ellsworth Kelly's Blue,
Green, Yellow, Orange,
Red. 1966 Actual size

7
8
9

10-11 Advanced Economics project, designed and published in limited edition by Experimental Jetset / Netherlands / 1998 / The project appears to be a complete corporate-identity program. Closer reading reveals a darker undertone, as every single item contains a story of corporate misery.

12 *Decembergedachten* (December thoughts) stamps / Royal Dutch Mail / Netherlands / 2002

13-14 Covers, *The People's Art-A Arte do Povo* exhibition catalogue / Witte de With / Netherlands / 2001 / The catalogue featured twenty different dust jackets wrapped on top of each other.

15-17 Catalogue and exhibition design, *Display* exhibition on contemporary jewelry design / Stedelijk Museum / Netherlands / 2002

Experimental Jetset

Sara Fanelli creates the children's books that all designers wish they'd owned in their formative years. Her illustrations are wonderfully rich. More like paintings. The visual landscape is there to be explored. What seems initially quite simple in structure is full of content and information. Her layered and collage-style illustration is full of graphic surprises. Each element is rich with unique characteristics that provide individual and collective messages. Her illustrative techniques combine the traditional mediums of painting, drawing, and printmaking. While her work is all about ideas, the interpretation is highly personal. Her commercial projects have clearly benefited from the lessons of her self-initiated projects, where she has had the freedom to experiment and explore more creatively rewarding territory—areas that under the pressure of deadlines would be seen as dangerous. The combination of typography and image is seamless; often the text is the image.●●Born in Florence, Italy, Fanelli arrived in London to study design and illustration. Since her graduation from the Royal College of Art in 1995 she has worked as a freelance illustrator. She has also written and illustrated several award-winning children's books, including *Dear Diary*, *First Flight*, and *Mythological Monsters*. While Fanelli's work has reached great heights in its development, one senses the best is still to come. ●●Ken Cato●●

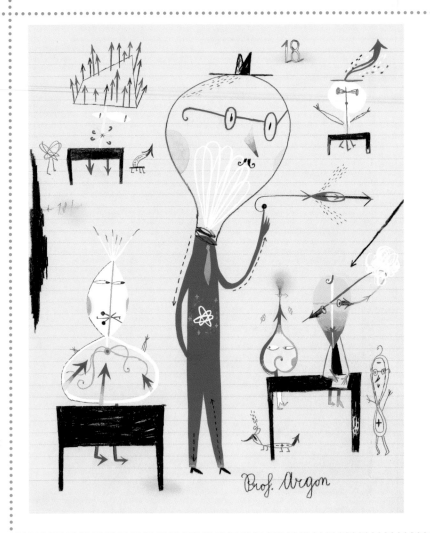

1-3 Illustrations for annual report of Swedish chemistry board Kemikontoret / Bark Design / Sweden / 2001
4 Cover and spreads from *Dear Diary*, written, illustrated, and designed by Sara Fanelli / Walker Books / United Kingdom / 2000
5 Spreads from *Mythological Monsters*, written, illustrated, and designed by Sara Fanelli / Walker Books / United Kingdom / 2002

Sara Fanelli

London

6   Cover, *The New Faber Book of Childeren's Verse*, edited by Matthew Sweeney / Faber and Faber / United Kingdom / 2001

7   Cover, *Kraven Images*, by Alan Isler / Vintage / United Kingdom / 1998

8   First-class stamp celebrating the emancipation of woman through the invention of the bicycle / Royal Mail / United Kingdom / 1999

9   Cover, *Where Are You, Robert?*, by Hans Magnus Enzensberger / Hamish Hamilton / Untited Kingdom / 2000

10   Cover, *The Prince of West End Avenue*, by Alan Isler / Vintage / United Kingdom / 1996

11   Poster for play *The Magistrate*, by A. Wing Pinero / Royal Exchange Theatre, Manchester / United Kingdom / 2001

12   "Airport" personal piece / 2000

13   Page from *A Dog's Life*, written, illustrated, and designed by Sara Fanelli / Heinemann Young Books / United Kingdom / 1998

14   "Six Characters in Search of an Author" personal piece / 2002

15   Print advertisement for Nat West bank air-miles program / Nat West / United Kingdom / 1999

Sara Fanelli

12

13

14

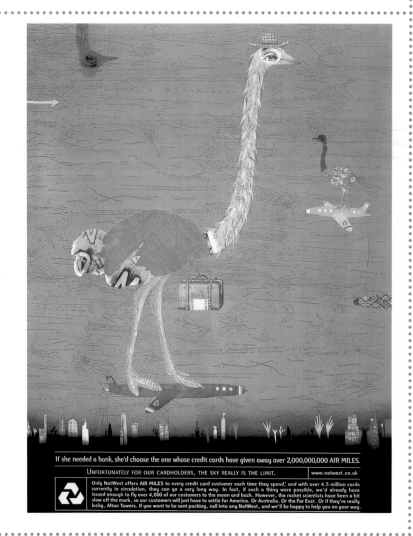

15

The first clue about Isidro Ferrer is his own personal symbol: a sharpened pencil bound by string to a triangular section of wood. The combination of elements creates the form of a gun, menacing and ready for action. It is so appropriate for someone who communicates so simply and so spontaneously and who is ready for the next opportunity and the next solution. His work is full of information, often combining found items with simple graphic elements. The solutions are eclectic, whimsical, and diverse.●●Born in Madrid in 1963, Ferrer initially studied drama. Somewhere between completing his acting studies and starting his design studio, he developed his illustrational craft in the workshop of graphic designer Peret in Barcelona. And then in partnership with three other designers he founded the Studio Camaleon in Zaragoza. Since 1996 he has run his own studio in Huesca where he applies his talents to a diverse range of projects. Editorial design, animation, artistic direction, exhibition design, comics, and work for television leave him with a broad spectrum of graphic design-solutions. To date he has had seventeen books published, in France, Portugal, and Spain. His work has been the subject of numerous national and international exhibitions. In the year 2000 he was inducted into the Alliance Graphique Internationale (AGI). To my mind he is one of a rare breed of graphic designer who has the ability to dramatically communicate a message and at the same time bring a smile to those who encounter his works.●●Ken Cato●●

①

②

Isidro Ferrer

Huesca, Spain

1900-2000

Luis Buñuel

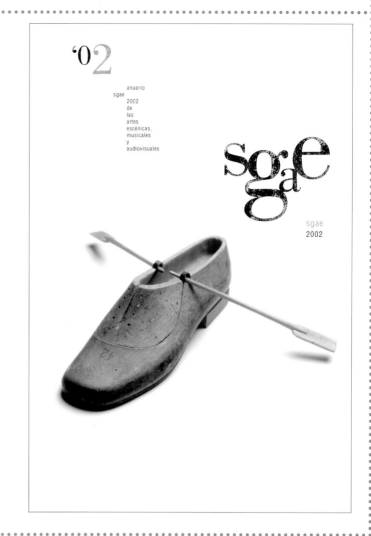

'02

anuario
sgae
2002
de
las
artes
escénicas,
musicales
y
audiovisuales

sgae

sgae
2002

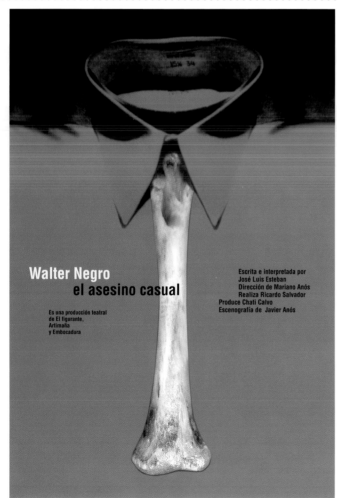

Walter Negro
el asesino casual

Escrita e interpretada por
José Luis Esteban
Dirección de Mariano Anós
Realiza Ricardo Salvador
Produce Chati Calvo
Escenografía de Javier Anós

Es una producción teatral
de El figurante,
Artimaña
y Embocadura

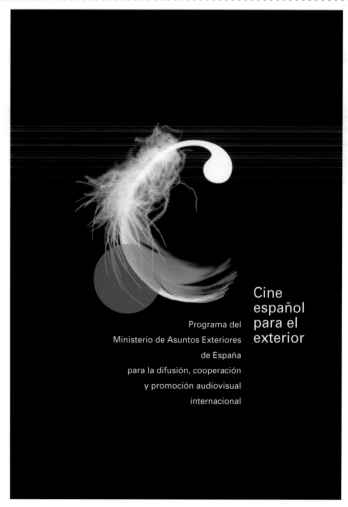

Programa del
Ministerio de Asuntos Exteriores
de España
para la difusión, cooperación
y promoción audiovisual
internacional

Cine
español
para el
exterior

Dante **La Divina Comedia**
Santillana Clásicos Universales

Goethe **Fausto**
Santillana Clásicos Universales

Shakespeare **Hamlet**
Santillana Clásicos Universales

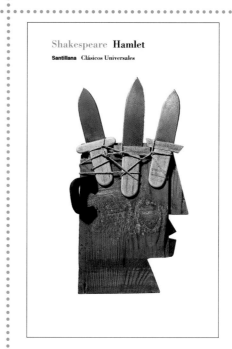

Moliere **Tartufo**
Santillana Clásicos Universales

Sófocles **Edipo rey** | **Antígona**
Santillana Clásicos Universales

Boccacio **El Decamerón**
Santillana Clásicos Universales

7-12 Book covers for Clásicos Universales paperback
collection / Editorial Santillana / Spain / 1999–2000
13 Poster for paper-recycling festival in Zaragoza / Fundación
ecología y desarrollo / Spain / 2000
14 Poster for South Pyrenees music festival / Diputación
Provincial de Huesca / 1999
15 Poster for Jeanne d'Arc festival in Rouen / Municipality of
Rouen / France / 2002
16 Poster for 12th theater festival in Aragon / Government of
Aragon / Spain / 1998
17 Poster homage for Toulouse-Lautrec's centennial /
Nouveau Salon des Cent / France / 2001
18 Poster for play *Ubu Rey*, by Alfred Jarry / University of
Zaragoza / Spain / 1996
19 Poster for bullfighting festival / DDI-AEPD / Spain / 2002
20 Cover, *La illustración* magazine / Asociación Española
de Ilustradores Profesionales / Spain / 1998
21 Antiwar poster / Instituto Europeo de Design / Spain / 2001
22 Poster for exhibition on Spanish graphic design in Berlin /
DDI-SEACEX / Germany / 2002
23 Poster for exhibition of Isidro Ferrer's work / Universidad
Nacional a Distancia / Spain / 2003

Isidro Ferrer

12
feria de
teatro
en
aragón

Huesca del 3 al 7 de noviembre de 1998

NOUVEAU SALON DES CENT EXPOSITION INTERNATIONALE D'AFFICHES.
HOMMAGE À TOULOUSSE-LAUTREC

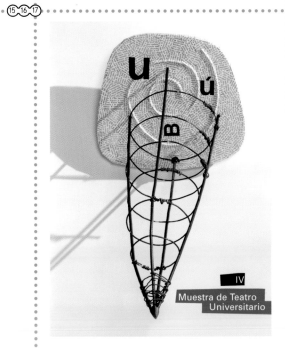

IV
Muestra de Teatro
Universitario

FERIA DE
SAN ISIDRO

2002

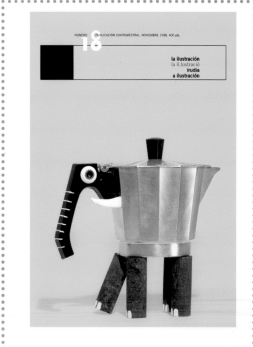

NÚMERO   PUBLICACIÓN CUATRIMESTRAL. NOVIEMBRE 1998. 400 pts.

la ilustración
la il.lustració
irudia
a ilustración

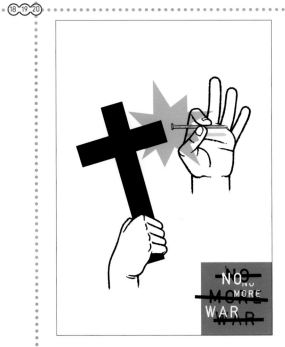

NO
NO
MORE
MORE
WAR
WAR

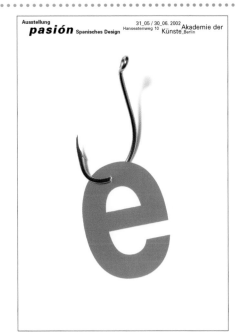

Ausstellung
pasión Spanisches Design
31_05 / 30_06. 2002
Hanseatenweg 10   Akademie der
Künste_Berlin

sala de exposiciones
de la UNED, argensola
55, barbastro

del 15 de noviembre
al 12 de diciembre

UNED
FUNDACIÓN 'RAMÓN J. SENDER'
BARBASTRO

Laurent Fétis developed an original visual language informed by vector art, photography, graffiti, airbrush, and Kippenberger. (Martin Kippenberger is quoted prominently in *ABC+*, Fétis's new monograph: "*Jetzt geh ich in den Birkenwald, denn meine Pillen wirken bald*" [Now I'll head for the birch forest as my pills will be taking effect soon].) ••Producing work for all the magazines a young designer wants to be featured in (*Dazed and Confused*, *The Face*, etc.) and working for all the clients a young designer would like to be associated with (Beck, Björk, etc.), he sits at that interestingly blurred border where design and art meet.••Fétis sees tight analogies between design and pop music: "Each has its codes, its skeleton, its format, and finds itself in a situation of permanent research. One radically transformed the twentieth-century music scene. However, if you open a general encyclopedia of music, it takes up only a few lines. For its part, graphic design—more so than art—has transformed the visual scene of the past twenty years, yet it remains excluded from the history of art and is for this reason de-contextualized."••One of his most striking pieces is a poster for Audiolab, a daring typographic tour de force synthesizing different stylistic and formal questions into an organic whole. "I am led only by the idea of making the things I wish to see exist at a given time. It remains very intuitive. I am far from being a formalist, to my regret, moreover, as everything would be so much more simple." ••Stefan Sagmeister••

1-3　CD packaging, *Rocker's Delight* compilation (with Elisabeth Arkhipoff) / Quatermass / Belgium / 2002
4-6　Cover and spreads, *ABC+* by Laurent Fétis / Die Gestalten Verlag / Germany / 2002
7-10　Cover and spreads, *Ronan et Erwan Bouroullec–Catalogue de raison*, by Laurent Le Bon / Editions Ceo and Editions Images Modernes / Paris / 2002

Laurent Fétis

Paris

Laurent Fétis

Field Study came to my attention through an eccentric self-promotional mailer that landed on my desk last summer: an old-fashioned buff board document folder containing a pleasingly motley collection of printed papers and photographs fastened upon two metal binding prongs. The cover carried a text printed in brown and promoted the simple virtue of knowing your subject. This modest piece of softsell projected the aura of a school classroom; items gathered on a field trip and presented for inspection. Inside were two business cards; a sixteen-page leaflet folding down to the size of a postcard emblazoned with the word *Study*; two color photographs, one of stuffed llamas, the other of stuffed ibex; and, visible underneath that, an off-white cotton-fiber letterhead, rubber-stamped in silver at the top left corner and laser-printed with a letter addressed to UNA from someone called Roy Brooks who claimed to know me. He said he had participated in a workshop I held at North Carolina State University more than six years before. In fact his name was familiar, but for a different reason. It turns out this was the same Roy Brooks whose design assistance was credited on a significant number of J. Abbott Miller projects we had just laid out for the "Reputations" interview in *Eye* no. 45, which had been sent to press just days before. ● ● Through this mailer, Brooks was informing me that he had set up his own company with fellow NC State grad Matthew Peterson. Here he was reporting in with the evidence of original research gathered from his and his partner's formative graphic-designing experience so far. It was impressive. It turns out that Peterson has had an equally challenging, rewarding, and enviable apprenticeship to write home about; he worked under Andrew Blauvelt at the Walker Art Center in Minneapolis. With that in mind, we should all be expecting a hell of a lot from them. ● ● The Field Study mailer seems to emerge out of a documentary ethos, from a gentler age, free of spin. It's a dialect in which design is more about the articulation of contents (fragments of raw material) that speak through being unmodified, remaining in their original, unadulterated form, rather than becoming subsumed by the rules of an aesthetic system susceptible to valuing only uniformity. For Field Study, it's the pure, untutored charm of formats unalloyed with the prevailing design canon that hold their attention. ● ● Nick Bell ● ●

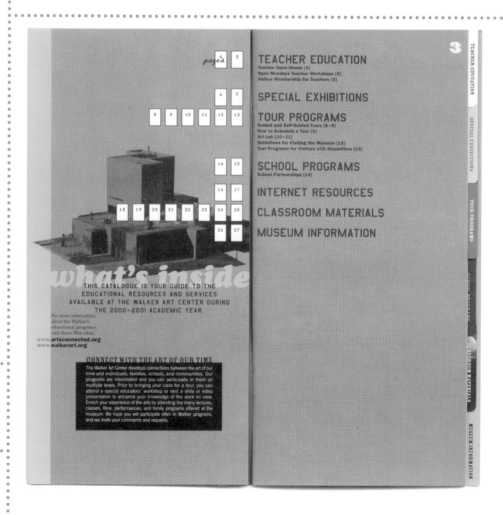

1-2 Spreads from Walker Art Center 2000-2001 education catalogue (with Andrew Blauvelt) / Walker Art Center / USA / 2000
3 Poster for the GraficEurope:Pan-European Graphic Design Conference / Spain / 2003
4-6 Poster and CD packaging, *Lullaby for Sue*, by Clogs / Brassland Records / USA / 2003

Field Study

Assuming risk in
hope of gain

Meditating on or
pondering a subject

Suggesting, testing
and examining

Curiosity and
questioning

Theorizing vs.
demonstrating

Speculative Chicago
A Compendium of Architectural Innovation

Field Study

In beginning a study of the trees the student should be careful to confine himself to well-established facts. Once started he should proceed slowly, assimilating each new discovery before seeking another. He should begin with the trees nearest home, and, as he gradually grows to know these in all their aspects, should extend his trips afield. Not only should he be able to name the trees when they are fully clothed in their summer dress, but he should know as readily these same trees when the leaves have fallen and only the bare branches stand silhouetted against the sky. Then, and only then, will he derive the utmost satisfaction from his efforts.

From "Michigan Trees," by Charles Herbert Otis

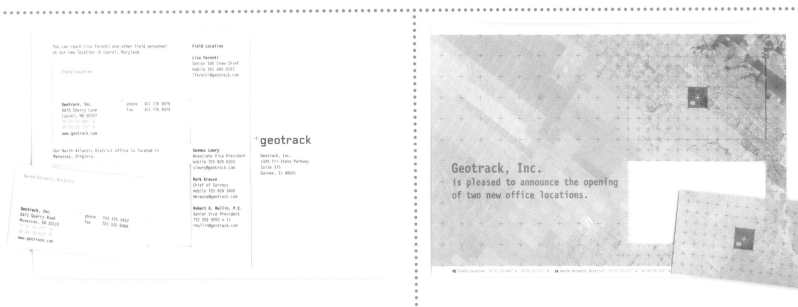

You can reach Lisa Feronti and other field personnel at our new location in Laurel, Maryland.

Field Location

Geotrack, Inc.
8675 Cherry Lane
Laurel, MD 20707
www.geotrack.com

Our North Atlantic District office is located in Manassas, Virginia.

North Atlantic District

Geotrack, Inc.
8471 Quarry Road   phone 703 335 2622
Manassas, VA 20110   fax   703 325 6466
www.geotrack.com

Field Location

Lisa Feronti
Senior SUE Crew Chief
mobile 301 440 4727
lferonti@geotrack.com

Seamus Lowry
Associate Vice President
mobile 703 929 6203
slowry@geotrack.com

Mark Krause
Chief of Surveys
mobile 703 929 3400
mkrause@geotrack.com

Robert A. Mullin, P.E.
Senior Vice President
732 202 9050 x 11
rmullin@geotrack.com

+geotrack

Geotrack, Inc.
1325 Tri-State Parkway
Suite 375
Gurnee, IL 60031

Geotrack, Inc.
is pleased to announce the opening
of two new office locations.

Like most designers today, Lizzie Finn does not work without a computer, but the first tools she uses are pencil and paper, followed by needle, thread, and sewing machine. Finn has long loved the century-old history of traditional household crafts but was further inspired by 1970s feminists who adopted domestic stitching in their protest signs for equal rights. Sewing became a symbol the oppressed domestic female used to fight male dominance. A certain subversiveness in Finn's work is evident, but her passion for sewing, do-it-yourself, and the handmade would last and strive far beyond all sex battles.●●Finn's unique interest emerged in 2000 with a CD cover for the British house band Moloko. A beautiful cross-stitched logo on top of a dense group shot of about thirty colorful rag-doll animals. The title she proposed with the design was "Things to Make and Do," which is also the title of her favorite do-it-yourself magazine. The group loved both design and title. The inside CD booklet corresponds to the cover language and is equally surprising. In typical do-it-yourself style, Finn gives instructions for cutting and sewing one of the rag cats on the cover. Later, a few of the animals were used as solo primary subjects for promotional singles.●● "Things to make and do" became Finn's working philosophy. The nature of her work naturally attracted the international clothing and textile industries that commission both communication and product design. Editorial illustrations for cutting-edge trend and fashion magazines were another source of work. Technique and form seem to deeply influence the content of her output.●●In her recent "Eye Spy" pages for *Dazed and Confused* she brilliantly pushed further in her effort to discover new speculative dimensions by combining sewing, patchwork, and erotic imagery. In considering Finn's provocations the question to ask could be, Design by woman or woman by design?●●Omar Vulpinari●●

1–3   "Eye Spy" spreads, *Dazed and Confused* magazine (photography Clare Shilland) /
       Dazed and Confused / United Kingdom / 2003
4–9   CD packaging and design, *Things to Make and Do* album and singles "Indigo"
       and "Pure Pleasure Seeker" by Moloko / The Echo Label–Chrysalis / United
       Kingdom / 2000

Lizzie Finn

London

Lizzie Finn

10 Illustration for *150 B&T*, book published by printer Butler and Tanner in celebration of their 150th anniversary / Butler and Tanner / United Kingdom / 2001

11–12 "Sit back & Relax" stitch and spread for *Relax Magazine* / Relax Magazine / Japan / 2002

13–14 Stitch and opening spread on UK fashion brand Silas for *Relax Magazine* / Relax Magazine / Japan / 2001

15 Front and back cover and spreads from Silas promotional catalogue, autumn/winter 1999–2000 / Silas / United Kingdom / 1999

Amy Franceschini comes from a paradoxical Californian background. Her father was a corporate farmer (owner of a pesticide company), and her mother left him to embrace the worlds of organic farming and New Age philosophy. "I grew up bouncing between these conflicting logics," she recalls. "I spent half of my childhood with my father, cultivating 3,000 acres of irrigated farmlands, and the other half with my mother cultivating our consciousness through ideologies derivative of Rudolf Steiner, Sai Baba, Permaculture, and the like."••In her design/art practice Franceschini thinks of herself as a biodynamic farmer. "Biodynamic farming is a model that speaks to a philosophy of mind, body, and spirit that I would like to employ into whatever I do: [It] involves restoring to the soil a balanced living condition through the application and use of the completely digested form of crude organic matter known as stabilized humus." She named her studio Futurefarmers and titled the anthology of their work published in 2002 *Harvest*.••Another project, Games for the Masses, reveals a strong interest in social interaction. "Games for the Masses was an experiment in social interaction [...] I placed this fake game in the gallery and started it with a simple set of rules but told the players they could make up rules as they pleased. Over the course of one night the game evolved from a purely fantastical game played with seven kids to a complex gambling game played by four adults."••In the project Holding Pattern, Franceschini combines social interaction with her innate concern for nature. "Holding Pattern addressed environmental problems suffered by wetlands and migratory birds as a result of population growth and economic expansion." Through her love for the intricate systems of nature, Franceschini works to create an awareness about the fragility of these systems.••In her most recent work Franceschini has been trying to find the simplest way to get people to play together. "I recently made a 14-inch seesaw in a gallery show. A seesaw is really the simplest interactive architecture. It involves a certain amount of immediate cooperation and trust.••Technology is an important factor in her work, but her relationship with it definitely remains love/hate. "On one hand I am completely fascinated and excited about new technologies, and on the other hand I want to run back to the forest. A piece of work should begin with an idea or a feeling about something. This idea should dictate the form and technology. A pencil is still a very powerful tool."••Omar Vulpinari••

1 Games for the Masses at Jack Hanley Gallery, San Francisco / USA / 2003 /
The game begins with three "open" rules that change while playing, allowing it to evolve at random to increasing intricacy.
2 Poster for *Communication What* exhibition, Venice / Italy / 2002
3 Logo for Amy Franceschini's design studio Futurefarmers / USA / 2002
4 "Seeds of Inspiration" poster for *Communication What* exhibition / Italy / 2002

Amy Franceschini

San Francisco

SEEDLINGS

SEEDS ARE THE MEMORY BANK OF NATURE

CONSERVE THE GENETIC DIVERSITY FOR THE FUTURE.

Seeds are magical; given proper stewardship, they will acclimate to specific areas over time. By growing them out, we weave the stories of our lives and seeds into an unending chain of community, tradition, and history.

WE NEVER SLEEP

5   Cover illustration for *Design Plex* magazine / Design Plex / Japan / 2002 / The illustration is a portrait of
      Amy Franceschini, Josh On, Sascha Merg, and Michael Swaine, all members of Futurefarmers.
6–8 "Hydrogen" poster series for *Communication What* exhibition, Venice / Italy / 2002
9   "T(h)ree" illustration, study for Futurefarmers logo / USA / 2002
10 Cover and spreads from *Harvest* / Futurefarmers and IdN / USA and Hong Kong / 2002 / The book is an
     anthology of Futurefarmers projects from 1995 to 2002. It includes a CD-ROM and the toy "Pinga."

Amy Franceschini

Born in Brighton, England, Vince Frost was educated in graphic design at West Sussex College of Design. After working freelance for some time, he joined Pentagram in 1989 but returned to private practice and started his own London-based design consultancy, Frost Design, in 1994. In independent practice, Frost's work attracted attention due to its innovative use of photographic images combined with clean, crisp typographic elements. He has gained international recognition through his editorial work for *P Magazine*, a Polaroid publication aimed at professional photographers, and further in *Big Magazine*, a dual-language publication. This work led to the opportunity to design the *Saturday Independent Magazine*. His publication work continues through numerous publishing houses around the world. ●●Like so many before him, Frost believes the profession is not just about making money. He realized at an early age that it was about making the most of every opportunity that came his way. Clearly he has done this. Strong ideas, well executed, resulting in highly effective pieces of communication: a formula that can lead only to success. ●●During his development as a designer he has worked on a diverse spectrum of projects including stamps for the Royal Mail, television advertising, the development of signage systems, and corporate identity and promotional programs. Frost is also a very active member of the design community, lecturing at conferences around the world, conducting design workshops, and participating as a judge at international design competitions and exhibitions. Frost is a designer of influence, now and for the future. ●●Ken Cato●●

1   Cover and spreads, *Some Trains in America*, by Andrew Cross / Prestel / United Kingdom / 2002
2   Cover and spreads, *D&AD Annual Report* (illustration Marion Deuchars) / D&AD / United Kingdom / 2002
3   Cover and spreads, D&AD magazine *Ampersand* (with Matt Willey) / D&AD / United Kingdom / 2002

Vince Frost

London

WHAT'S THE POINT?

D&AD FROM A
CLIENTS POINT OF VIEW

WE COMMISSION
INDEPENDENT RESEARCHERS TO PROVE THE
COMMERCIAL EFFECTIVENESS OF D&AD
AWARD WINNING DESIGN AND
ADVERTISING PROJECTS

CREATIVITY WORKS

TOP-OF-MIND
THUNDERSTRUCK
HAIR-RAISING
MESMERISING
MIND-BLOWING
EYE-POPPING
BREATHTAKING
RIGHT-ON-THE-NOSE
MOUTHWATERING
LIPSMACKING
TONGUE-IN-CHEEK
JAWDROPPING
SPEECHLESS
DUMBSTRUCK
HEAD-TURNING
KNOCK-OUT

40
41

'70's
80's

OUR MISSION:
TO SET CREATIVE STANDARDS
IN DESIGN AND ADVERTISING,
TO EDUCATE
AND NURTURE THE NEXT CREATIVE
GENERATION,
TO COMMUNICATE
TO BUSINESS THE IMPORTANCE OF
GOOD DESIGN
AND
ADVERTISING

6
7

D&AD FROM A
MEMBERS POINT OF VIEW

12
13

rewind review

To celebrate the
publication of our
40-year review of
legendary design
and advertising,
Lakshmi Bhaskaran
invited a handful of
creatives to pick their
personal favourites

60's

IBM

Vince Frost

Tom Gauld's work belongs to a long and rich tradition, yet his approach to that tradition is remarkably refreshing. His commercial work includes projects for *The Guardian*, *WISH* magazine, and publishers such as Penguin and HarperCollins. However, it's work such as Move to the City—a comic strip that appears weekly in the London edition of *Time Out*—and the work he publishes via his own company, Cabanon Press, that provides Gauld with the ideal medium for his eccentric vision.••Gauld is a wonderful storyteller. Stories like "Outside," for example, in which an explorer falls just short of what could be the promised land because the safety rope is not quite long enough; stories where warrior robots discuss the possibility of doing something other than fight or where two wrestlers kill time before a match by visiting a park and feeding stale muffins to ducks. Often, the joke requires only one frame, one image, one gesture, and a small amount of text to work. In one piece, two astronauts on the surface of a distant planet have had an argument. All we have—and it's all we need—is one line: "Oh come on...I was joking."••Gauld's work never fails to bring a smile to your face. He has a less-is-more approach that, on the surface at least, often appears quite surreal, but all you have to do is scratch that surface to realize that the humor comes from the everyday. He engages his audience by presenting not a world a million miles away, but our own.••As a draftsman his style is direct and honest, presenting his stories and characters in a straightforward manner that echoes the economy and deadpan delivery of his comedic vocabulary. Comprising predominantly black-and-white line drawings, his work has veered well clear of technological advances. Maybe it would be easy to skim the surface and regard Gauld's style as pedestrian; but all you have to do is look a little closer.••Fernando Gutiérrez••

1   "Dante's Inferno," illustration for *The Guardian* newspaper / The Guardian / United Kingdom / 2002
2   Hilltop handkerchief design for Japanese retail brand / United Arrows / Japan / 2002
3–4 Pages 1 and 2 of 6-page comic strip "Cat, Bear and Ghost" in *Sturgeon White Moss* magazine / Sturgeon White Moss / United Kingdom / 2003
5   "Seven Robots Go to the Shops" illustration for *Graphics International Diary* (unpublished) / Graphics International / United Kingdom / 2002
6   Billboard, Happiness in Brockley project / United Kingdom / 2001 / Project organized by artist Simone Lia for which artists produced cheerful billboard pieces to be displayed in Brockley, South London.

Tom Gauld

London

Tom Gauld

CHARACTERS FOR AN EPIC TALE

THE HERO · THE PIRATE · THE THREE WITCHES · THE MESSENGER · THE WRESTLERS · THE OLD MAN · THE GIRL · THE MONKEY · THE MIDGET · THE TWINS · THE CONVICT · THE HERMIT · THE KING · THE PRIEST · THE ESCAPIST · THE INVALID · THE NURSE · THE QUEEN · THE CORPSE · THE RINGMASTER · THE DANCING BEAR · THE WANDERERS · THE APPARITION · THE HEADLESS MAN · THE GIANT · THE GENIUS · THE MINOTAUR · THE BIRD MAN · THE VISITORS · THE KNIGHT · THE FLOATING SKULL · THE FREAKS · THE INNKEEPER · THE URCHINS · THE GOLEM · THE PROPHET OF DOOM · THE MAGIC COW · THE SNIPER · THE LOVER · THE HAIRY BEAST · THE NUDIST · THE SKELETON · THE NECROMANCER · THE DANDY · THE HUSBAND · THE GIANT CAT · THE METAL MAN · THE BOY · THE TART · THE GUARDS · THE DEVIL · THE SCARECROW

WWW.TGTOKYO.COM

THERE GOES TOKYO

SMALL PRESS

BIG MONSTERS

BOATING ACCIDENT · GYPSY CURSE

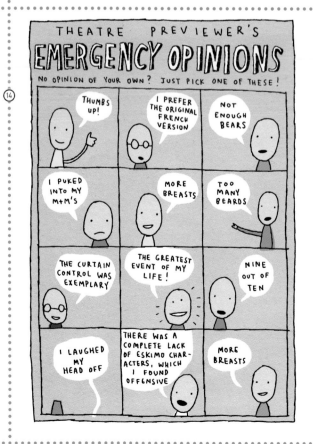

THEATRE PREVIEWER'S
EMERGENCY OPINIONS

NO OPINION OF YOUR OWN? JUST PICK ONE OF THESE!

THUMBS UP! · I PREFER THE ORIGINAL FRENCH VERSION · NOT ENOUGH BEARS

I PUKED INTO MY M+M'S · MORE BREASTS · TOO MANY BEARDS

THE CURTAIN CONTROL WAS EXEMPLARY · THE GREATEST EVENT OF MY LIFE! · NINE OUT OF TEN

I LAUGHED MY HEAD OFF · THERE WAS A COMPLETE LACK OF ESKIMO CHARACTERS, WHICH I FOUND OFFENSIVE · MORE BREASTS

Juli Gudehus's little calendar *Mindestens Haltbar bis* 31.12.1999 (Best Before 12/31/1999) is one of the smartest time lines I've ever seen: The countdown of the last year of the millennium using nothing but expiration dates of food products.••A different product goes bad on every calendar sheet on every day. Some of the products, shown in tight crops in order to transform the date itself into the hero, are still recognizable: On 14 February the mousse au chocolat is fresh no more, on 23 April butter cookies turn stale, the white bread gets moldy on 5 January, and Windsor Tea is off by 5 August.••The typographic diversity and the variation of application techniques are also incredible: embossed, tampon-printed, stamped, offset-printed, letterpressed, flexi-printed, ink-jetted, and debossed expiration dates are included. Gudehus painstakingly collected all the items, products she likely would have never bought were it not for that missing date in her collection.••The resulting round-cornered calendar, ordinary everyday designs put into a different context and shrinkwrapped into a green foamcore tray, is simply breathtaking in its simplicity. It fulfills the requirements for good design: an original idea well executed.••Or take her smart and hilarious retelling of Genesis: She retells God's creation of the earth and the skies using only corporate logos, directional icons, and pictograms. Gudehus is probably the purest conceptual designer I know.••Stefan Sagmeister••

1

1   *Gestern War Heute Morgen* (Yesterday Was Today Tomorrow) project for *Die Zeit* newspaper / Die Zeit / Germany / 1999 / Commentary on the millennium and what it holds for the future.
2-4 Cover and spreads, *Genesis*, by Juli Gudehus / Lars Mueller Publishers / Switzerland / 1997 / The biblical story of the Creation told in modern hieroglyphics.

Juli Gudehus

Berlin

Lars Müller Publishers Juli Gudehus

GENESIS

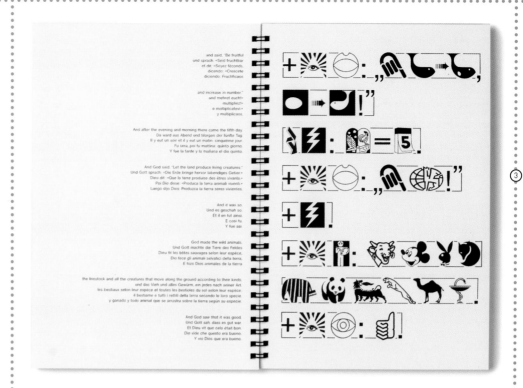

and said, "Be fruitful
und sprach: »Seid fruchtbar
et dit: «Soyez féconds,
dicendo: «Crescete
diciendo: Fructificaos

and increase in number"
und mehret euch!«
multipliez!»
e moltiplicatevi»
y multiplicaos.

And after the evening and morning there came the fifth day.
Da ward aus Abend und Morgen der fünfte Tag.
Il y eut un soir et il y eut un matin: cinquième jour.
Fu sera, poi fu mattina: quinto giorno.
Y fue la tarde y la mañana el día quinto.

And God said, "Let the land produce living creatures."
Und Gott sprach: »Die Erde bringe hervor lebendiges Getier.«
Dieu dit: «Que la terre produise des êtres vivants.»
Poi Dio disse: «Produca la terra animali viventi.»
Luego dijo Dios: Produzca la tierra seres vivientes.

And it was so.
Und es geschah so.
Et il en fut ainsi.
E così fu.
Y fue así.

God made the wild animals.
Und Gott sah, dass es gut war.
Dieu fit les bêtes sauvages selon leur espèce.
Dio fece gli animali selvatici della terra.
E hizo Dios animales de la tierra

the livestock and all the creatures that move along the ground according to their kinds.
und das Vieh und alles Gewürm, ein jedes nach seiner Art.
les bestiaux selon leur espèce et toutes les bestioles du sol selon leur espèce.
il bestiame e tutti i rettili della terra secondo le loro specie.
y ganado y todo animal que se arrastra sobre la tierra según su especie.

And God saw that it was good.
Und Gott sah, dass es gut war.
Et Dieu vit que cela était bon.
Dio vide che questo era buono.
Y vio Dios que era bueno.

The Creation
Die Schöpfung
La création
La creazione
La creación

In the beginning God created heaven and earth.
Am Anfang schuf Gott Himmel und Erde.
Au commencement, Dieu créa les cieux et la terre.
Nel principio Dio creò i cieli e la terra.
En el principio creó Dios los cielos y la tierra.

And the earth was without form and void
Und die Erde war wüst und leer,
Or la terre était vide et vague,
La terra era informe e vuota,
Y la tierra estaba desordenada y vacía

and the deep was covered in darkness
und es war finster in der Tiefe,
les ténèbres couvraient l'abîme
le tenebre coprivano la faccia dell'abisso
y las tinieblas estaban sobre la faz del abismo

and the Spirit of God was hovering over the waters.
und der Geist Gottes schwebte auf dem Wasser.
un vent de Dieu tournoyait sur les eaux.
e lo Spirito di Dio aleggiava sulla superficie delle acque.
y el Espíritu de Dios flotaba sobre la faz de las aguas.

And God said "Let there be light,"
Und Gott sprach »Es werde Licht.«
Dieu dit: «Que la lumière soit.»
Dio disse: «Sia luce!»
Y dijo Dios: Sea la luz;

and there was light.
Und es ward Licht.
Et la lumière fut.
E luce fu.
y fue la luz.

cheerful T

⑥

crest-fallen T

T

well-balanced T

Juli Gudehus

5   Christmas card for printer and publisher / Druck- und Verlagshaus Wienand / Germany / 1997 / The card lists 453 variations of the key colors white, blue, yellow, red, and black.

6   *Aus dem Leben des T* (From the Life of T) project for *100 T-Variationen*, book on the letter T / Verlag Hermann Schmidt / Germany / 2000

7   *Mindestens Haltbar bis 31.12.99* (Best Before 12/31/99) calendar / Verlag Hermann Schmidt / Germany / 1998 / Each day of the year is represented by the expiry date taken from package of a general household product.

Mittwoch

mindestens haltbar bis:
31.12.1999

ein Kalender von Juli Gudehus im Verlag Hermann Schmidt Mainz

⑦

Sonntag Valentinstag

Freitag

Freitag

Samstag

Mittwoch

Sonntag

Dienstag

Dienstag

Montag

Donnerstag

Samstag

Donnerstag

Dienstag

During Soviet times, there was not much design in the USSR, yet there were many designers. New times came with black humor: Design now exists, but there seem to be no designers. Yuri Gulitov is one of the few masters who refuses to fit into this gloomy paradox. He is a professional and observable personage with his own creative position.••In the Russia of the 1990s, graphic design suddenly became a popular and prestigious profession. It woke up famous, propelled into the limelight by the favorable conditions of the growing market economy. To satisfy the needs of the advertising boom, huge quantities of graphic design were generated from nothing. Unfortunately, the design required in commercial advertising is one that sells fast, that indulges the wild tastes of the client, not design as a culture-preserving and culture-creating profession.••In the midst of all this, Gulitov continues to defend the honor of graphic design. He fights for the trade's right to play an independent cultural role. His typefaces, posters, logos, advertising booklets, journals, and newspaper layouts are never limited simply to a series of decisions pertaining to the piece's problems and functionality. He is always in search of something greater. Each work is an artistic experiment, one more opportunity to "foster the idea."••This "idea" is about the particularities of national design; about core archetypes of visual culture and the Russian field being shaped by graphic design; about the unsolved specificity of our Slavo-Greco-Latin Cyrillic alphabet. Gulitov is interested in the character and nature of the Russian "inside-outness" that begins with the mirror-image appearance of letters in our alphabet. Font is a model of national cosmos.••The graphic particularities he embraces were born in the street and can be traced back to his native Sebastopol, in Crimea. The specific, widespread style of graffiti that exists in this southern city made a lasting impression on him. Like street graphics, Gulitov's designs breed energy and are characterized by a dynamic and unpredictable nature. They have a touching naiveté, sincerity, and credulity and break down the barriers between the author and the audience. They are saturated with an atmosphere of real freedom. This deeply personal inspiration places Gulitov's designs in the context of not only "predesign era" Russian visual culture, but also today's postmodern design concepts, which embrace regionalisms. As a result, his quest is more relevant than ever.••Serve Serov••

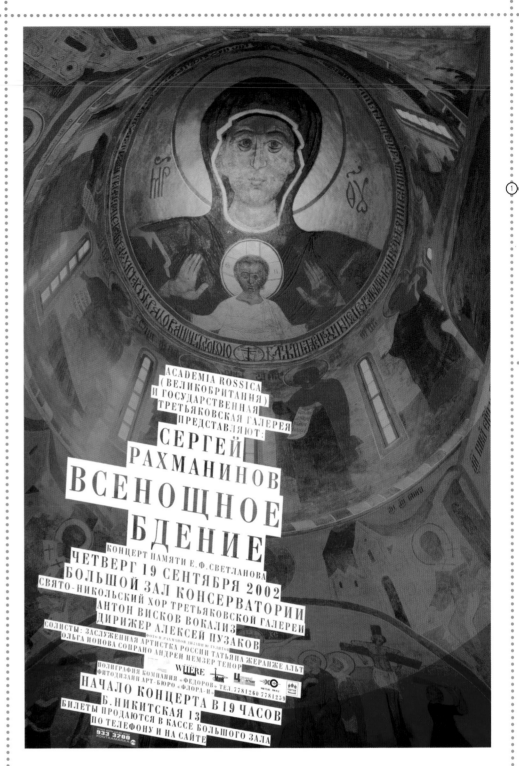

1   Poster for concert, *Vespers* by Sergei Rachmaninov / St. Nikolai Church Choir of the
    State Tretyakov Gallery / Russia / 2002
2-3 Logos for art gallery ST-ART and advertising agency ODA / Russia / 1995-96
4   Front and back of invitation and poster for the *Russian Design 99* competition and
    exhibition / Design Union of Russia / 1999
5   Poster for solo exhibition *Yuri Gulitov–Beach Pictures* / Russia / 2001

Yuri Gulitov

Moscow

④

⑤

Yuri Gulitov

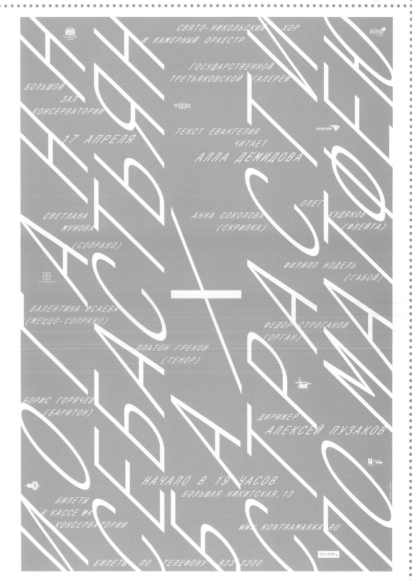

Julia, the wondergirl in New York with the perfectly English-sounding name Hasting can be found in a high-rise building in Manhattan, where, for some years now, she has been designing appallingly beautiful books for a publisher with the lyrical name Phaidon.••Phaidon was a pupil of Socrates. Four hundred years before Christ, Phaidon founded his own philosophy school in Elis. Plato named his dialogue on the immortality of the soul after him.••Hasting was a pupil of Gunter Rambow. She began her studies at the famous art university in Kassel (Kasseler Schule) in 1990 and in 1992 followed Rambow to the newly founded university for design (HfG) in Karlsruhe. After receiving her diploma in 1997, she emancipated herself from her master and developed her own forms of expression.••Hasting was successful right from the start. Her particular love for typographic detail becomes clear in all of her work. The same can be said for the surprising way she stages text and image. While still a student, she designed an excellent corporate identity for the EIKK (European Film Institute Karlsruhe), which was soon decorated with an award.••In fact, there are very few projects of Hasting's that have not been awarded prizes and received corresponding international publicity. Perfectly equipped with the recognition of the design scene, she quickly landed a job at the number-one publishing address for art and design: Phaidon in London—where else?••The "master" Rambow soon remembered his pupil, who had by now become Phaidon's art director in the newly opened New York office. In the role of a "godfather," he nominated her to be a member of the Alliance Graphique Internationale (AGI). Chance had it that I was then part of the AGI jury. She was unanimously voted in and became the youngest member of the Alliance. ••Since 2001, Hasting has had her own students. She teaches Publication Design at the renowned Cooper Union School of Art in New York. And she naturally continues to make beautiful books, conscious of the immortality of her typographic soul.••Uwe Loesch••

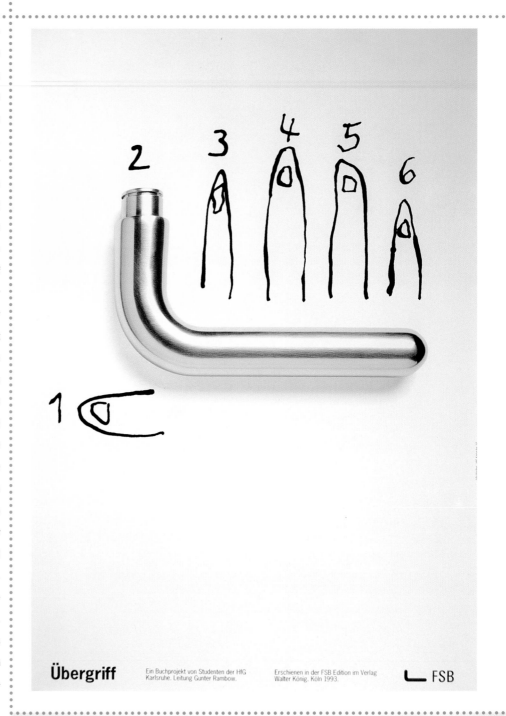

Übergriff   Ein Buchprojekt von Studenten der HfG   Erschienen in der FSB Edition im Verlag   ⌐ FSB
Karlsruhe. Leitung Gunter Rambow.   Walter König. Köln 1993.

1   Poster for door-handle manufacturer FSB / FSB / Germany / 1993
2   Book and packaging, *Cream–Contemporary Art in Culture* / Phaidon Press / United Kingdom and USA / 1998
3   Book, *10x10–10 Critics, 100 Architects* / Phaidon Press / United Kingdom and USA / 2000
4   Book, *Vitamin P–New Perspectives in Painting* / Phaidon Press / United Kingdom and USA / 2002
5   Book, *Magnum⁰* / Phaidon Press / United Kingdom and USA / 1999
6   Book, *Gordon Matta-Clark* / Phaidon Press / United Kingdom and USA / 2003
7   Inflatable point-of-sale and book, *Fresh Cream–Contemporary Art in Culture* / Phaidon Press / United Kingdom and USA / 2000
8   Book, *Robert Capa–The Definitive Collection* / Phaidon Press / United Kingdom and USA / 2001

Julia Hasting

New York

Julia Hasting

9-12 Cover and spreads, *Andy Warhol Catalogue Raisonné–Volume I: Painting and Sculpture, 1961–1963* / Phaidon Press / United Kingdom and USA / 2002

13-16 Cover and spreads, *Blink. 100 Photographers, 10 Curators, 10 Writers* / Phaidon Press / United Kingdom and USA / 2002

17-19 Poster series for exhibition *Die 100 Plakate des Jahres 1994* (The best 100 posters of 1994), Berlin / Germany / 1994

20-22 Poster series for student ball at design academy Hochschule für Gestaltung Karlsruhe (with Thomas Mayfried) / Hochschule für Gestaltung Karlsruhe / Germany / 1998

23-25 Posters and catalogue, part of corporate identity for the European Film Institute Karlsruhe (EIKK) / EIKK / Germany / 1998

Fons Hickmann appeared one day in my seminar at Wupperthal University, although he had already received a degree from the excellent university in Düsseldorf. Hickmann didn't just want to learn something, he also wanted to shake things up, so it didn't come as a surprise that I was soon correcting the typography of a poster he had designed for Bazon Brock, a professor in the school's department of aesthetics. One year later he was on the move again. In his luggage he had a fantastic poster series for the silent-movie festival in Graz, which was soon awarded gold medals around the world.••Hickmann wore a T-shirt on which was written "Fons." Small wonder that he has now become a professor himself, teaching at the University of Applied Arts in Vienna and running its institute for design. He is not only an excellent designer with the ability to create a *Gesamtkunstwerk*, but also an admirable communicator. In his biography he writes: "Fons M. Hickmann was born somewhere among the coal heaps of the Ruhr area. Afflicted by bouts of typographic fever, after falling into a bowl of alphabet soup as a child. 1972: beginning of school career spent on soccer pitches between Dortmund and Schalke. Travels in distant lands. 1987: start of attempts at studying philosophy, Germanic philology, photography, art and design, leading to a diploma in graphic design. In 1991, crowned as 'Guaredisch the First' by the Düsseldorf Typographic Society and dubbed Typographic Knight for Life. Established design offices in Düsseldorf and Berlin, with virtual stations in Dortmund and Essen. Currently 'Fons Hickmann m23' in Berlin [...] 1997: appointments as a lecturer and professor at various universities, lecture tours, participation in juries, numerous publications. Received innumerable design awards and honours...."••He who so confidently and unconventionally reflects on his designer life with such critical and ironic distance must be able to present work that is up to the highest standard. Hickmann does this! What's more, his output in poster and corporate design is increasingly living up to his aspirations. His work has been represented at biennials and exhibitions around the world, and in 2002 he won the prestigious corporate design commission for the Kieler Woche, Europe's most important sailing regatta.••Hickmann now lives in Berlin and Vienna with the illustrator Gesine Grotrian-Steinweg and a small Fontissima with the lovely name Uma Malina. And when one meets him, one always has the impression that he is just at the beginning.••Uwe Loesch••

1–3 Poster series for Kieler Woche sailing regatta / Festival Kieler Woche / Germany / 2002
4–6 Poster series for concerts, *St John Passion*, by Johann Sebastian Bach, *Messiah*, by Georg Friedrich Haendel, and *Requiem*, by Giuseppe Verdi (photography Wolfgang Bellwinkel) / Johanneskantorei / Germany / 2001–2002
7 *Als Augen noch sprechen konnten* (When Eyes Could Still Speak) poster series for silent-film festival in Graz, Austria / Stummfilm Tage Graz / Austria / 1996

Fons Hickmann

Berlin/Vienna

STUMMFILM-TAGE GRAZ

Als Augen noch sprechen konnten

96.30.10.2010.

STUMMF.TAGE G

11.20.10.

S1 GRAZ 2

FILM-

LETTRE À L'ATELIER

Fons Hickmann

8–10   *Anonyme Idylle* (Anonymous Idyll) poster series for open-air concerts at the Freibad Rheinstadion, Düsseldorf / B8 / Germany / 2000

11   Poster for *Lettre à l'atelier* exhibition of the Franco-German artist group Théâtre Parlant / Théâtre Parlant / France / 1998

12   Poster for Hickmann lecture in Beijing (illustration Gesine Grotrian-Steinweg) / Central University of Fine Arts, Bejing / China / 2002

13   Poster for lecture by Hickmann at the Hochschule für Gestaltung Offentbach / Hochschule für Gestaltung Offentbach / Germany / 2002

14   Poster announcing Hickmann's website (photography Simon Gallus) / www.fonshickmann.com / Germany / 2002

15–20 Posters for exhibitions, concerts, and lectures in Düsseldorf / Labor für Soziale und Ästhetische Entwicklungen / Germany / 1999–2002

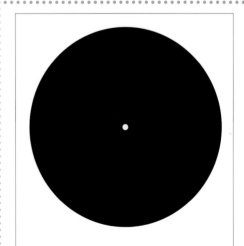

1. Reihe: **Seltene Platten**
Samstags 14 Uhr
19. 2. 2000 Bruce Haak, The Electric Luzifer, 1968 Moog Sounds
26. 2. 2000 Silver Apples Spectrum, Spaceman 3

Labor für Soziale und Ästhetische Entwicklung
Berger Kirche, Bergerstrasse Ecke Wallstrasse, Düsseldorf
In Zusammenarbeit mit Hitsville

I first saw Kim Hiorthøy's work when I gave a workshop in Bergen, Norway, and asked which young designers were now the Norwegian graphic trailblazers. From between the fjords, Kim arose, a young designer who is in his element in the country's music scene. At his tender age he has already published a book on his work, which suggests a similarly defiant feel for self-promotion as David Carson's did: it talks to its own audience, in codes that can be recognized and unraveled by that audience.●●Kim's designs are completely incompatible with my own musical background of Blue Note (Reid Miles) and Verve (David Stone Martin), with their brilliant record sleeves, but Kim's style is certainly his own, especially in the case of covers that he draws in wispy lines or conceives with the sparsest of colored planes. He may not be unique, but he is a good representative of the "Bruna generation": young designers who use the most minimal of means to make something "readable." In this case, readable means recognizable by people who know and appreciate the music and who will immediately comprehend the visual codes on Kim's covers. Apart from that, he is an excellent draftsman, who, in his best works, maintains a sense of space in his drawings, preventing them from becoming clogged. He represents a somewhat peripheral culture, which through travel, the Internet, and publications still manages to keep track of the rest of the world—and feeds back to it through the same channels. And the fact that Kim has found a client (Rune Grammofon) who lets him do what he wants—that, of course, is spectacular!●●Anthon Beeke●●

Kim Hiorthøy

1–4   Wall designs for restaurant in Roppongi, Tokyo / Thisisrealart and Peter Smith / Japan / 2002 / The designs are mounted on a "Venetian blind"-like billboard that rotates every fifteen minutes displaying the different flower designs.
5   CD cover, *Genetic Engineering*, by Phonophani / Rune Grammofon / Norway / 2001
6   CD cover, *Duck-Rabbit*, by Alog / Rune Grammofon / Norway / 2001
7   CD cover, *Den øverste toppen på en blåmalt flaggstang*, by Spunk / Rune Grammofon / Norway / 2002
8   CD cover, *Veggie*, by Food / Rune Grammofon / Norway / 2002
9   CD cover, *Scorch Trio*, by Björkenheim/Flaten/Nilssen-Love / Rune Grammofon / Norway / 2002
10   CD cover, *Free Music*, by Monolight / Rune Grammofon / Norway / 2002

phonophani
genetic engineering

alog
duck-rabbit

6

SPUNK

food
veggie

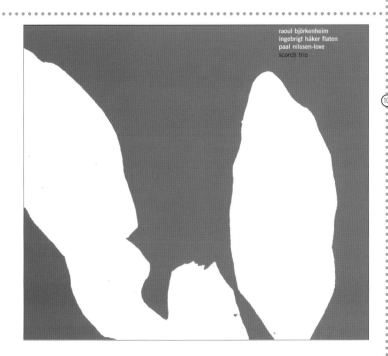

raoul björkenheim
ingebrigt håker flaten
paal nilssen-love
scorch trio

monolight
free music

(11)

(12)

(13)

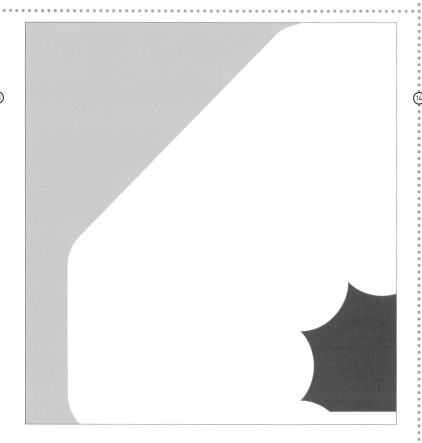

(14)

Kim Hiorthøy

11 Early version of CD cover for *The Stix*, by Jaga Jazzist / Smalltown Supersound and Ninja Tune / Norway / 2003

12 CD cover, *Various Artists: The Smalltown Supersampler* / Smalltown Supersound / Norway / 2002

13 CD cover, *Voice*, by Maja Ratkje / Rune Grammofon / Norway / 2002

14 Cover illustration, *2001 D&AD Award Winners* booklet / Creative Review / United Kingdom / 2001

15–16 Illustrations for March/April and July/August programs of the Oslo Cinematheque / Oslo Cinematheque / Norway / 2002

17 Poster for exhibition *Jeg er nesten alltid redd* at the Photographers' Gallery, Oslo / Norway / 2003

18 Promotional poster for album *Hei*, by Kim Hiorthøy / Smalltown Supersound / Norway / 2000

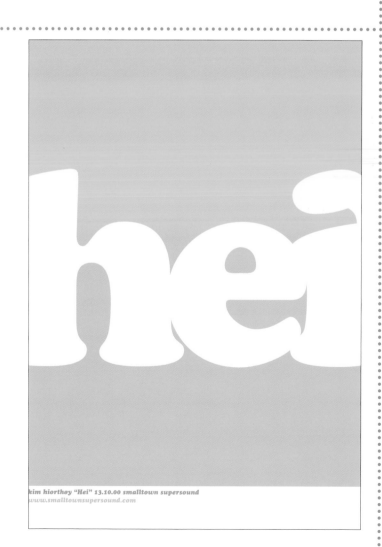

On a cold winter morning, a thin, clear film of ice forms in the shallow flower basin in the garden. When I try to scoop the fragile ice with my hands, it melts away in my palm. Keiko Hirano's works do not by any means melt away. They have a firm presence with their delicate but deep, penetrating colors. Are they the colors of the surface of the sea when a mermaid looks up from the depth of the ocean? Are they the colors of the universe when an angel casts a glance from atop a cloud? They are strange, clear colors. **Hirano's graphic designs, packaging designs using varied materials, and display spaces all transcend the idea conceived on the designer's worktable. Their abstract composition, which may appear too clean, and their delicate construction result in great works that seem to firmly reflect a strong creative ideology. **In the noisy and flashy advertising business of Japan's declining economy, Hirano's designs have a gentle, soft touch that appeals to the heart. They make us recall the long-forgotten virtue of good style and grace. **Her ability is demonstrated in the logo of the National Museum of Modern Art, Tokyo and the overall art direction for Qiora cosmetic products . She is one of the new powers who will change the direction of graphic design in Japan. **Shigeo Fukuda**

1   Packaging, bottle, and logotype for Awai sake brand (bottle design together with Aoshi Kudo) / Gekkeikan / Japan / 2002
2   Four of nine variations of CD packaging for *Dogs*, by Kenji Ozawa / Toshiba EMI ltd. / Japan / 1997
3   Logo, invitation cards, vinyl bags, and banner for National Museum of Modern Art, Tokyo / Japan / 2002

Keiko Hirano

Tokyo

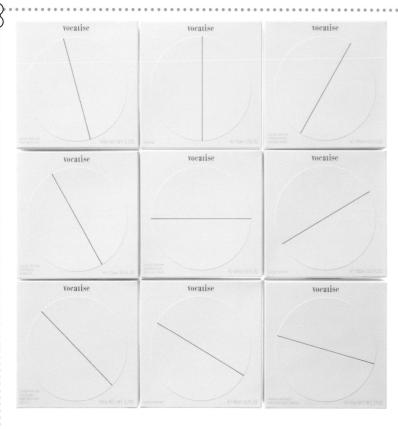

4–5   Logo and packaging for Vocalise perfume / Shiseido / Japan / 1997
6–7   Poster series for beauty salon / Shiseido Beauty Saloon / Japan / 1994
8–9   Poster, banner, and flyer for *Graphic Wave 1998* exhibition at Ginza Graphic Gallery / Dai Nippon Printing / Japan / 1998
10–13 Visual identity including logo, stationery, shop facade, and display-unit system for cosmetic brand Qiora / Shiseido / Japan / 2000–2001

Keiko Hirano

SHISEIDO BEAUTY SALOON
TOKYU BUNKAKAIKAN 3F
SHISEIDO BEAUTY SALOON
TOKYU BUNKAKAIKAN 3F

キンザ・グラフィック・ギャラリー第148回企画展

Graphic Wave 1998

蝦名龍郎　平野敬子　三木健

1998年9月1日(火)　9月26日(土)

ggg

DAI NIPPON PRINTING

Graphic designers are engaged in works that represent the entire culture of their society. Their works cover areas from business communications to leisure activities with no boundary in applications. Thus, a designer faces an extremely difficult task to satisfy all the needs of different objectives. He must have a good understanding of his client's needs, he must have a good grasp of the society at large, and above all he must possess the unyielding spirit of an avant-gardist with full command of the techniques of the formal arts.••Hon Bing-wah has overcome all these difficulties. I have full confidence that he is one of those creators who will bravely deal with new challenges in the future. He has demonstrated his talent in such areas as figurative illustration, abstract photography, creative typography, and three-dimensional design.••In Hong Kong, where the design business is fiercely competitive, Hon has successfully demonstrated his broad vision combining the tradition of Asia with a modern sensitivity. We learn from his passionate works that graphic design transcends the business world to the culture of a city, country, and society.••Shigeo Fukuda••

1–5 Cover and spreads, *Image of Shanghai* / Information Office of Shanghai Municipal People's Government / China / 1999 / The book was part of the campaign Shanghai in the Eyes of the World's Top Photographers, which celebrated the fiftieth anniversary of the liberation of Shanghai.
6 Kiss or Kill poster for *Peace Poster Exhibition 2001, Taiwan* / Taiwan Poster Design Association / Taiwan / 2001
7 Profession of Perfection poster for *10th Hong Kong Awards Poster Exhibition* / Heidelberg Printing Machine Co. / Hong Kong / 1998
8 Poster for *Suzhou Image Poster Exhibition* / Suzhou Graphic Designers Association / China / 2000
9 Redeeming Culture poster for *Living Heritage* exhibition / Hong Kong Heritage Museum / Hong Kong / 2001

Hon Bing-wah

Hong Kong

10   Slipcase, cover, and spreads, 60th Anniversary commemorative brochure / Hong Kong Printers Association /
     Hong Kong / 1999
11   Set of transportation cards with Chinese zodiac theme / Shanghai Public Transportation Card Co. Ltd. / China /
     2000 / The set was designed for the first anniversary of the Shanghai Public Transportation Card System.
12   Cover and spreads, information brochure to promote Shanghai's bidding for the World Expo 2010 /
     Expo 2010 Shanghai China Bidding Office / China / 2002

Hon Bing-wah

Inkahoots began as a government-assisted community screenprinting workshop and was founded as a public-access poster collective in 1990 by three self-taught graphic designers—Chris Stannard, Geoff Heller, and Robyn McDonald—during a chronic housing shortage in Brisbane. For five years the posters designed for, with, and by local community groups were characterized by an often crude yet vibrant and raw immediacy that reflected the urgency of their messages and Inkahoots's passionate, card-carrying commitment to addressing social inequalities. Their active participation in protest and debate about aboriginal land rights, gay rights, women's rights, labor issues, war, housing, and ecological matters gives real substance to the tagline they use to describe themselves, "direct design action". At a time when anthologies of the "new typography" were showing how a new generation of designers questioned the polite modernist principle of service by foregrounding artistic self-expression, Inkahoots had already rejected the service principle. While proponents of postmodernism engineered opportunity for their own aesthetic obsessions, this band of Australian idealists created a platform for their political beliefs.●●The arrival of Inkahoots's first college-trained graphic designer, Jason Grant, followed the enforcement of Brisbane's anti-bill-posting laws in 1994. Out of the grassroots poster collective had emerged a graphic-design practice free of the binds of state funding and able to tackle broader communication problems. Grant brought with him ideologically compatible professional design values that enabled Inkahoots to bring to their social work a highly sophisticated visual language. This was a combination powerful enough to provoke right-wing extremists into action; their studio was burned down in 1998. More recently with the addition of young graduates Lucas Surtie, Ben Mangan, and Joel Booy, the practice places increasing importance on the use of design as a seductive tool. With new graphic approaches married to an informed use of irony and biting wit, Inkahoots have proved that a critical stance need not be a didactic one. They understand how best to engage an audience, what American activist David Solnit calls "show, don't tell."●●Nick Bell●●

1   Poster protesting the harassment of the homeless by local authorities / Inner Brisbane Housing Network / Australia / 2000
2   CD packaging, *Quietly Building an Empire*, by The Carousel / The Carousel / Australia / 2001
3   Visual identity/promotional poster for company planning Australia's first zero-emission residential community / Ecodomo / Australia / 2001
4   Visual identity/promotional poster for Australia's oldest ethical investment institution / Foresters ANA Friendly Society / Australia / 2000
5   Cover, annual report for group organizing emergency accommodations for migrant women / MWESS / Australia / 2002
6   Spread from booklet promoting resources for young parents / Young Mothers for Young Women / Australia / 2002

Inkahoots

Brisbane, Australia

NATURAL **LIVING**

PASSIVE DESIGN PRINCIPLES | RENEWABLE ENERGY | WATER CONSERVATION | COMMUNITY, EMPLOYMENT & SOCIAL INTEGRATION | SENSITIVE LAND MANAGEMENT

ECO**DOMO** ecological developments

eco**domo** ™

FORESTERS ANA
FRIENDLY SOCIETY

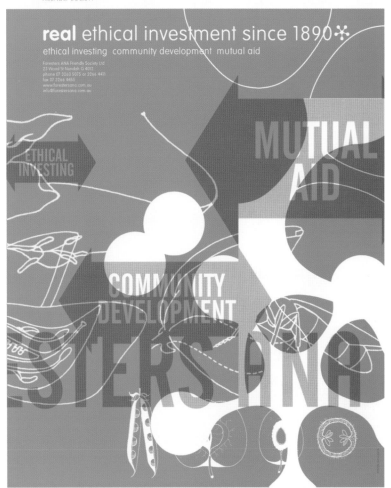

real ethical investment since 1890

ethical investing community development mutual aid

Foresters ANA Friendly Society Ltd
23 Wood St Nundah Q 4012
phone 07 3260 5075 or 3266 4411
fax 07 3266 4455
www.forestersana.com.au
info@forestersana.com.au

ETHICAL INVESTING

MUTUAL AID

COMMUNITY DEVELOPMENT

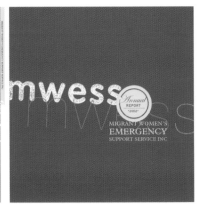

mwess

Annual REPORT 2002

MIGRANT WOMEN'S
EMERGENCY
SUPPORT SERVICE INC

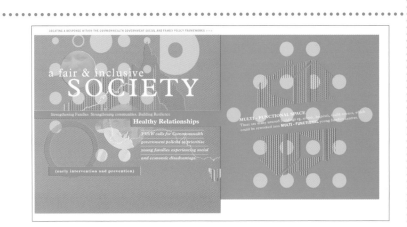

a fair & inclusive
SOCIETY

Strengthening Families. Strengthening communities. Building Resilience.

Healthy Relationships

MWW calls for Commonwealth government policies to prioritise young families experiencing social and economic disadvantage.

(early intervention and prevention)

MULTI - FUNCTIONAL SPACE

Inkahoots

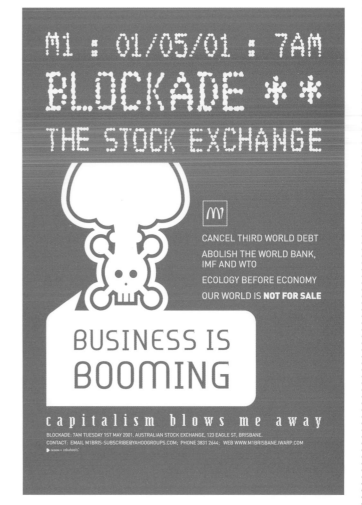

What do you get when two young designers, one Icelandic and one German, get together and set up a graphic-design studio in Manhattan? The answer: Karlssonwilker Inc. In order to introduce their new studio in late 2000, Hjalti Karlsson and Jan Wilker distributed a rather interesting mailing. Printed on newsprint, it featured a portrait of the two designers—stiff as boards, all very Gilbert and George—and an animated diagram with layer upon layer of information (including contact details, sound bites, and illustrations) on the reverse. It captured the studio's eclectic personality to a T and brought a number of jobs to their door.**A glance at their well-rounded portfolio reflects the convergence of cultural backgrounds, the European aesthetics, and the myriad stimuli of Manhattan's voracious cultural landscape. It is a recipe that encourages eclecticism and makes it impossible to pigeonhole their work. They aren't afraid to try a new direction, so long as it will achieve the most appropriate and relevant solution for the client, and for themselves.**
The CD covers and promotional program they developed for the Vines have taken their work into a huge arena. Karlssonwilker created an appropriate graphic language, with shaky hand-drawn typography suggesting the edgy, postpunk ethic of the band. One of the CDs was shrinkwrapped in plastic that was printed in three colors. To spend time, effort, and resources on an element of the packaging that will end up in most people's wastebaskets says a lot about Karlssonwilker.**The firm's solution for a collection of live recordings by the psychedelic rock-jazz cult band Kraan is particularly appropriate. The graphic language suggests contemporary "psychedelic rock-jazz" without resorting to stereotypical psychedelic graphics. *Curious Boym*—a book designed for industrial-design studio Boym & Partners—has a die-cut cover, and the waste circle from that cut was subsequently used as an invite/coaster for the book's launch party. A fun, practical, and cost-effective solution.**
Are they space cadets or just plain, run-of-the-mill eccentrics? In 2001, they were invited to design a lamp for auction as part of an annual design benefit to fund scholarships for disadvantaged students. They created Doglamp, which is...a dog in a lamp, or rather a dog with a protective shade on its head, turned into a lamp. You have to admire that. There is no grand gesture involved, no pseudo-intellectual crap; just good, clean, twisted fun.
Fernando Gutiérrez

1–4 Promotional poster and CD packaging, *Live 2001*, by Kraan / Kraan and Bassball Records / USA / 2001
5–8 Book, cover, spreads, and promotional party invitation/coaster, *Curious Boym* by Studio Boym & Partners, New York / Princeton Architectural Press / USA / 2002 / The invitation/coaster is the cutout of the die-cut cover.

Karlssonwilker

New York

9 Cover and spreads, second Karlssonwilker Inc. mailer / USA / 2002
10 CD packaging, *Elemental Chill* compilations / Kriztal Entertainment / USA / 2002 /
   The circles on the CDs serve as the bar code.
11 CD packaging, *Highly Evolved,* by The Vines / Capitol Records / USA / 2002

Karlssonwilker

ELEMENTAL CHILL

VOL. 1   FIRE

ELEMENTAL CHILL

VOL. 3   AIR

ELEMENTAL CHILL

VOL. 4   WATER

ELEMENTAL CHILL

VOL. 2   EARTH

Maverick! Siobhan Keaney has been described as a lone woman pioneer in London. She prides herself on the ability to remain independent and her knowledge that creative freedom is more important than just making money. This complete freedom from restrictions on her creativity allows her to approach each project in a distinctive way. She believes her route forward should be experimental. Keaney describes her method of working as "steering well clear of the mainstream." Whatever her approach, the resulting work is powerful and direct. Very now. The numerous awards, exhibitions of her work, and invitations to speak nationally and internationally stand testament to a consistent quality of work and a commitment to its standards. She also has strong links to design education, having lectured at the Royal College of Art in London and consulted for Leeds University and Bath Spa University. She also currently tutors at the University of Brighton. In 1997 she became a member of Alliance Graphique Internationale (AGI). Keaney is a designer who continues to reemerge, and her road of experimentation should establish her as one of design's innovative and influential forces in years to come.
••Ken Cato••

Siobhan Keaney

London

Siobhan Keaney

7   Postcards aimed at communicating the value of intangible assets and their importance in building a successful business / Design Council / United Kingdom / 2001

8   Self-promotional poster / United Kingdom / 1999

9   Print advertisment for postproduction company / The Mill / United Kingdom / 1997

10–12 Millennium poster and images produced for Millennium Dome brochure / New Millennium Experience Company / United Kingdom / 1999

There is something particularly nostalgic about the work of London-based duo Frith Kerr and Amelia Noble, but to describe it as old-fashioned would be way off the mark. Their work shows a willingness to experiment and reinvent traditional elements of graphic design in order to achieve the most appropriate and relevant solution. They certainly aren't afraid of mixing the myriad elements that inform their visual vocabulary.●●A prime example of this is the map/guide they designed for British Television's Channel Four riverboat trip in 1999, which utilizes typography to create the shape of the River Thames as it flows through London. It is a basic concept that has been explored before, but you'd struggle to find an example that feels as fresh.●●The riverboat trip map/guide is an elegant, understated example of print design that openly suggests a nostalgia entirely appropriate for content of this nature. The Thames reeks of history, which is why Kerr/Noble sourced a poem—"A Description of London," written in 1738 by John Bancks—and set the poem in the shape of the river in a variety of classic serif typefaces. You can't help but sense the history; then again, you can't look at a piece like this without feeling refreshed.●●Typography plays an important role in the way Kerr/Noble communicate information, personality, and content. Take, for example, the cover of *Accommodating Change*, a book designed to accompany an Architecture Foundation exhibition of the same name. Rather than adorn the cover with one project, the team opted for a democratic solution that communicates the diverse nature of the work in the exhibition. The name of each firm is set in a different typeface—ranging from clean sans serifs to more rounded, psyche-delic typefaces—which suggests the individual personalities and qualities of each company as well as the diverse nature of the exhi-bition. All communicated with a sense of wit and clarity that can be found time and time again in Kerr/Noble's work.●●Fernando Gutiérrez●●

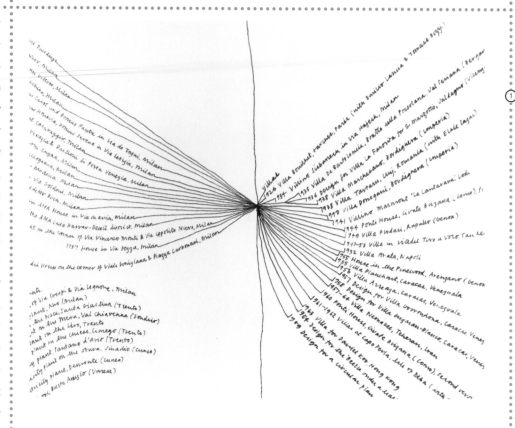

1 Hand-drawn mural for *Gio Ponti–A World* exhibition / Design Museum, London / United Kingdom / 2002 / The "tree" is a register of Ponti's works, detailing every project he worked on, in the style of his own handwriting.
2–3 Title wall designs for *Gio Ponti–A World* exhibition / The leaf is taken from Ponti's 1974 "Facade with Leaves" on a building in Hong Kong.
4 Front of *Accommodating Change: Innovation in Housing* exhibition guide / Architecture Foundation / United Kingdom / 2002
5 Short-film viewing aperture made of translucent cast resin, part of exhibition design for *Accommodating Change: Innovation in Housing* / Architecture Foundation / United Kingdom / 2002
6 Opening spread, *No More Rules–Graphic Design and Postmodernism*, by Rick Poynor (illustration Edward Fella) / Laurence King Publishing / United Kingdom / 2003 / Kerr/Noble's Modified Pop typeface featured in the book was based on Neville Brody's Pop font and created especially for the project.

Kerr/Noble

London

No More Rules

Graphic Design and Postmodernism

Rick Poynor

Laurence King Publishing

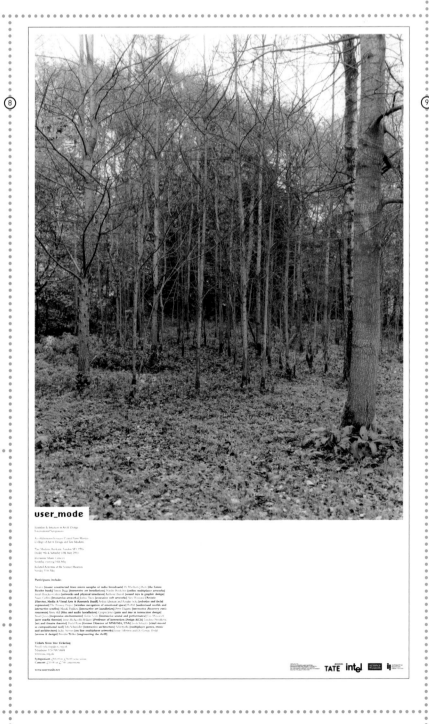

7   Foldout souvenir for riverboat trip on the Thames / Channel Four Television / United Kingdom / 1999 /
    The foldout features the poem "A Description of London," by John Bancks (1738).
8   Poster for open gig of film director Tony Kaye's rock band K at Cannes Film Festival (with Ian Wright) /
    Tony Kaye / United Kingdom / 2001
9   Poster for international symposium on emotion and intuition in art and design (photography Amber
    Rowlands) / Central Saint Martins College of Art & Design and Tate Modern / United Kingdom / 2003
10-12 Spreads and front and back cover, self-published magazine *Lost But Not Forgotten* (photography Clare
    Shilland) / Kerr/Noble / United Kingdom / 2002 / Kerr/Noble designed a special font for the magazine,
    which was inspired by a day trip to London's Highgate Cemetery. The title of the magazine is revealed to
    the reader throughout the publication.

Kerr/Noble

Lost But Not Forgotten
Concept, Design & Art Direction: Kerr/Noble
Contributors: Scott Bradley, Tom Geens, Chosil Kil, Chris Petersen & Clare Shilland
Copyright 2002.

ISBN 1-85332-187-7

9 781853 321870

The first thing Rene Knip did, within half an hour of entering my studio as an apprentice, was blow up the only computer we had. He thought that would get him fired on the spot, but I didn't care that much. I hadn't hired him for his computer skills, but for his typographic talent, which he engaged for us for over three years. Knip exemplifies a new generation of designers. His theme is the architecture of letters—he is deeply fascinated with letters as three-dimensional objects. Today we have slightly forgotten about the way letters used to be employed on buildings in the 1930s, and in reclaiming the field of spatial typography, Knip revives an old craft. He polishes as long as it takes to find the right form.**His point of departure as a designer is handwriting; he writes beautifully and is an ardent correspondent. But in the end, that handwriting results in very precisely constructed typography, with a very peculiar sensibility for color.**Knip is a bit brainy, but also someone who embraces modern life to the fullest—he loves sailing, good cooking, is a social guy and an excellent host. He is one of those rare people who knows how to share.**Like so many intelligent people, Knip is also a bit lazy. He knows exactly what he wants and hates wasting time with nonsense or, in other words, working for clients or projects he doesn't believe in. Knip is not a career planner. He might just decide to go sailing around the world for a year or to pick up studying again. He once said that if he could start over, he would become an architect. This feeling for architecture, for space, is superbly expressed in a calendar he made, a cube, exactly 12 x 12 x 12 centimeters—the matrix of the months. He researched paper stock until he found the weight to get exactly 12 centimeters of height with 365 pages. The year 2003 has been cut out in the sides of the block and each month has a different diecut in the middle of the page, so that almost every day has a different form. Typographically, it's a beauty as well: a masterpiece! I'm glad that—besides being his good friend—I am working with Knip again, now as a teacher in my communication department at the Design Academy in Eindhoven.**Anthon Beeke**

ABCDEFGHIJKLM
NOPQRSTUVWXYZ
1237890¡¡¡¡⊥@?
LAUNDRY SANS

ABCDEFGH
IJKLMNOP
QRSTUVWX
YZ!O1234
56789E·?

1, 3 Hanging typeface Laundry Sans used for *Mooi Maar Goed* exhibition on graphic
design at Stedelijk Museum, Amsterdam / Stedelijk Museum / Netherlands / 1999
2, 4 Terra-cotta tile typeface HEMA used by Merkx + Girod Architects for restaurants
in HEMA department stores / Merkx + Girod Architecten / Netherlands / 1998
5 Self-commissioned project "Firebasket" (with Edgar Knip) / Netherlands / 2002 /
Laser-cut steel basket composed of words: zinc, moss, silence, dust, bone, moon, etc.

Rene Knip

Amsterdam

⑤

6 Six-volume set with slipcase, "Dutch Design 2000–2001" / BIS publishers and the Association of Dutch Designers (BNO) / Netherlands / 2001 / The set comprises of individual books on graphic design, environmental design, industrial design, packaging design, illustration, new media. Knip specifically developed a different "illustrative" typeface for each book.

7 Calender cube designed for Dutch printers Calff & Meischke / Calff & Meischke / Netherlands / 2003 / Every month is cut in a different form.

8 Aluminium house-number design developed for Merkx + Girod Architects as a gift for clients in celebration of their fifteenth anniversary / Merkx + Girod Architecten / Netherlands / 1999

Rene Knip

Since the use of a hip typeface or the application of a new Photoshop filter is often misinterpreted as innovation, it is becoming increasingly rare for a piece of graphic design to be truly exciting. ● ● The mysteriously dark blue Musik Box Elisabeth Kopf designed for the Vienna Art Orchestra is one of those very few pieces that blew me away: It not only packages music beautifully, but performs music itself, thereby creating a conversation between design and content I have nowhere else experienced so elegantly. Kopf commissioned thirty short compositions, ten relating to Vienna, ten to art, and ten to orchestra. Each piece is performed on an ingenious harmonica system when one of the limited-edition CD packages is opened. The musicians of the Vienna Art Orchestra produced a live music piece utilizing the packaging as instruments, a conceptual loop that blurs the borders not only between art and design, and between content and packaging, but also between music and object. This *is* innovation. ● ● Many of Kopf's less lavishly conceived and produced packages are also little performance pieces, graphics that not only visualize the music perfectly but expand on it. ● ● While working on the exhibition design for the *Arbeitersamariterbund*, a small Austrian version of the Red Cross, she learned from the client that in situations requiring first aid, many people are willing to help but afraid to do the wrong thing; that first-aid course was a while back, after all. All those booklets containing first-aid rules did little to reduce that fear. The rules must be reiterated all the time to make people aware of them. Kopf's response was to print a different first-aid rule on each and every graphic-design piece her studio produces, be it a CD cover, a theater poster, or a lecture invitation. If a client refuses to have the rule printed on their project, they have to donate to the *Arbeitersamariterbund* to remain one of her clients. ● ● I am very tempted to steal that idea. ● ● Stefan Sagmeister ● ●

1   CD packaging, *Segmente*, by Peter Herbert and David Tronzo (with Werner Korn) / Aziza Music / USA / 1999 / The cover print consists of two images placed on top of each other. The hidden image can be revealed by scratching off the top layer.
2   Four pieces from personal project "Scratch Gallery," collection of scratched *Segmente* CD covers by friends and colleagues / 1999–present
3   CD packaging, *Peter Herbert & Aktionstheater Ensemble 2000* / Aziza Music and Aktionstheater Ensemble / USA / 2000 / In this packaging for a CD of theater music, the wide black curtain revealed inside the unfolded hardcover contains a booklet. When one flips through it, the curtain gradually opens and shows a one-act theater scene. The curtain is also a bar code saying, "It's art when you can't add and you can't reduce anymore little theater for music by elisabeth kopf for peter herbert."

Elisabeth Kopf

Vienna

4–5 Personal project "Air Cigarettes," do-it-yourself paper cigarettes / 2002 / Kopf's stance against nicotine.

6   Announcement for lecture and exercise "How to check for consciousness/unconsciousness" held by
Elisabeth Kopf at the anniversary symposium "75 Years Design Austria" / Austria / 2002 / The lecture
formed part of Kopf's personal "First Aid" project.

7   "Little Orchestra" CD packaging, unique edition of thirty handmade CD cases (with Werner Korn) / Vienna
Art Orchestra / Austria / 1997 / Created for the twentieth anniversary of the Vienna Art Orchestra, the CD
packaging itself makes music by using the air flow produced through opening and closing. Each case plays
its own tune, the complete collection creating a full orchestral composition. The orchestra performed live
with the musical CD boxes during its Anniversary World Tour.

8   Packaging for CD featuring performances of the Little Orchestra musical CD boxes / Austria / 1997

Elisabeth Kopf

⑦

⑧

Ji Lee took it upon himself to produce and pay for the production of 15,000 speech-bubble stickers, large and small. He glues them everywhere he goes but mostly on posters around town that feature people, thus giving those flat heads a voice and transforming a one-way communication into a dialogue. Everybody wins: The advertiser gets more people to look at its (now personalized) posters, the public finally gets a chance to talk back to the advertisers, and the rest of us are able to enjoy these little jolts of joy by seeing and reading the transformed posters. ● ●And how much more interesting they become. Take a regular record-release poster, the likes of which hang around New York City by the hundreds, announcing that the new CD by Glenn Lewis will be available on March 19. Whoever wrote the text in Lewis's (really Lee's) speech bubble, "I am concerned that my CD will not sell more than 200,000 units and that, as a result, my recoupable advance from my label will be taken away from me, after which my contract will be canceled and I'll be back doing Journey covers on Bleecker Street," transformed a dull promotion into an apt comment on the music industry. ● ●Lee uses every medium available to him. One moment he dedicates himself fully to developing a revolving alphabet that invites viewers to decode it in three dimensions; the next he is busy inventing the Abstractor, basically a TV whose screen is covered with two black cardboards leaving only a small slit visible, thus transforming any dull program into "a beautiful and pleasant experience at any time with any channel." You have to see it to believe it. ● ●Lee has a day job as an art director for one of the big advertising conglomerates where he produces fine but less remarkable work. In a way the speech-bubble campaign can be seen as a nightly atonement for sins committed during the day. ● ●Stefan Sagmeister● ●

ABSTRACTOR

INSTANTLY TRANSFORMS YOUR TV VIEWING INTO A BEAUTIFUL AND PLEASANT EXPERIENCE AT ANY TIME, WITH ANY CHANNEL. TRY WITH YOUR TV. IT'S EASY.

①

Ji Lee
writetojilee@hotmail.com

②

Where did I meet him?		How do I know him?	
Age group:	Profession:		Marital Status: ☐ M ☐ S ☐ D

What can I get from him?
☐ PROF. HELP ☐ SEX ☐ DRUGS ☐ NOTHING ☐ OTHER:

What does he seem to want from me?
☐ PROF. HELP ☐ SEX ☐ DRUGS ☐ NOTHING ☐ OTHER:

Sex appeal (circle one):	1	2	3	4	5	6	7	8	9	10
Intelligence:	1	2	3	4	5	6	7	8	9	10
Financial/Social status:	1	2	3	4	5	6	7	8	9	10

When to contact him: ☐ TOMORROW ☐ IN 2 DAYS ☐ WAIT ☐ NEVER

Ji Lee

New York

1   Abstractor project / USA / 2002 / "An easy way to transform TV viewing into a beautiful and pleasant experience."
2   Ji Lee's business card / USA / 2002
3   Speech-bubble sticker project in New York City / USA / 2002-present / Blank speech-bubble stickers placed on posters, ads, public signs, etc. throughout the city invite passersby to fill them with comments.

④

⑤

⑥

⑦

Ji Lee

There is no national boundary in human emotion (joy, anger, sadness, and pleasure), and humor can be one of the most important elements in visual communication. Graphic designers throughout the world attempt to deliver messages in a humorous manner. However, it is difficult to incorporate humor in a single poster. Humor can be delivered through concrete expression, and success depends on the wisdom and ability of a designer in upending the common sense and anticipation of the audience.●●Ken-Tsai Lee has been concentrating on this area throughout his career. He can courageously shut out colors and sideline words in order to achieve the desired effect. Look at, for instance, the simple and clear visual messages he created for his client, E+E (Earth and Environment) Paper. One of the posters shows a leaf composed of empty bottles and cans of chemical products in black. The tip of the leaf is contaminated and shown in red. In another poster, the veins and nerves of the human body are connected to a blue plant growing out of the top of the figure's head. Lee's youthful sensitivity is on display in these works.●●In our global era saturated with the influence of all-purpose computers, I am not the only one to have great expectations for Lee and his creative, humorous philosophy.●●Shigeo Fukuda●●

1   Logo / Ken-Tsai Lee Design Studio / Taiwan / 2001
2–3 Two posters from "My Name is Ken-Tsai" Lee street-poster series / USA / 2003 / Self-promotional effort during three-month stay in New York City. Every week Lee hung posters all over the city with designs of his name written in the native tongue of the people he had met. Here in Korean and Bangladeshi.
4   Network Snake poster for poster-design exhibition / Taiwan Poster Design Association / Taiwan / 2001

Ken-Tsai Lee

Taipei

⑤

⑥

⑦

⑧

Ken-Tsai Lee

5-8   Posters for public Chinese AIDS-prevention campaign / Chinese Society of Preventive Medicine–Living with
       Hope Organization / Taiwan / 2001
9-10   "Peace–China and Taiwan" and "War–China and Taiwan" posters for poster-design exhibition / Taiwan Poster
       Design Association / Taiwan / 2001
11-12 Posters promoting recycled E+E (Earth and Environment) Paper / Fonso Enterprise / Taiwan / 2001

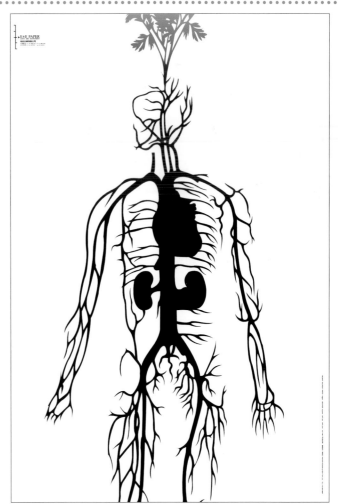

Anette Lenz is an insider's secret. Since she has been living in Paris for more than a decade now, she could nearly pass for being French. But in reality, she is a legal alien in the city of lights.••Her biography is as impressive as her work. After finishing her visual communication studies in Munich, Lenz began her career as a graphic designer for a Munich-based design agency. In 1989 she moved to Paris, where she first worked for Grapus with Alexander Jordan and then cofounded Nous Travaillons Ensemble. For three years she worked within this graphic-design collective and played an important role designing books, posters, and corporate identities for cities and cultural institutions. Finally, in 1993, she set up her own studio in Paris. Her list of clients included the town of Blanc-Mesnil, for which she created a poster series for the exhibition *Approches* that was seen in Chaumont, Paris, and many other European cities. Thanks to this exposure, numerous cultural institutions became aware of her work, and she began collaborating with new clients. For AFAA (the foreign ministry) she embarked on a yearlong campaign for the Saison Culturelle du Maroc, and for the city of Chaumont Lenz developed a corporate identity and a set of graphic guidelines. From 1998 to 2001 she designed the communication materials of the Théâtre de Rungis, a job that, in 2002, earned her a gold medal at the international graphic-design biennial in Brno. Since 2000 she has been working for Radio France, and in 2001 she joined forces with Vincent Perrottet for the Théâtre d'Angoulême. Together with Hervé Binet, with whom she shares an interest in literature and poetry, she established "editions 23," a collaborative effort focusing on book projects that combine typography, poetry, and text. Lenz joined the Alliance Graphique Internationale (AGI) in 1999.••She is special because she is truly her own person. Headstrong, she developed her own style, hardly revealing her influences. On the one hand, I discover in her work typically German forms of expression, especially in her handling of typography. On the other hand, I find her work very French. Sometimes I wonder whether she would have had the same opportunities and acclaim in Germany or whether it is precisely the symbiosis of French delicatessens and German wine that is the secret to her success.••Throughout her career Lenz has done so many notable projects that I find it difficult to select my favorites. I would even go so far as to say that I am jealous of her beautiful, intelligent posters.••Uwe Loesch••

1–2 Poster series for Radio France concerts for the 2000–2001 season (2 of 9) /
Radio France / France / 2001
3 Poster announcing the 2000–2001 theatrical season / Théâtre de Rungis /
France / 2000
4–8 Poster series announcing individual plays for the 2000–2001 theatrical season
(5 of 17) / Théâtre de Rungis / France / 2000

Anette Lenz

Paris

3

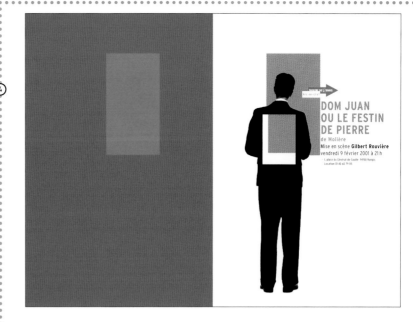

4

DOM JUAN
OU LE FESTIN
DE PIERRE
de Molière
Mise en scène **Gilbert Rouvière**
vendredi 9 février 2001 à 21 h
1, place du Général de Gaulle 94150 Rungis
Location 01 45 60 79 95

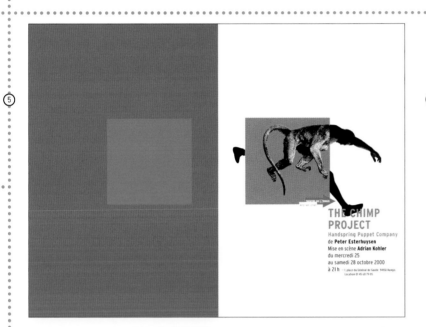

5

THE CHIMP
PROJECT
Handspring Puppet Company
de **Peter Esterhuysen**
Mise en scène **Adrian Kohler**
du mercredi 25
au samedi 28 octobre 2000
à 21 h 1, place du Général de Gaulle 94150 Rungis
Location 01 45 60 79 95

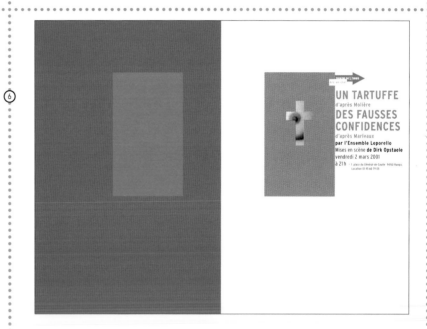

6

UN TARTUFFE
d'après Molière
DES FAUSSES
CONFIDENCES
d'après Marivaux
par l'**Ensemble Leporello**
Mises en scène **de Dirk Opstaele**
vendredi 2 mars 2001
à 21 h 1, place du Général de Gaulle 94150 Rungis
Location 01 45 60 79 95

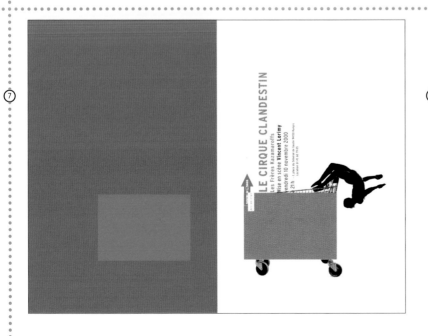

7

LE CIRQUE CLANDESTIN
Les Frères Kazamaroffs
Mise en scène **Vincent Lorimy**
vendredi 10 novembre 2000
à 21 h 1, place du Général de Gaulle 94150 Rungis
Location 01 45 60 79 95

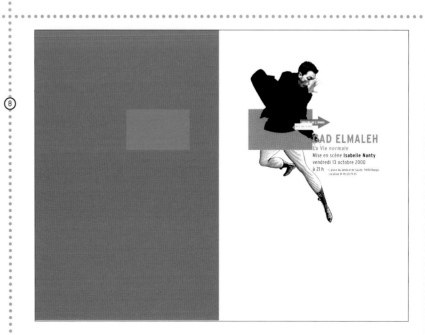

8

GAD ELMALEH
La Vie normale
Mise en scène **Isabelle Nanty**
vendredi 13 octobre 2000
à 21 h 1, place du Général de Gaulle 94150 Rungis
Location 01 45 60 79 95

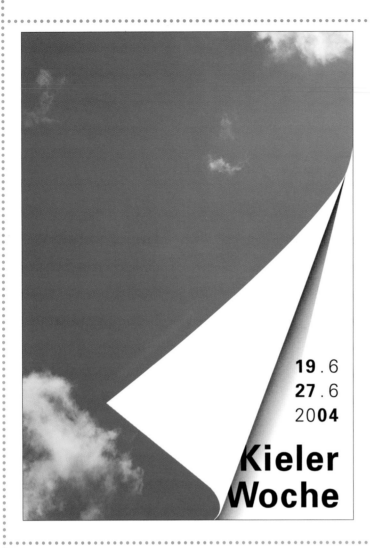

19.6
27.6
2004

Kieler Woche

Anette Lenz

You cannot cut a giant tree with a sickle, and you cannot reap rice plants with a saw. Experts must choose their tools and deliberate their means. The tasks imposed on a graphic designer are various and diverse, almost limitless. Sometimes a designer is asked to deliver a message visually to many people in a beautiful manner without words, and sometimes this means struggling with his or her own creative ideology as a graphic designer.●●Apex Lin is one of those praiseworthy people endowed with common sense, sensitivity, and the capacity to tackle these difficult tasks. He has a natural understanding of how to communicate with a given target audience. One can observe this ability for persuasion in the way he switches the meaning of characters on his posters. He demonstrated his creative wisdom by giving the middle letter *A* of PEACE a sense of eternal future though his use of perspective. Equally impressive is the exquisite red cross formed by the combination of *F* and *E* in LIFE.●●The era of communication to limited audiences is already history for graphic design. It is now plunging into communication on a global scale. Lin's philosophy of fine arts will enable him to develop his creativity in the new vortex.●●Shigeo Fukuda●●

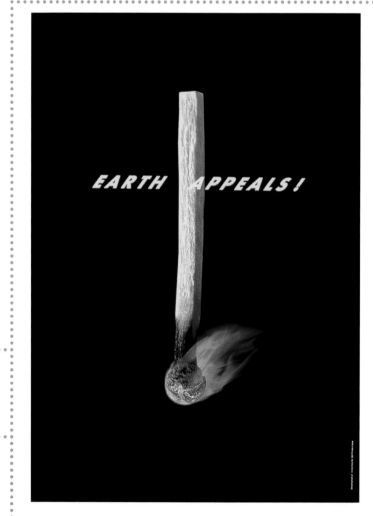

1　Poster commemorating victims of Taiwan's 21 September 1999 earthquake / Taiwan 921 Earthquake Reconstruction Committee / Taiwan / 2001
2　Earth Appeals poster / Apex Design Consultant Corporation / Taiwan / 1997
3–6　Formosa? Republic of Casino, Illusion of Taiwan, Green & Life, and Levitating Taiwan posters from "Taiwan" series / Taiwan Image Poster Design Association / Taiwan / 1993–96

Apex Lin

Taipei

多彩的世界‧迷失的台灣！

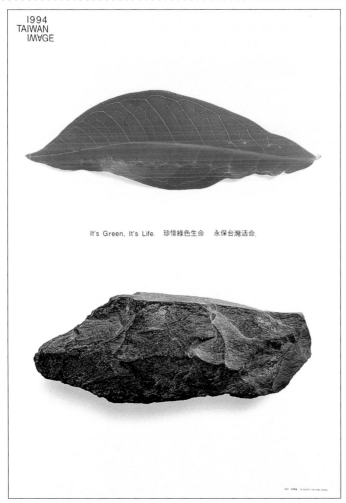

1994
TAIWAN
IMAGE

It's Green, It's Life.　珍惜綠色生命　永保台灣活命.

7 Poster for Shanghai's bid to host the World Expo 2010 / Expo 2010 Shanghai Committee / China / 2002
8 Promotional poster for NACPES / National College of Physical Education and Sports / Taiwan / 1989
9 Logo / Greatwall Oil Corporation / China / 1996
10 Discover Asia, Discover Taipei poster / Taiwan Poster Design Association / Taiwan / 2002
11 Life poster / Apex Design Consultant Corporation / Taiwan / 1998
12 Poster for Apex Lin exhibition in Macau / UNESCO Center of Macau / Macau / 1999
13 Green in Your Heart poster / Apex Design Consultant Corporation / Taiwan / 2001
14 Peace–One Way of the World poster / Taiwan Poster Design Association / Taiwan / 2001

Apex Lin

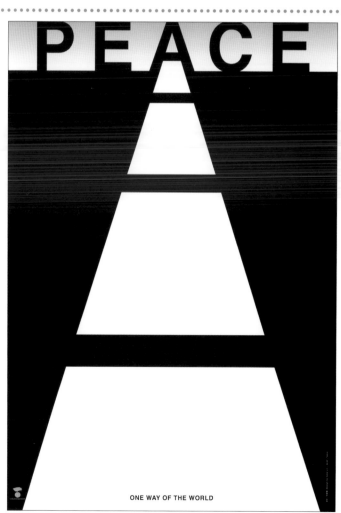

In the late 1990s, Moscow designer Andrey Logvin became famous in the international design community for his witty, bright, energetic posters. In 1996 he received the gold medal at the international poster biennial in Warsaw. The New York journal *International Design Magazine*, which devotes one issue each year to artistic profiles of masters pushing the boundaries of the profession, added him to this distinguished list in 1998, the first Russian designer to be so honored. In 1999 Logvin was admitted into the prestigious Alliance Graphique Internationale (AGI). ••But professional recognition alone does not satisfy him. With his posters he constantly tries to break through to the general public. Above all, he dreams of success for the social poster. In the USSR, such poster art was called "sociopolitical." For decent designers, the genre was discredited as communist propaganda and remained indecently untouchable. ••Meanwhile in the West, creating social posters is not shameful even for the stars of international design. In the fall of 1994, during a workshop offered by jury members of the Moscow Golden Bee graphic-design biennial, Logvin's idol, Uwe Loesch, showed slides of his green environmental posters all around Düsseldorf. Thus Logvin discovered that poster art is a means of mass, not elitist, communication. He started the project Moscow-poster, in which a group of young designers, at their own discretion, created sociopolitical posters and the young firm LiniaGrafik funded, printed, and plastered two hundred of them. But Moscow is not Düsseldorf. Two hundred posters are not enough to blanket a capital. ••In another campaign, seven national and seven international design celebrities visually interpreted the fiftieth anniversary of the victory in World War II. This time the posters didn't even make it to the field. Moscow authorities did not allow their posting, afraid that they would not be "understood by the people." ••Recently Logvin participated in the large-scale poster project "I don't want to hate." His contribution showed Christ, Muhammad, and Buddha sharing a meal. The poster was displayed in various Russian cities, but religious orthodoxy organized pickets against it. ••Logvin is not discouraged. He still believes that his efforts will fuel a rebirth of the visually and socially active street poster. ••Serge Serov ••

1   Poster for *Russian Design 95* competition and exhibition / Design Union of Russia / Russia / 1995
2   Self-commissioned Life Was Successful poster / Russia / 1996 / The phrase written in caviar ironically refers to a Russian idiom on success in life.
3   The Best in the World poster for caviar retailer / Russian Alaska Company / Russia / 1997
4   Poster for artist Stas Ishenko's In the Cube exhibition / Stas Ishenko / Russia / 1999
5   Poster for international poster project "10 Graphic Designers for Human Rights" / Ministère de l'Éducation nationale / France / 2001
6   It's Sad Without a Label poster for *The Label 95* exhibition organized by printing company LiniaGrafic / LiniaGrafic / Russia / 1995
7   Bear Up, Egory poster celebrating Moscow's 850th anniversary / LiniaGrafic / Russia / 1998 / Egory is Moscow's patron saint.

Andrey Logvin

Moscow

ne sera soumis à la torture, ni à des peines ou traitements cruels, inhumains ou dégradants.

Revolution is in Danger! The Russian History 1917-1993

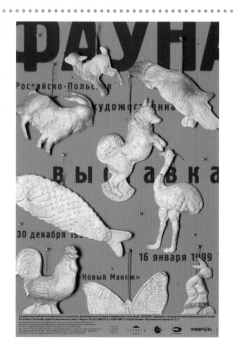

8   Poster advertising workshops offered by jury members during 5th Moscow Golden Bee poster biennial / Golden Bee Committee / 2000
9   Poster for puppet show *Cowboy Story* / Saratov Puppet Theatre / Russia / 1991
10   Poster for *Revolution Is in Danger! The Russian History 1917–1993* exhibition / National Center for Contemporary Art / Russia / 1995
11   Poster for *Fauna* exhibition / National Center for Contemporary Art / Russia / 1998
12   Poster for concert by the band Mouse Trap / Mouse Trap / Russia / 2002
13   Poster for festival celebrating the 100th anniversary of Vladimir Mayakovski / futurism.ru / Russia / 2002
14   Poster for Swiss-Russian art project Supremus / Supremus Foundation / Russia and Switzerland / 2002
15   Poster for *Serials* exhibition / National Center for Contemporary Art / Russia / 2000

Andrey Logvin

Most graphic design strives to balance the views of society and a general sense of beauty, but Victor Hugo Marreiros's design is an exception. Many of his works demonstrate a magic that reminds us of watching a circus performance. They are pleasant, humorous, and at the same time bewitching. The poster in the series created for the 12th Macao Arts Festival is a masterpiece. It looks like both a face and an instrument, and amazingly you can visualize music from the rhythmically composed surface. The well-controlled variations of a string instrument, a piano, melody, and dance are truly exquisite. The new talent of this exceptional designer is likewise demonstrated in his poster for the Macao Youth Musician Contest and in the series of posters for the Luís de Matos magic show. ••Marreiros is one of the most precious and most dangerous and interesting designers in the global graphic-design world, like a creature from another planet. His designs do not require many words or explanation. They should be savored silently, just like listening to music. ••Shigeo Fukuda••

1   Poster for XII Macao Arts Festival / Macao Cultural Institute / China / 2001
2   Cover illustration for *Oriente Occidente–East West* magazine no. 4 / International Institute of Macao / China / 2001
3   Poster series for fourth Chinese Drama Festival in Macao / Macao Cultural Institute / China / 2002

Victor Hugo Marreiros

Macao, China

Victor Hugo Marreiros

I met Malte Martin during the preparations for my exhibition *Zwischenkieferknochen (Os Intermaxilliare)* at the Galerie Anatome in Paris. When speaking he switched effortlessly between perfect French and German, making it difficult for me to figure out where he was really from. He soon hinted that once upon a time, long ago, he had come to Paris without any intention of staying and had never left. I was even more impressed when he handed me a literary journal that he publishes himself, self-designed, of course, with every typographic subtlety.**Later, we bumped into each other again in the small city of Chaumont in the French heartland. Chaumont has dedicated itself to the art of postermaking and once a year hosts an international poster festival. Martin was standing on a ladder surrounded by many helping hands: a large-scale poster-mounting operation, a sort of typographic manifesto, that spread over the entire city. The posters and banners were poetry for the eye. This type of operation is typical of Martin.**In his graphic design studio he devotes himself to contemporary theater, dance, and music. In a permanent dialogue with his clients he conceives new signs and images, always developing his preference for experimentation and new technologies, such as digital picture processing. At the same time, he does not shy away from using traditional techniques like photograms.**Another project to which Martin dedicates himself is the Agrafmobile, a sort of mobile visual theater that creates and organizes artistic processes and prefers forms of expression that work well in public spaces. Martin, often in collaboration with other artists, such as sound designers, composers, writers, dancers, and performers, provides the visual concepts. With this "visual theater" he hopes to win back public areas as "agoras"—creative spaces for the people who live around them.**Uwe Loesch**

1   Installation *Quoi de neuf Denis*, Chaumont, France / Agrafmobile / France / 2002 /
    One of several installations distributed throughout Chaumont showing a young
    citizen's face accompanied by a quote from philosopher Denis Diderot.
2   Installation *Takalefaire*, Chaumont, France / Agrafmobile / France / 2001 /
    Installation in front of the town hall for the centenary celebration of the law on
    associations, which established freedom of association in France.
3–6 Program spreads, poster, and bus design for 2002–2003 theatrical season (with
    Stéphanie Schuller) / La Comédie de Reims / France / 2002
7–8 Poster/program cover and spread for theater festival *La mousson d'été* (spread
    image Julien Cochin) / La maison européenne des écritures contemporaines /
    France / 2001

Malte Martin

Paris

le diable
en partage
Fabrice Melquiot
Emmanuel Demarcy-Mota
création "En diptyque avec l'inattendu"

Une machine
à broyer
les corps et
les âmes,
une famille
prise dans le
désert de
leur rêve. Un
théâtre du
vertige.

Emmanuel Demarcy-Mota

bouli miro
Fabrice Melquiot
Patrice Douchet
jeune public création

bouli miro : C'est un drôle de boulot de grandir.
Surtout quand les filles partent de pleurécssion et qu'on
a Sharon Stone à ses trousses. Un drôle de boulot d'être
encore petit. Surtout quand on aime sa cousine Pétula Clark
"à la vie de la mort des requins qui tuent". Oui, c'est un drôle
de boulot d'aimer. Surtout quand l'amour est à ce point dérai-
sonnable... Véritable terrain de jeux, Bouli Miro sont bon la
nostalgie - ce pays où les ours voyagent en train sur les
genoux des jeunes filles en fugue, où le son des boîtes à
musique couvre le "smack" d'un premier baiser et, si cruauté
il y a, c'est que le monde est cruel. Melquiot n'hésite pas à
parler de la guerre, des ruptures, de la dépression, du cha-
grin, mais il écrit sur du papier tendresse, avec un petit vent
d'humour qui sèche vite les larmes. Après Le Diable en partage et L'inattendu, Bouli Miro sera le troisième texte de
Fabrice Melquiot à découvrir, troisième voyage dans son
univers, cette fois encore différent puisque destiné d'abord
au jeune public.

Patrice Douchet

mardi 4 février à 19h,
mercredi 5 à 15h,
jeudi 6 à 14h30
vendredi 7 à 14h30,
et à 19h,
samedi 8 à 15h

Bouli Miro,
je l'ai rêvé comme ça,
idéalement :
un lien de théâtre des
petits aux grands, comme
un Fil d'Amour
à Durée Eternelle.

Fabrice Melquiot

ro,

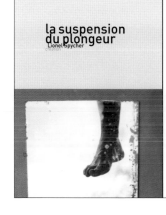

la suspension
du plongeur
Lionel Spycher
création

La Sus-
pension du
plongeur :
natation,
politique,
affaires et
cham-
pagne !

la Comédie
de Reims
vous invite à l'envol
de la saison 02/03

que le regard
et des idées
qu'ils

théâtre

personne n'a ra

un conflit famil

des blagu

chine à broyer la Coméd

Alexandre :
Je paierai l'autob
Jovan : On prend
le bus pour y alle

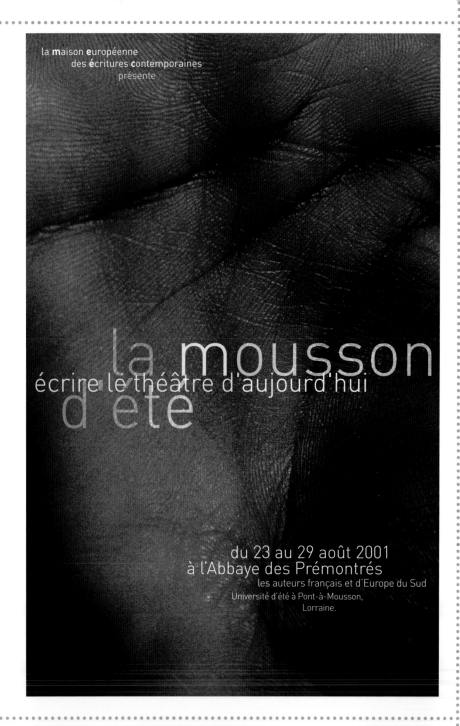

la maison européenne
des écritures contemporaines
présente

la mousson
d'été

écrire le théâtre d'aujourd'hui

du 23 au 29 août 2001
à l'Abbaye des Prémontrés
les auteurs français et d'Europe du Sud
Université d'été à Pont-à-Mousson,
Lorraine.

3
4
5
6

7
8

9-10 Installations and performances, *Instants Mobile*, Chaumont, France / Agrafmobile / France / 2001 / Multidisciplinary performances featuring a dancer and paper juggler.

11-12 Typographic installation, *Galerue*, Paris / Agrafmobile / France / 2002

13 Installation and performance, *Théâtre des Questions*, Chaumont, France / Agrafmobile / France / 2002 / Multidisciplinary performance conceived with the students of the Lycée d'Arts Appliqués.

14-15 Poster/program cover and spread for dance and theatre festival (photography Romeo Castelucci and Michel Chassat) / Festival d'Avignon / France / 2002

16-17 Cover and spread of review for art foundation Royaumont (with Bruno Bernard; photography Michel Chassat) / Royaumont / France / 2002

18-19 Program cover and spread for 1999-2000 season of contemporary-music orchestra (photograms with Costanza Matteucci) / 2E2M / France / 1999

Malte Martin

Kei Matsushita seeks the root of graphic design in Japan among the ukiyo-e works of the Edo era. Ukiyo-e use only outlines of plane figures, and it is in this unique world that Matsushita pursues his graphic activities and finds his ideological inspiration. He is a new breed of designer and rejects perspective-drawing techniques. He accomplishes three-dimensional images by using a two-dimensional technique.••In the history of graphic design, the most difficult tasks are faced during a chaotic economic slump. In this environment, Matsushita has been delivering all sorts of fresh messages. He cleverly chooses ordinary houses, rooms, and furniture, which attract the interest of ordinary citizens, and at the same time he exercises his wisdom of realizing his two-dimensional expression. No other designer is so committed to using living space as the basis of his works, and no other work gives us such joy in appreciating the skillful renderings of that space. Here is the lesson of the importance of having a theme in creative work. In the cheerfully colored spaces created in Matsushita's work, one can see a four-dimensional pleasure beyond the scope of three dimensions. Matsushita's creative activities may represent the future direction of visual communication.••Shigeo Fukuda••

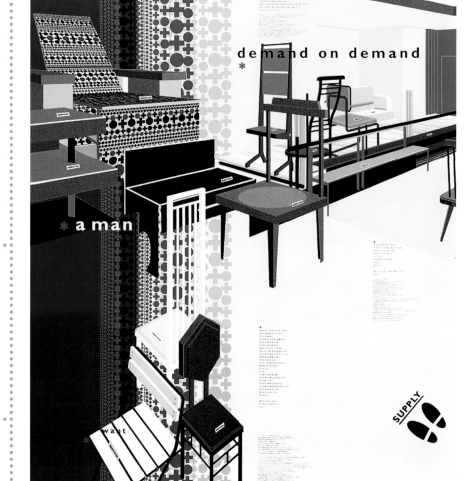

1–2 Promotional leaflets for paper-processing company PCM Takeo / PCM Takeo / Japan / 1997
3–4 Posters advertising the entertainment robot AIBO / Sony Creative Products Inc. / Japan / 2001
5–6 Posters for the *30x100* meeting and architecture exhibition / Japan Institute of Architects / Japan / 1997 / The *30x100* events focus around the work of 100 architects in their thirties.

Kei Matsushita

Tokyo

30代 建築家 100人展

30×100 architects展は30×100 meetingでの言葉を空間に置き換えたものです。
30代の視座から切り取られた風景を100個の定点で観測する場です。
その肯定点に意味を生じさせるのはわれわれにあると考えます。

1997年11月6日(木)→12日(水)

⑪

⑫

THE DORAEMON

Doraemon from all levels atrata

7-10 Poster series "Nipponjin" for the exhibition *Close-up of Japan*, Museu de Arte de São Paulo / Mitsui Public
Relations Committee / Japan / 1995
11 Calendar conceived for the Takeo Paper Show / Takeo Co. / Japan / 2001
12 Poster for *The Doraemon* exhibition, Suntory Museum, Osaka (© Fujiko-pro and Kei Matsushita) /
Executive Committee for *The Doraemon* Exhibition / Japan / 2002 / Doraemon is an animation character
that has been highly popular in Japan since the 1970s.
13-15 Posters for Kei Matsushita exhibition *DI+VISION* at the Ginza Matsuya Design Gallery, Tokyo / Japan
Design Committee / Japan / 2002

Kei Matsushita

Let Ω be a abstract space and ~ be an equivalence relation.
Then we can obtain a topological space in a natural way from Ω.
We call it "quotient space" of Ω, and describe it as Ω/~.
The points of Ω/~ are equivalence classes,
and the topology is the strongest one such
that the projection map is continuous.

SPEED
& TIME
+ACCELERATION

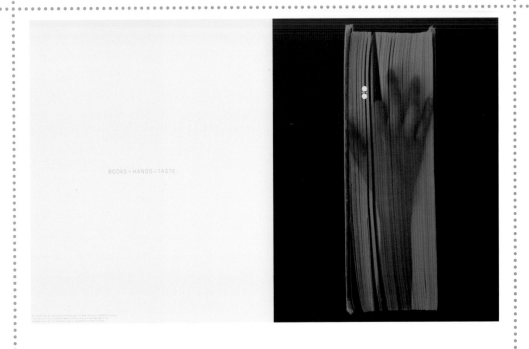

BOOKS + HANDS + TASTE

As I leafed through books and magazines over the years, my eye often stopped at the work of Chaz Maviyane-Davies from Zimbabwe. Each time I was struck by his powerful, intriguing images. Early in 2001, I asked Maviyane-Davies to contribute to an exhibition and book celebrating the hundredth anniversary of the death of Henri de Toulouse-Lautrec, and he happily agreed. ••Although I regrettably have yet to meet him, we have developed a bond that deepened when in 2002 he started his "Portal of Truth" campaign. For one month, we and others around the world received a new poster each day via E-mail. Each day a new indictment against Robert Mugabe's ZANU-PF party in Zimbabwe, and a call to Maviyane-Davies's fellow countrymen to go out and vote. Each morning, that day's poster was printed out at our studio and discussed with all collaborators. My admiration for Maviyane-Davies's one-man guerrilla campaign grew with each new poster; day in, day out, he succeeded in engaging us with the elections in his country. In the end, it didn't have the political effect he wished it would, but not for lack of effort! ••Maviyane-Davies combines a great knowledge of craft with a deep insight in the power of words and images. And he knows how to use the Internet to reach a lot of people. With these skills he is one of the rare voices speaking out on the deplorable political situation in Zimbabwe. He demonstrates that graphic design can be fatally dangerous—because to be openly critical in Zimbabwe can get you killed. Against this background, Maviyane-Davies wisely moved to the United States; he now teaches at Massachusetts College of Art in Boston. ••In January 2003, I learned that I played a role in Maviyane-Davies's life long before our first acquaintance. He sent me a photo of his studio in Harare as it was back in 1983, and on the wall was a copy of my Leonce en Lena poster, from 1979. I was moved by the sight of my poster on a twenty-year-old photo from a faraway country. Now I feel even more like we have known each other for a long time, and I want more than ever to meet Maviyane-Davies in the flesh. ••Anthon Beeke ••

1   Self-commissioned poster commenting on a speech by Sri Lankan Prime Minister
    Ratnasiri Wickremanayake / Zimbabwe / 2001
2   Poster for exhibition at the 12th World AIDS Conference in Switzerland / Aujourd'hui
    pour demain / Switzerland / 1998
3-6 Self commissioned "Rights" poster series (4 of 12; photography Ian Murphy) /
    Zimbabwe / 1996 / The posters are based on the United Nations Articles on Human
    Rights as seen from an African perspective.

Chaz Maviyane-Davies

Boston/Harare, Zimbabwe

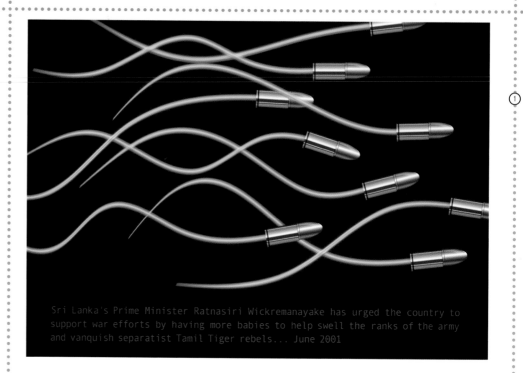

Sri Lanka's Prime Minister Ratnasiri Wickremanayake has urged the country to support war efforts by having more babies to help swell the ranks of the army and vanquish separatist Tamil Tiger rebels... June 2001

I AM NOT MY DISEASE

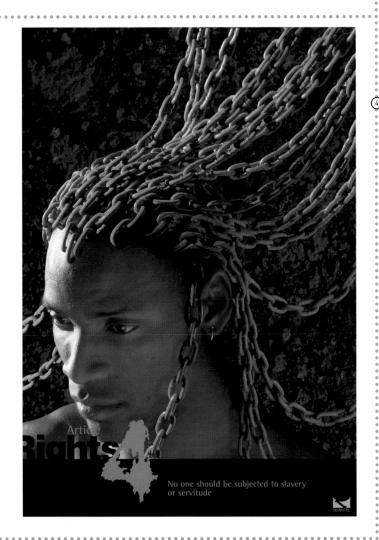

Article
Rights 4

No one should be subjected to slavery or servitude

QUANTEL

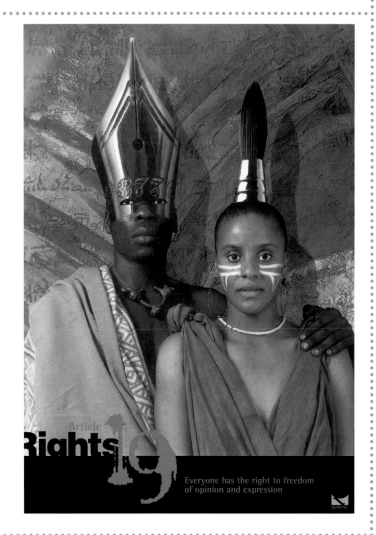

Article
Rights 19

Everyone has the right to freedom of opinion and expression

QUANTEL

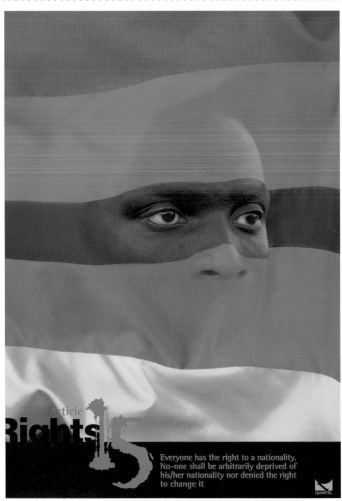

Article
Rights 15

Everyone has the right to a nationality. No-one shall be arbitrarily deprived of his/her nationality nor denied the right to change it

QUANTEL

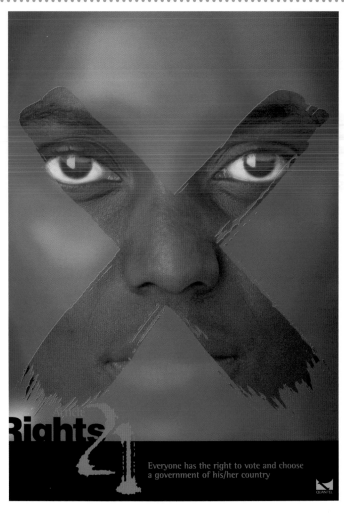

Article
Rights 21

Everyone has the right to vote and choose a government of his/her country

QUANTEL

the cure
for
impotency

Don't be intimidated
Use your vote
It's your secret weapon

"we have degrees
in violence..."
Robert Mugabe president of Zimbabwe

take courage: VOTE

...If you think you are too small to make a difference, try sleeping in a closed room with a mosquito...

African proverb

7-9 Self-commissioned posters from resistance campaigns "Graphic Commentary" and "Portal of Truth" /
      Zimbabwe / 2000 and 2002 / During the thirty days before the Zimbabwean parliamentary elections in 2000
      and presidential elections in 2002, Maviyane-Davies created graphic commentaries on a daily basis. Due to
      lack of funding and fear of persecution, these posters were originally diffused through the Internet.
10   Cover, *Jacaranda* magazine / Nippon Club / Zimbabwe / 1997 / *Jacaranda* is the publication of a Japanese
      social group in Zimbabwe.
11   Poster homage for Toulouse-Lautrec's centennial (photography Steve Hammon) / Nouveau Salon des Cent /
      France / 2001
12   Illustration for university journal *Rhodes Review* special edition created for race summit in South Africa /
      Rhodes Review / Zimbabawe / 2001

Chaz Maviyane-Davies

ジンバブエ日本人会会報
第9号
1997年11月発行

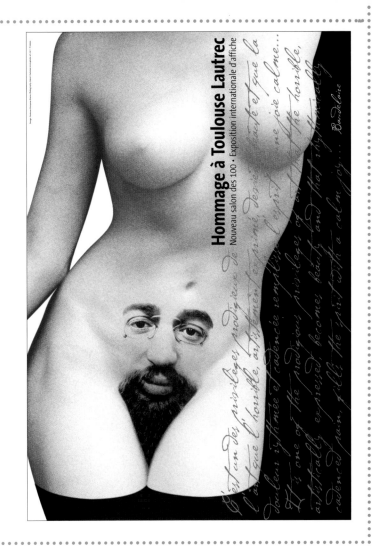

Hommage à Toulouse Lautrec

Nouveau salon des 100 · Exposition internationale d'affiche

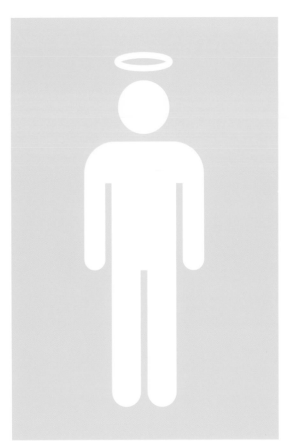

It is very rare that the highly-cultivated techniques used in artistic sketches can be applied to graphic design to successfully deliver messages. Instead, the established means of illustration, typography, and layout are considered the integral tools of the trade. The work of Ung Vai Meng makes for a wonderful exception. Although he clearly masters all of the more conventional graphic-design techniques, his beautiful, fresh posters live in a world quite far from the established concepts. The artistic strokes of his pen run through half-concrete and half-abstract shadow, and letters float up into two-dimensional space. I have seldom seen posters that can convey a feeling of such free joy.●●Moreover, it is impressive that these unique posters are done for such public organizations as the Macao Cultural Institute, the Macao Museum of Art, and the Cultural Foundation for Music.●●The stance Meng takes by confronting us with works of such hand-drawn beauty must be appreciated in a design field where the artificial technicians that are computers are commonly employed to guide creative endeavors. True originality remains an essential element within the culture of graphic design and Meng's works will surely leave an enduring mark in the global history of posters.●●Shigeo Fukuda●●

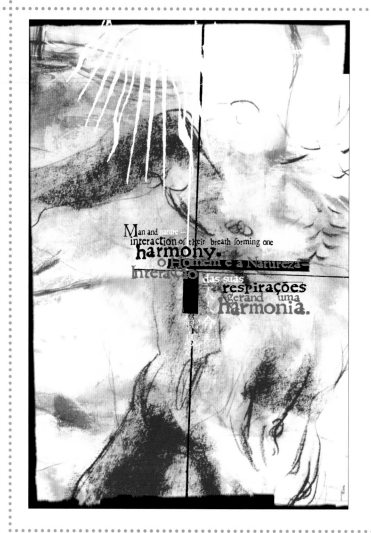

1   Self-commissioned Man and Nature poster / China / 1999
2   The Macanese-Blood/Language poster conceived for the 3rd International
     Macanese Congress / Leal Senado do Macau / China / 1999 / The poster was
     designed as a tribute to the unique culture in Macao and was given to the partici-
     pants of the congress.
3   Poster for XII Macao International Music Festival / Macao Cultural Institute /
     China / 1998
4   Poster for performances by the Macao Chinese Orchestra / Macao Cultural
     Institute / China / 1998
5   Cultural Epicenter poster promoting the Museum of Macao / Museum of Macao /
     China / 1998
6   Self-commissioned Macau poster / China / 2002

Ung Vai Meng

Macao, China

Ung Vai Meng

GREEN BEIJING · GREAT OLYMPICS

Every year, the small French town of Échirolles, a ski resort along the Swiss border, organizes a poster festival. In 2002 French graphic designer and guest curator Alain Le Quernec invited a number of designers from Iran for the exhibition *Le graphisme en Iran*. The work by Saed Meshki in the exhibition was, in my view, representative of graphic work now emanating from Iran: romantic, poetic, craft-inspired. In Meshki's work one sees, apart from a few obvious Western influences, a personality formed outside the reach of the Dutch, the Polish, the Swiss, and the American designers that have defined the trade of graphic design worldwide. Meshki's subjects are painterly. Some look like they were made a thousand years ago and just excavated; others seem to be sampled from abandoned scraps, left next to the copying machine; and sometimes they look like watercolors.°°Apart from being poetic, Meshki's work is also of its time. Everything is made on the computer from scanned elements. Despite the obvious limitations of clients and technology, this is vital work that demands to be seen far beyond the borders of Iran.°°Meshki is a kind man and an honest designer, just like his colleagues in the exhibition, who all demonstrated exceptional qualities and who, in France, were on a mission to another world. They were glad to be in contact with associates from quite different cultures and in return offered their gift of a graceful spirituality. I hope to be able to visit them in their own country soon.°°Anthon Beeke°°

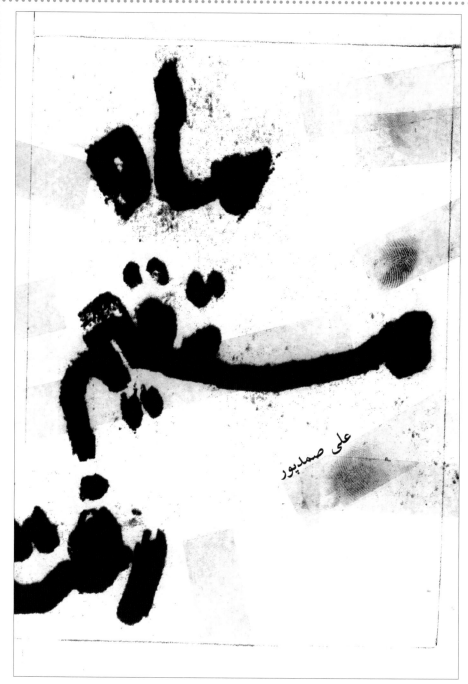

1   Book cover, *Lost Paradises*, poems by Jorge Luis Borges / Mahriz Publications / Iran / 2002
2   Book cover, *Mah mostaghim raft* (The Moon Went Directly), by Ali Samadpour / Mahriz Publications / Iran / 2002
3   Book cover, *Vahemehaye bi nam o neshan* (Imaginations Without Any Name and Trace), by G. H. Saedi / Mahriz Publications / Iran / 2001
4   Book cover, *Bi Eshgh, Ma Sang, Ma hich* (Without Love, We Are Stone, We Are Anything), by Bahman Rafei / Goftman Publications / Iran / 2001
5   Book cover, *Yek Manzoomeye Diryab dar Barf o Barab yaft shod* (A Rare Poem Was Found in the Rain and Snow), by A. R. Ahmadi / Mahriz Publications / Iran / 2002
6   Book cover, *Agar in Mahian rangi naboodand* (If These Fishes Weren't Colored), by Bahman Rafei / Goftman Publications / Iran / 2002

Saed Meshki

Tehran

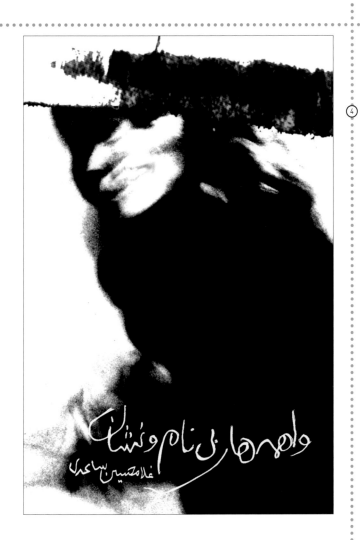

واژه‌های بی‌نام و نشان

غلامحسین بهادری

بی عشق، ما سنگ و ما هیچ

بهمن رافعی

احمدرضا احمدی
۱۳۸۱

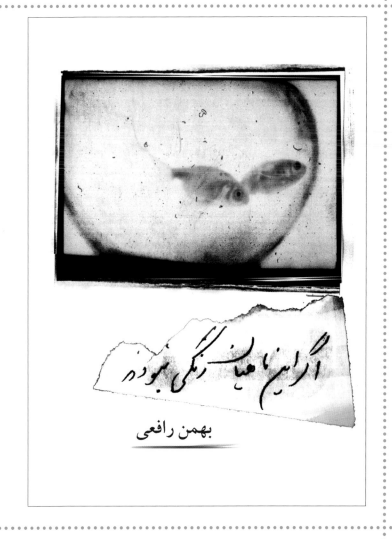

اگر این نام‌ها سنگ زندگی بود در

بهمن رافعی

7   Logo / Apple and Mirror Film Studio / Iran / 1999
8   Logo / Theatre Festival of Iranzamin / Iran / 2000
9   Logo / Roozgar Publishing / Iran / 1999
10 Logo / Avay-e-Doost Cultural Center / Iran / 2001
11 Logo / Sunlight magazine / Iran / 1999
12 Poster for movie LEYLI bahaneye nagozir / Farabi Cinema Foundation / Iran / 2001
13 Poster for 3rd International Theatre Festival of Iranzamin / Theatre Festival of Iranzamin / Iran / 2001
14 Poster for Abadan Film Festival / Iranian Ministry of Culture / Iran / 1999
15 Poster for 3rd Kish Documentary Film Festival / Kish Documentary Film Festival / Iran / 2002

Saed Meshki

No one is interrogating modern graphic design quite like Maureen Mooren and Daniel van der Velden. In fact they are torturing it. This is nothing for them to feel queasy about, since they see graphic design as comatose anyway. By trampling on it, poking fun at it, tearing it apart, and reassembling it in new and formidably grotesque mutations, Mooren and van der Velden shoot a million volts through the veins of its twitching body. This crazy experiment will, they hope, help catapult their visual communication beyond the generic, the hackneyed, and the merely representative toward what they call a "new and immediate personal communicative relevance."••Person-to-person messaging is the ideal they apply in their design. Mooren and van der Velden are greatly concerned with the "personal space in between design and its user" at a time when, with the help of the Internet, "the status of information, and therewith, the information object, has degraded to something close to trash." They confront the user of their design with a multitude of possibilities for interaction (see *Archis* magazine). The invitation to interact is skewed by the appropriated design convention that is employed as the information carrier. Sound confusing? It is. I'll try to simplify.••First of all, it is important to point out that Mooren and van der Velden, conceptually driven designer/writers that they are, have managed to liberate themselves from the inhibitions of good taste. It's like they believe that design conventions, together with their respective information objects (for example, signage, newspapers, posters, and books), are now so familiar as information carriers that they have become impotent, or at least they don't engage us in the vital way Mooren and van der Velden would like. In response they have chosen to mess with this accepted duality by altering the context within which design conventions and their concomitant information objects are usually found. For instance, a passport masquerades as a catalogue, an invented crossword puzzle carries the events program of an art gallery, a fax sheet operates as a poster, and an architecture magazine aspires to the form of a document file bursting with loose sheets of information. Transposing these formats into unfamiliar territory produces a clash that throws their associated conventions into relief. This makes the user question them and in so doing question the process of communication. The experience of the familiar in these unexpected realms is a form of poetry, one that Mooren and van der Velden call "fictional functionalism."••Nick Bell••

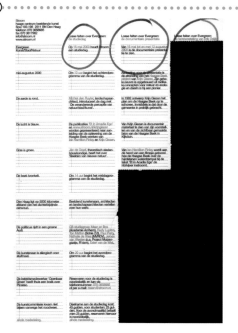

Mooren + van der Velden

1   Flyer for Rotterdam Design Prize 2001 events and exhibition at the Museum Boijmans Van Beuningen / Rotterdam Design Prize / Netherlands / 2001

2-3 Front and back of invitation for *Evergreen* conference and exhibition on public space and art in relation to nature / Evergreen / Netherlands / 2000 / The invitation is conceived as a perforated A4 card made up of smaller cards on which all information pertaining to the event is written.

4-6 Invitations for different events at the Maastricht-based art space Marres / Marres / Netherlands / 2002 / An A3 sheet of paper is folded down in different ways to create the various invitations. Functional information is provided in the crossword puzzle.

7-9 Informational publication accompanying Droog Design project for a small hotel presented at the Salone del Mobile, Milan / Droog Design / Italy

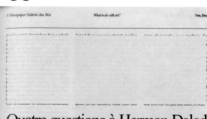

10–12 Cover and spreads, *Oscillations*, by Manon de Boer, Annemiek de Haan, Chloé Martin, Maureen Mooren, and Daniel van der Velden / La Lettre Volée / Belgium / The book collects conversations between two friends. The starting point for the design and editorial approach, however, is not the content of the conversations, but the complex interplay between the book's five collaborators.

13–17 Covers and and spread of newsletters for the Jan Mott Galerie, Brussels / Jan Mott Galerie / Belgium / 2001–present / The newsletter takes the form of a downsized newspaper.

18–20 Covers of architectural magazine *Archis*, issues 5, 2001, and 4, 5, 2002 / Archis / Netherlands / 2001–2002

21–23 Spreads from *Archis* magazine, issue 4 / Archis / Netherlands / 2002 / The publication is designed as a tear-out magazine focusing on the layering of interactive reading elements.

Mooren + van der Velden

Good graphic design polarizes, and so does good theater. When Barbara Mundel became the new director of the Luzerner Theater, Lucerne began to boil. Her new concept surprised both actors and the subscription audience and put pressure on the town administration. She is a person who demands complexity and exhibits it. She is direct and without frills, and in this spirit commissioned the agency Velvet, and its principal Peter Moser, to develop a new corporate identity and campaign for the theater. Peter Moser's concept team sat down and got going. ●●For the seasonal theme "homely, secretive, eerie," Velvet took the Lucerne telephone book, wrote down names of professions and associations from the area, visited them, took photos, and completed the posters. For the cycle "happy, the man of the future," Velvet took the actors, photographed them unclothed and without makeup, and produced another series of engaging posters. For the "money, power, nature" season, Velvet went onto the street and photographed people in the pose of Rodin's Thinker. ●●Peter Moser is bold and provocative. Peter Moser tapes over his own posters (see *Tatort* project). Or, Peter Moser makes a poster, and therein the model wears a knit hat, and at the speed of light this absurdity becomes a cult object in Lucerne, and swiftly the clever people from Velvet bring multiple reproductions of the hat into circulation. Or, Peter Moser satirizes advertising clichés for a communications museum exhibition and turns a female butcher into a Claudia Schiffer double; rarely was a poster in Switzerland so widely discussed in the media. ●●Peter Moser is somebody who balances the sharp directness of advertising with a tenderhearted and soulful graphic design and combines what sensibly should not be separated anyhow. He profits from his studio's internal distribution of work and the separation of profit and nonprofit segments. Thus large clients—by hiring Velvet—might well be supporting those who mock them, for indirectly they are supporting subculture, they are supporting theater. Velvet is a tremendously smart way to effect persistent influence. ●●Werner Jeker ●●

1-3 Cover and spreads, *Sedel 1981–2001* / Velvet-Edition / Switzerland / 2002 / Book commemorating the first twenty years of the Sedel music center in Lucerne, Switzerland. Set in a former prison, Sedel was a fertile ground for the punk scene during the eighties. The book has a heat-sensitive cover and is accompanied by a CD.
4 Poster for art event "Eros/" at the Plattform für Zeitgenössische Kunst (PZK), Lucerne / PZK / Switzerland / 2001
5 Poster for exhibition *Happy–Das Versprechen der Werbung* (Happy–The Promise of Advertising), Bern / Museum für Kommunikation / Switzerland / 2001
6 Poster for exhibition *Frankensteins Kinder–Film und Medizin* (Frankenstein's Children–Film and Medicine) / Museum für Gestaltung Zürich / Switzerland / 1997
7 Poster for exhibition *Ich & Du–Kommunikation und neue Medien* (Me & You–Communication and New Media) / Museum für Gestaltung Zürich / Switzerland / 1996

Peter Moser

Lucerne, Switzerland

④

⑤

Musée de la communication
Museum für Kommunikation

HAPPY

Das Versprechen der Werbung
La promesse de la publicité
07.09.01–28.07.02

MfK

www.mfk.ch

⑥

⑦

11

12

Peter Moser

8–10 Poster series for 2002 Viper Basel International Festival for Film Video and New Media / Viper / Switzerland / 2002

11–12 Posters and informational flyer for exhibition *Tatort* (Crime Scene) / Museum für Gestaltung Zürich / Switzerland / At first, only the simple poster showing a real crime-scene photo of the Zurich police was posted. Two days later, it was "cordoned off" with mock yellow police tape. The flyer is packaged in a plastic bag similar to the ones used for forensic evidence.

13–15 Poster series for performances at the Luzerner Theater under the 1999/2000 season theme, *heimatlich–heimlich–unheimlich* (homely–secretive–eerie) / Luzerner Theater / Switzerland / 1999

16–18 Poster series for performances at the Luzerner Theater under the 2001/2002 season theme, *geldmachtnatur* (money, power, nature) / Luzerner Theater / Switzerland / 2001

19–21 Poster series for performances at the Luzerner Theater under the 2002/2003 season theme, *transit* (transit) / Luzerner Theater / Switzerland / 2002

luzerner**theater**→
frost→ schauspiel nach
thomas bernhard→
ab 22.09.99

luzerner**theater**→
die tödliche blume→
oper von salvatore sciarrino→
ab 05.11.99

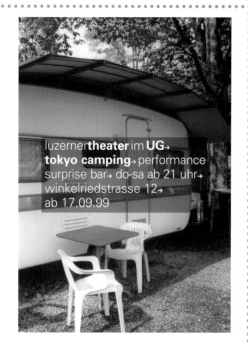

luzerner**theater** im **UG**→
tokyo camping→ performance
surprise bar→ do-sa ab 21 uhr→
winkelriedstrasse 12→
ab 17.09.99

luzerner**theater**→
die pest→
schauspiel nach albert
camus→ ab 08.03.02

luzerner**theater**→
stallerhof→
oper von gerd kühr→
ab 10.11.01

luzerner**theater**→
geld und geist→
schauspiel nach jeremias
gotthelf→ ab 17.11.01

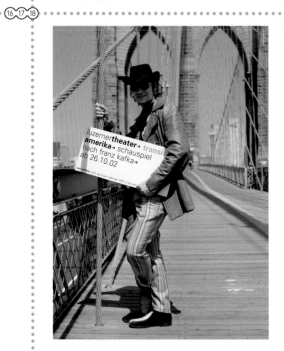

luzerner**theater**→ transi
amerika→ schauspiel
nach franz kafka→
ab 26.10.02

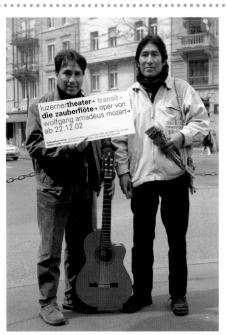

luzerner**theater** → **transit**→
die zauberflöte→ oper von
wolfgang amadeus mozart→
ab 22.12.02

luzerner**the**__→ **transit**→
carmen→
oper von georges bizet→
ab 12.10.02

While Melanie Mues was studying at the Academy of Art in Bremen, one of her teachers, Peter Rea, advised her to relocate to London in order to "loosen up." It seems to have been sound advice. She graduated in 1995, spent a year freelancing in Berlin, and moved to London in 1996. Following five years of valuable experience in some of London's leading design studios, she decided to go freelance again.••In recent years, she has worked on a variety of projects including book design, invitations, posters, promotional programs, and exhibitions. Her passion for the work and her resourcefulness have led her to some great projects. Recent projects for the V&A and, in particular, Tate Modern also allowed Melanie to develop her skills as an exhibition designer.••She recently created an identity for a Tate exhibition of work by the sculptor Eva Hesse that recalls the light, transparent nature of the show's subject. She also designed the exhibition space, a guide, and an interpretation area, where visitors experience the materials used by the artist. The Hesse interpretation area is a fine example of how resourceful Melanie is: The boxes and display cases were made from Plexiglas left over from previous shows at the Tate. Her cost-effective solution reflected Hesse's aesthetic. The graphics at the entrance to the show continued the theme, with the artist's name built out of transparent Plexiglas.••Melanie recently also entered the world of publishing design, with *Sanctuary: The Temples of Angkor*, a book she designed for Phaidon in 2002. *Sanctuary* features Steve McCurry's evocative photography of Buddhist temples in Angkor, Cambodia. Melanie's sensitive approach resulted in a landscape-format book that allows the quality of the photography to shine.••When necessary, her work can be playful and often bears the influence of British design. Take, for example, the Garden Party invitation she designed for Omni Colour—a lawn-green card that opens to reveal a pink gingham tablecloth. Simple, playful, and very English. It seems as if Peter Rea's advice was perfect: living and working in London may have loosened her up a little. It has allowed her to grow as a designer and amass a body of work that clearly indicates her talent and potential.
••Fernando Gutiérrez••

1–3 Café type installation, reading-room type detail, and reading room with run-around type and specially designed furniture, as part of *Eija-Liisa Ahtila* exhibition design / Tate Modern / United Kingdom / 2002
4 Poster, print advertisment, exhibition guide and invitation, and signage, as part of *Eva Hesse* exhibition design / Tate Modern / United Kingdom / 2003
5–6 Classic Design Award voting wall at Victoria & Albert Museum, London / Victoria & Albert Museum / United Kingdom / 2003 / The voting wall is designed to allow V&A visitors to vote for "The People's Award" given away by the magazine *Homes and Gardens*.

Melanie Mues

London

Melanie Mues

In Basel a distinct dialect of Swiss-German is spoken. Here syllables aren't swallowed like elsewhere.●●Basel is home to one of the largest art fairs in the world, Art Basel. Basel, geographically situated in a basin, is committed to the chemical industry and about as endangered by an earthquake as Kobe, Japan. Basel has never been politically volatile, like, for example, Zurich in the 1980s and 1990s. Because Basel lies in close proximity to the borders with Germany and France, Basel is aware of the other, lives with the foreign. Basel knows no boundaries.●●Müller + Hess are from Basel. Müller + Hess communicate in a precise, thoughtful, and traditional design language; they don't allow themselves any aesthetic shortcuts; they are independent and therefore better than other graphic artists. This was also noticed by Art Basel, which has used their talents for five years now. Others clients have followed suit and don't regret it. Müller + Hess, acknowledged with prizes, have also been honored with an exhibition at the Design Museum London. They are atop the Mount Olympus of graphic artists.●●Beat Müller and Wendelin Hess are fabulous tailors of thoughts, images, colors—and above all typomaniacs through and through. "During our education we experienced a dedication to thoroughness and the beauty of the detail that continues to set the standard for our work today. Yet we are always exploring, in search of something new, never backward-looking," comment Müller + Hess in an interview on the occasion of their exhibition at the Design Museum. For these two, graphic design is a world circled by the sun, a world that provides and destroys meaning at the same time. Therefore, the most exacting customers are their favorite ones, those who work with them on the content, the ones who reject artifice. Their interest in debate- and process-oriented products have led—logically—to redesigns for no less than three prominent Swiss monthly and weekly magazines. It's the world in reduction, in the very precise reproduction of the now and today. Müller + Hess are relentless in their aestheticism—but they are also smart and have soul.●●Werner Jeker●●

1-3   Cover, spread, and book-launch invitation, *Art Directors Club Schweiz* yearbook 2001 (with Ludovic Balland) / Art Directors Club Switzerland / Switzerland / 2001
4-7   Poster and invitations for exhibition *Richard Paul Lohse-Konstruktive Gebrauchsgrafik* / Museum für Gestaltung Zürich / Switzerland / 1999
8   Poster and invitations/programs for 1996-97 exhibitions at the gallery Kaskadenkondesator, Basel / Kaskadenkondensator / Switzerland / 1996-97 / A year's worth of programs was printed initially featuring just the events of the first month. Some were relesed for immediate use. The remainder was overprinted on a monthly basis in a different color, each time adding the following month's events and crossing out what had already taken place.

Müller + Hess

Basel, Switzerland

VORWORT JEAN ETIENNE AEBI, JUBILÄUMS-ANSPRACHE JOSEF ESTERMANN
AUSZEICHNUNGEN   PUBLIKUMSANZEIGEN 1-ER UND 2-ER SUJET
PUBLIKUMSANZEIGEN SERIEN   FACHANZEIGEN   AUSSENWERBUNG 1-ER UND 2-ER SUJET   AUSSENWERBUNG SERIEN   WERBEFILM
TV-TRAILER UND TV-DESIGN   RADIOSPOTS   DIREKTWERBUNG I
DIREKTWERBUNG II   VERKAUFSFÖRDERUNG   DESIGN
EDITORIAL UND BUCHGESTALTUNG   FOTOS, ILLUSTRATIONEN UND GRAPHICS
ELECTRONIC PUBLISHING   PUBLIC SERVICE 1-ER UND 2-ER SUJET
PUBLIC SERVICE SERIEN   EIGENBEDARF   GESAMTKAMPAGNEN
PRESSEPREIS   SONDERPREIS   GASTMITGLIED   JAHRESRÜCKBLICK
MITGLIEDER   JAHRBÜCHER   SPONSOREN   EINSENDER,
AUFTRAGGEBER UND AGENTUREN   MACHER   GÖNNER UND BUCHMACHER

Richard Paul Lohse
Konstruktive Gebrauchsgrafik

27. November 1999
bis 5. März 2000

Museum für Gestaltung Zürich
Ausstellungsstrasse 60

Richard Paul Lohse
Konstruktive Gebrauchsgrafik

27. November 1999
bis 5. März 2000

Museum für Gestaltung Zürich
Ausstellungsstrasse 60

④

⑤ ⑥ ⑦

[LISTE 98 – THE YOUNG ART FAIR] >[10.06.–14.06.] 13–21h: Kaskadenkondensator präsentiert sich gemeinsam mit HOTEL (Zürich) / KIOSK (Bern) / KONSUMBÄCKEREI (Solothurn) / KUNSTRAUM AARAU (Aarau) / Vernissage: 09.06., 16–22h

⑧

KASKADENKONDENSATOR | Warteck pp | Burgweg 7 | 4058 Basel | Tram Nr. 2 bis Wettsteinplatz |
>1 | VÉRONIQUE ZUSSAU | BLANC COMME NEIGE | 12.10.–03.11.96 | Vernissage: 11.10.96, 18 Uhr | Werkgespräch: 01.11.96, 19 Uhr | >2 | ARIANE EPARS | INS BLAUE HINEIN | 16.11.–08.12.96 | Vernissage: 15.11.96, 18 Uhr | >3 | POUR LE CLAVIER | JEAN-JACQUES DÜNKI (Klavier, Clavichord) in eigenen Werken | Matinée | So 24.11.96, 11 Uhr | >4 | SUSANNE FANKHAUSER | 14.12.96–05.01.97 | Vernissage: 13.12.96, 18 Uhr | Werkgespräch: Do 19.12.96, 19 Uhr, ab 16 Uhr geöffnet | geschlossen: 23.12.96–02.01.97 | >5 | HEINRICH LÜBER | DOWNLOAD | Performance | 14.01.97, 18–21 Uhr | >6 | ERNST THOMA | INSTANT SOUND NETWORK | Konzert | Do 16.01.97, 20.30 Uhr | >7 | PASCALE GRAU/SIMONE KURZ/ ANDREA SAEMANN | LEIBLIEB VARIATIONEN | 20.01.–02.02.97 | Vernissage: 19.01.97, 17 Uhr | Werkgespräch: 31.01.97, 19 Uhr | Finissage und Performance: 02.02.97, 17 Uhr | >8 | SIBYLLE HAUERT UND NUDA MATHIS | THE PLOT – DIE VERSCHWÖRUNG, HEY MARY JANE, WHERE ARE YOU GOING WITH THIS SCISSORS IN YOUR HAND | 22.02.–16.03.97, 10–21 Uhr | Vernissage: 21.02.97, 18 Uhr | Werkgespräch: 14.03.97, 19 Uhr | >9 | CHRISTOPH BÜCHEL | ZU VERMIETEN | 05.04.–20.04.97, Do–So 16–21 Uhr | Vernissage: 04.04.97, 18 Uhr | >10 | CHIARENZA & HAUSER & CROPTIER | HEUTE IST ES ÜBERALL SCHÖN | 02.05.–25.05.97 | Vernissage und CD-Taufe: 02.05.97, 19 Uhr | Kunst und Öffentlichkeit. Thematisches Werkgespräch mit Philip Ursprung (Zürich) und Gästen: 23.05.97, 19 Uhr |

Der Kaskadenkondensator wird unterstützt von: Migros Kulturprozent | Schweizerische National-Versicherungs-Gesellschaft, Basel | Stiftung für kulturelle, soziale und humanitäre Experimente, Binningen |
Öffnungszeiten: Fr–So | 16–19 Uhr | (wenn nicht anders vermerkt) | oder nach Vereinbarung | T 061 693 26 48 | >3 | T 061 692 94 51 | >4 | T 061 322 19 26 | >5/6/7 | T 061 381 39 12 | >8 | T 061 691 86 24 | >9 | T 061 261 89 72 | >10 | T 061 261 89 72 |

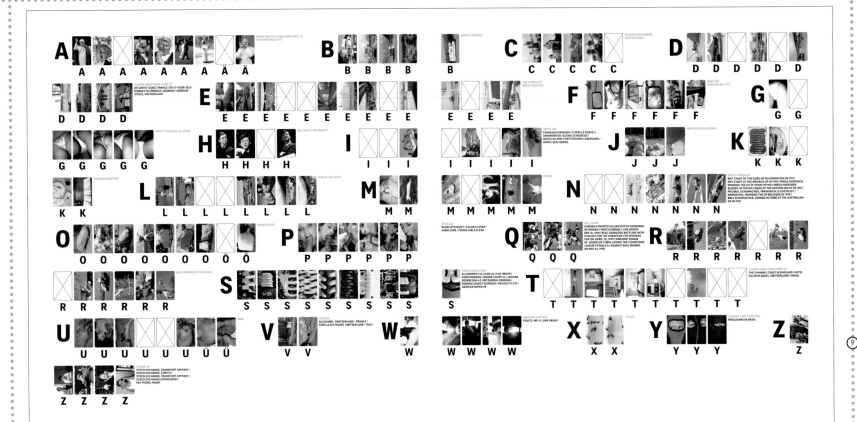

9 Spread from "Dismantling the Basel Principle," *Eye–The International Review of Graphic Design*, no. 32 /
Eye–The International Review of Graphic Design / United Kingdom / 1999
10 Issues of *Das Magazin*, redesigned and art directed by Müller + Hess / Tamedia AG, Das Magazin /
Switzerland / 1999–2002
11–13 Cover and spreads, *Grenzwert* magazine, no. 3 / Bar Grenzwert and Müller + Hess / Switzerland / 1998 /
The magazine is wrapped in a protective plastic bag, which, together with the magazine, has a hand hole
punched through it. The motto of the issue was "sex, crime, and violence."
14–16 Poster and program spreads for music festival Neue Musik Rümlingen / Neue Musik Rümlingen /
Switzerland / 1997

Müller + Hess

The highly sophisticated design world of Japan nurtures many new design talents. Standing out in such a competitive environment, however, requires talent and determination. Something special. Hideki Nakajima has those qualities. In his view, new technology demands new means of expression and new ways of communicating—not just in graphic design, but in all fields of creative endeavor. He assigns himself the most difficult task of developing something that is truly unique. He searches for an orginal form, something that has not been seen before, that will endure and influence our visual vocabulary over the next decade. Clearly Nakajima seeks to lead and influence the designers of the world. He began his career at Misami Shimizu Design Office before establishing his own practice, Nakajima Design, in 1995. Since then his work has received national and international acclaim resulting in exhibitions and the publication of his work in numerous books and magazines. In 1999 he became involved in the Code group with Ryuichi Sakamoto, Shigeo Goto (editor), and Norika Sora (creative director). The Code group has been actively campaigning for the production of goods that put little or no strain on the earth's resources, foods without chemical additives, and experimental art books. In 2002 the group's first large-scale exhibition *Code: New Village* was held in Tokyo, Osaka, and Kyoto.●● In 2000, Nakajima became a member of Alliance Graphique Internationale (AGI). He strongly believes that design has many brand-new possibilities. He is a pioneer of the future we will watch with anticipation.●●Ken Cato●●

①

1-8 Cover and spreads, "Re-cycling," *IDEA* magazine no. 295 / IDEA / Japan / 2002 / The images are abstractions and mutations of previously created work.

②

Hideki Nakajima

Tokyo

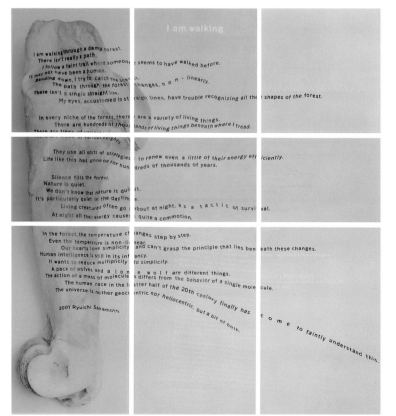

9   Poster from "S/N" series for *Code: New Village* exhibition held in Tokyo, Osaka, and Kyoto (with Ryuichi Sakamoto) / Code / Japan / 2002 / Code is a project established by Ryuichi Sakamoto, Shigeo Goto, Norika Sora, and Hideki Nakajima to organize and distribute a wide range of art forms in cooperation with people from different artistic fields.

10 I am Walking poster for exhibition organized by paper manufacturer Takeo (with Ryuichi Sakamoto) / Takeo Co. / Japan / 2001 / The poster is made up of nine different types of paper.

11-14 Posters from "S/N" series for *Code: New Village* exhibition held in Tokyo, Osaka, and Kyoto (with Ryuichi Sakamoto) / Code / Japan / 2002

Hideki Nakajima

Working, doing, and producing were fundamental tenets of Dylan Nelson's childhood in a small mill town. Son of a carpenter, Nelson grew up among rugged craftsmanship, wood, hammers, nails, and the sound of Metallica—the tools and environment of his father's trade that deeply influence his own life and work today. ••The Cranbrook Academy of Art is the other primary influence in his art and design, supplying him with new "tools." Mind-opening conceptual instruments that enabled him to "let loose" and create work untouched by complex theoretical bindings. Days and nights of thinking, making, and breathing work straight from the heart became natural and liberating. His attention expanded from two-dimensional design to writing, from furniture design to installation art. Nelson explores any realm where mind and body can be inspired and energized by "just doing." Life and work become one. ••In applying what he absorbed from Cranbrook, today his most original and personal creations come from the conscious materialization of his intimate contrasts from the past. Bright Disney-like wonderlands of wilderness and harmless fairy-tale animals that were distant during his restricted childhood are provocatively juxtaposed with carpentry tools, chains, studs, and stuffed deer heads. Professional practice becomes dream reality and introspective escape. ••But it's not only "what you see is what you get." Environmental concerns are also explicit. Many of his pieces carry a distinct pro-wildlife message. His cynical usage of hunting references raises questions and sparks debate. Through his idiosyncratic creations Nelson does not search for a prescribed reaction from his audience, but he wants people to understand and investigate. Behind both his commercial and research work the philosophy is, "Do it right for yourself, and you'll do it right for the world." ••Omar Vulpinari ••

Dylan Nelson

Portland, Oregon

⑤

⑥
⑦
⑧
⑨

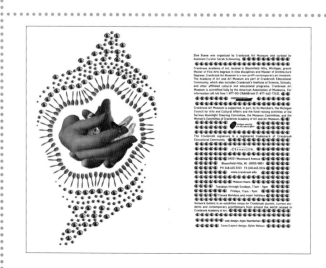

5   Poster for *Zine Scene* exhibition at the Cranbrook Art Museum's Network Gallery / Cranbrook Art Museum /
      USA / 2002
6–9 Back and front cover and spreads, *Zine Scene* exhibition guide / USA / 2002
10–12 Self-commissioned pieces Untitled and Basketball Stylos and installation / USA / 2002

Dylan Nelson

When I look at certain images, I hear sounds. The messages of Yves Netzhammer's images are, however, mute. Looking at them, I feel alienated, as if a capsule were closing in on me and blocking out the outside world. In this sensory-deprivation tank, I am absorbed in pure contemplation. Results, realizations occur only through the reflection with my own world of experience. I am inside a dream. In this metaphysical dimension, the surprising connection of elements reveals simple processes or provides sudden insight into extremely complex occurences. Netzhammer is able to put into images that which causes us to stumble even when we try to put it in words. ••He asks these somnambulistic questions. He asks for meaning with such directness that it often seems embarrassingly naked. As soon as the observer gets somewhat used to this nakedness, however, he realizes with consternation that he has already been taken possession of. With the inquiries Netzhammer undertakes about the functioning of things and with his complete, plausible, linear answers to them, he stirs up depths quietly rotting away in our society and ourselves. Netzhammer looks into his own backpack and therefore knows exactly what we others carry around with us. He looks, feels, smells, and thinks with accuracy, scientifically, clinically. He is someone who walks along the border, a storyteller who lovingly yet emphatically gives back to my heart things put away carelessly. He is someone who makes me think, and I like that. ••Werner Jeker••

1   Illustrations from *Was sich erzählen lässt wird verbessert werden* (What Can Be Told Will Be Improved), by Yves Netzhammer / Verlag Ricco Bilger / Switzerland / 1997
2   Poster for 2001 international Frankfurt Book Fair / Frankfurt Book Fair / Germany / 2001
3–5 Poster and front and back of invitation for *Curators' Digest* exhibition at the Helmhaus, Zurich / Helmhaus Zürich / Switzerland / 1999
6   Poster for exhibition *Der Abgelenkte Blick–Malerei* (The Distracted View–Painting) at the Helmhaus Zürich / Helmhaus Zürich / Switzerland / 2000
7–9 Poster and front and back of invitation for Yves Netzhammer exhibition *Wenn man etwas gegen seine Eigenschaften benützt, muss man dafür einen anderen Namen finden* (If One Uses Something Against Its Characteristics, It Must Be Renamed) at the Museum zu Allerheiligen, Schaffhausen / Museum zu Allerheiligen / Switzerland / 1999

Yves Netzhammer

Zurich

Yves Netzhammer

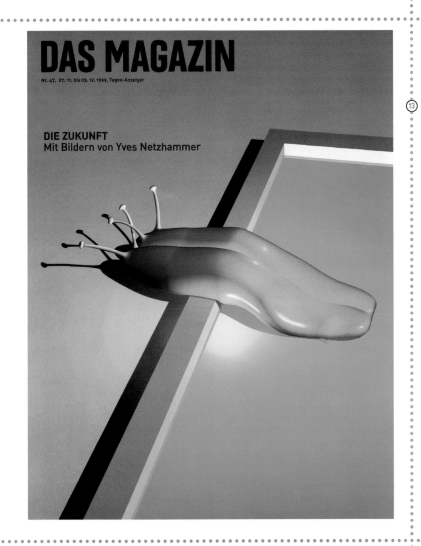

DAS MAGAZIN

Nr. 47, 27. 11. bis 03. 12. 1999, Tages-Anzeiger

DIE ZUKUNFT
Mit Bildern von Yves Netzhammer

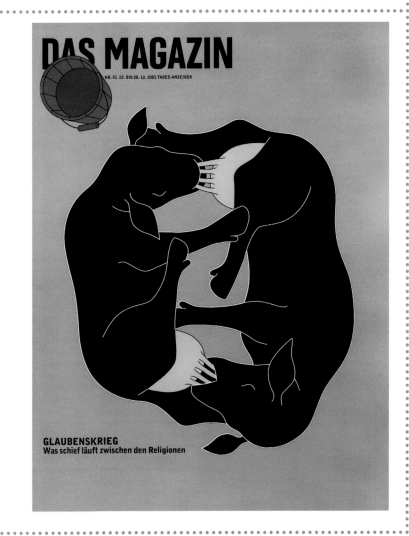

DAS MAGAZIN

NR. 51 22. BIS 28. 12. 2001 TAGES-ANZEIGER

GLAUBENSKRIEG
Was schief läuft zwischen den Religionen

Ideas, ideas, ideas! For me Christoph Niemann was an easy selection. His talent and training guarantee the quality of his output. Heinz Edelmann, Paul Davis, and Paula Scher have all been his mentors. His illustrative approach to design is genuinely idea-driven. "I have always been a designer who has to solve problems with illustration," he says. He doesn't hold back. Be it political, satirical, humorous, it's always pointed. What's more, he is versatile enough to adopt an illustrative language best suited to make the idea even more potent. He has been described as a dedicated storyteller. The wonderful part of it is that he does it in his own way. His keen intelligence and respect for the traditions that have come before him allow him to constantly reinvigorate styles that have been forgotten in the computer-driven illustrative environment.••Born and educated in Stuttgart, Germany, he now lives and works in New York. He teaches a class in conceptual graphic design at the School of Visual Arts in New York, and in collaboration with Nicholas Blechman he publishes a series of limited-edition books entitled *100%*. It is a highly suitable and appropriate title given Niemann's tendency to squeeze every last drop out of an idea and pursue it relentlessly until he has found the ultimate graphic expression to make it work.••Ken Cato••

1–4 Chapter-opening illustrations, *F-Stop* / Font Shop International / Germany / 2003 / *F-Stop is* a stock-image catalogue designed by Stefan Sagmeister.
5   Illustration, *The New York Times Magazine*, 8 April 2001 / The New York Times / USA / 2001
6   Cover illustration, *The New York Times Book Review*, 25 April 1999 / The New York Times / USA / 1999
7   Poster for exhibition held on occasion of the 2001 Alliance Graphique Internationale (AGI) congress in Paris / AGI / France / 2001
8   Opening illustration for article on innovation, *Fortune Small Business* magazine, April 2001 / Fortune / USA / 2000
9   Cover illustration, *The New York Times Book Review*, 10 September 2000 / The New York Times / USA / 2000
10   Illustration for campaign advertising the Parsons School of Design's continuing-education program / Parsons School of Design / USA / 1999

Christoph Niemann

New York

11–12 Cover Illustrations, *The New Yorker* magazine, "Style Japan" issue, 18 March 2002 and "Independence Day" issue, 9 July 2001 / The New Yorker / USA / 2001–2002

13 Illustration for "Worst Websites Ever," *Rethinking Design* journal, "Subculture" issue / Mohawk Paper / USA / 2000

14 Cover Illustrations, *The New Yorker* magazine, "Down and Out" issue, 7 October 2002 / The New Yorker / USA / 2002

15 Wine label created on occasion of an Alliance Graphique Internationale (AGI) conference in San Francisco / AGI / France / 2002

16 Cover illustration, *The Nation*, "Bush Goes Nuclear" issue, 1 April 2002 / The Nation / USA / 2002

17–18 Illustrations for *American Illustration 20* annual / Amilus Inc. / USA / 2001

Christoph Niemann

Nagi Noda is arguably the brightest new design star on the Tokyo design scene. In her late twenties, she is sparkling and funny and quirky, just like her work.••Noda is able to mix small cultural projects with huge advertising campaigns. All the more surprising is that the large projects remain as quirky as the small stuff—a rarity in a world where the usual rule is, "The more money involved the blander the outcome."••Her "I'm a Kaugirl" campaign for the Tokyo department store Laforet is built not only on a sweet wordplay (the Japanese word *Kau* means "shopping"), but also features a cowgirl twirling her three-meter braided lock of hair like a lasso. The whole scene is surrounded by beautifully braided custom typography.••Her stylistic scope is remarkable: From the expert art direction of a Nike swimwear campaign (when was the last time you saw sports visualized in a truly original way while still showing hero shots of the product?) to her polka-dotted-Christmas-tree-Mexican-wrestler masks or the most elegant, heartfelt, hand-drawn typography on the Spring 2001 campaign for Laforet, she seems to get even the most outrageous formal compositions just right. How can you not like the typography entirely made out of sperm she created for the Sperm Palace project?••Noda mixes her own idiosyncratic illustration with an idiosyncratic logo design into a remarkable program for Colorbar. And her Shungiku Uchida books featuring abundances of braided bookmarks leave me with only one wish: that I had thought of them myself.••Stefan Sagmeister••

1   Book jacket variations, *It's Good Because It's Love*, by Shungiku Uchida / Koudansha / Japan / 2001
2-3   Posters for Tony Tanaka Holistic Beauty hair salon / Tony Tanaka Holistic Beauty / Japan / 2000
4   Poster for Japanese department store Laforet's spring season 2001 / Laforet Harajuku / Japan / 2001
5-6   Poster and packaging design for Colorbar beauty products / Colorbar / Japan / 2000

Nagi Noda

Tokyo

NEW OPEN!

The woman
with physical strength.

The way a beautiful woman
is seen seems to be changing.
Introducing, Nike swimwear.

The woman
with healthy appetite.

The way a beautiful woman
is seen seems to be changing.
Introducing, Nike swimwear.

The woman with vitality.

The way a beautiful woman
is seen seems to be changing.
Introducing, Nike swimwear.

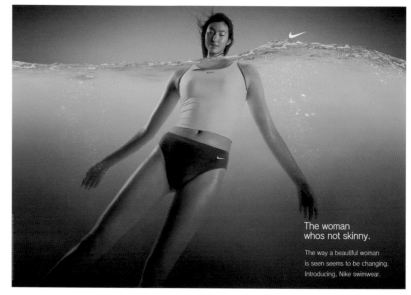

The woman
whos not skinny.

The way a beautiful woman
is seen seems to be changing.
Introducing, Nike swimwear.

7   Poster series for Nike Japan's women's swimwear campaign / Nike / Japan / 2001
8   Poster for Japanese fashion brand Theatre PRODUCTS' opening fashion show / Theatre PRODUCTS /
     Japan / 2002
9–10 Poster series "I'm a Kaugirl" for Japanese department store Laforet's Autumn season 2001 / Laforet
     Harajuku / Japan / 2001
11   Poster for Japanese fashion department store Laforet's Christmas season 2001 / Laforet Harajuku /
     Japan / 2001

Nagi Noda

I'm 買うガール
LAFORET
AUTUMN

I'm 買うガール
LAFORET
AUTUMN

MERRY X'mask. LAFORET.

The work of the Swiss designers Dimitri Bruni and Manuel Krebs is definitely not "in the norm" as their studio name might make one think. Coming from a sound Swiss education with maximum respect for the days of Joseph Müller-Brockmann, they claim that the importance of structure, hierarchy, and readability is unquestionable but also that graphic design of the present cannot replicate that of the past. ●●Their intentions are diverse and go from crystal-goblet information design to irritating, confusing, subversive, and mischievous speculation, depending on the nature of the effort. But whether it's public service work for an airport signage program or a self-initiated research project, their concern never focuses on formal matters like the mere choice of a typeface or specific image treatment. It will rather be toward a distinctive conceptual approach where visual clarity and attention to detail are fundamental ingredients. Never unifying, constantly diversifying. ●●Norm started with *Introduction*, a specific research project but mainly a quest for freedom from the mainstream design they had done at the firms they worked for at the beginning of their careers. They craved a conceptual domain of their own where they could escape the conventional art-director-over-designer concept and finally set their own "norms." Being able to define the rules as they feel necessary gives them the liberty and power to play and (why not?) break the rules as they please. ●●The recent prize-winning book *The Things* was written, designed, and published by Norm. It defines an eye-punching, mind-blowing visual analysis not only for the Latin alphabet but also for universal, everyday, three-dimensional objects. This project demonstrates how a system can be pushed very far and make solution finding automatic, doubtless, and surprising at the same time. It can become an operational mode capable of ironing out the decision-making process and possible errors. "The more restrictions we have," Norm tells us, "the happier we are." ●●Omar Vulpinari ●●

1–5 Pages from *The Things*, by Norm / Norm Publishers / Switzerland / 2002 / Pages taken from the "*Kritik*" part of the book, which analyzes and reviews the letters of the Latin alphabet.

Norm

Zurich

LITHFE   ZYNKAM
XVW   UDPBGJ   R
OCS   Q

ZYNKAM   R
XVW
LITHFE
UDPBGJ   OCS

			Key
	1		Key
	2		Keyboard
	3		Standard
	4		Inner Structure
	5		Outer Structure
	6		Description Signs *
	7		Construction Text *
	8		Construction *
	9		GRID P9/C16
	10		GRID P9/C16 norm-choice
	11		Pixel *
	12		Helvetica Thin
	13		Helvetica Lasso
	14		Conflict *
	15		Developpement
	16		Ranking
	17		Scrabble *
	18		Handwriting *
	U		Upper Cases
	L		Lower Cases

* Figure in Ranking

A A B b C c

		1	Key		5	Outer Structure
		2	Keyboard		12	Helvetica Thin
		3	Standard		13	Helvetica Lasso
		4	Inner Structure		M	Max Miedinger

N N N

N 12 n 04

Two vertical lines, leading from the baseline to the upper height, connected by a diagonal line leading from the upper end of the vertical line to the left, to the lower end of the vertical line to the right.

n n

N

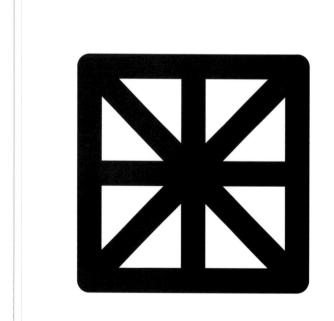

8

C16-00001

6   Poster for contemporary-art gallery Planet 22, Geneva / Planet 22 / Switzerland / 2002 / The poster can be
    divided up to create various smaller posters, flyers, and business cards.
7–8 Pages from *The Things*, by Norm / Norm Publishers / 2002 / After the analysis of the Latin alphabet, this part
    of the book presents collections of newly generated signs with high "letter" potential. The last sign has
    sixteen connections.
9   Poster for *Transmission02: Utopia* exhibition and publication / :phunk / Singapore / 2002

Norm

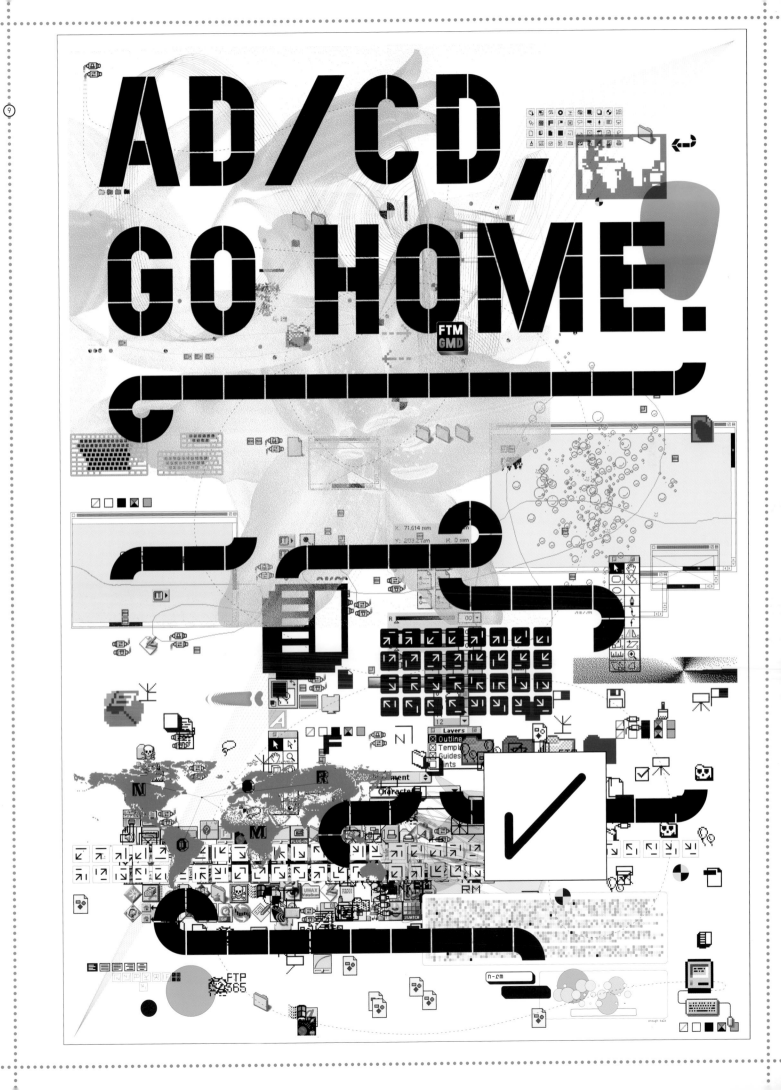

When at the end of the twentieth century Philip Teufel stumbled upon my former students Petra Knyrim and Stefan Nowak at the University of Applied Arts in Düsseldorf, I was already long gone and teaching at the university in Wupperthal. Teufel was the successor chosen to fill my empty chair in Düsseldorf. Within the design scene, this new Bermuda Triangle of communication—named Nowakteufelknyrim—soon became known for its exceptionally original concepts and creations for museums and exhibitions. I particularly remember the publicity material for an open house by Düsseldorf artists, as it stood out from the overload of bad information about cultural institutions. It was a blue folder full of white dots. Later I discovered the corresponding poster. Each dot represented an artist on the map of Düsseldorf, finely calculated and placed with cartographic and typographic precision.°°By now there is hardly a museum along the banks of the Rhine for which Nowakteufelknyrim has not designed a comprehensive exhibition and developed the communication materials. They also conceive special orientation systems. For the city of Dresden they created cultural maps and guides that use the pavement surface as informational space—a project that was immediately honored with the Josef Binder Award. And to finally come into some money without further detours, they designed a money museum and information center for the Deutsche Bundesbank.°°Equally notable and artful is their publication dedicated to their field of work: Entitled *Einszueines. Positionen zum Austellen* (One to One. Positions on Exhibiting), it is hard to make better publicity for oneself.°°The work that is shown here represents only a fraction of Nowakteufelknyrim's complex output. Their systematic approach, their deep understanding of the topic at hand and its graphic and typographic interpretation, cannot be displayed so succinctly. Therefore, there is only one solution: you must go to the next exhibition that Nowakteufelknyrim superbly conceives and designs—or at least order the catalogue! °°Uwe Loesch°°

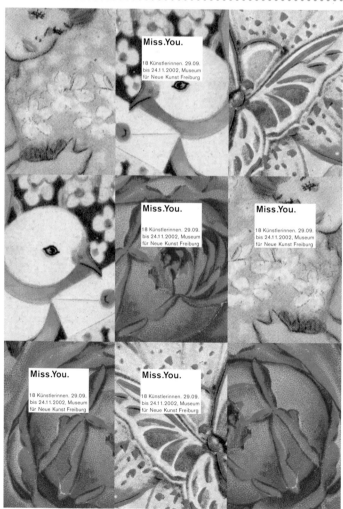

1   Poster for *Kunstpunkte* (Art Points) open-house event in which four hundred artists opened the doors of their ateliers to the public / Kulturamt Düsseldorf / Germany / 2000
2   Adhesive Flyers for *Miss.You.* exhibition featuring the works of eighteen female artists / Museum für Neue Kunst Freiburg / Germany / 2002
3–5 Spread from exhibition guide, train design (unrealized), and ground orientation guides for exhibition *Continental Shift* / Ludwig Forum Aachen, Bonnefantenmuseum Maastricht, Musée d'Art Moderne Liege, Stadsgalerij Heerlen / Germany, Netherlands, Belgium / 2000 / The exhibition focused on artists who came from other continents to work and live in Europe. It was shown at four museums in three different countries.
6–8 Posters for exhibition *Continental Shift* / 2000

Nowakteufelknyrim

Düsseldorf

AACHEN

AKASHI

CONTINENTAL SHIFT / 21 05–10 09 2000 /
Ludwig Forum AACHEN / Eine Reise zwischen
den Kulturen / JAPAN / KOREA /
An Exhibition of Contemporary Art

Ludwig Forum AACHEN / Jülicher Straße 97–109 / D 52070 Aachen / Information +49 (0) 241 1807 0 / www.continentalshift.org
/ Design: grafikbüro / DANKE ▶▶

CONTINENTAL
SHIFT 21 05 –
10 09 2000

A voyage between cultures / AACHEN
/ MAASTRICHT / HEERLEN / LIÈGE /
An Exhibition of Contemporary Art

Eine Reise zwischen den Kulturen / Een reis tussen culturen / Un voyage entre les cultures / Ludwig Forum AACHEN
Bonnefantenmuseum MAASTRICHT / Stadsgalerij HEERLEN / Musée d'Art moderne LIÈGE / Information +49 (0) 241 1807 0
/ www.continentalshift.org / Design: grafikbüro / DANKE ▶▶

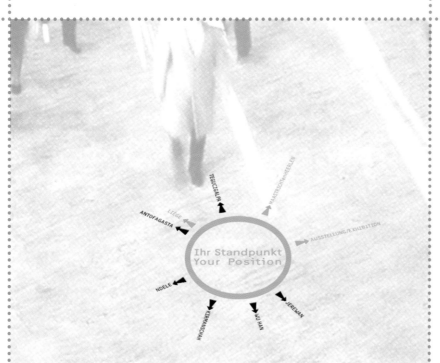

Ihr Standpunkt
Your Position

AACHEN

AZUL

CONTINENTAL SHIFT / 21 05–10 09 2000 /
Ludwig Forum AACHEN / Eine Reise
zwischen den Kulturen / LATEINAMERIKA /
An Exhibition of Contemporary Art

Ludwig Forum AACHEN / Jülicher Straße 97–109 / D 52070 Aachen / Information +49 (0) 241 1807 0 / www.continentalshift.org
/ Design: grafikbüro / DANKE ▶▶

5

9   Pedestrian orientation system "Pylon" for the historic city-center of Dresden, Germany (unrealized) /
      Municipality of Dresden / Germany / 2001 / Three pylons are conceived to convey different specificity levels
      of orientational information. The pylons themselves also work on various levels, showing maps on the
      ground, written information in the middle, and the general location at the top.

10   Posters for different phases of *Totale 2000* exhibition / Museum für Neue Kunst Freiburg / Germany / 2000 /
      The exhibition showcased the museum's entire collection. Due to space limitations it was impossible to
      show all the works at once. Therefore, Nowakteufelknyrim conceived a system of hanging the artworks on
      top of each other. There were three layers, each representing a different period: 1900–40s, 1950s–1970s,
      and 1980s–1990s. One by one, at specific opening events, the layers were "peeled off."

Nowakteufelknyrim

TOTALE 01 02
03 5 Feb bis 7
Mai 00 27
Mai bis 10 Sep
00 30 Sep bis
31 Dez 00
Das Jahrhundert im Blick
der Sammlung 00er 10er 20er
30er 40er Jahre 50er 60er
70er Jahre 80er 90er Jahre
Museum für Neue Kunst
Freiburg Marienstrasse 10a
www.mnk-freiburg.de/TOTALE

TOTALE 01 02
03
Mai 27
Mai bis 10 Sep
30 Sep bis
31 Dez 00
Das Jahrhundert im Blick
der Sammlung
80er 90er Jahre
Museum für Neue Kunst
Freiburg Marienstrasse 10a
www.mnk-freiburg.de/TOTALE
Städtische Museen Freiburg. Museum für Neue Kunst. Marienstrasse 10a, 79098 Freiburg. Tel 0761 2012581. Di bis So 10 bis 17 Uhr geöffnet. Einzelbesucher 8 DM. ermäßigt 5 DM. Dauerkarte 10 DM. Familienkarte 15 DM. Freier Eintritt für Mitglieder des Fördervereins und Besitzer des Oberrheinischen Museumspasses. Vielen Dank an Rhodia Acetow GmbH Freiburg. Partner des Museums für Neue Kunst. ©grafikbüro 2000

TOTALE 02
27
Mai bis 10 Sep
00
Das Jahrhundert im Blick
der Sammlung
50er 60er
70er Jahre
Museum für Neue Kunst
Freiburg Marienstrasse 10a
www.mnk-freiburg.de/TOTALE
Städtische Museen Freiburg. Museum für Neue Kunst. Marienstrasse 10a, 79098 Freiburg. Tel 0761 2012581. Di bis So 10 bis 17 Uhr geöffnet. Einzelbesucher 8 DM. ermäßigt 5 DM. Dauerkarte 10 DM. Familienkarte 15 DM. Freier Eintritt für Mitglieder des Fördervereins und Besitzer des Oberrheinischen Museumspasses. Vielen Dank an Rhodia Acetow GmbH Freiburg. Partner des Museums für Neue Kunst. ©grafikbüro 2000

TOTALE 02
27
Mai bis 10 Sep
00 30 Sep bis
31 Dez 00
Das Jahrhundert im Blick
der Sammlung
50er 60er
70er Jahre
Museum für Neue Kunst
Freiburg Marienstrasse 10a
www.mnk-freiburg.de/TOTALE
Städtische Museen Freiburg. Museum für Neue Kunst. Marienstrasse 10a, 79098 Freiburg. Tel 0761 2012581. Di bis So 10 bis 17 Uhr geöffnet. Einzelbesucher 8 DM. ermäßigt 5 DM. Dauerkarte 10 DM. Familienkarte 15 DM. Freier Eintritt für Mitglieder des Fördervereins und Besitzer des Oberrheinischen Museumspasses. Vielen Dank an Rhodia Acetow GmbH Freiburg. Partner des Museums für Neue Kunst. ©grafikbüro 2000

Fabio Ongarato belongs to the emerging generation of designers from Down Under. As with so many of his predecessors, what really drives him is a passion for design. His work reflects a love of and belief in the power of contemporary photography and architecture. It is not difficult to detect the influence of Op Art and Kinetic Art. He is one of the new true collaborators, seeking input from those around him and remaining open to comment and new views that might influence the direction of the work. Through thoughtful and incisive art direction he eliminates the unnecessary. All that remains is that part of the communication that genuinely sends the message. Never losing sight of the content or the idea is essential. Analyzing the brief in search of the single idea is natural to his method. While he is very process-driven, there is an undeniable spark of intuition, a sensitivity to creative subtlety that invades his work. He speaks enthusiastically of a passion for the craft of design and the beauty of the printed medium. It is also evident that his work allows him to explore the alternative disciplines of design. The willingness to cross boundaries is innate.●● Like so many designers in this publication, Ongarato is much honored locally and internationally. Most notable among his acclamations is his ISTD London award for the *Lineage* project and exhibition dedicated to the work of architect Daniel Libeskind. Ongarato's company, Fabio Ongarato Design, is based in Melbourne, Australia. Despite the geographic isolation, I am sure the impact of his work will be felt on more distant continents.
●● Ken Cato ●●

1-2 Front and back of foldout poster for *Fashion Photography Now* exhibition (photography Sølve Sunsbo) / Melbourne Fashion Festival / Australia / 2002
3   Signage for *Fashion Photography Now* exhibition / 2002
4   Poster for the Melbourne Art Fair 2002 / Melbourne Art Fair / Australia / 2002
5   Poster for the BMW Festival of German Cinema in Melbourne and Sydney / Goethe Institute / Australia / 2002
6   Cover, *Big Magazine* no. 44, "Australian issue" / Big Magazine / USA / 2002
7   Poster/corporate identity for architectural firm Elenberg Fraser / Elenberg Fraser / Australia / 2001

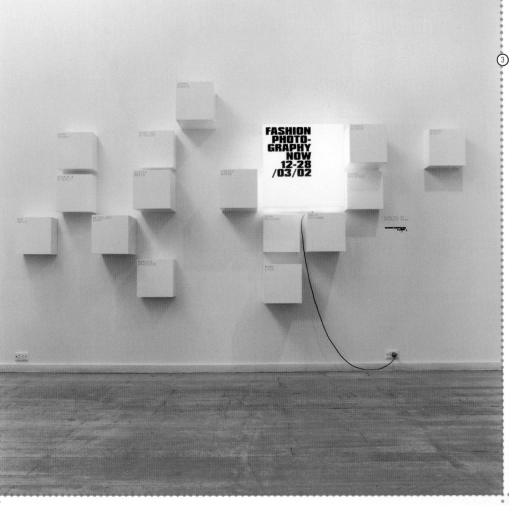

Fabio Ongarato

Melbourne

4

MELBOURNEARTFAIR**2002**
2-6 OCTOBER

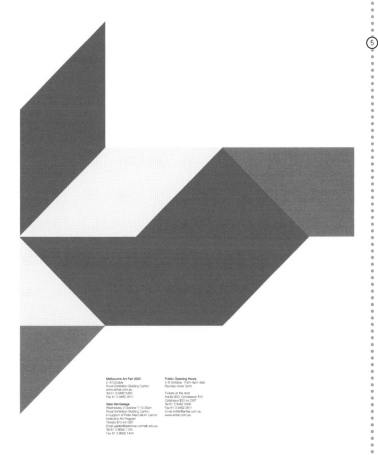

Melbourne Art Fair 2002
2–6 October
Royal Exhibition Building Carlton
www.artfair.com.au
Tel 61 3 9482 5400
Fax 61 3 9482 2611

Gala Vernissage
Wednesday 2 October 7-10.30pm
Royal Exhibition Building Carlton
In support of Peter MacCallum Cancer
Institute's Art Program
Tickets $75 inc GST
Email galafxt@artemisc.unimelb.edu.au
Tel 61 3 9656 1124
Fax 61 3 9656 1444

Public Opening Hours
3–6 October, 11am–9pm daily
Sunday close 7pm

Tickets at the door
Adults $20, Concession $15
Catalogue $20 inc GST
Tel 61 3 9482 5400
Fax 61 3 9482 2611
Email artfair@artfair.com.au
www.artfair.com.au

BMW
FESTIVAL
OF GERMAN
CINEMA
2002

Melbourne
September 13-22
Palace Como

Sydney
September 13-24
Palace Verona

Big

AUSTRALIA

WWW.BIGMAGAZINE.COM
Printed in Spain
US $15 Canada $20

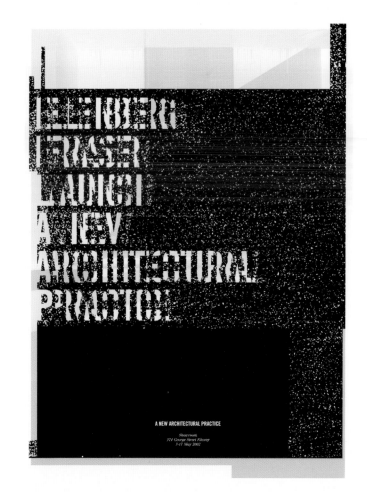

A NEW ARCHITECTURAL PRACTICE

Shearroom
324 George Street Fitzroy
3-17 May 2002

8   Poster for *Lineage: The Architecture of Daniel Libeskind* exhibition / Jewish Museum of Australia / Australia / 2000
9–12 Boxed-set exhibition catalogue with foldout posters, *Lineage: The Architecture of Daniel Libeskind* / 2000
13   Unfolded poster from exhibition catalogue *Lineage: The Architecture of Daniel Libeskind* / 2000
14–16 Book cover and spreads, *Red* / Australian Centre for Contemporary Art / Australia / 2001
17–19 Unfolded cover, spread with foldout, and individual pages from spring/summer catalogue of fashion designer Karen Walker /
       Karen Walker / New Zealand / 2001
20   Poster for Karen Walker Spring/Summer campaign / Karen Walker / New Zealand / 2001

Fabio Ongarato

17
18
19

14
15
16

20

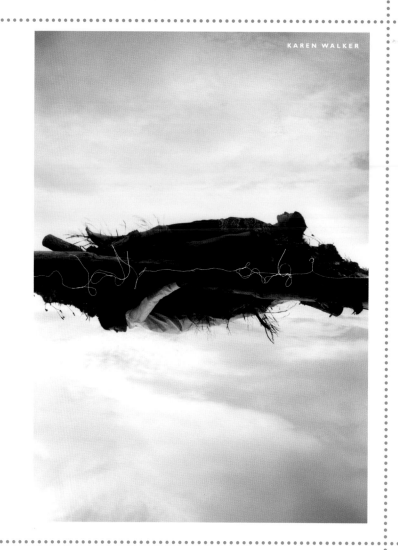

Switzerland is a special country for graphic design. It may seem that its moment in the sun came and went in the middle of a century now left in the past, when the Swiss school was synonymous with graphic design. But as the years go by and the world changes, what remains constant is that this small country continues to produce wonderful young talents.••At the Moscow graphic design biennial Zolotaya Pchela (Golden Bee) I received a large series of silver-gray posters, covered with entrancing patterns, and I immediately noted this new name, Tania Prill, especially since it sounded so Russian. ••But Prill's posters are distinctly Swiss, even if at a brief glance they don't seem anything like the works of Müller-Brockmann or Armin Hofmann, or Ralph Shraivogel or Rudolph Lutz. Their origin is expressed not so much in the stylistic particularities and shapes of their composition, but in the special treatment of letters, lines, and text. I would call this approach typographical postulation, as if all the answers in this discipline were already provided by the Swiss themselves.••The Swiss never seem to tire of marveling at the everyday miracle of a line connecting with a sheet of paper. For them, each time this union occurs is a question, and each time everything starts anew. Again and again, the text becomes a problem of composition and image. And typography, again and again, becomes the main hero of the poster. It is precisely this way in Prill's work.••Moreover, her designs seem very fresh. The text creates a lush intellectual environment, a quivering, vibrating, living texture. Prill's lines fly and streams of information flow, forming the finest pulsating ether. Prill's posters and books are also permeated by the special charm of precise, careful work. They seem filled with a flickering light, quiet and warm.••This delicate virtual ether, this environment, this light, this sound, this music delights me and seems extraordinarily pertinent to the developments in international design today.••Serge Serov••

1-2   Posters for project *Kunst am Bau in der Universität Irchel* which invited artists to
      conceive works for dedicated spaces at the University Irchel / Hochbauamt Kanton
      Zürich / Switzerland / 2000
3-4   Pages and poster from All Blues! project (4 of 12) / Verein Schichtwechsel /
      Lichtenstein / 1999 / A visual translation of a twelve-part text by Norbert Haas, All
      Blues! is made up of twelve unbound pages and a poster in which all pages are
      featured. The project was commissioned by the cultural association Verein
      Schichtwechsel as a gift for its members.

Tania Prill

Zurich

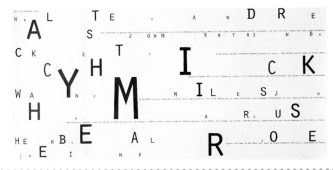

MEINE FREUNDIN UND ICH,

Ein Text von Norbert Haas · Herbst 1996

wir mussten ja nicht gleich nach Paris ziehen. Es stand wirklich in unserem Ansinnen, uns umzusehen, unabhängig alle hielten vielleicht am Anfang alles für möglich, wir kamen und und ein Ziel zu erreichen, auch gelegentlich mittel vergessen, ja wer denkt wer ist mehr, und ich roh und auch und eine und und selbst einem einen Atem einen Atem der Geschichte eingebracht hat, wie es in eurem Nachruf auf Amalie Pinkus heisst, der oder wie hat es verkauft, die unter Umständen über das Leben entscheidende Information weitergegeben, dass die Geschichte nicht einfach einen Atem hat, sondern den jüngeren immer ins Gesicht hustet. Wenn ihr euch schon mit (revolutionärer?) Geschichte beschäftigt, dann tut es doch selber und lasst euch dabei nicht führen. Denkt auf eure eigenen Kosten. Denn wo es um biographische Eitelkeiten geht, lügen die älteren alle. Amalie Pinkus kannte ich nicht, aber Theo Pinkus. Als ich ihn zusammen mit drei anderen Berlinern 1968 in Zürich besucht habe, versuchte er uns zu schocken, indem er gleich zu Beginn der Entstalinisierung in der Aera Chruschtschew auch geblieben. Wir waren aber nicht geschockt. Wir waren einfach stocksauer über eine solche Eröffnung. Irgendwie muss Theo gemerkt haben, dass ein Abchecken von Gesinnung damals nicht mehr lief. Er begann zu reden wie ein Wasserfall. Lauter Repertoire, mit komischen Einlagen dazwischen. Wir standen nur da. Ich muss zugeben, dass ich irritiert war. Heute bin ich froh darüber, dass wir die Nerven hatten, eine Stunde lang nur da zu stehen und kein Wort zu sagen.

DISCOGRAFIE Was lief, während ich geschrieben habe.

James Cotton with Joe Louis Walker and Charlie Haden · Deep in the Blues · 1996 Gitanes/Verve

Detroit Gary Wiggins & Fabrice Eulry · Paris Jook · 1996 Syncope

Cowboy Junkies · The Caution Horses · 1990 BMG Music Canada Inc.

Holly Cole · Temptation · 1995 Metro Blue Capitol Records

Original Funk · Le Son de la Nouvelle Orleans · 1996 Novapress

All Blues!

Ein Text von Norbert Haas · Herbst 1996

Marianne Faithfull · A Secret Life · 1995 Island Records

Miles Davis · Get up with it · 1974 Coline Records

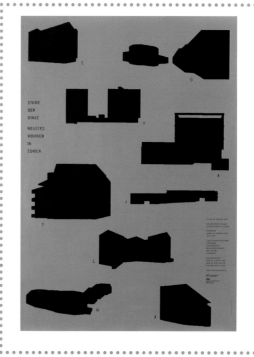

5   Cover and spreads, exhibition publication *Die Schweizer Autobahn* (The Swiss Highway) / Museum für Gestaltung Zürich /
     Switzerland / 1999
6–8 Posters for exhibition *Stand der Dinge: Neustes Wohnen in Zürich* (The State of Affairs: New Living in Zurich) / Hochbauamt Kanton
     Zürich / Switzerland / 2002
9   Self-commissioned poster Faxaction conceived in memory of Swiss typographer and teacher Hans-Rudolf Lutz / Switzerland / 2002 /
     In January 1998, while working on the conception of his exhibition *Werkschau Hans-Rudolf Lutz*, Hans-Rudolf Lutz passed away. His
     friends followed through with the exhibition, which took place in the Visosuisse Factory, Emmenbrücke, a few months later. A fax
     machine was installed in the exhibition space, allowing people from around the world to react to the loss. The faxes became part of
     the exhibition and a selection was used to make up this poster.

Tania Prill

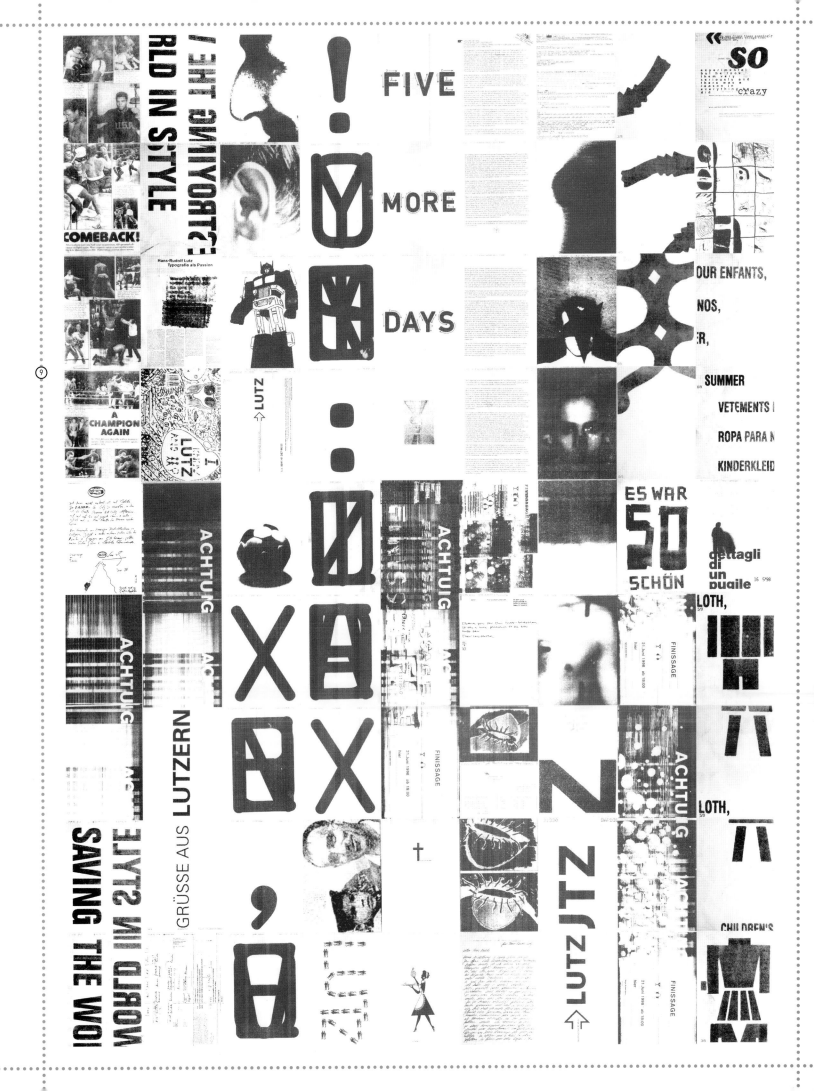

Read from left to right, QWER are the first four letters on a standard keyboard. QWER is also the symbiosis of two graphic designers who communicated with one another until they had their own studio and a beautiful baby. The studio was founded in a day, when they won the commission for the corporate design for the Expo 2000 in Hannover. Their concept was as unusual as it was convincing. Instead of a logo they presented an optical impulse—not a conventional sign, but rather an ever-changing structure. This important success right at the beginning of their careers served as both an obligation and a motivation. It therefore comes as no surprise that their Cologne-based studio now takes on projects for reputable corporations and cultural institutions. ° °Iris Utikal and Michael Gais studied communication design at the Academy for Applied Arts in Düsseldorf and received their diplomas in 1992 under my auspices. After this they worked in my studio for several years. Even their final-year projects were worth seeing: Among other things, Utikal directed a movie about the belly button, and Gais designed a razor-sharp book about the sociocultural meaning of shaving. During their studies they separately gathered experience in renowned design and advertising agencies from London to Tokyo. Since then both have become professors of typography and book design at Cologne's International School of Design. ° °Their work has received numerous awards at national and international competitions—not least for its excellent typographic design. Particularly characteristic of them, however, is their ambition to understand even boring assignments as creative challenges. They are not afraid to embrace the consistent application of a design system: for example, the corporate design manual that they created for the Expo 2000 is heavy enough to bend your bookshelf. Since they are untiringly committed and active, I am already looking forward to their future work. ° °Uwe Loesch ° °

1–2 Airplane design and poster series for Expo 2000 Hannover World Exposition / Expo 2000 Hannover / Germany / 1996–2000
3 Logo detail, brochure, design for stationery, and invitations to various events of the *Stiftung Kulturregion Hannover* (Foundation of the Cultural Region Hannover) / Stiftung Kulturregion Hannover / Germany / 2001
4–5 Box set of paper-sample booklets and cover variations for paper company Zanders / Zanders Feinpapiere AG / Germany / 1997–present

QWER

Cologne, Germany

Zentrum
Internationaler
Skulptur

Stiftung
**Wilhelm
Lehmbruck
Museum**

⑥⑦⑧

⑨⑩⑪

6–8 Logo and posters for exhibitions *Bruce Nauman* and *Alexander Rodtschenko und die Raumkonstruktion im 20. Jahrhundert*, Wilhelm
Lembruck Museum, Duisburg / Stiftung Wilhelm Lembruck Museum / Germany / 2000–2002
9–11 Posters for exhibitions *Holub Ludens–Kunst für Kunst*, *Unter der Haut*, and *Nam June Paik–Fluxus und Videoskulptur* / Stiftung
Wilhelm Lembruck Museum, Duisburg / Germany / 2001–2002
12 Logo application on facade of Wilhelm Lembruck Museum, Duisburg / 2000
13–14 Logo variations and street campaign for *Rotterdam 2001, Cultural Capital of Europe* (unrealized) / Rotterdam Cultural Capital 2001 /
Netherlands / 2001
15–17 Poster, magazine cover, and spread for *Rotterdam 2001, Cultural Capital of Europe* campaign (unrealized) / 2001

⑫

rotterdam 2001

culturele hoofdstad van europa

rotterdam 2001

cultural capital of europe

rotterdam 2001

culturele hoofdstad van europa

network diversity on the move

decentralize sampling significant

dimensions connections exchange reflection transparency

rotterdam 2001 sound language beat

expression variety stimulation

light symphony energy

global dynamic floating

r.001

het festival de stad en het leven

rotterdam 2001

Samuel Nyholm and Jonas Williamson from Sweden, Laurent Benner from Switzerland: three middle-class western Europeans with a common sense of humor, knack for music, and passion for high and low culture. Federico Fellini blended Kafka and *piadina romagnola*; Reala do something similar with the *Tractatus Logicus Philosophicus* and Superman. Their inspiration emerges from their not-so-distant teenage days, art school, friends, and daily lives. Nyholm states, "Work becomes pretty playful, but with strict rules. We often pick up systems/objects from the backyards of human culture, as signifiers of different themes. We try relate to the subject, assignment, in the most obvious way. Trying not to be too clever. This point of view helps us to find the signfiers that later become a system around which we can build our work."●●Reala are your friendly next-door-neighbor designers. They want to present information in a nice costume. "Like Limburger cheese," explains Williamson, "you may not like it at first, only to then realize that the taste is very complex, rich, and mature." They want to elicit strong emotional reactions (see "I love to meet you"), obviously not through market logic, but through sincere and instinctive human activities. Such as "sleeping, cooking, fixing your bike, phase shifts, listening to yet another pile of garbage from a son of a bush, stealing chairs, Gore Vidal, having a cup of tea, having a pint, rewinding, selecting, busting," in the words of Benner.●●Omar Vulpinari●●

1   Portrait illustrations for weekly segment in the culture section of Swedish newspaper *Svenska Dagbladet* / Svenska Dagbladet / Sweden / 2002
2–3 Thematic spreads "global/regional/local," *Benzin–Young Swiss Graphic Design*, published by Lars Müller Publishers / Lineto.com / Switzerland / 2000
4–5 Posters for contemporary-art event "After Shopping," Kulturhuset, Stockholm / After Shopping / Sweden / 2002
6   Promotional poster for Japanese jeans company Edwin Jeans / Yotsugi Yasunori Incorporation and Edwin Jeans / Japan / 2002
7   Poster for short film *She is Dead*, by Henry Moore Selder and Sara Lundén / Pinguin Film / Sweden / 2002

Reala

London/Stockholm

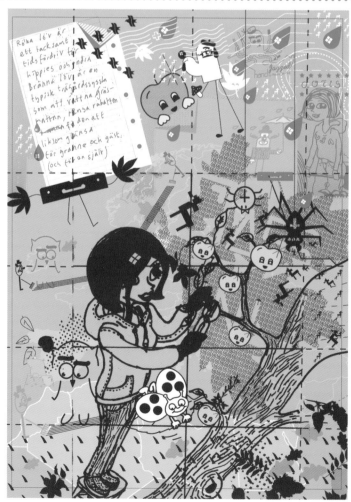

8-10 Cover illustrations for winter, summer, and autumn menus of the Lydmar Hotel restaurant / Lydmar Hotel / Sweden / 2000-2001

11-12 Posters for Payam Sharifi and Alan Clarke's exhibition and short film *Hall of Fame*, held and shown at Fanclub, Amersterdam, and the Stockholm Film Festival / Payam Sharifi / France / 2002

13 Official poster for exhibition *I love to meet you–New graphic design* held at Palazzo Fortuny in Venice / Studio Camuffo / Italy / 2002

14 Poster/calendar created as Reala's Christmas card / United Kingdom and Sweden / 2002

Reala

Casey Reas's research examines abstractions of biological and natural systems by means of various digital media such as software art, print media, and animation. As a member of John Maeda's Aesthetics and Computation Group (ACG), he researches the conception and execution of intelligent, interactive, mobile sculpture (behavioral kinetic sculpture). He designs independently, and is a professor at the newly founded Interaction Design Institute in Ivrea, Italy.••Reas is constantly looking for new forms. Every day he reacquaints himself and practices with the computer, with this illustration tool, which for many of us has very set limits. He peeks behind each byte, he tinkers with the zeros and ones, strums around on them. For him all barriers regarding the pure function of the computer have fallen completely, allowing him a fascinating ease and freedom with its applications. He knows how to work the machine, about its possibilities, the way the rest of us know paper and pencil. But he clearly goes even further: It is as if, in order to draw a line with a pencil, we were to start by hewing a tree or grinding lead. Listening to Reas talk about his research, I quickly understand that computers are open books, that computers are generated, natural systems, that computers are also just human beings. He is an addict, a maniac. His output is more than impressive. He is someone who *must* do research. He is a real explorer, because he works without a specific goal: He is not in a binding commitment to any company, no enterprise has bought him.••Werner Jeker••

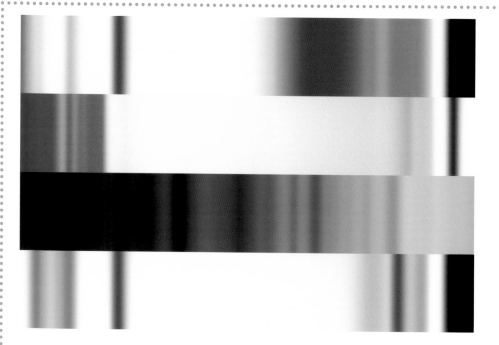

1–3   Print series "Mediation" / Group C / United States / 2002 / In this series the representational and symbolic content of a photograph is systematically obscured and replaced with an empty surface.

4–6   Print series "Path" / Group C / United States / 2001 / The prints explore the movement of four synthetic systems reacting to different stimuli. Each image is a frozen moment in time from this continually shifting ecology.

Casey Reas

Ivrea, Italy

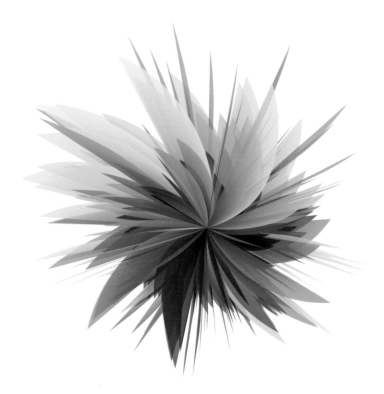

7-8 Print series "Seed" / Group C / United States / 2001 / Each image is the result of a synthetically cloned seed growing in a unique environment.
9-10 Prints from RPM project / IAMAS / Japan / 2001 / The prints represent kinetic forms created through manipulation of location, phase, speed, and transparency of the same moving object.

Casey Reas

R Studio, David Richmond's graphic-design company, is currently based in a converted church near Camden. Introducing the company on their Web site, Richmond says that while this may be quite strange, they believe that "divine intervention on any project is always welcome." I've known Richmond since we were both students at the London College of Printing, and he's always had a dry, northern sense of humor. He has managed to filter that into his work, bringing a distinctive personality to the kinds of products that usually end up looking tired, bland, and faceless. • •His humor is evident in his work for the Food Doctor, which offers advice and information on all aspects of nutrition, and their own line of healthy food products. Richmond developed an identity and range of packaging that capture the essence of the brand. The identity is modern, approachable, and suggests authority, while the packaging is warm and friendly, bringing a distinctive personality to an area that is highly commercialized and increasingly competitive. Products were given breezy names such as "A Bit on the Side" mayonnaise, "Well Dressed" salad dressings, or "Good Morning" cereals. The humorous language acts as an icebreaker, giving the brand more appeal than other, more sober-looking health-food lines. • •He recently created a new look for the store-brand food packaging of the English department store Selfridges. With it, he hoped to challenge people's perceptions of how food should be packaged. He has truly succeeded, with an approach that engages the consumer and builds on the customer experience. No fancy food photography here, just bold, bright typography on a black ground—an audacious solution that is incredibly effective. • •His work extends beyond the world of brand packaging. His identities—such as those designed for Martin Pritchard (a dentist) and Sara Bruce (a food consultant)—display his ability to create warm, humorous solutions, with an approach that is consistently direct and human. The dentist's logotype transforms his name into a smiling mouth. It's as simple as that. No frills. Just a friendly identity that makes you smile. • •Fernando Gutiérrez • •

1 Identity for food consultant Sara Bruce / Sara Bruce / United Kingdom / 2002
2 Packaging for flavored olive oil brand Inventory Oils / Inventory Oils / United Kingdom and Spain / 1999
3 Branding and packaging for UK supermarket Selfridges's in house product range / Selfridges / United Kingdom / 2002

David Richmond

London

SELFRIDGES&Cº
RUNNY HONEY WITH HONEYCOMB

SELFRIDGES&Cº
CLEAR RUNNY HONEY

SELFRIDGES&Cº
CRANBERRY & ORANGE SAUCE

SELFRIDGES&Cº
APPLE & MINT SAUCE

SELFRIDGES&Cº
PURE GROUND KENYAN GETHUMB-WINI COFFEE
sharp, bright, invigorating
strength 5

SELFRIDGES&Cº
PURE GROUND COLOMBIAN EMERALD MOUNTAIN COFFEE
soft fragrant richness, smooth
strength 2

SELFRIDGES&Cº
PURE GREEN TEA 20 TEA BAGS
naturally purifying and uplifting
strength 2

SELFRIDGES&Cº
SINGLE ESTATE DARJEELING TEA 20 TEA BAGS
full flavoured Champagne of teas
strength 2

SELFRIDGES&Cº
CHRISTMAS PUDDING WITH CHAMPAGNE
produce of England

③

SELFRIDGES&Cº
MERLOT VIN DE PAYS D'OC 2001

SELFRIDGES&Cº
CHARDONNAY VIN DE PAYS D'OC 2001

SELFRIDGES&Cº
HANDMADE PANETTONE

④

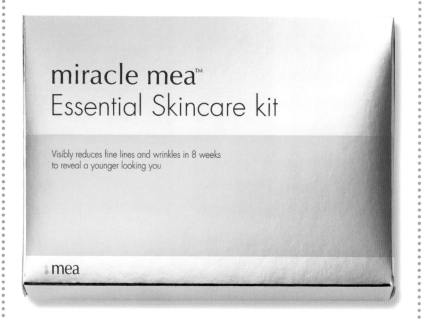

miracle mea™
Essential Skincare kit

Visibly reduces fine lines and wrinkles in 8 weeks
to reveal a younger looking you

⑤

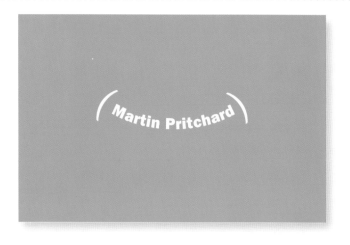

Martin Pritchard

David Richmond

4   Identity and packaging for new range of Mea makeup and skincare products / Mea / United Kingdom / 2000
5   Identity/business card for Martin Prichard's dental pratice / Martin Prichard / United Kingdom / 2000
6   Identity, packaging, and posters for UK food brand The Food Doctor / The Food Doctor / United Kingdom / 2002

A fresh start

Feeling low? Your environment affects your immunity for which you need antioxidants on a daily basis. What you eat makes all the difference.

Find out how to get the most out of your life with a 'one-to-one' nutrition consultation. Please ask at reception for details.

THE FOOD DOCTOR™
A Recipe for Health & Vitality

www.thefooddoctor.com

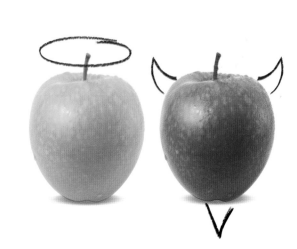

Is your food good to you?

Food intolerance testing available
You may love food, but does your food love you?
Few people actually have allergies, but many can react badly to the food they eat.

THE FOOD DOCTOR™
A Recipe for Health & Vitality

www.thefooddoctor.com

Sanja Rocco. I came across this beautiful, rolling name—sounding Latin and Slavic at the same time—when two posters were received at the Moscow international graphic-design biennial Zolotaya Pchela (Golden Bee): a black one and a white one, produced for the Croatian Typhlology Museum. The text can only be seen when illuminated from an angle, because it's set in raised dots of braille. A poster for the blind! It was hard to imagine. A poster you can perceive by touch. I was very impressed.••Graphic design often provokes both visual and tactile sensations: the heaviness of fine paper stock in a magazine or book, the textured cardboard of packaging, or the smoothness of an invitation card. These pleasures are grander than mere information by itself.••In postmodernism this quality becomes one of the most relevant today. The fact that we are in contact with the whole world through mobile phones, faxes, electronic mail, and the Internet is more important than the information we receive through these channels. Connecting is more important than communicating. The Internet makes this fact obvious, felt by fingertips on a computer keyboard.••Paradoxically, the key underpinnings of modernism and postmodernism—"grid" (modular grid) and "net" (Internet)—are almost synonyms. Meanwhile they belong to two different cultural epochs.••The growing importance of tactile sensations and of subtle physical contact in postmodernism is visualized through such traditional concepts as "texture." In Sanja Rocco's work for the Jordan Catalogue, the texture of the canvas seeps through to the surface, demonstrating that painting is born on the resilient, animate base of this sort of organic "net" rather than the strict modular "grid" that fits the nature of graphics.••It seems to me that this quality is part of feminine nature. And when Sanja Rocco allows this nature to spread its wings, "texture" and "painting" make her work privy to the actualities of postmodernism. On the Rundek CD cover, the hero has closed his eyes. This doesn't mean he doesn't see anything. It simply means that he's looking inside, into himself.••Serge Serov••

1–4 Annual report with CD-ROM for telecommunications company Ericsson / Ericsson Nikola Tesla Croatia / Croatia / 2002

5–6 Black and White posters for the Croatian Typhlology Museum / Croatian Typhology Museum / Croatia / 1991 / The braille type is embossed on the posters.

Sanja Rocco

Zagreb

7   Poster for Radio Drama's Second International Festival of Radio Play and Documentary / Croatian Radio /
    Croatia / 1998
8   CD cover, *Ruke*, by Darko Rundek / Menart / Croatia / 2002
9   Poster for play *How the Other Half Lives*, by Alan Ayckbourn / National Theater of Varazdin / Croatia / 1997
10 Variations of the Raiffeisen Bank Smart Card / Raiffeisenbank Croatia / Coatia / 2001

Sanja Rocco

Mexican-born graphic designer Gabriela Rodriguez comes from a land where the bold use of bright color is second nature. Yet her work also embraces the subtlety and refined use of colors outside the obvious local palette. While being proudly Mexican, she is a citizen of the world. She is a multitalented designer and artist. Following her graduation from design school, she worked mainly in the design of books, magazines, and assorted print material. While producing many excellent works, she was not content to be confined to the restrictions of the printed page. She has since moved on to produce bold, daring, and provocative posters for political and social issues—things that relate directly to her country. In executing these works she has not been afraid to use the tools of graphic design to confront her public. Her work is simple, strong, bold, and very much to the point. Beyond the surface there is an undercurrent of messages that revolve around carefully planned imagery relating to various aspects of the culture, the country, and the particulars of the project itself.••More recently she has collaborated internationally on a number of projects, adding a cross-cultural element while exploring new areas such as architectural graphics and exhibitions. Opening up new horizons is something that she is very familiar with. She is constantly searching for the next lesson and the next big idea. She is continually involved in activities that promote and educate the practitioners and consumers of graphic design in Mexico. There is always a strong sense of history, achievement, and culture that often blends both the old and the new. Sometimes it is subtle, other times blatant, but always relevantly applied. She is a natural leader and champion of the profession in a country that is naturally graphically rich but naive to the more commercial aspects of the design profession.••Ken Cato••

1   Poster for XL *Muestra Internacional de Cine* (International Film Festival), Mexico City /
     National Film Archive of Mexico / Mexico / 2002
2   Poster for festival on occasion of André Breton's centennial / National Council
     for Culture and Arts (CONACULTA) and the French Embassy / Mexico / 1996
3   Poster inviting young artists to apply for National Foundation of Culture and Arts
     (FONCA) scholarships / CONACULTA / Mexico / 1999
4   Poster for cultural-exchange project and exhibition *Goya Posada* / Mexican Ministry
     of Foreign Affairs and the Mexican Institute, Madrid / Mexico and Spain / 2002
5   Promotional poster for book *Miradas sobre el Aborto* (Views on Abortion) / Grupo de
     Información de Reproducción Elegida / Mexico / 2001
6   Poster homage for Toulouse-Lautrec's centennial / Nouveau Salon des Cents /
     France / 2001

Gabriela Rodriguez

Mexico City

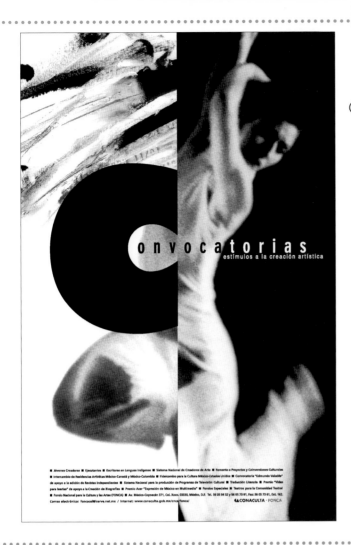

onvocatorias
estímulos a la creación artística

MIRADAS SOBRE EL ABORTO

I don't need legs
if I have wings for flying
Frida Kahlo

7   Back and front cover, *I and My Circumstance* exhibition catalogue / CONACULTA and the Montreal Museum of Fine Arts / Mexico and Canada / 1999

8–9   Ceiling design and installation, Monterrey International Airport, Mexico (with Ken Cato) / Grupo Aeroportuario Centro Norte and Eduardo Terrazas / Mexico / 2001

10   Identity for *Festival Cinema Europa* 2002 / Delegation of the European Commission, Mexico / Mexico / 2002

11   Cover for brochure accompanying the 2000 Alliance Graphique Internationale (AGI) congress in Oaxaca, Mexico / AGI / France / 2000

12   Contribution to promotional calendar for Mexican paper company / Pochteca Group / Mexico / 1999

13   Cover, *Fronteras* magazine, spring 1997 / CONACULTA / Mexico / 1996 / *Fronteras* is a Mexican cultural magazine dedicated to the regions around the country's northern and southern borders.

Gabriela Rodriguez

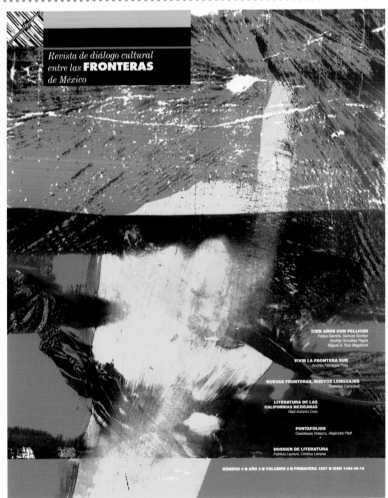

Joe Sacco's comic books leave me thinking that news is overrated. Labeled with the words "Breaking News" or "LIVE," the world crisis du jour is being delivered instantly to our screens. Why is so much value pinned on the immediacy of news when so often it is later proved to be inaccurate or grossly misleading? Why are we glued to the thousands of bulletins of this saturated coverage when it is failing to stack up, form a bigger picture? When "official" phrases like the purposely vague *collateral damage* and the crazy *mutually assured destruction* start to be used on the major TV networks, it is even more important that self-respecting journalists like Joe Sacco manage to avoid the clichés and strive to employ a specific language that actually tells us what is happening.●●Sacco inhabits another time zone. Topicality is not one of his concerns despite his enthusiasm for placing himself in the thick of the world's hot spots; from Bosnia to Palestine to, most recently, Ingushetia. In 1993, Sacco spent two months in the Occupied Palestinian Territories holding interviews and taking reference photographs. Once this information—typically for Sacco, always a complexity of the extraordinary shot through with the mundane—was collected, he returned home to Portland, Oregon, and spent months meticulously drawing it up, carefully re-creating his experience for us all to share in a series of nine comics called *Palestine*. Only now, because all the comics have been brought together and published in a single book, is *Palestine* getting the attention it deserves—just as relevant now as it was ten years ago.●●Sacco choreographs your gaze across the frames of his pages like a film director in control of a lens. He achieves this by fragmenting commentary and dialogue text into short sentences that are carefully placed, so that as you read, the details he wants you to notice are dwelled upon in a lingering sequence he has complete mastery of—details such as the individualized faces of people in crowds, the particular texture and pattern of their clothes, the miserable state of the ground they walk on, and the precarious condition of the roofs that shelter them.●●Sacco is a cartoonist who became a journalist who favors "humanizing people who are broadly labeled 'terrorists' or 'victims.'" Sacco feels that while journalism's main aim is to inform, why should people care when so little of it is moving? Sacco's art is about redress—for peoples and places mis- and unrepresented by the mainstream media. It's ironic that Sacco has pulled it off in a medium often dismissed as kids' stuff.●●Nick Bell●●

1-3   Spreads, *Safe Area Gorazde–The War in Eastern Bosnia 1992-95*, by Joe Sacco / Fantagraphics Books / USA / 2000 / *Safe Area Gorazde* details Sacco's trips to the Bosnian town of Gorazde during the aftermath of the war.
4   Spread from *The War Crimes Trials*, a six-page story for *Details* magazine / Details / USA / 1998 / The story focuses on the Bosnian War Crimes Trials in the Hague.

Joe Sacco

New York

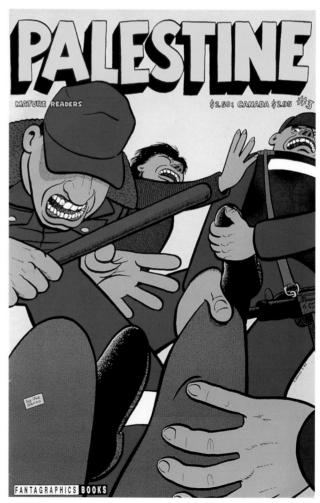

5–7 Covers, first three issues of nine-issue comic series *Palestine*, by Joe Sacco / Fantagraphics Books / USA / 1993–94 / *Palestine* details Sacco's two-month stay in the Palestinian occupied territories.

8–15 Cover and spreads, *Palestine*, by Joe Sacco / Fantagraphics Books / USA / 2001 / The book is a collection of all nine issues of the *Palestine* comic series.

Joe Sacco

At the turn of the millennium, Korean designer Ahn Sang-Soo managed to coin a new word in international design: Oullim.●●Oullim suggests absolute harmony of nature, humanity, and technology; of the past, present, and future; east and west, north and south. But this simple word is not as empty or as favorable as may seem at first glance. Behind it hides a deep crisis through which our culture, civilization, and design are living.●●Twentieth-century design, according to Sang-Soo, developed from Bauhaus ideology, industrialization, and mass production. These developments took place in opposition to nature and in aesthetic terms can be described as having created "contrast." Such contrast, in the end, led to ecological destruction, increasing cruelty, and other frictions between man and his surroundings. As a result, we now find ourselves in search of new ideals, a new design paradigm for the twenty-first century. This new conception of design must be found in the delta of Eastern rather than Western philosophical traditions. The design of the new millennium must break the fetters of contrasts that bound it in the twentieth century and establish a balance between "all of you" and "me," between the society and the individual, between the skies and the earth.●●Sang-Soo tries to solve these difficult philosophical dilemmas within the framework of his main professional specialty—typeface design and typography. Or, rather, he constantly strives to step outside this framework in search of the cultural meaning of graphic design: His typographic experiments often include dance, architecture, sculpture, and music. Innovative and elegant, his works appear wise and bright, like Sang-Soo himself. They instill hope and appease.●●One of his latest experimental works is called "From Alpha to Huit." Huit is the last letter in hangul, the Korean alphabet. Thus, instead of the common expression "from alpha to omega," Sang-Soo offers an alternative and redirects Greco-Latin civilization eastward.●●In another project we see this idea as part of a live performance in which letters disappear and emerge again behind a semitransparent wall. We thus experience a work that speaks about itself and engages us in the intellectual and aesthetic process of its creation.●●Serge Serov●●

1–3   Typographic installation and performance "From Alpha to Hiut" held at the Rodin Gallery, Seoul / Korea / 2002 / Huit is the last character of the Korean hangul alphabet.
4   Black Planet poster for *Kyoto Environmental Poster Design Exhibition* on occasion of United Nations environmental summit in Kyoto, Japan / Korea / 1997
5   Poster for concert by saxophone player Kang Tae-Hwan / Kang Tae-Hwan / Korea / 1997
6   Poster series promoting Korean arts and culture magazine *bogoseo/bogoseo* / bogoseo/bogoseo / Korea / 2001 / *Bogoseo* is Korean for "report."
7–9   Poster series as part of advertising campaign for Korean fashion brand / Ssamzie / Korea / 1999

Ahn Sang-Soo

Seoul

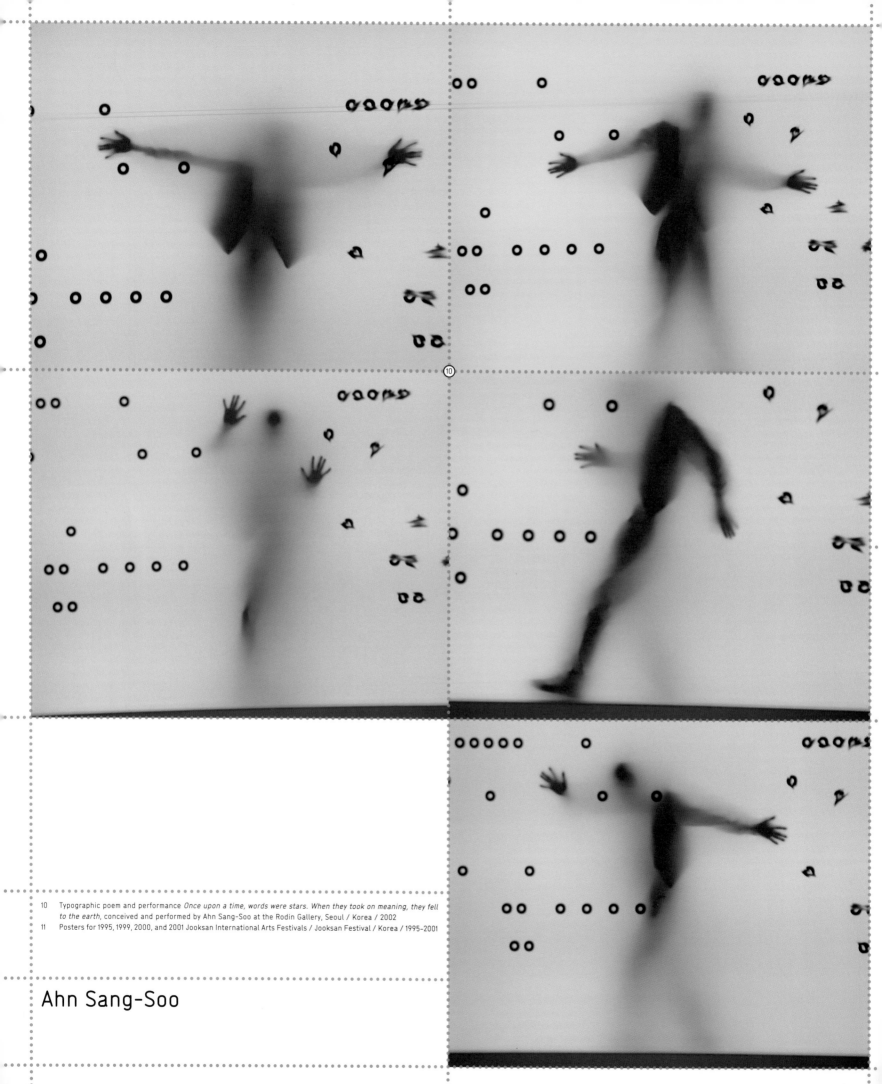

10   Typographic poem and performance *Once upon a time, words were stars. When they took on meaning, they fell to the earth*, conceived and performed by Ahn Sang-Soo at the Rodin Gallery, Seoul / Korea / 2002
11   Posters for 1995, 1999, 2000, and 2001 Jooksan International Arts Festivals / Jooksan Festival / Korea / 1995–2001

Ahn Sang-Soo

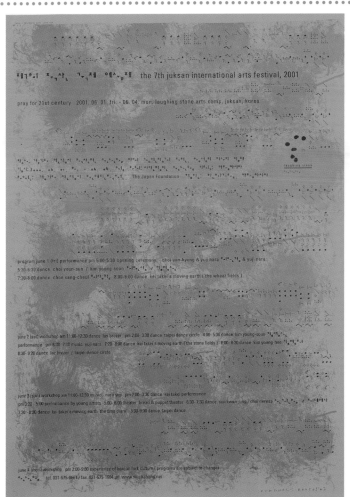

In the Japanese martial arts of swordsmanship, kendo, there is a position called *gedan-no-kamae*. Instead of swinging the sword above one's head to slash it down, one dangles it low on the right side, inviting the opponent to attack. In the sphere of Japanese graphic design, Yasuhiro Sawada's style is unquestionably *gedan-no-kamae*.●●Sawada is a new talent who has consistently been demonstrating his unique sensitivity through his graphic creations. His works are based on ordinary forms such as circles, squares, rectangles, polka dots, and so forth, and he uses commonplace materials such as fabric and wood. Like the *gedan-no-kamae* position, they appear to be ordinary and harmless. In reality, however, Sawada's works create highly effective messages owing to their well-thought-out composition.●●There is a Japanese expression that describes the subtle relationship created between two people before embarking on a task they are going to undertake together. By observing each other closely, they don't have to speak to communicate. Just like a question-and-answer session of Zen priests that is beyond the comprehension of outsiders, Sawada's work communicates with the viewer while letting him or her feel and think freely.●●I imagine Sawada stepping onto a stage. One of his works fills the space around him, forming the set. "I cannot find anything new," our hero declares. I would like to say to him, "Why, you yourself are the new material."●●Shigeo Fukuda●●

1-7 Posters for architectural consultancy / Kosaka Giken Co., Ltd. / Japan / 1998-2000
8 New Year's poster for Japanese fashion brand / VIVRE / Japan / 1994
9-10 Posters for exhibition *4 from Tokyo* held at the Art Directors Club Gallery, New York / Art Directors Club New York / USA / 1997

Yasuhiro Sawada

Tokyo

1·2

3·4

5·6

KOSAKA GIKEN CO.,LTD.

ベスト。

あなたと、
あなたの愛するすべての、
ベストになりたい。
平成五年一月一日

VIVRE

GRAPHIC POSTERS EXPOSITION · "4" FROM TOKYO
KATSUHIRO KINOSHITA / TADASHI KONDO / YASUHIRO SAWADA / SIGEL SHIMO'OKA
MARCH 10-14,1997 · ART DIRECTORS CLUB GALLERY
250 Park Avenue South, New York, N.Y.10003
Open Monday through Friday, 10a.m.-5p.m./Closed Saturday, Sunday and National Holidays.
212-674-0500

GRAPHIC POSTERS EXPOSITION · "4" FROM TOKYO
KATSUHIRO KINOSHITA / TADASHI KONDO / YASUHIRO SAWADA / SIGEL SHIMO'OKA
MARCH 10-14,1997 · ART DIRECTORS CLUB GALLERY
250 Park Avenue South, New York, N.Y.10003
Open Monday through Friday, 10a.m.-5p.m./Closed Saturday, Sunday and National Holidays.
212-674-0500

11 Poster for exhibition celebrating the two hundredth birthday of Japanese ukiyo-e artist Sharaku held at the Shibuya Parco Gallery, Tokyo / Mainichi Newspapers / Japan / 1994
12 Poster for exhibition *The Design Spirit of Japan* held at the University Art Museum, Tokyo / Tokyo National University of Fine Arts and Music / Japan / 2001
13 Poster designed to be sold at fund-raising event organized by the International Commissioner for the Protection of Fundamental Human Rights / Amnesty International / Japan / 1991
14–15 Poster series "Trimming" for *Graphic Wave 2002* exhibition held at the Ginza Graphic Gallery, Tokyo / Japan / 2002
16–17 Pages from catalogue for Yohji Yamamoto's fashion brand Y's for men / Y's for men / Japan / 1989

Yasuhiro Sawada

Graphic Wave 2003
Ginza Graphic Gallery
September 4(Wed.)–30(Mon.)

Graphic Wave 2003
Ginza Graphic Gallery
September 4(Wed.)–30(Mon.)

PEA COAT/WF-J09-129/¥32,000/ ●MOCHA ●DARK BROWN ●BLACK

THIS COLOR IS MOCHA

JEANS/WF-P06-054/¥9,000/ ●BLUE ●BLACK

THIS COLOR IS BLUE

The term personal computer implies that the computer is personal rather than impersonal, more human than machine. "Personal computer" means "humanist technology." Indeed, the arrival of the PC coincided with a mental evolutionary jump. Technology that delivers an end result in no time, eliminating the slow and methodical progression of ideas from prologue to epilogue, changes the thought process itself. ••Throughout the twentieth century—a century in which the Swiss school formed an important apex of graphic design—technology attempted to demystify the world and turn it into a machine to serve life. At the threshold of the twenty-first century, however, technology opened the window to the magical world of the virtual, showing us its inexhaustible depths and spellbinding mystery. ••Claudia Schmauder is a designer whose work clearly demonstrates this development. With the Swiss design school at her core, she extracts and creates images of modernity—or, more correctly, of postmodernity, images of the new computer age. ••The American "new wave" that started mastering digital images in the 1980s saw that what was most important was the background's openness, its context, its medium. The Swiss graphic designer Schraivogel in the 1990s increased the depth of field and discovered the astonishing density and richness of light spaces. Claudia Schmauder continues this journey, advancing postmodernism and pushing the boundaries of the paradigm. ••At the same time, Schmauder is a typical representative of the Swiss graphic school. In the depths of the chaos of her works, strict Swiss composition is always visible; at the core of the magical effects is a rational framework. What can you do? The personal computer is, after all, a machine. ••Serge Serov ••

1–2   Front and back of invitation for exhibition *Silberreflexe* (Silver Reflexes) / Johann Jacobs Museum, Zurich / Switzerland / 1996
3–4   Shopping-bag designs from personal project "Food Culture" / Switzerland / 1997
5   Poster for exhibition *Silberreflexe* (Silver Reflexes) / Johann Jacobs Museum, Zurich / Switzerland / 1996
6   Poster for exhibition *Am Limit–Kaffeegenuss als Grenzerfahrung* (At the Limit–Coffee as a Border Experience) / Johann Jacobs Museum, Zurich / Switzerland / 2001
7   Poster for exhibition *Café Mundo* / Johann Jacobs Museum, Zurich / Switzerland / 2000
8   Perforated invitation/unfoldable poster for open-air contemporary-art exhibition *Passagen* on the half-island Au / Au Konsortium / Switzerland / 2001

Claudia Schmauder

Zurich

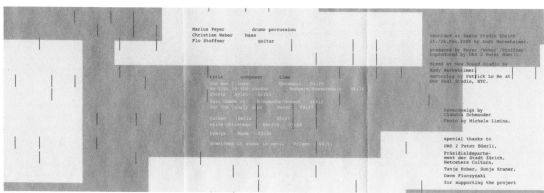

Claudia Schmauder

9 Mailer/unfoldable poster announcing Claudia Schmauder's new studio location / Switzerland / 1999
10–11 CD cover and booklet for *Unsung Songs* by jazz trio Peyer, Weber, Stoffner / Peyer, Weber, Stoffner and Unit Records / Switzerland / 2000
12 Front and back of invitation and poster for exhibition *Das Kaffeetrinken und der Blick der Kunst* (The Drinking of Coffee and the Eye of Art) / Johann Jacobs Museum, Zurich / Switzerland / 1997
13 Front and back of invitation and poster for exhibition *Coffee Talks* / Johann Jacobs Museum, Zurich / Switzerland / 1999

(12)

(13)

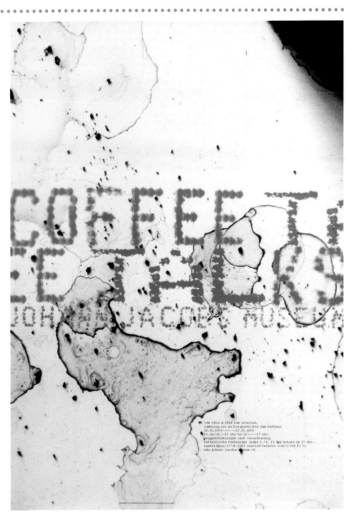

Nico Schweizer lives inside a colossal beast, in an abyss of infinite variety. Here, nothing is impossible, except, perhaps, for smoking. He lives and works in New York. New York is the excess of options, a giant Moloch, a monster, and also the old world. New York compels, focuses, splits open, caresses, polishes, curses, dances, grinds its teeth, and laughs. New York lives. Boundless impressions perish, a multitude of ideas emerge, the cold facts of life set boundaries. Schweizer sits in this billowing giant entity and works.●●Schweizer incorporates, his detailed creative observations draw from analyses of actual visual conditions. These transformations and adaptations take well-known paths. For instance, when he turns to the redesign of common commercial typefaces, they gain a contemporary relevance, the aesthetic of which yields substantial successes; *Wallpaper* magazine uses his fonts exclusively.●●The previously mentioned "known paths" are certainly not to be misunderstood as the beaten track, as the highways of a generally preferred taste. Schweizer confronts and builds on his Swiss roots as a graphic designer and illustrator and likes to orient himself therein when constructing his work. This discrete yet persistent self-reliance, which is strongest in his interpretations that break new ground, forms one aspect of his mode of working; his elegant, sober executions, the carefully thought-out color choices, and the weighting of tactile moments form the other, slightly more playful side. Schweizer's works are convincing because they employ such well-rounded—at times trendy—forms and always look and feel so wonderfully rich and complete.●●Werner Jeker●●

1–2   Posters for typography exhibition *Postscript* / Künstlerhaus Wien / Austria / 2002
3–4   Cover and spread, *Room 606–The SAS House and the Work of Arne Jacobsen*, by Michael Sheridan / Phaidon Press / United Kingdom and USA / 2003
5   Record cover, *Kamaal/The Abstract*, by Q-Tip (unrealized) / Arista Records / USA / 2002
6   Invitation for presentation of Hugo Boss Eyewear collection at the Fiera di Milano / Hugo Boss / Germany / 2000
7   Record cover, *Kamaal/The Abstract*, by Q-Tip / Arista Records / USA / 2002
8   Record cover, *Young Lawyer*, by French Kicks / Startime Records / USA / 2001

Nico Schweizer

New York

11

12

9–11   Front and back of poster and catalogue cover, *Young Guns 3* design exhibition / Art Directors Club
       New York / USA / 2001
12   Book cover, *Goldfinger*, by Ian Fleming / Flagstick Publications / USA / 2000
13   Type specimen, Typ 1441 Stencil / Mediadub.com / USA / 2001
14   Type specimen, LeCorbusier Bold / Mediadub.com / USA / 2002
15   Type specimen, Deluxe Script / Lineto.com / Switzerland / 1999–2003
16   Type specimen, Typ 1451, Typ 1441, Typ 1461 / Lineto.com and Mediadub.com / USA / 1995–2002

Nico Schweizer

Emerging countries must ultimately breed emerging designers. Twenty years ago in China there was virtually no such thing as graphic design. In the period that has followed, a graphic design community has rapidly come to life and developed. Highly influenced by the aesthetics of the trade's more evolved and design-conscious communities, however, the output of this young group has not always been characterized by originality.••Shaohua is aware of this, and his refreshing work comes as a welcome exception. His goal is to find direct and rapid mechanisms to communicate while searching for a new, inspring visual language.••Through his commitment and creativity, Shaohua has become one of the leaders of the new Chinese design community. He understands that design and business are partners and that designers have a role in helping the Chinese business community find a place in the international arena. Shaohua's work seeks to provide innovative identities for corporations, organizations, and branded products in an environment that previously disregarded such things. The 1980s Cultural Revolution in China changed this and significantly influenced Shaohua's career path. In 1987, discarding thoughts of engineering and science, he entered the Central Academy of Crafts and Art, Beijing, where he first encountered modern graphic design. At the beginning of the 1990s he moved to Shenzhen to pursue his chosen career. One senses that for Shaohua and for China, the journey has just begun.••Ken Cato••

1   Poster promoting traffic safety in Shenzhen / Advertising Association, Shenzhen Bureau of Industry and Commerce / China / 1997
2   Logo series for publication *China Annual Graphic Design* / Shenzhen CIS Type Association / China / 2002
3   Stamps designed on occasion of Fourth United Nations World Conference on Women, held in Beijing / Stamp Printing Bureau / China / 1995
4   Poster for first congress of the Shenzhen Graphic Designers' Association / Shenzhen Graphic Designers' Association / China / 1995
5   Poster for *Communication* invitational exhibition, Shenzhen / Shenzhen Graphic Designers' Association / China / 1996
6   Poster for *Graphic Design in China* exhibition, Shenzhen / China Industry Design Association and Package & Printing Magazine / China / 1992
7   Poster for the seventieth anniversary of the China Academy of Art / China Academy of Art / China / 1998

Chen Shaohua

Beijing/Shenzhen, China

④

⑤

⑥

⑦

8   Logo for Asian Development Bank meeting in Shanghai / Asian Development Bank / China / 2002
9   Poster for *9/11* invitational exhibition / Japanese Poster Museum, Tokyo / Japan / 2002
10   Logo / Shenzhen Commercial Bank / China / 2000
11–12 Logo and poster for 2008 Olympic Games in Beijing / Beijing Organizing Committee for the Games of the
      XXIX Olympiad / 2002
13   Self-commissioned poster protesting NATO's bombing of Yugoslavia / China / 1999
14   Poster for *01* invitational exhibition, Beijing / Beijing Poster Academy / China / 2001
15   Poster for Alliance Graphique Internationale (AGI) invitational exhibition / AGI / France / 2000
16   Poster celebrating the tenth anniversary of Chen Shaohua's design studio / Chen Shaohua Design /
      China / 2002

Chen Shaohua

13

New version of Humanitarism

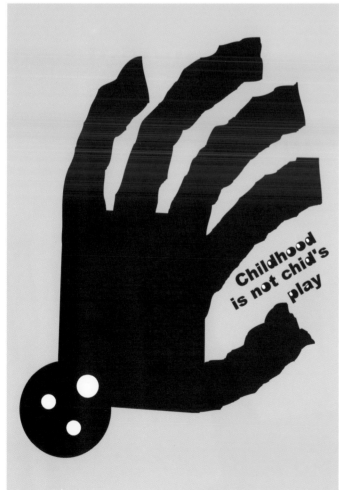

Childhood is not chid's play

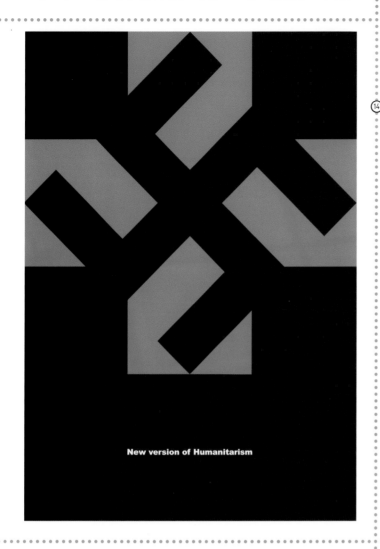

陈绍华设计十年

There is an old saying, "Those who fail to describe what they see cannot possibly express what is in their minds." It is my belief that drawing a picture is the very base of creativity, and, at the same time, through the course of continued drawing, one's individuality is cultivated. In graphic design, however, if one limits one's creative activities to this specific form of expression, one risks being confined to the field of illustration. Despite her talent and initial education as a painter, So Man-yee's creativity knows no such restriction. ●●The graphic worlds So creates are based on the lyricism of pictures and transparent colors. Traditionally, communication in the visual arts aims at an appeal of strength, of boldness. So, by contrast, is a great talent who has developed a unique graphic world through an appeal of depth and softness. ●●Her love of the trade is evident in the delightful tension she subtly instills in her numerous packaging designs, small graphic pieces, and calendars. Her graphic activities, which are supported by her delicate illustration techniques, represent a stone cast gently in today's loud communication world which runs at full speed on a global scale. ●●Shigeo Fukuda●●

1–2   Promotional calendar for paper company / Tai Tak Takeo Fine Paper Co. Ltd. / Hong Kong / 2000
3   Poster to promote the importance of environmental consciousness in the new millennium / Hong Kong Designers Association / Hong Kong / 2000
4   Poster for *Discover Asia International Poster Exhibition* in Taipei / Taiwan Poster Design Association / Taiwan / 2002
5   Poster in celebration of the reunification of Macao with China / Macao Designers Association / China / 1999

So Man-yee

Hong Kong

6 Poster for International Fashion Festival held in Ningbo, China / Ningbo International Fashion Festival Organization / China / 1999

7 Promotional calendar / Tai Tak Takeo Fine Paper Co. Ltd. / Hong Kong / 2002

8-9 Photo album and address book / H+S Gallery / China / 2002 / These items were designed for the gift shop of a traditional Shikumen house, a popular tourist desination in Shanghai.

10 Packaging for Blossom Garden Fine Tea / The Blossom Garden / United Kingdom / 2000

So Man-yee

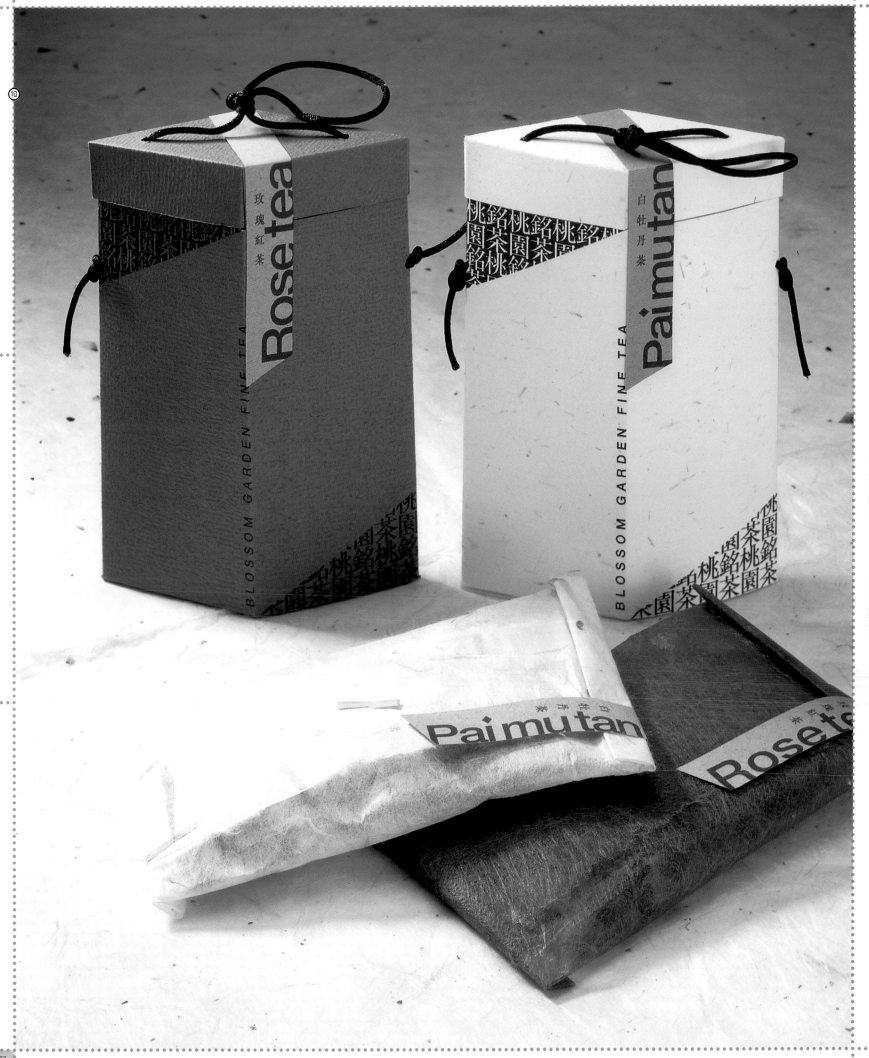

I discovered Leonardo Sonnoli one fine day, because he had discovered me and sent some of his recent work. At the international poster triennial in Toyama, Japan, I came across him again: after the jury decoded his Alphabeto Palindromo, the poster was awarded the silver medal. We finally met in person at a restaurant in Venice eating with Giorgio Camuffo, also a graphic designer, and Sergio Polano, a philosopher and sharp critic of the Italian design scene. The conversation was as inspirational as the food—a revelation! • •Unfortunately you cannot eat Sonnoli's work, but you can admire it. It arises from an unusual intellect seldom found in the world of design. To be raised in "bella Italia," to live and work there, represents a special pleasure ,yet also a commitment, since both Italian graphic designers and Italian universities for communication design have seen better days. • •Sonnoli found international acclaim primarily through his "manifestos." Appropriately, *manifesto* is the Italian word for "poster." Impossible to better convey the communication assignment of a rectangular surface of paper! Sonnoli's posters are indeed manifestos. They are message-conscious, stimulating attacks on our visual perception and understanding of language. • •Sonnoli was born in Trieste, a city that before the First World War was still part of the Austro-Hungarian Empire, equally influenced by German and Italian culture. Demonstratively and relentlessly implementing the influences of twentieth-century German typography, he reflects this particular cultural background in his work. He likes to call this "remixing—like a DJ." Existing typographic concepts, such as Jan Tschichold's *New Typography*, are not just mechanically imitated, but instead cited and rearranged in an original way. • •Sonnoli's passion for experimentation, his enthusiastic love of typography, and, last but not least, his unconventional use of text and image are remarkable. Beyond this, I share his fondness for "black on white." • •Uwe Loesch • •

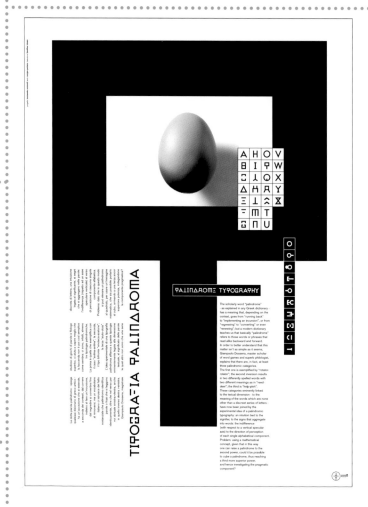

Leonardo Sonnoli

Rimini, Italy

Leonardo Sonnoli

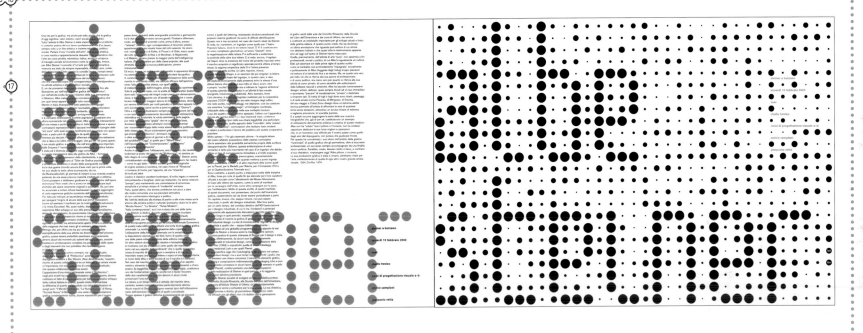

Wri-things periodic table by Dr. Soon Lin

©copyright 2000 by
Dr. Soon Lin's Laboratory
of Wri-things' Research,
University of Flatland

19

Ideas and the ability to think beyond graphic design were two of my self-imposed criteria for the selection of designers for this publication. Jennifer Sterling's strongly held views, together with her design excellence, demand her inclusion as one of the recently emerged designers who will influence the design scene in years to come. Since 1995 she has been the principal of Jennifer Sterling Design in San Fransisco. Her multidisciplinary practice has worked on a wide variety of design projects, including the development of brands, annual reports, publications, software, packaging, and Web sites. She is very willing to move from one design discipline to another. This has led her, more recently, to the development of her own product line.●●In Sterling's work one senses a pragmatic approach of conveying the message to maximum effect. At the same time, her graphic expression and execution are always stylish, contemporary, and appropriate. While she marvels at the diversity of design, she carries a concern that, in the current climate, it is in great danger of devaluation. She believes that graphic design has lost much of its ability to persuade clients to develop long-lasting or highly cherished items. Not the "us wealthy, you not so wealthy" kind, but the variety that could be created in an environment where design partners with smart technology to find wonderful new solutions that enrich our lives at an affordable cost. High ideals indeed. Sterling also believes that the excessive "branding" of items has demanded more accountability of designers. The increased branding has become the "blanding" of graphic design.●●While Sterling is highly idealistic, she is also accountable. Among her numerous achievements, Sterling serves on the San Fransisco Museum of Modern Art's Architecture and Design Accessions board, and in 2000 was invited to become a member of the national registry of "Who's Who in America." In 2000 she was elected to the Alliance Graphique Internationale (AGI). More recently, the San Francisco Museum of Modern Art hosted a three-month solo exhibition of her work. ●●Ken Cato●●

1   Poster for performance by Wim Vandekeybus and Ultima Vez at Yerba Buena gardens / San Francisco Performances / USA / 1999
2   Poster for performance by Eiko and Koma and the Kronos Quartet at Yerba Buena Gardens / San Francisco Performances / USA / 1999
3   Stationery system for Sterling Design featuring microperforations, blind debossing, and stainless-steel business cards / USA / 1996–present
4   Five promotional brochures showcasing the work of Sterling Design enclosed in a metal mesh portfolio case / USA / 1996–present
5   CD packaging, *Trust Me*, by Bhoss / Bhoss and Actionpatch Music / USA / 1998 / A metal bolt holds together the CD and letterpressed, disc-shaped coasters featuring individual song lyrics.
6   Promotional catalogue for work of photographer David Maisel / Maisel Studios / USA / 2001

Jennifer Sterling

San Francisco

7   Poster for American Institute of Graphic Arts (AIGA) "Get out the Vote" campaign to encourage voter
    turnout in 2000 US presidential election / AIGA and Yupo / USA / 2000

8–11 Cover and spreads, *365: AIGA Year in Review* / AIGA / USA / 2001

12   Poster for spring lecture series offered at the Southern California Institute of Architecture (SCI-Arc) /
    SCI-Arc / USA / 1999

Jennifer Sterling

I would like to suggest that, from now on, we call the practice of graphic design "stolking," derived from the surname of my friend and colleague Swip Stolk.●●Why? Over many years, I have seen Stolk work frantically: not to get rich, but to make the "things" that he had in mind. He has designed books, posters, houses, packaging, calendars, and sets—far too much to list. Everything is done with the same dedication to high quality and has substance that lives up to the design. The current project always comes first and always remains above compromise. Stolk dreams graphic design in all colors and formats, eats typography in every conceivable font and size, drinks printing techniques, paper types, and binding. As a "craftsman," he has undertaken much technical research, which prompts many colleagues, when they study his work, to call out, "How on earth did he do that?" In other words, Stolk is not a graphic designer, he *is* graphic design. This attitude has enabled him to put together a sublime portfolio that measures up to the greatest in our profession. In the best of worlds, a graphic designer is a "stolker": A professional who unites passion, vision, skill, and artistry into a form of "visual intelligence."●●On my first visit to Stolk's tiny studio, he was busy with a design that involved lines made from complex curves. He drew the lines—with the aid of templates, a pen, and poster paint—by hand on thin transparent paper. Nothing special at the time, but what took my breath away was the fact that where those lines met, the intersection was completely invisible. My admiration grew when I realized that while his hand was clearly damp, there was not a trace of moisture on the extremely sensitive tracing paper. Most amazing, however, was that this display of technical virtuosity provided only a minor contribution to the stunning overall piece. Wonderful: he was barely twenty years old and already a master.●●It is striking that Stolk maintains very long-term relationships with both the companies he works with (lithographers, printers, etc.) and his clients. His collaboration with art historian and former museum director Frans Haks is one of the most beautiful. Together they put the Groninger Museum in the Netherlands on the map. You can only be grateful for something like that. Swip, you are rightly a "master forever."●●Anthon Beeke●●

1   Entrance tickets for the Groninger Museum (illustration Atelier Mendini) / Groninger Museum / Netherlands / 1995
2   Poster for *Peiling 4–Hollandse Nieuwe!* exhibition (illustration Micha Klein) / Groninger Museum / Netherlands / 1995
3   Corporate identity for Studio Swip Stolk / Studio Swip Stolk / Netherlands / 1998
4   Poster for *Mingei* exhibition / Groninger Museum / Netherlands / 1999
5   Poster for "Week of the Book," a promotional event to encourage reading (with Erwin Olaf) / CNPB / Netherlands / 2000

Swip Stolk

Zaandam, Netherlands

6, 9 Encoded flyer and decoder card as part of the Code-Encode project presented in *Stile* magazine no. 4 / IDlaser / Netherlands / 2002

7 Logo / Stile Magazine / Italy / 2002

8 Logo / Gallery Flatland / Netherlands / 2000 / The logo was made into a poster for the Swip Stolk exhibition *2nd Use* held at the Flatland Gallery, Utrecht.

10–12 Logo and covers, *Dutch Magazine*, nos. 19, 26, and 28 (photography Cometti) / Dutch Magazine / Netherlands and France / 1998–2000

13 Logo and cover, *Chiq–Navigator for Women* magazine no. 1 / Chiq / Netherlands / 1999

Swip Stolk

10

D U T C H

D U T C H

#19
1998

march / april 2000

26

D U T C H

D U T C H

#26
2000

ground zero

Yves Saint Laurent Rive Gauche Homme

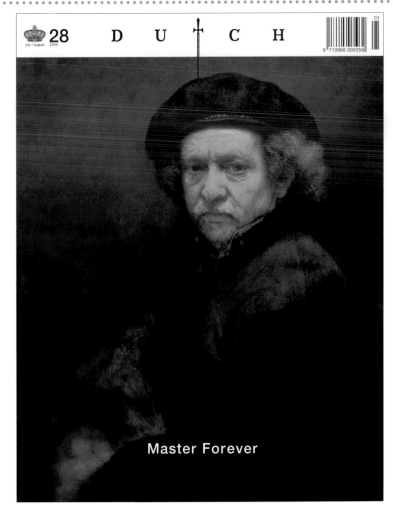

july / august 2000

28

D U C H

03

8 710966 000359

Master Forever

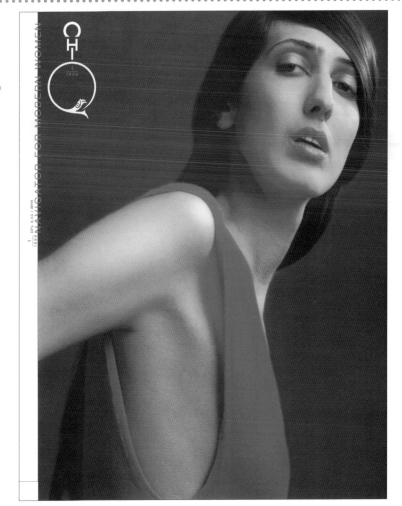

13

CH
Q

A NAVIGATOR FOR MODERN WOMEN

Remo Stoller appears to be of a new breed, a mutation of the canon-ical Swiss designer. When he was a student, the massive wave of new technology distracted his attention from the classic Swiss graphic design heroes and their theories on graphic systems and legibility. Today much of that seems to be popular again under an advanced form, but as Stoller missed out on the original school, he finds it difficult to understand what in these recent years has often been referred to as the neo-Swiss trend. ••His total elimination of typog-raphy makes him even more awkward in the land of the masters. His playful experimentation goes wild on photographic imagery of daily objects and human body parts. Manipulation, subtraction, addition, and crossbreeding are his tools. In his work, he says, "the element of play fits in mostly in the way the fragments are designed. I'm like a gardener starting to grow a plant, influencing its growth by crossing, combining, and putting together, being influenced myself by unex-pected results and shapes. I cut off unliked branches, go back to an older fork, and start again till it seems right to me and growth stops." ••Stoller is a discreet artist, with a rich inner dialogue. His imagina-tion concentrates on creating parallel realms of two-dimensional characters, each with his own role under the spotlight where Stoller is at the same time writer, director, and costume designer. He suggests, "they could be a collection of actors on the stage of an imaginary world, the result of trying to reproduce our world, trying to find structures, constants, and variables, to group things and produce versions. They could be fragments of possible stories or instructions on how to fill up the empty spaces in between, through my imagination. They could be exercise pieces to find out how to give shape to a fantasy without freezing it." Or perhaps a search for an undiscovered realm of life to better understand its terrestrial coun-terpart. ••Stoller knows his work cannot be divided without pain and loss of integrity. "It's not one particular piece. It's their accumu-lation, because in accumulation a piece or fragment creates another fragment again, and a new piece is shaped on a higher level. Every level brings it closer to what I want it to be." ••Omar Vulpinari••

Remo Stoller

Bern

1   Self-commissioned, untitled work / Switzerland / 2003
2   Self-commissioned, untitled work / Switzerland / 1999-2001

Remo Stoller

WILDE
WUNSME
NADEL.
DAS
GEHEIMNIS
DER N
AMENLISEN
DINGE.

Kosta Stratigos tries to be a good man to run into on the street or to deal with in business or personal matters. He will hold the door for you. He will meet his obligations how and when he says he will meet them. He will buy his mother flowers for Valentine's Day and pay her a visit. But his design pieces Scrambler, Dirty Whore Megastore, and The Representatives evidence a craze for rock 'n' roll, consumerism, girls, guns, and gears. "How right you are!" he exclaims. "Growing up and living in the Detroit area, I have been absolutely surrounded and immersed in industry. My father is an engineer and an electrician, so there were always electrical parts and devices all over the house when I was a kid. I guess the fascination begins there. In my practice as a designer now, I approach design as a sort of mechanical problem solving whereby certain elements are needed on a page and my job is to figure out how they fit and work together, like the parts of a machine. Soviet Constructivism has been a big deal to me in that regard....The consumerism piece stems largely from my reluctant relationship with progress and globalization....Now in the U.S., all of these little towns are being slowly absorbed in the suburban sprawl of the larger cities, and locally owned businesses are being driven out by national and international concerns. This upsets me."●● "Play" assumes a very interesting meaning in Stratigos's work. He explains, "My father introduced me to another use of the term 'play' when I was younger. He described the way that the steering wheel on my mother's car could be turned a bit before the wheels themselves would actually turn as the steering wheel having some 'play' in it. As this relates to design and the design process, I find it hugely beneficial to approach any design project with a bit of 'play.' By this I mean that when I start a new project, I think it's great to start working without having every little parameter mapped out and every move planned and every inch of the page designed in my mind. Previously, I've tried to work where I try to plan everything in advance and nothing ever gets done; now I try to just get to work and let the piece take shape on its own."●●For Stratigos, design is a personal playground, a place to indulge and investigate the connections that occur when people interact with one another face to face, the hazards of progress, the power of music, neurosis, and the strange ways that people deal with things.●●Omar Vulpinari●●

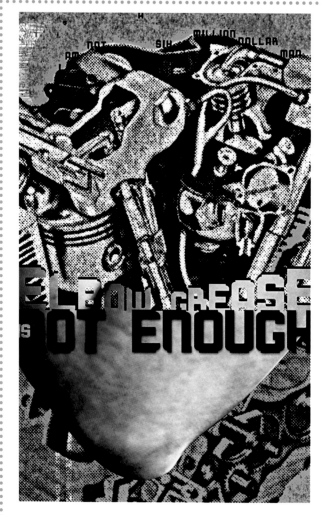

1   Promotional flyer for fashion show and exhibition *Composite* held at the Brooklyn 2000 Gallery, Detroit / Detroit Bitter / USA / 2000
2   Self-commissioned Elbow Grease poster, featuring Kosta Stratigos's typeface Heft / USA / 2000
3–4 Self-commissioned Scrambler and Howard Hughes posters / USA / 2001 / The posters represent an investigation into physical and cerebral lifestyles.

Kosta Stratigos

Detroit, Michigan

TO HAVE A CLOSET FULL OF SUITS INSTEAD OF A DUFFEL BAG AND A PAIR OF BOOTS

INSOMNIA

I will begin my great work this weekend

Did I charge my phone ?

WOULD I SLEEP BETTER AT NIGHT IF I WORKED WITH MY BACK INSTEAD OF MY HEAD

Whose Birthday am I forgetting ?

Did I turn off the lights ?

GEIGER & HUCKABY

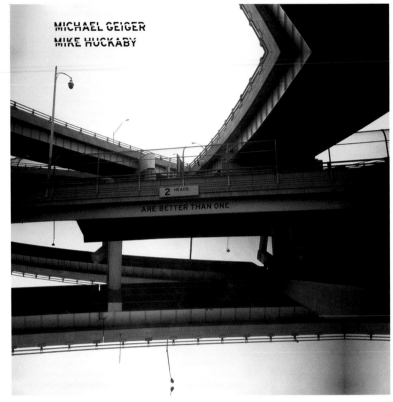

MICHAEL GEIGER
MIKE HUCKABY

2 HEADS

ARE BETTER THAN ONE

LECTURE
WEDNEDAY
MARCH 7
DESALLE
1 2 : 3

FROM THE NEW
INTERMEDIA CENT
HOCHSCHULE FUR
KUNSTE BREMEN,
GERMANY

Kosta Stratigos

5–6   CD covers for self-released house mixes by DJs Michael Geiger and Mike Huckaby / USA / 2003
7   Poster for lecture by Peter Rea at the Cranbrook Academy of Art / Cranbrook Academy of Art / USA / 2001
8   Poster for exhibition *The Representatives* held at the Cranbrook Academy of Art / Katrayna Randall, Moon-joo Lee, and Megan Mcginnis / USA / 2002
9–11   Cover and spreads, *Dirty Whore Megastore* zine / Medialuxe / USA / 2002 / The publication focuses on the death of locally owned businesses in suburban America.

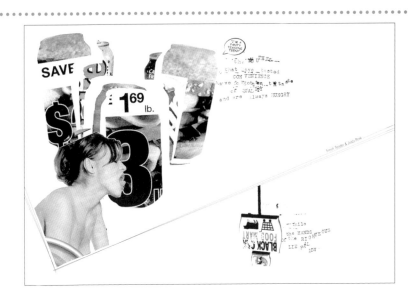

Yuri Surkov—or, as the signature on his works goes, "Suric"—is one of the prophets of Russian graphic design, which is enjoying an unprecedented commercial boom.**The prophet goes his own way. Suric is one of the few who continues to revere design as a demiurgical craft, a mystery. For him, design is labor of the mind, the means to understanding the world. It is the path, the truth, not just an ordinary profession for quirky characters. He wants to work for the glory of life, not for the glory of the client. He knows that the designer who indulges the caprices of a crude client is also raising the level of crudeness in life.**As a result, Suric doesn't have that many works—where do you find a customer whose purpose, like yours, is eternity? That's why a significant part of his posters are limited-edition esoteric investigations, free exercises, experiments for himself. These experiments have become possible thanks to the support of a handful of enthusiasts, such as the Moscow-based printing company LiniaGrafic, which printed collector's editions of a whole series of his posters.**A contemplative attitude in life and ethical priorities in art led Suric, rather organically, to such a burning issue as the environment. The theme permeates his work of recent years. During Soviet times, propaganda posters for protection of the environment, or for world peace, most often invoked a struggle against an outside enemy. Our peace dove was, so to speak, a bird of prey. Suric, on the other hand, sees the enemy within—in the depths of the human conscience and subconscious.**Suric's posters are marked by artistic erudition, by attention to the inner life of words, allowing him to extract unexpected visual effects from a literal foundation. Suric's artistic language has a propensity for minimalism. A minimum of color, a minimum of shape. Constructivist rhythms, actively working with contrasts. In Rodchenko's and Lissitsky's homeland, Suric is one of the very few who can be considered an heir to the Russian Constructivists.**But his is a slightly different type of minimalism, a different type of Constructivism—not so sober and realistic, but rather slightly mystical and virtual. In any case, his approach is different enough for his works to be considered as part of the future, not of the past.**Serge Serov**

1   Poster for international poster exhibition on occasion of Bertolt Brecht's hundredth birthday / Berliner Ensemble and Verband der Grafik-Designer e.V. / Germany / 1998
2   Poster for Moscow Film Festival / IMA Press-Print / Russia / 1992
3   Poster for exhibition on occasion of the Vladimir Mayakovski Festival, Moscow / Academy of Graphic Design / Russia / 2002
4   Poster promoting ecological awareness for the World Wildlife Fund for Nature (WWF) / WWF / Russia / 1995
5   Poster for exhibition celebrating of the fiftieth anniversary of the ending of the "Great Patriotic War" (1941–45), Moscow / Academy of Design / Russia / 1995
6   Poster contribution to exhibition on the importance and preservation of water / Association pour une banque d'images: l'eau pour l'humanité / France / 2000
7   Self-commissioned ecological poster series "Signature" / Russia / 1997

Yuri Surkov

Moscow

Dream Word

Museum on the Seam—for Understanding, Dialogue & Coexistence

Yuri Surkov

8   Poster for international exhibition organized by the Museum on the Seam, Jerusalem / Museum on the Seam / Israel / 2000
9–10 Idea and Form posters for exhibition at the MAR'S Gallery, Moscow / Russia / 2000
11   Self-commissioned poster for exhibition at the Golden Bee V, Moscow International Biennale of Graphic Design / Russia / 2000
12   Self-commissioned Nature Morte poster for the tenth anniversary of the Chernobyl radiation disaster / Russia / 1996

If there's one Dutch designer who deserves to be put on the world map, it's Dick Bruna. His designs and illustrations radiate order, purity, and clarity on all sides. Bruna's telltale style is principally one-dimensional: one typeface, Helvetica; four "proper" colors plus a bit of black for the lines; and a standard page format of 15.5 x 15.5 centimeters. Bruna is a "brand" in the best sense of the word. When I asked him if he had finally finished his illustrated children's charac-ter Miffy—after over a hundred versions of the rabbit—and if it was not time to slaughter the little creature, Bruna answered, "Oh no, there's still development—I'm still simplifying it!"**But I digress—this was to be about Thonik. Thomas Widdershoven and Nikki Gonnissen look a bit like Bruna—in their work, that is. They have appropriated his generic modus operandi. They, too, prefer standardized formats, one typeface (Avenir), and a limited range of colors. But that's where the comparison ends, because Bruna's cuddly simplicity—read and understood by millions of toddlers around the world, mind you!—transforms into a style front in the hands of Thonik, a cheerful cover for a message that tells the passerby exactly what the client wants to communicate.**I first noticed Widdershoven years ago because of the experimental and witty forms he devised for the irregular poetry magazine *De Zingende Zaag* (The Singing Saw). Sometimes packed in cigar boxes with loose pages and funny objects, sometimes a strange printed object—always with a taste of dry poetic humor that often surpassed the quality of the published poems. That dry sense of poetry is characteristic of Thonik, the studio Widdershoven and his partner, Gonnissen, run. Their fearlessness with regard to contro-versy is evident from their explosively orange studio in Amsterdam, designed by cutting-edge Dutch architecture firm MVRDV, which has provoked much dispute. For a younger generation, Thonik is a source of inspiration, which makes them one of the more influential design studios in the Netherlands today.**Anthon Beeke**

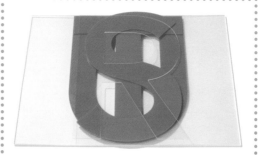

1   Three-dimensional manuscript for Vedute project / Vedute / Netherlands / 2001 / The Vedute project invites designers and architects to express their views on space in a "three-dimensional manuscript" that must fit in a 44 x 32 x 7 centimeter area. Thonik's entry employs the twenty-six letters of the alphabet. All letters are orange, except for those that make up the name of the employed font, Avenir.
2   Poster forming part of campaign for exhibition *Over The Edges* in Ghent / S.M.A.K. / Netherlands / 2000 / The exhibition invited fifty-two artists to create works of art on the street corners of Ghent, the Netherlands.
3   Book, *Apples & Oranges 2001*, a yearbook of graphic design in the Netherlands / BIS Publishers / Netherlands / 2001
4   Book, *Eternally Yours–Visions on Product Endurance* / 010 Publishers / Netherlands / 1997
5   Book, *Thonik–New Dutch Graphic Design*, part of a series of monographs dedicated to young Dutch design groups / BIS Publishers / Netherlands / 2001
6   *Narcisse Tordoir* exhibition catalogue (with De Designpolitie) / Centraal Museum, Utrecht / Netherlands / 1997
7-10 Cover and spreads, *Less+More–Droog Design in Context* / 010 Publishers / Netherlands / 2002

Thonik

Amsterdam

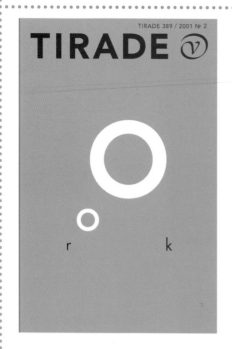

TIRADE 389 / 2001 Nr 2

r   k

TIRADE 390 / 2001 Nr 3

Wat moet ik doen?
het andere ogen lezen?
gevoelens van paniek?
e roerdomp in het riet?

TIRADE 370 / 1997 Nr 4

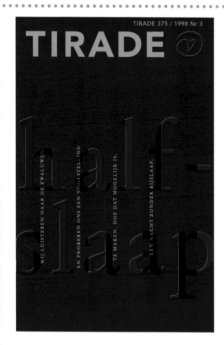

TIRADE 375 / 1998 Nr 3

half-
slaap

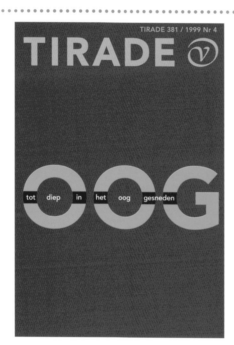

TIRADE 381 / 1999 Nr 4

tot diep in het oog gesneden

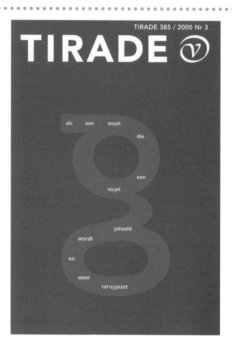

TIRADE 385 / 2000 Nr 3

als   een   vogel
die
geen
vogel
gehaald
wordt
en
weer
teruggezet

Thonik

11–16 Covers for Dutch literary magazine *Tirade*, issues 389, 390, 370, 375, 381, and 385 / Tirade / Netherlands / 1997–2001
17   Identity, exhibition and event posters, invitations, and newspaper / Centraal Museum, Utrecht / Netherlands / 1996–present / In order to increase the overall recognizability of the Centraal Museum's relatively autonomous five collections (old masters, modern art, local city history, costume, and design) a new identity was conceived. This identity program is modified and adapted to accommodate the museum's various events and promotional items.

Among all the fluff that is available out there, it is rare for a design project to touch my heart. TRUE has managed this unlikely and incredibly difficult feat a couple of times.••One is a project that took place within the New York subway. As in most public transport systems, the NY subway has a slew of official signs and stickers to tell you what you should and should not do. TRUE printed up a range of additional stickers imitating the look of the official ones but designed his to be rather more philosophical in content.••The reason they touched me was their location: riding on a train, staring in the air, being bored, looking at but not reading a directional sign, slowly realizing the message is different from the one expected, enjoying the content, happily anticipating others' reactions. I might have been able to come up with an idea like that, but I would have made the content cynical, critical of the mayor's office or the Metropolitan Transit Authority. It is a testament to TRUE's genius to have opted for unfashionable optimism. People I know mentioned that when they saw his "Strive to be Happy" sign, it actually made them feel better.••For the campaign, TRUE met every Wednesday at midnight with fifteen to twenty friends at the same subway stop, and they divided up the different subway lines among them. One group would do the A line, another the F, and so on. Being a true humanitarian he also equipped all of his helpers with fake Transit Authority IDs and even made up fake authorization letters so his friends would not get arrested. None did.••For another piece, he changed the wording of the "Walk/Don't Walk" pedestrian signs at specific sites all over New York. After he was through, the one in front St. Patrick's Cathedral said "Sin" and then started blinking "Repent." On Malcolm X Boulevard in Harlem it said "Strive" and "No Limits."••The power of these urban postings comes directly out of their anonymous, non-corporate heritage. They were produced selflessly, with little but the joy of the process to be gained for TRUE. A Nike logo on those subway stickers would have ruined the entire campaign.••Stefan Sagmeister••

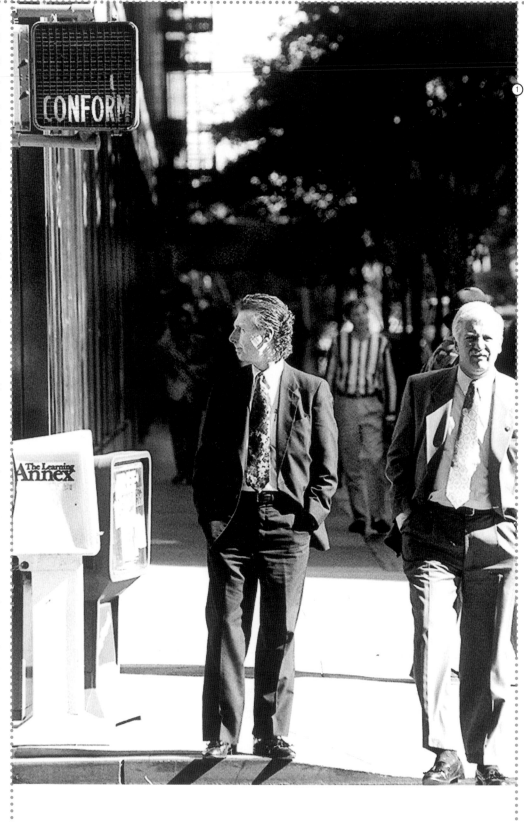

TRUE

New York

1   Self-commissioned Consume/Conform project / USA / 1993 / A pedestrian traffic sign in front of Gap store in midtown Manhattan was altered to read "Consume/Conform" rather than "Walk/Don't Walk."
2   Self-commissioned No Limits/Strive project / USA / 1993 / A pedestrian traffic sign on the corner of Malcolm X and Martin Luther King Jr. Boulevards in Harlem was altered to read "No Limits/Strive."

Life Instructions

| Have fun | Do not hurt people | Do not accept defeat | Strive to be happy |

Please

Do not hold grudges

Karma Conditioned Car
Please watch what you do

VOLUNTEER
Officially Authorized

MTA

SIGNATURE

Riding with despair prohibited

ATTENTION:
This sign has been commissioned by
The Department of Cultural Affairs in cooperation
with the City of New York and The New York Department
of Transportation. To remain until further notice.
DO NOT REMOVE

3–6 Adhesive subway signage created for self-commissioned New York Subway Sticker project / USA / 1994 /
Designed to look like conventional Metropolitan Transit Authority (MTA) signage, these stickers were
applied in subway cars throughout New York.
7 Laminated MTA volunteer card created for participants in the Subway Sticker project as protection against
MTA officials / 1994
8 Sticker created to avoid immediate removal of the new subway signage / 1994
9 Adhesive subway signage created for New York Subway Sticker project / 1994
10–11 TRUE and his friends applying new signage in a New York subway / 1994

TRUE

Keep hopes up

2x4 is a design group. That might sound like an obvious statement but consider for a moment that many other design groups aren't. A group, that is. Instead, many, like Pentagram for instance, are a collection of individuals who remain as separate principals running several groups within one. 2x4, on the other hand, is a studio of creative directors, writers, designers, and programmers who through collaboration claim to have managed "to a certain extent" to "erase personality and expression" from their work. This is not 2x4 riding the backlash against the insular, self-indulgent design that characterized the 1990s. 2x4 wants to be known as much for the organizational process they employ on projects as the fruits that result from them. They want to "make process the product" because this makes collaboration with big companies like Rem Koolhaas's Office of Metropolitan Architecture much easier. "Often our role is laying out the diagram of the project that is often filled in by the other people working alongside us." ● ●2x4 represent a new model for a design group, one where design ideology has been replaced by what they call a "sensibility." On the evidence of their portfolio, this seems to give them a greater elasticity of response to the challenges that their mainly cultural clients place before them. The gamut is wide, from the understated yet simultaneously bold layout of *Charrette* (a book for OMA/MoMA) to the frenetic detail on the covers of the Any book series to the dramatic, kaleidoscopic environmental graphics for both Prada and Vitra. The key to 2x4's approach, their resistance to design dogma, has something to do with the founders' unorthodox paths to becoming graphic designers; Michael Rock via a humanities degree and later as a design critic, Susan Sellers as a cultural critic, and Georgie Stout via furniture design. This background, says Rock, has given them a healthy skepticism that "informs everything we do." The distance they maintain from design prevents it from overshadowing the content they are asked to communicate. And that's fortunate, since they have an enviable list of clients who have interesting things to say. ● ●Nick Bell● ●

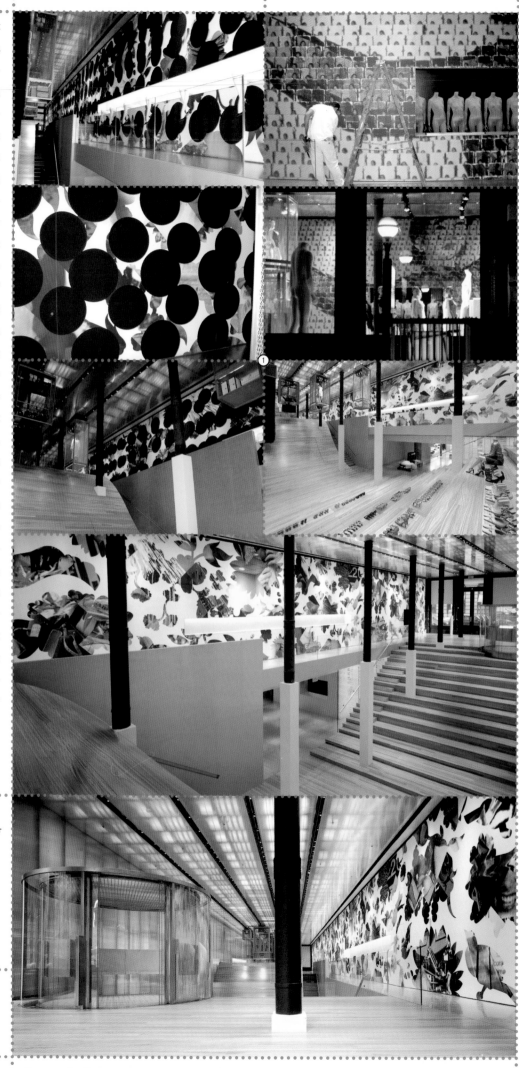

1   Wallpaper designs for Prada boutique in New York / Prada / USA / 2001 / The wall-
     paper is changed every season.
2   Identity system and Mies van der Rohe elevation as part of environmental design for
     the Illinois Institute of Technology McCormick Tribune Building (with the Office of
     Metropolitan Architecture and Petra Blaisse) / Illinois Institute of Technology /
     USA / 2003

2x4

New York

③

④

⑤

⑥

⑦

3–5 Installations in design store Vitra's showroom, Los Angeles / Vitra / Switzerland / 2002
6 Spread, Vitra publication *Workspirit* no. 8 / Vitra / Switzerland / 2003
7 Installation in design store Vitra's showroom, Los Angeles / 2002
8–11 Cover, wraparound jacket and spreads, *Philip Johnson's Glasshouse* / YKK and Tadahiro Yishida / Japan / 1998
12–13 Covers, architectural magazine *Any* no. 18, "Public Fear," and no. 20, "The Virtual House" / Any / USA / 1997
14 Book cover, *Anything* / Any / USA / 2001 / The book documents the "Anything" conference of contemporary architecture and urbanism held in New York, 2000.

2x4

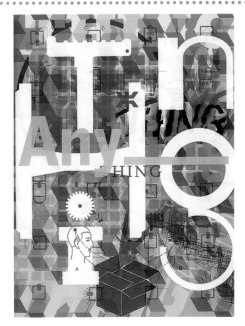

When Yuichi Miyashi and Naoyuki Suzuki cofounded Tycoon Graphics in the early 1990s, they were one of the first graphic-design groups to initiate their own experimental projects on a regular basis. They decided to become graphic authors before the term became ubiquitous. Who could ever forget the photographs of two of their members in the Tokyo subway system dressed up in American football uniforms carrying signs stating, "No more bad design"? ••While you can draw slight connections to Fluxus, Dada, and even Deconstructivism, the work does not seem to be directly influenced by any precedent in design or art. It really does inform itself. From the magically realistic photographic paintings for the Gokujo Hybrid CD cover to the TyGun vending machine, Tycoon often chooses to go down their own individual road.••There is an innocent fun about much of their work, a lovely sincerity that differentiates itself beautifully from all the staid professionalism so prevalent in graphic design today.••Stefan Sagmeister••

Tycoon Graphics

Tokyo

1   Poster contribution to exhibition *VERSUS EXHIBITION 02* at the Parco Museum, Tokyo / Japan / 2002
2–5 Lucky Strike advertising campaign including cigarette packaging, posters, ashtrays, lighters, picture books, and other promotional items / British American Tobacco Japan / Japan / 2002
6   CD packaging, *Gojuko Hybrid*, by Bird / Sony Music Associated Records / Japan / 2002

② ③ ④

⑤ ⑥

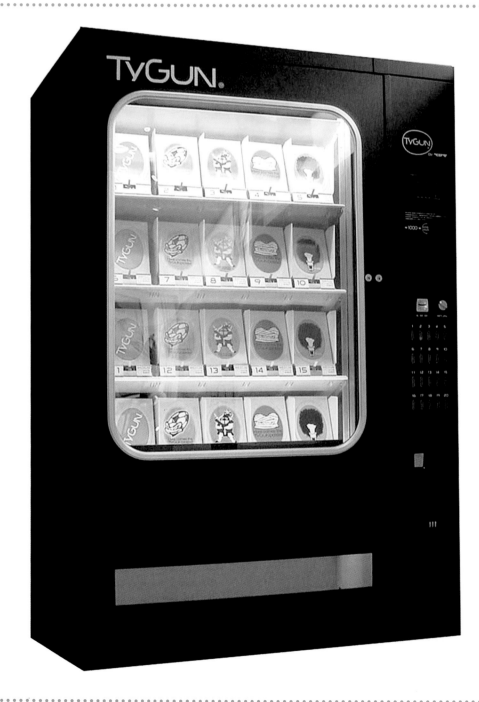

7   Tygun paper bags, book, and vending machine / Tycoon Graphics / Japan / 2002 / Tygun is a brand created by Tycoon Graphics, featuring a group of illustrated comic characters that appear in monthly Tygun publications and on various media such as bags, stickers, and T-shirts. In addition to being distributed at Tokyo cafés and book and record stores, Tygun items are sold through a special vending machine installed in Tokyo's modern-furniture store Daikanyama.

8–10 Print advertisment and posters for the Atehaca Home Appliances Project / Toshiba Corporation and United Arrows / Japan / 2002 / The Atehaca Home Appliances Project, together with the Intentionallies architectural design office, focuses on creating a new line of attractive home appliances that harmonize with Japanese gastronomic culture.

Tycoon Graphics

Design, like pop music (but unlike, say, architecture), is a young person's profession. Many talented professionals create their best, breakthrough work before they are forty and spend the second half of their careers either managing other designers or producing competent but ultimately irrelevant work.●●One of the very few designers who is experimenting at fifty and pushing at all the corners is Rick Valicenti. While it is exhausting to work on the edge for a couple of years, it requires a different kind of stamina altogether to keep going and going for decades: Rick = our very own Energizer bunny.●●His four-letter-word magazine has a forever-changing title (*FINK*, *WANT*, *MYTH*, etc.) and a constant mixture of content you have not experienced before with formal treatments you have not seen before.●●Some animations he developed for trade-show presentations are formally and technically so inventive that I felt sorry they were stuck inside a trade-show screen. You would have hoped for them coming alive at MoMA.●●For a talk in New York organized by the American Institute of Graphic Arts (AIGA), he designed a video in which he asked a woman on a porn Web site to form all the letters of the alphabet with her body. While she was contorting into A, B, and C, he took screen shots and later animated them into one of the freshest and most daring pieces of typography to come along in some time. Large parts of the audience were outraged and left without applauding.●●Stefan Sagmeister●●

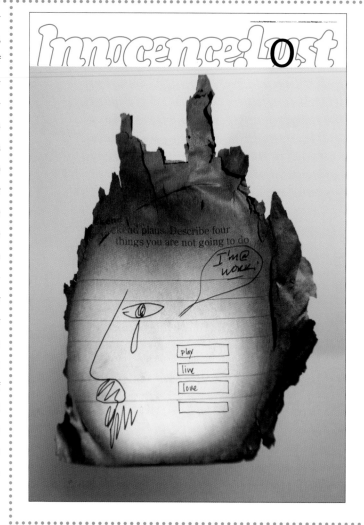

1 Poster introducing font design Oz, by Patrick Giasson / Thirstype / USA / 2000 /
   The font is based on Oswald Cooper's Cooper Font Family.
2 Poster to commemorate the introduction of North Star Printing's eight-color press /
   North Star Printing / USA / 1993
3-4 Spread illustrations from *FINK*, second issue of the "**** (four letter word)"
   magazine series / Thirstype / USA / 1997
5 Poster for lecture series organized by paper manufacturer Gilbert Paper / Gilbert
   Paper / USA / 1994

Rick Valicenti

Chicago

④

Heaven's Gate: America

SEDUCE ME

WONDERBOY

Rick Valicenti

6   Page from press kit for *Ray Gun* and *Bikini* magazines / Ray Gun Publishing / USA / 1998
7   Illustration commenting on sexism for MTV Music Awards catalogue / MTV / USA / 1993
8   Typeface design Handsome (with Brian McMullen) / Thirstype / USA / 2000
9   Logo for teen fashion brand (with Chad Johnston) / Wonderboy / Japan / 2003
10   Illustration for *ESPN The Magazine* (with Matt Dally) / ESPN / USA / 1998
11   Filmstill-based typography Just My Type for AIGA conference in New York (with Gregg Brokaw) / USA / 1999

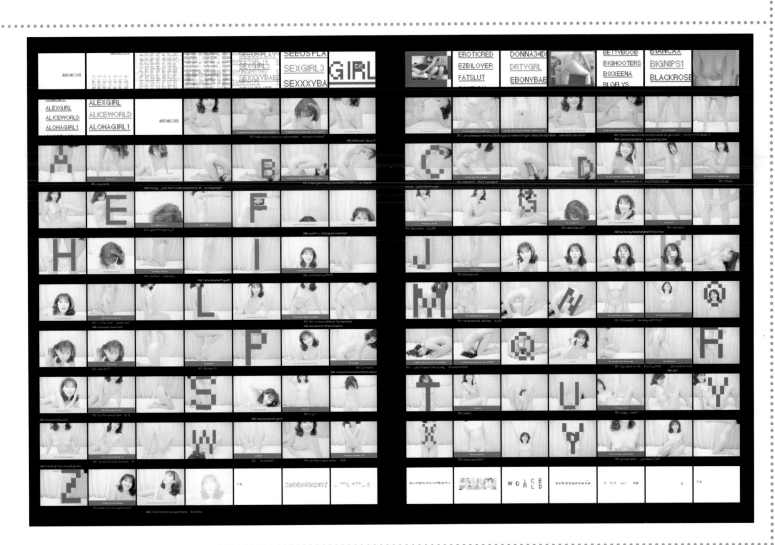

Seemingly few people know Alberto Vieceli's name, but the wonderfully discreet and quiet books he designs keep winning prizes. Vieceli always puts himself completely at the service of his projects, bringing out everything he has to offer in order to provide a book's content with its optimal form. He interprets each assignment carefully, seriously, without encroaching on the subject matter, but with an intuition that speaks volumes.••It might be appropriate to compare Vieceli to an accomplished pastry chef. Not just any pastry chef, of course, and certainly not one who deals with ready-made products. He studied his profession seriously and thoroughly—all the beautiful ingredients, colors, forms, as well as the care and respect for the material. This knowledge allows him to bake beautiful little cakes. These "book cakes" have the advantage that they can be picked up, their texture can be felt, they can be smelled and read over and over again. Vieceli likes variation in his recipes, not in order to create overly rich artifices—he is careful with his use of butter, cream, and sugar—but to approach every project's content with new, subtle flavors. Without much fuss and with an enviable consistency, he seems to imbue one book design after the next with higher blessings.••Vieceli has been collaborating with Tania Prill for more than a year now. Together they have already won several graphic-design competitions, created an award-winning poster, and made an award-winning book. Still waters run deep.••Werner Jeker••

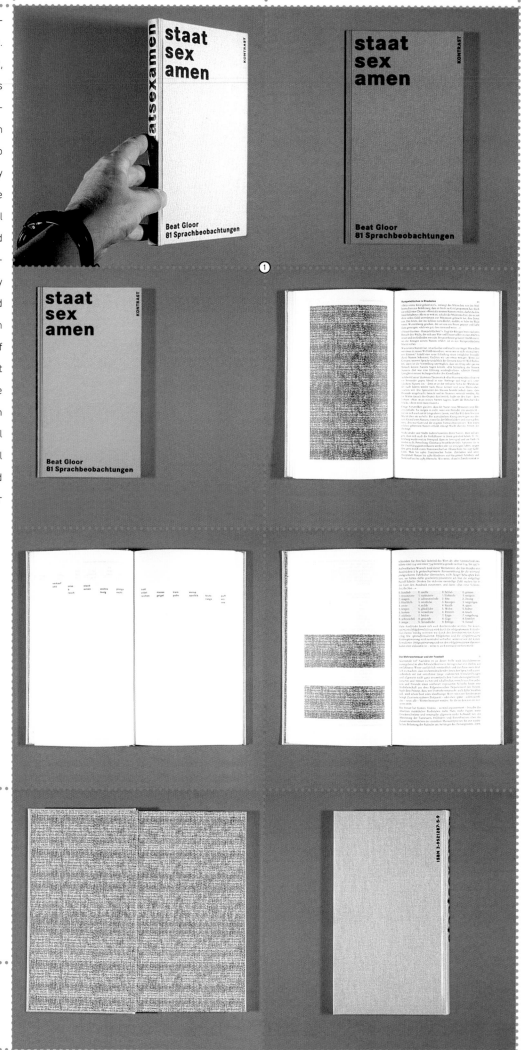

1 Silver, copper, and gold edition covers and spreads, *Staatsexamen–81 Sprachbeobachtungen* (State Examination–81 Linguistic Observations), by Beat Gloor / Kontast Publishing / Switzerland / 1999–2001
2–5 Cover, spreads, and back cover, *Die Tage gehen vorüber und klopfen mir nur noch nachlässig auf die Schulter–365 Tage Buch* (The Days Go By and Pat Me Only Indifferently on the Shoulder–365-Day Book), by Beat Gloor / Kontrast Publishing / Switzerland / 2002
6–9 Back and front cover and spreads, *Khadi–Textile of India*, by Manuel Bauer and Berard Imhasly (with Tania Prill) / Kontrast Publishing / Switzerland / 2002

Alberto Vieceli

Zurich

Alberto Vieceli

Volker Hesse und Stephan Müller führten das kleine Theater Neumarkt zu grossem Erfolg. Es gilt heute als eine der profiliertesten deutschsprachigen Bühnen. Zahlreiche Texte, Bilder und Dokumente aus der Zeit ihrer Direktion in Zürich von 1993–1999 ergeben das überraschende A–Z dieses Almanachs.

Thomas Hürlimann, Ruth Schweikert, Peter Weber, Urs Widmer sowie Kritiker-Innen und MitarbeiterInnen formulieren ihre Sicht auf das Theater Neumarkt.

Sehr gut ✓
CD mit 37 Tondokumenten von der Neumarkt-Bühne
237 Abbildungen in Schwarzweiss und Farbe

ISBN 3-9521287-4-0

Das Beste kommt noch

Theater Neumarkt Zürich

1993–1999

Eine Hinterlassenschaft

KONTRAST

‹Top Dogs›

Theater Neumarkt Zürich

ENTSTEHUNG · HINTERGRÜNDE · MATERIALIEN

ISBN 3-9521287-1-6

KONTRAST

I first met Garth Walker at the annual International Design Indaba in Capetown, South Africa. I had seen his irregular magazine *i-jusi* before and became fascinated by the work he presented at the conference: a series of images of cemeteries and richly decorated graves, set within a context of his own typography and locally inspired visual signals. The work suggested that he is reinventing the craft of graphic design.●●Walker's medium for doing this is the aforementioned magazine *i-jusi*, a publication replete with extraordinary visual and typographic experiments, based on southern Africa's enormous wealth of visual cultures. Often it has published excerpts from Walker's growing collection of images from these cultures, images featuring everything from traditional decorative patterns to hand-lettering on shabby cardboard announcements in townships and rural communities. Walker's work, and that of his colleagues, is streetwise, primitive, and direct but also subtle, intelligent, and visually literate—and definitively South African.●●You can't upset Walker more than by suggesting (as some do) that he, as a white guy, colonializes the cultural heritage of the indigenous black peoples of South Africa. He'll retort, emotionally, "I was born and raised as a South African. This *is* my culture!" He is also an important supporter of young South African typographic designers (both black and white) who show and distribute their work in *i-jusi* and other, often Web-based places. He is a stone in the water over there, making a splash that you hope will result in a new graphic style. Maybe this will happen, despite the enormous pressure in South African design to follow the established Western European and American models.●●Anthon Beeke●●

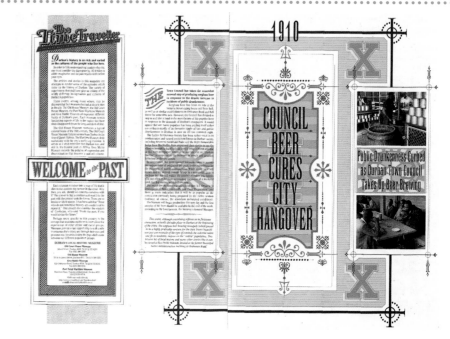

Garth Walker

Durban, South Africa

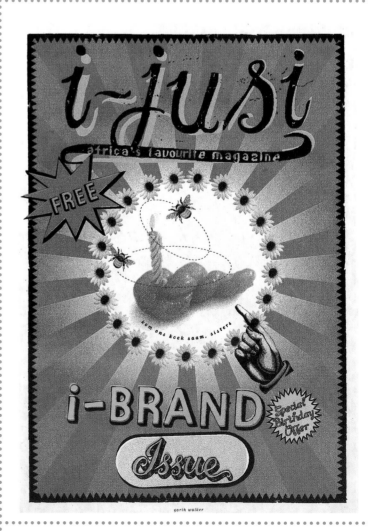

9   Cover, *i-jusi* magazine no. 2, "Durban issue" / Orange Juice Design / South Africa / 2001
10 Cover, *i-jusi* magazine no 12, "Death issue" / Orange Juice Design / South Africa / 2001
11 Cover, *i-jusi* magazine, special "i-Brand" issue celebrating advertising agency Ogilvy & Mather's fiftieth anniversary / Orange Juice Design / South Africa / 2001
12 Spread presenting Winky typeface by Garth Walker, *i-jusi* magazine no. 15, "Porn issue" / Orange Juice Design / South Africa / 2001
13 Spread presenting Vassie Naidoo typeface by Garth Walker, *i-jusi* magazine no. 17, "Typography issue" / Orange Juice Design / South Africa / 2002

Garth Walker

13

Some graphic designers were beginning to think that the conventions of design were constricting their capacity to surprise. There was concern that audiences had become accustomed to codes. Sometimes design itself seemed to be getting in the way. This led many designers to experiment with less designed approaches. Attentions turned toward a nostalgic aesthetic of the everyday that carried comfort in the amateur, the homemade, the uncrafted, and obsolete technology. It was not long, however, before laggards followed the early adopters and this aesthetic—the pinnacle of fashion for a while—had itself become yet another design convention. Although the trend has now blown over, it has left remnants of an austerity that can still be detected while the pendulum swings back the other way.●● Thankfully, comic artist Chris Ware obsesses over unrepentantly luscious forms. Present in his work is much that is now missing in graphic design, probably as a result of his being completely oblivious to the trend mentioned above. If you are a graphic designer and suspect that your medium has lost its facility to engage, take a look at a few pages of *Jimmy Corrigan, The Smartest Kid on Earth* and you'll be left feeling that you're not trying hard enough. Once you've picked yourself up off the floor, consider for a moment what makes these pages so effective. There is the lovingly crafted typography, hand-drawn in a broad range of late-nineteenth- and early-twentieth-century commercial-display styles. There is the quirky yet meticulous illustration style that, as its creator explains, is "more like typography, a mechanical sort of picture lettering." And, of course, there is the wonderfully subtle and sophisticated use of color, the carefully proportioned and controlled page layout, and the studied composition of frames hung off a grid so versatile you would be forgiven for thinking that it was created by the staunchly modernist studio Eight Five Zero. Within the frames, there are stunning changes of scale as we are hurled forward to inspect a detail, held there for several counts, pulled back to view the action in silhouette, shown a plan view, and then, in the next frame, the lights are turned off.●● Ware might be a comic artist, but he demonstrates what graphic design can be...just in case you had forgotten.●● Nick Bell●●

1–2 Comic strips *Building Story* and *Branford Bee*, featured in *The Acme Novelty Library*, by Chris Ware / Fantagraphics Books / USA / 2001–2002
3   Cover, *The Acme Novelty Library* no. 15, by Chris Ware / Fantagraphics Books / USA / 2001
4   Cover, *Untold Tales of Kavalier and Clay*, by Michael Chabon, featured in *McSweeney's* no. 7 / Michael Chabon and McSweeney's Publishing / USA / 2001
5   Exterior signage design for Quimby's bookstore, Chicago / Quimby's / USA / 1997

Chris Ware

Chicago

Chris Ware

Martin Woodtli is perhaps the most accomplished representative of the new design scene in Switzerland, where the joy of the design process (as opposed to monetary reward) seems to determine the direction of the studios. Swiss designers would rather work for small cultural projects to which they are often connected personally than to fall into the trap of large advertising conglomerates. While at first glance this may seem to be a complete break with all traditions of the famed Swiss International Style, the roots of the new generation are still firmly grounded in the world of Brockmann and Bill. • •Woodtli does not subscribe to the silly adage circulated by many of his colleagues about the computer being just a tool; he sees it simply as a process. He is also the only person I know who can actually think with the keyboard. His proficiency in various programs is such that he sketches with the keyboard as quickly and uninhibitedly as with pencil and paper. • •Having worked with many artists within the art market, he has no interest in following them but happily remains in the design world. He considers graphic design a "wonderful medium in which you can create friction within the existing world." To work within that world, to intervene and throw it just slightly out of balance, is his biggest challenge. • •Woodtli is obsessive. He seems to have taken to heart that line from Brian Eno's diary that a good way to create something original is to do something so incredibly painstaking and time-consuming that nobody else bothers. Woodtli notes, "Sixteen-square-foot black paintings made with a very fine (6H) pencil would qualify." Woodtli's black squares manifest themselves in complex typographic plays and manically layered, dense patterns of everyday objects produced in perplexingly exact silk screens. • •After spending a couple of months as an intern in my New York studio, he returned to Switzerland, buried himself in a two-year excess of work, and created a beautifully conceived monograph. He also became the youngest member of Alliance Graphique Internationale (AGI), that most venerable group of the international design establishment. • •I knew I was old when our intern became an AGI member. • •Stefan Sagmeister • •

Martin Woodtli

Zurich

1–3 Informational flyers for contemporary-art event *On The Spot*, Bern / Kiosk and Stadtgalerie Bern / Switzerland / 2000
4 Back and front cover and spreads, *Soda Magazin* no. 11 / Soda Magazin / Switzerland / 1999 / The spreads form part of the Martin Woodtli special feature "Millennium Starter Kit (MSK)."

TRAINIER-KAMMER

KAMPFBAHN

JAHRTAUSENDCODE ****

Martin Woodtli

5   Flyers for various vernissages and exhibitions at the art gallery Kiosk, Bern / Kiosk durch Kunstkanal / Switzerland / 1996–99

6   Demonstrations of the font design WoodtliUnivers / USA / 2001

7   Poster for the font design WoodtliUnivers / USA / 2001

KONTRASTE

DAS SCHNITTPROGRAMM DER WOODTLIUNIVERS GEZEIGT AM BUCH-
STABEN U 「MARTIN WOODTLI ATELIER WOODTLI ZUERICH」
MIT DER WOODTLIUNIVERS HAT DER TYPOGRAPH DIE MOEGLICHKEIT
KONTRASTWIRKUNGEN INNERHALB EINER SCHRIFT ZU ERREICHEN
DAS PROGRAMM ERMOEGLICHT FOLGENDE KONTRASTWIRKUNGEN
MAGER_FETT LINIE_FLAECHE SCHMAL_BREIT HELL_DUNKEL GERADE_KURSIV
STATIK_DYNAMIK

CONTRASTS

THE DESIGN PROGRAMME FOR WOODTLIUNIVERS ILLUSTRATED WITH
REFERENCE TO THE LETTER U 「MARTIN WOODTLI ATELIER WOODTLI
ZURICH」 WOODTLIUNIVERS AFFORDS THE TYPOGRAPHER AN
OPPORTUNITY OF ACHIEVING CONTRASTS WITHIN A SINGLE FAMILY
THE PROGRAMME PROVIDES THE FOLLOWING POSSIBILITIES OF
CONTRAST LIGHT_BOLD LINE_SURFACE NARROW_WIDE LIGHT_DARK
UPRIGHT_ITALIC STATIC_DYNAMIC

There was a time when Michael Worthington's own brand of practice might have led a writer to call him an artist and then launch into some interminable debate about the difference between art and design. Over the last fifteen years graphic-design criticism has learned to deal with designers like Worthington. Receiving commissions from companies and organizations much like any other designer, he is particularly good at finding ways to secrete his own personal voice—be it a judgment on the content he is asked to deliver or, more commonly, the spice of his own aesthetic concerns—into a client's message. His work is conceptually driven, not in compensation for any insecurity with form, but always through joyful experimentation with it. In fact, irrespective of context, his impetus always seems to come from his restless desire to make things. Before starting on the Lyrics project (made possible by a grant from the City of Los Angeles), for instance, he wrote, "I knew I wanted to make something purely typographic."**Worthington is very much a graphic designer and one who wants to forge a new form of graphic-design criticism. "Personal Modernism," his eight-page contribution to the book *Restart*, is a recent example of his critical methodology. Contrary to the journalistic ideal of distance, Worthington is, in his own words, "trying to use design to talk about design" and "to create designs that do what they are talking about." We would all like to see more designers participating in critical debates. "Personal Modernism" is a critique on the style fetish of modernist methods of systematizing, a crutch for so many of us. Worthington does not dismiss modernism for this, but develops a visual argument for ways in which what he calls the "generic" can be personalized. "Stylistic individuality," he writes, "exists within a system consisting of preformed components, only when the concept is thoroughly considered."**In the West, brought about by our desire for economy and convenience, we live in a highly mediated, shrinking world saturated with representation, with fake images of people we supposedly would like to be. Taking refuge in our personal imagination to ponder alternatives could make life a bit more interesting, especially if our personal armory of visual devices, ideas, and approaches were as amazingly rich as Worthington's. His response to all his commissions is specific, beautiful, and original every time. Considering half his studio time is eaten up by teaching, that is quite a feat.**Nick Bell**

1-2 Front and back of inflatable poster for fall lecture series at the Southern California Institute of Architecture (SCI-Arc) / SCI-Arc / USA / 2000
3-5 Back and front covers, *X-TRA* magazine 2, no. 3, "Beauty and Criticism" (illustration Brad Spence); no. 2, "Gardens" (illustration Patrick Nickell); no. 1, "Lost and Found" / X-TRA / USA / 1998-99

Michael Worthington

Los Angeles

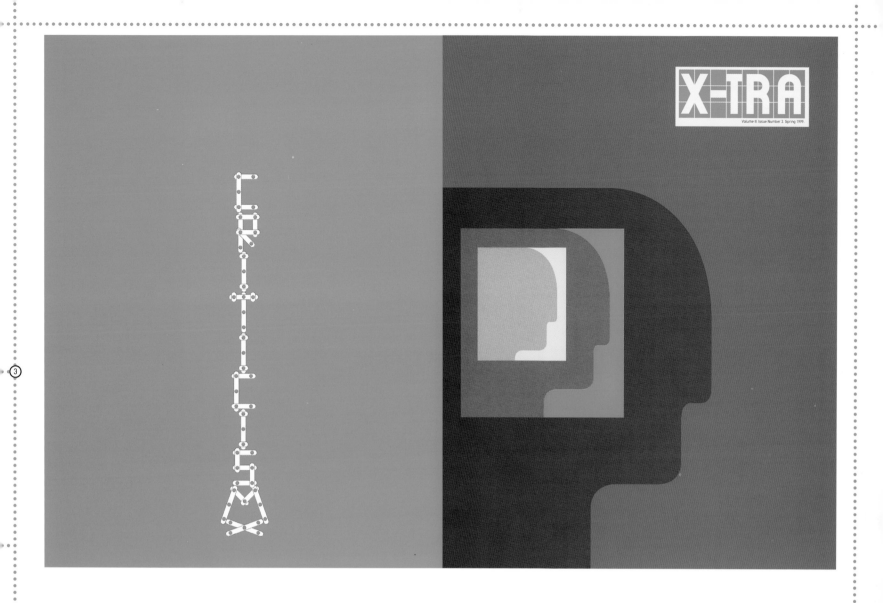

X-TRA

Volume II, Issue Number 3, Spring 1999.

Michael Worthington

6–7 Back and front cover and spread, California Institute of the Arts bulletin (type design Jon Notaro) / California Institute of the Arts / USA / 2001

8 Spread from "Personal Modernism" book feature, *Restart: New Systems in Graphic Design* (type design Lee Schultz) / Thames & Hudson / United Kingdom / 2001

9–11 Posters from Lyrics project for exhibition at the Japanese American National Museum, Los Angeles (made possible by a grant from the City of Los Angeles) / USA / 2002

12–13 Exterior and interior of record sleeve for *Landscape Number 2*, part of the multidisciplinary art project Song Poems (type design Jon Notaro) / USA / 2001

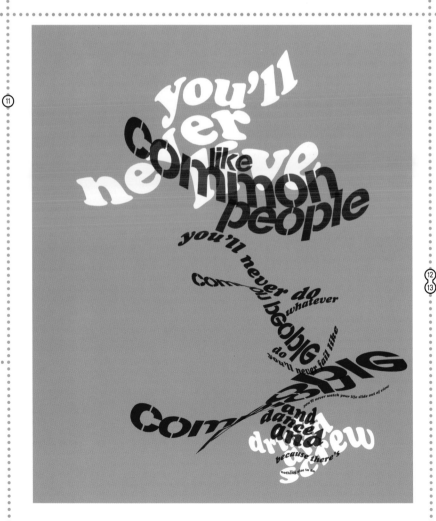

Looking at the works of Chinese designer Wang Xu is like staring at a freshly washed window. Behind it opens a different dimension. It's clean and airy, with lots of transparent light and a steady breeze. Using the stamp of truism, one can say that this is light from the East, wind from the East.●●It seems as if Xu has been offered the highest truth, which God hid from the wise and gave instead to children and people with simple and pure hearts. Those who know him personally will no doubt forever remember that booming silver laughter that reveals his inner harmony and happiness.●●His delicate, elegant works seem very Eastern, Chinese, I would even say ancient Chinese. And at the same time they're absolutely Western, stylish, acutely modern. In them, organic nature stridently joins with the techno-genetic civilization.●●How does the designer achieve such a union? It's a mystery. But I think it is no coincidence that the journal that Xu published, edited, and laid out was called *Design Exchange*. That excellent, oversized magazine was the window to the world for Chinese designers, uniting West and East.●●Spilling from behind the Great Wall of China, which for a long time acted as an iron curtain, Chinese design was the last to join the ranks of world design. It spread quickly, calmly, without fuss. It seems the Chinese, as did the Russians in their time, feel themselves "laborers of the eleventh hour" as in the evangelical parable, workers who appear last on the world stage but stand next to the first, awarded not for merits but by the grace of God. I'm not sure whether the Chinese are aware of the parable, but they hold themselves with undeniable dignity.●●Chinese design succeeds also thanks to its sensitivity to different kinds of breezes and winds, to its openness and readiness for different cultural inflows. With the conviction of "laborers of the eleventh hour," Chinese design reaps where it didn't sow and, as a result, appears as a kind of weathervane of cultural interests in the new epoch—the epoch that chose as its slogan the combination of the uncombinable. When all of this falls on a pure heart, the result turns out organic and harmonious.●●Serge Serov●●

1-3   Spreads, *Artistic Conception Writing* / China Youth Press / China / 2000 / The book is dedicated to the characters of the Chinese alphabet and all of its cultural facets.
4-9   Promotional poster series for the book *Artistic Conception Writing* / China / 2000
10-12 Poster series for *Ambiguity* exhibition and book launch, Beijing (illustration Quan Zi) / Now Design Club / China / 2003

Wang Xu

Beijing/Guangzhou, China

15

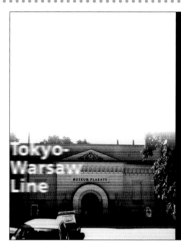

The **1994** edition of the International Poster Biennale in Warsaw has presented a larger number of Japanese graphic artists compared to their Polish counterparts. At the same time the Warsaw Academy of Fine Arts has granted the honoris causa doctorate to Yusaku Kamekura and the National Museum of Poznan has dedicated an important retrospective to the history of the Japanese poster. Meeting with Yusaku Kamekura and Lech Majewski, I ask them the meaning of the encounter between two visual cultures that may appear far apart.

Tokyo-Warsaw Line

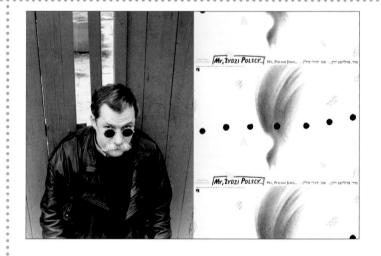

Wang Xu

13–15 Cover and spreads, new edition of *Design Exchange* magazine no. 15 / China Youth Press / China / 2000
16–18 Cover and spreads, new edition of *Design Exchange* magazine no. 12 / China Youth Press / China / 1997
19   Poster for thematic workshop "Water" / Shanghai Graphic Designers Association / China / 2000
20   Poster for *Chinese Character* exhibition, Taipei / Taiwan Poster Design Association / Taiwan / 1995
21   Poster for *Paper* exhibition, Taipei / Taiwan Poster Design Association / Taiwan / 2001
22   Poster for Second International Ink Painting Biennial of Shenzhen / China / 2000

when the
well is dry
we know
the worth
of water

1995
TAIWAN 漢字
IMAGE 庫

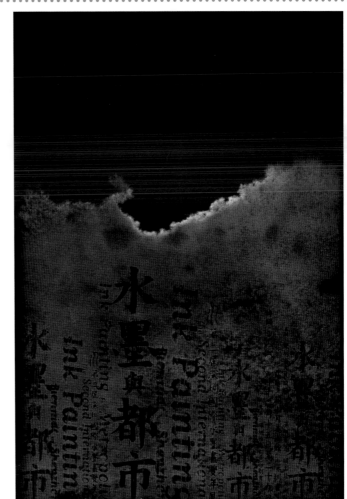

It is always a pleasure to spend time with Catherine Zask—be it in her atelier on the Rue du Faubourg-Saint-Martin in Paris, where her fantastic posters hang from the ceiling, drying like washing in Naples, or at a symposium at the other end of the world, where she never fails to impress the audience with her intelligent typographic experiments.••To truly understand her work, however, one must have seen her dance or watched how she rolls herself a perfect cigarette with great ease. In short, I am a big fan of Zask, her work, her way of being. She is a one-woman show. She is a master of play-fully using letters and words to interpret the world. Some of her work even borders on witchcraft. In the Middle Ages she would have surely been burned at the stake: like every artist, she is independ-ent and free in her work and bound only to herself.••Zask clearly knows how to defend herself with much élan and energy against the superficial premise of graphic design, against the small-minded requirements of the marketing world or even the unimaginative desires of some clients. Her work is the expression of a mentality that is uninterested in decorative sensationalism. Through her generous use of the surface she demonstrates the possesive claim for space that characterizes words. With her sophisticated trimming and cutting of the individual letters she creates a unique sign language. Even the breathing time, the space between the words, is an object of her creativity.••Her current client roster reads like a "who's who" in the administration of intellectual interests in France: L'Hippodrome, scène nationale de Douai, Université de Franche-Comté, Ministère de la Culture, the list goes on and on.••One of her best poster series was awarded the 2002 Grand Prix at the interna-tional poster biennial in Brno, Czech Republic. To everybody's delight, she flew in right away, because parties must be celebrated as and when they occur. À la prochaine, ma chère Catherine!••Uwe Loesch••

1   Poster for play *Macbeth*, by William Shakespeare / L'Hippodrome, scène nationale de Douai / France / 2001
2   Poster for dance performance *Rain*, by Anne Teresa de Keersmaeker / L'Hippodrome, scène nationale de Douai / France / 2001
3   Poster for musical juggling performance *Le chant des balles*, by Rémi Balagué / L'Hippodrome, scène nationale de Douai / France / 2001
4   Poster for play *Tête d'or*, by Paul Claudel / L'Hippodrome, scène nationale de Douai / France / 2001
5   Poster for dance performance *La tribu Iota*, by Francesca Lattuada / L'Hippodrome, scène nationale de Douai / France / 2002
6   Poster for Merce Cunningham Dance Company performance / L'Hippodrome, scène nationale de Douai / France / 2002

Catherine Zask

Paris

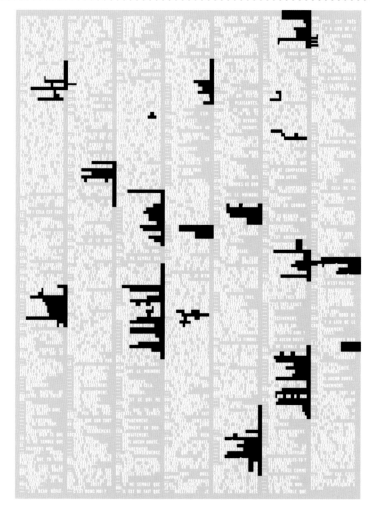

7   Poster for performance by the Philharmonic Orchestra of Strasbourg / L'Hippodrome, scène nationale de
    Douai / France / 2002
8   Poster for play *Platonov*, by Anton Chekhov / L'Hippodrome, scène nationale de Douai / France / 2002
9   Self-commissioned Alcibiade au téléphone poster / France / 2000
10 Spreads from various programs for the Société civile des auteurs multimedia (Scam) / Scam /
    France / 2001–2002

Catherine Zask

032c is a groundbreaking magazine designed, edited, and art directed by the 032c workshop, an "office for creative direction" based in Berlin. The name derives from the Pantone reference for the studio's house color, the only color other than black and white to grace the pages of *032c*. It is a confident editorial approach, understated but honest and direct. The standard of photography is high, as is the quality and relevance of the writing, and even when the subject matter lies in the past, it is somehow relevant to the here and now.••The first three issues of *032c* were tabloid format, printed on newsprint-quality paper, each with more or less the same cover: heavy black sans serif type on a white ground, with a large off-center red square covering almost three quarters of the cover's surface; it is incredibly striking. The tabloid format and inexpensive paper suggest the ephemeral, reflecting the fast-moving nature of contemporary culture, a subject at the heart of *032c*. Issue 4 is a rather different proposition. It has a glossy cover and includes several full-color, full-bleed ads for brands such as Lee jeans and Camper. However, it is a sideways move into the commercial world that hasn't affected the quality of the design or content, nor blunted its subversive edge.••Each issue concerns itself with one "umbrella" theme. Issue 4, for example, asks readers to "Embrace Instability," and if the modern world can be summed up in one word, then instability wouldn't be far from the mark. The themes of earlier issues, such as "Destruction" (issue 2) and "What's Next?" (issue 3), suggest the ethos of *032c*. It communicates the way in which contemporary culture is in a constant state of flux.••*032c* is a document of our times. More specifically, it is a declaration of how a new creative spirit is placing Berlin at the forefront of contemporary culture. Many of the photo stories and essays represent the viewpoints of young Berliners and the new opportunities that are opening up for them. It will be interesting to see where *032c* magazine goes next and how that informs the commercial work of the 032c workshop. If the exceptional standard maintained over their first five issues continues, then there's an awful lot to look forward to. ••Fernando Gutierrez••

1–4 Cover and spreads, *032c*, issue 1, "Professionalism" / 032c / Germany / 2000
5–8 Cover and spreads, *032c*, issue 2, "Destruction" / 032c / Germany / 2001
9–12 Cover and spreads, *032c*, issue 3, "What's Next?" / 032c / Germany / 2001

032c

Berlin

032c

2ND ISSUE "DESTRUCTION", BERLIN SUMMER 2001.
F 1 www.032c.com

032c

3RD ISSUE "WHAT'S NEXT?", BERLIN WINTER 2001/2002
F 1 www.032c.com

RECONSTRUCTION AS DESTRUCTION

THE NATURE OF THINGS

ENDLESS MUTATIONS ON COMPUTERS
UNLEASH MONSTERS: ARCHITECTS ARE
INVENTING AN AESTHETIC FOR THE
BIOTECHNOLOGICAL AGE

BERLIN DESTRO YERS

WE POSED FIVE QUESTIONS TO BERLINERS WHO
ARE BUSY DESTROYING THE IMAGE OF NEW BERLIN
TRUE DESTROYERS. THEY PROVIDE A KALEIDO-
SCOPIC VIEW ON BERLIN BEYOND THE HYPE BY
TALKING ABOUT THEIR JOBS.

THE SEARCHING STAYS WITH YOU

13   Cover and spreads, *032c*, issue 4, "Embrace Instability" / 032c / Germany / 2002

14   Cover and spreads, *032c*, issue 5, "Shanghai Desire" / 032c / Germany / 2003

032c

UNDERCOVER
JUN TAKAHASHI

REFLECTION
By Aileen Hanjiang

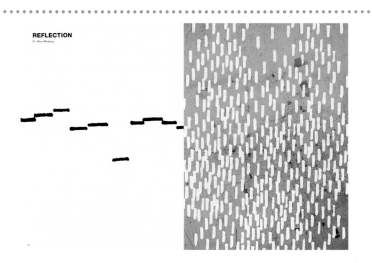

The real estate dilemma

Shanghai citizens who think local apartment prices are disproportionately high compared to their incomes

Shanghai citizens who think the present prices are much higher than they expected

11.2 percent of the households in Shanghai plan to buy an apartment within a year. Of these,
59% would live to buy a new apartment
41% a second-hand one

24.7% plan to pay below 200,000 yuan (about US$ 24,088)
56.1% pay between 200,000 and 400,000 yuan (US$ 48,196)

China's urban self-image

Beijing is traditional, with a long history and strong cultural ambiance
Shanghai is modern, international and fashionable
Guangzhou is open

Residents identified the most symbolic buildings in their cities:
the Great Wall/Beijing, the Oriental Pearl Tower/Shanghai, China International Trust and Investment Co (CITIC) Plaza/Guangzhou

32% of Beijing residents were satisfied with their living conditions
33% of Shanghai residents said they were satisfied with their living conditions
37% of Guangzhou residents consider their living conditions to be mediocre

76% of residents in Beijing love their city
93% in Shanghai
96% in Guangzhou

of Chinese people under the age of 19 have a good impression of Shanghai
of people above the age of 50 prefer Beijing

When asked why they love their own cities, survey respondents gave different reasons:
Beijing: infrastructure and humane environment, harmonious relations between neighbors, and good education for children
Shanghai: power network, children's education
Guangzhou: housing and communications

Shanghai under construction

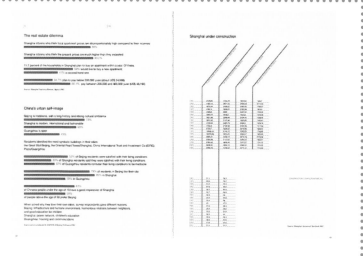

Ms. Viola Zimmermann is a speedy woman, for the pulse of the times races inside her. Her career is full of sophistication, but with just enough edge to keep it from being predictable. She is wide awake and for me something like a "She-J" of the graphic possibilities of everyday life, which, unfortunately, sounds so extremely dry—and inadequate—that I will have to start right at the beginning. ••When it was still customary to spend a career in one single profession, when too many changes of employment were considered a sign of indecision or immaturity, when popular wisdom said that successful people find their place by the age of thirty—already then Zimmermann was working according to her searching, active spirit, hopping from agency to agency, from party to party. ••Since then quite a few things have changed. The commissions she receives have become as diverse as the expectations are high. All this might not seem to be that unique, but someone who, with these opportunities, with this specific set of instruments, manages to create an innovative, beautiful, even intelligent song, sparks something inside of me. Zimmermann's compositions are multitonal and contemporary. Her designs concentrate on the everyday, on all the "designed communications" that life may require. ••Zimmermann got her start with parties and all that they entail: She has built up more than just one trendy music club DJ-ing, cooking, creating posters and flyers, and animating her environment with her serious bravado. Zimmermann is able to bring a project to life, accompany it, and then let it go like few others. ••Today her concerns are taking the new, interesting, and edgy direction of political awareness. She has courage. Nothing is less sexy in our profession than becoming politically active as a designer. Clients want the moldable, happy designer, the clean-cut designer, in short, the polished mirror in which their interests are sure to be perfectly understood and reflected. Clients sometimes forget that independent thinking and responsible action make graphic designers so much more exciting. ••Werner Jeker ••

1-3 Corporate design and informational bulletin for organization Authors of
Switzerland / Autorinnen und Autoren der Schweiz (AdS) / Switzerland / 2002-2003
4-5 Entrance ticket and T-shirt for Zurich drum 'n' bass club SNOT / SNOT /
Switzerland / 1997
6 Skateboard designs / Airflow Skateboards / Switzerland / 2002-2003

Viola Zimmermann

Zurich

Schweizergasse 22
Sonntag ✝ 20-01 h

24. A..

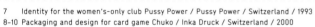

7   Identity for the women's-only club Pussy Power / Pussy Power / Switzerland / 1993
8-10 Packaging and design for card game Chuko / Inka Druck / Switzerland / 2000
11-14 Covers and spreads, *Outlet–Interventionen im Stadtteil VI, Bern Bümpliz* and *Outlet–Interventionen in der
MesseStadt München Riem* / Hochschule für Gestaltung, Kunst und Konservierung (HGKK) / Switzerland /
2002-2003 / The publication accompanies an exchange project between students of the HGKK, Bern, and
the Academy of Fine Arts, Munich, dedicated to artistic interventions in both cities.
15-18 Promotional postcards for short-story and poetry competition organized by Zurich's Department of Public
Transport / Verkersbetrieb Zürich (VBZ) / Switzerland / 2002

Viola Zimmermann

010 design classics

When I was a boy of about sixteen, I went on a holiday to France with a friend of mine. I drove a bike pieced together from a dozen other bicycles, with a three-speed Sturmy Acer gear, two side bags, and a tent. Armed with a huge cap (I didn't have money for sunglasses), I cruised France with my mate, along country roads and through small villages. In every town or village there would be a couple of blind walls, and without exception these walls would be covered with a gigantic painted advertisement. Colorful images, monumental lettering—the kind of brazen sales pitch one wouldn't see in Holland. The most fascinating of those images looked like they were fragments of an even larger whole: mysterious parts of messages that, on these enormous surfaces, contrasted sharply with the expansive landscape. I was so impressed that I started to look out for these strange emblems. I had no idea what they meant. Sometimes you saw only letters—"Saint," or "aël"—other times just a stylized waiter, sometimes a fat, short one, sometimes thin and tall. It completely escaped me. But I did recognize they belonged together. You never got the whole picture, but you knew it was something special. I tried to memorize the parts and imagine how they would fit together, but didn't succeed. Until I came across an enameled announcement, in Paris, that for the first time revealed the complete image: two little waiters, each with a tray held at shoulder height on which sat a stylized glass. On top of that, the brand name: Saint-Raphaël. Three colors—black, red, white—and that characteristic hand-painted French lettering...I thought it was marvelous! I had no idea of the existence of a craft named graphic design or typography, but I was fascinated by these bold, graphic signs in the landscape. I thought it must have something to do with Cubist art—a kind of street version of Picasso, about whom I had read something somewhere. ••I still have an ashtray and a clock at home with that splendid logo of the two waiters and those beautiful letters, but I have never tried the drink. I'm afraid that its taste could spoil the illusion of the image and, with that, the experience of one of the most beautiful and intriguing pieces of public graphics I have ever come across. To this day I don't know who made these superb images, but whoever it may be, he still inspires me. Thank you!

St. Raphaël Quinquina
by Charles Loupot

Anthon Beeke

Transport, a typeface designed by Jock Kinneir and Margaret Calvert, was introduced in 1965 as part of their firm's design program for British road signs. It exists in two weights—Heavy, for use in dark colors on white backgrounds, and Medium, for reversal out of dark backgrounds in light colors—which appear of equal weight when in use. The font's purpose was to remain legible to drivers who were by now traveling at faster speeds on a modern road network. According to a contemporaneous report on roadway signage, signs needed to be "clear at a glance so that the driver's attention is not distracted from the task of driving." That these signs still work and look fresh and modern some forty years later is testament to their logical layout and simple color coding, but especially to their skillfully drawn, thoroughly detailed, "invisible" yet distinctive typeface.●●Transport is a rare example of a typeface that is both functional and humane. By "humane" I mean the letterforms exhibit an aesthetic sensibility that is skeptical of the overrationalized and which therefore tempers the coldness of their inherent structural geometry. Achieving this balance requires highly skilled drawing. Transport is very warm for a sans serif typeface and, as Phil Baines said of it recently, well ahead of its time. Baines wrote, "mainstream typefaces following this 'softer' approach such as Lucida and Meta were not produced until 1985 and 1991 respectively."●●To understand the particular character of Transport's letterforms it helps to compare them with other typefaces. Beside Akzidenz Grotesk, Transport's lowercase letters are narrower yet surprisingly softer and more open. The circular dot over the *i*, the curl at the foot of the *l*, and the curving tail of the *a* lend the font a childlike, youthful, and friendly appearance. Compared with cold Helvetica, it has a monolinear naïveté and makes Helvetica counters look oversize and clumsily attached to their verticals. Interstate (the face for road signs in the U.S. and closest in appearance to Transport) looks self-consciously mannered with its diagonally sliced terminals and tall x-height. The German Din, beside Transport, looks like the result of a dogmatic adherence to a system, ugly and compromised by its predetermined mechanical structure. The design of Transport has captured within it the history of Britain's own diffident courtship of modernism. It reflects how designers in postwar Britain received modernism with a healthy measure of doubt and suspicion, but also diehard conservatism.●● Nevertheless, today in Britain many graphic designers are fascinated by modernism—well, at least by the glittering sheen of functionalism, now that the ideology has been stripped away over the years. Today, functionalism seems merely the adaptation of form to create the *appearance* of purpose as if in compensation for the fact that so much of the information that is thrown at us has no urgent need (unless you are a shareholder benefiting from a company chalking up its quota of media appearances every day on the back of it, that is). Despite that, various intriguing mutations of modernism crop up in my choice of ten graphic-design practices from around the world: personal (Michael Worthington), fictional (Mooren & van der Velden), neutral (Experimental Jetset), skeptical (2x4), and as if it hadn't happened yet (Field Study). All ten understand the difference between purpose and mere function as exemplified here by this choice of design classic.

Transport

by Kinneir Calvert

Nick Bell

There have been numerous works in each generation of graphic design that influence, inspire, and are the beacons of our profession. To choose one is a near-impossible assignment. Thinking back to the beginnings of my career, there were several works that made me pause, assess my own work and understand my shortcomings, and impelled me to more inventive solutions. My choice of real influence, however, comes from a designer I was fortunate to meet in the early 1970s, when the piece in question had already been done. Through this work I discovered that type wasn't simply the vehicle for writing the words. With thought, interpretation, and the craft of typography, words could come to life and impart emotion and meaning way beyond an assembly of letters. ● ● Herb Lubalin was a true master. For me his work throughout the 1960s and 1970s was particularly influential. I could have chosen many of his creations as my favorite piece, but his identity for a never published magazine stands out: it not only states the magazine's name, but graphically interprets the message and enhances its meaning. *Mother & Child* is a simple enough and universally understood concept. When I first saw it, the words leaped off the page. The inspired use of the ampersand as an implied fetus form inserted into the letter *o* spoke fondly and dramatically about the closeness of the relationship. The significance of this work is profound. ● ● In the computer age, when the convenience of technology so often overrides the culture of the typographer's craft, this work serves as a timely reminder that our profession is largely about communication and the designer's obligation to deliver the message in a far more potent way. I also love the work for its simplicity and clarity of message. In stark contrast to the more prevalent overlaid images being generated by many of today's practicing designers, this work delivers instantly. ● ● It was always meant to be. Its ability to communicate across cultures and language barriers justifies its position as an outstanding global work and demands inclusion as one of the best works of any generation. The only hesitation in regard to its selection was the fact that the magazine was never really produced. I have often commented and lamented that the graphic-design profession is all too ready to dispense awards to works that are not, in a sense, real projects. The award shows are full of them. A lot of self-congratulations for what are essentially our own projects. Despite not being published, this work has generated numerous awards and been included in the permanent collection of the Museum of Modern Art. ● ● After struggling to write these inadequate words, ultimately I think the work has to speak for itself. Like all great design, it really doesn't need explanation or justification. It's quite simply "great."

Mother & Child

by Herb Lubalin

Ken Cato

In the 1950s posters and advertisements of superb quality created by American and European designers were introduced to Japan through design and trade magazines and shocked and stimulated the Japanese design field. During this era, organizations such as the Tokyo Art Directors Club and the Foundation of Advertisement and Arts were established, and numerous design magazines were launched. It was a trying period for me, as I, a student, was attempting to express humor in designs, although the prevailing philosophy was to emphasize beauty. ● ● It is then that I came across an article on an exhibition of illustrations for advertising posters by Bernard Villemot and Raymond Savignac held in Paris in 1949. It was quite a shock to me. Most shocking was Savignac's powerfully humorous poster titled Cochon, in which the belly of a hog is sliced into ham. The hog wears an incredibly humorous expression. I told myself that the creative spirit behind this work was the very one I should pursue. ● ● "A design should be as free and interesting as this work": This belief has been the backbone of my creative activities for the past fifty years.

Cochon

by Raymond Savignac

Shigeo Fukuda

When the first issue of *Octavo* was published in 1986, it was way ahead of its time. *The Face* magazine was seen more as the epitome of 1980s editorial design, but for me, everything changed when *Octavo* appeared. If Neville Brody's graphic language for *The Face* reflected the loud, brash, futuristic elements of the 1980s, then *Octavo* provided the perfect antidote. ●●The standard of *Octavo*'s content was incredibly high: the first issue featured essays on Anthony Froshaug, Richard Long, groundbreaking computer-generated type by April Greiman, and a page of monograms belonging to twentieth-century artists and designers. The design, with its subtle visual poetry and attention to detail, reflected the exceptional quality of the content. ●●*Octavo* was designed and published by Eight Five Zero (Simon Johnston, Mark Holt, Michael Burke, and Hamish Muir) as a "serious forum for the discussion of matters, both contemporary and historical, relating to typographic design." *Octavo*'s life span was limited to just eight issues, with a print run of three thousand per issue. Each issue retained the same format but differed in design according to its content. ●●I first found *Octavo* in the library at the London College of Printing, and it really leaped off the shelf. Compared with it, the other publications looked tired and conventional. It presented an elegance and clarity lacking in 1980s editorial design that tended to be quite decorative, ostentatious even. *Octavo* went completely against that trend, referencing the ordered grids and visual vocabularies of European modernist design. The type was exclusively sans serif, while the color palette was restricted to black, gray, red, and white, an approach that gave the content an understated, authoritative tone. It recalled the work of designers such as Anthony Froshaug and made typographers such as Tschichold relevant again, breathing life into figures who had been consigned to the history books. ●●Perhaps the most eye-opening spread from the first issue is the one featuring several quotations from leading typographers/designers such as Tschichold, Froshaug, Weingart, Bill, and Moholy-Nagy. The layout is rational yet animated, and the type is set in a variety of weights of Helvetica in black and gray (with notes in red) on a white ground that has been divided into sections, subtly defined by different varnishes. The use of sans serif typography and large, unbroken areas of white space was incredibly radical. ●●*Octavo* was a breath of fresh air and still stands out as a true design classic.

Octavo Journal of Typography
by Eight Five Zero

Fernando Gutiérrez

Graphic designers are filtering systems with hearts. ● ● They absorb unbelievable quantities of informational particles, sort through them, divide them up, put some in small piles, others in large piles, keep what they want, and dump large quantities back into the primordial soup. Graphic designers store things you and I don't think, don't see, don't hear, smell, and at times don't even feel. Good graphic designers are better people than you and me. Yes. ● ● More important, graphic design is a high-tech regulative force in today's industrialized world. Its visual channels build media empires and influence our way of thinking. Graphic design is an instrument that yields power. ● ● A profession that has such a diverse sphere of action, with fingers in so many pies, must assume a special ethical responsibility.

Political Street Flyers

anonymous

Werner Jeker

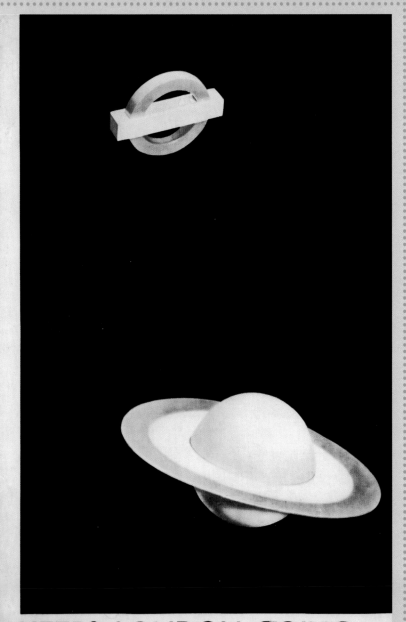

-KEEPS LONDON GOING

The author of my classic lived on another planet. Born in Philadelphia in 1928, he spent his life on both sides of the Atlantic but primarily in Paris. He was one of the all-around geniuses of the twentieth century, the conjurer of Dada, the protagonist of Surrealism. With boundless imagination, he was a master of ironic ambiguity in painting, collage, film, and poetry. Photography in particular owes him many of its decisive creative impulses: With the obsession of an alchemist he invented the Rayogramme, a self-named new form of expression—photography without a camera. ● ● He was also an excellent typographer and a highly talented poster designer, but I only discovered this in 1988 during the legendary Museum of Modern Art exhibition *The Modern Poster* in New York. His Keeps London Going poster from 1932 anticipates nearly all the design principles valid today, some of which I even temporarily believed I had invented myself! ● ● The unconventional use of the poster surface alone is astounding: It is cut on two sides, thereby pointing toward an "event space" outside the picture. The illustrations on the inside are also placed in a rather unexpected way, following the "principle of optical disappointment." The connection between illustration and meaning, between image and text, is unmistakable. The prefixed dash in the subhead prompts the viewer to complete the beginning of the sentence by free association, for example, "The Heavenly Underground —KEEPS LONDON GOING." ● ● The uncovering of a formal relationship between the logo of the London Underground and the representation of the planet Saturn is a stroke of genius. Both images presuppose motion. Their symbolic content opens the gates to a fantasy world that stimulates our imagination with both poetry and irony. The axes of these planet meet outside the format in eternity. ● ● Above all, however, the poster's minimalist use of "sign language" is extremely striking to the eye—even without the text. In this sense, it is a nonverbal poster, timeless in its virtue. Regardless, its designer remains immortal. ● ● Who was this six-letter man?

Keeps London Going

by Man Ray

Uwe Loesch

I picked the *Sticky Fingers* album design for the Rolling Stones by Andy Warhol and Craig Brown for many reasons: First, it uses the album-cover format to its best advantage, a twelve-inch sleeve with an innovative front, back, and inner sleeve—a site-specific design. Second, I admire the obvious trouble the designers, the band, and the record company were willing to go through to affix that actual zipper to the front cover. And it took a lot of determination to keep that zipper in regular production for decades, unlike the "limited edition" designs nowadays that are mostly produced as a promotional item for radio DJs and journalists. ••The zipper wound up scratching other albums in people's record collections, a fact that likely was not part of the concept but worked—not only with the Stones' abrasive bad-boy image of the time, but also with the rough and grating sound of the music. ••This memorable* cover left many questions open: Are these really Mick's jeans, is that actually his body underneath, and most important, will we see his privates when we open that zipper? (Sorry, no.) The fact that the music is thought of by many as the greatest album by the world's greatest rock 'n' roll band did not hurt either. Katherine McCoy's adage that design can never rise above its content is all the more true in the music industry: If the music is crap, the best cover won't make a difference. ••Questions about content are now at the forefront of graphic design. While we were busy in the 1980s talking about layouts and lifestyles, lived through the 1990s discussing readability, layering, and money (!), there is now finally time to think about what we do and for whom we do it. This not only is evident in the enormous impact of the First Things First manifesto, which in 2000 urged designers to redirect their creative efforts away from promoting unfettered consumerism, but is also underlined by luminaries such as Peter Saville bemoaning our "monthly culture" and proclaiming the "crisis of the unnecessary." ••The first sentence in Victor Papanek's influential book *Design for the Real World* is as true today as it was when he wrote it twenty years ago: "In persuading people to buy things they don't need, with money they don't have, in order to impress others that don't care, advertising design is probably the phoniest field in existence today." ••There are people in this book who try to do something about that.

* Not everybody thought this design so memorable. Twenty-five years later my studio designed a CD cover for the Stones. In an initial meeting, Mick Jagger answered my question about his three favorite Stones album covers with "*Exile on Main Street*, *Some Girls*, and *Sticky Fingers*." Charlie Watts leaned over to Jagger and whispered, "What's ON *Sticky Fingers*?" ••"Oh, you know, the one with the zipper, the one that Andy did."

Sticky Fingers

by Andy Warhol + Craig Brown

Stefan Sagmeister

Jazz Festival Willisau

by Niklaus Troxler

Why did I decide to present a series of jazz posters by the Swiss designer Niklaus Troxler as a classic work of international graphic design? There are three reasons. ● ● First, because Troxler works with the fundamental basis of twentieth-century graphic-design language. All his life, only this: the bare outlines, the essence, the distilled dots and lines that make up an expression, form a face. Troxler is in love with pure graphics, with points and lines, and he's unafraid to tell everyone about this love. Decades of visual exploration of expressive possibilities in elementary geometry; precise, functional decisions; subjectivity that accurately hits the target each time: For thirty-five continuous years, Troxler has not only organized the annual jazz festival in his native Willisau, he has also designed the posters for it. The works form a legitimate artistic dissertation, dedicated to the instruction of graphic design. Troxler's minimalism is never boring. What else, it would seem, could one do with a line? But his virtuoso inventiveness is overwhelming. It seems to know no limits. ● ● Second, because Troxler, remaining true to himself, reflects in this series, which encompasses many years, the changing times. Each new work is fresh and timely. Postmodern multilayers and articulation of meaning in the background, qualities that are seemingly the exact opposite of classical design composition, have both organically entered his works. During his first visit to Moscow in 1998, I managed to interview him. "How is this possible?" I asked, about this fusion of modernism and post-modernism. "I don't know," answered the maestro. "I rely more on spontaneity than logic." ● ● Third, and this is the most important reason, I next asked Troxler about what he thought most important in design. "The heart." And then he added, "I only do that which my heart dictates. I never take on a project if my heart is not with it." Swiss precision? We know the watches. Swiss quality? Exactly, Swiss knives. Swiss dependability? Right, the banking. But Swiss tenderness of the heart...Never heard of anything like that before. But what else do Troxler's dazzling posters represent if not genuine cardiograms? Broken, flexible, pulsating lines. His posters are alive with open color and light, radiating energy and purity. Where does it come from, this lightness, this sincerity, this artistry, this absolute organity? Clearly, from a pure heart.

Serge Serov

O

THE FOOL.

Tarot cards arrived from India, from China, or from Spain, where they were introduced by the Arabs. They were imported by the Crusaders, or perhaps they were found in the only book that survived the dispersion of the Egyptian libraries, delivered to our day through the pythagoreans, the agnostics, and the alchemists. The origins of tarot cards are obscure, but what really matters is that the images they carry correspond with the symbols of the cosmogonies and the oldest antique mythologies of all humankind. Their roots lie deep in the timeless collective unconscious. Tarot cards attract me because they tell stories, which is what communication is all about. One tarot figure intrigues me particularly and guided me in my selection of ten designers for this book. That figure is the Fool. I curiously detect that this character personifies the necessary essentials that will influence the creativity and graphic design of the future. The Fool I'm presenting belongs to the set conceived by Arthur Edward Waite, drawn by Pamela Coleman Smith, and published for the first time in London in 1910 by Rider & Co. This set is so open and direct to our contemporary sensibility that it is one of the most popular today. The Fool is central. The Fool is all and none. He is the projector, the director, the screen, and the spectator. He is the beginning, the end, the alpha, and the omega. The Fool is the Salt Man of the Buddhist tradition who wanted to see what the ocean was made of. He dove into it and never emerged again. Contrary to the more conventional card sets that depict the Fool as ugly with a dog or cat or lynx tearing at his trousers and exposing his rump, Waite gives a positive interpretation to the madness of the Fool, expressing clearly his sublime duality of madman and enlightened sage. The Fool, with his one foot over a cliff, reminds me of a famous Zen story: A man walking along a path encountered a tiger. He started running, chased by the tiger. Reaching a cliff, he grasped the root of a wild vine and let himself hang over the edge. The tiger smelled him from above. The man looked down trembling. At the bottom of the drop another tiger was waiting to devour him. Only the vine was holding him. Two mice started nibbling the vine little by little. The man discovered next to him a magnificent strawberry. Clasping the vine with only one hand, with the other hand he picked the strawberry. How sweet it was! At the beginning of the game the Fool is the unconscious conscience, at the end he is the conscious unconsciousness. The controlled madness of Casteneda's Don Juan. The Fool stands on a cliff with one foot over. He is suspended, and he is not aware of it. He is watching the stars and is happy. His head is full of dreams. He is carrying four sacred symbols on his shoulders but does not even know that they are there, nor what they are. They are the jungle, the forest, the garden and the home. Hindu symbols for the four stages of research and truth. Behind him unreachable peaks. The Fool becomes searcher of truth, meditating in isolation from the world that considers him mad and idiotic. His only friend is a joyful little dog that runs alongside him, representing instinct and animal nature. His clothes are green. They recall the mysterious influences of springtime, related to purity, innocence, and the freshness of a new beginning, a new cycle and also play and irresponsibility (April Fools). I am a designer to be a Fool.

The Fool

from a deck of tarot cards

Omar Vulpinari

biographies

Majid Abbasi Born Tehran, Iran, 1965. Lives and works in Tehran education 1992–96 B.A., Graphic Design, Fine Arts Faculty of Tehran University practice 1998–present Web Site Assistant and Web Designer, Iranian Graphic Designers Society (IGDS)••1989–present Art Director, Did Graphics Inc., Tehran••2003 Professor of Graphic Design, Fine Arts Faculty, Tehran University••2002 Member of editorial board of *Neshan* quarterly, Iranian graphic-design magazine••1998 Assistant Professor of Basic Design, Fine Arts Faculty, Tehran University••1986–89 Freelance graphic designer selected projects 2001 Art direction and design, *Graphic Design Iran 1*, Iranian Graphic Designers Society (IGDS), Tehran••2000 Official Web site of Iranian Graphic Designers Society (IGDS), graphiciran.com, Iranian Graphic Designers Society (IGDS), Tehran••1996 Identity and promotional campaign, Behrizan door-handle company, Isfahan, Iran••1996 Campaign for Cheshmak facial tissue, Pars Crepe Company, Tehran••1996 Identity campaign, Yazd Tire Company, Tehran••1995 Identity and packaging design for Varian lubricants, Guilan Oil Refining Company, Tehran selected bibliography 2002 *Graphic Design Iran 1*, Iranian Graphic Designers Society, Tehran••2002 *7th Biennial of Iranian Graphic Designers*, Iranian Graphic Designers Society, Tehran ••2002 "*Graphisme en Iran*," *Création Numérique* magazine, Paris••2002 "*Réveil Iranien*," *Étapes Graphiques* magazine 87, Paris selected exhibitions 2002 18th International Poster Biennale Warsaw, Poster Museum Wilanow, Warsaw••2002 20th International Biennale of Graphic Design Brno••2002 *Un cri persan*, Echirolles Visual Communication Center, Echirolles, France••2000 6th Biennial of Iranian Graphic Designers, Tehran Museum of Contemporary Art, Tehran awards 2000 Advertising and Packaging Design awards, 6th Biennial of Iranian Graphic Designers, Tehran memberships 1998 Iranian Graphic Designers Society (IGDS)

Reza Abedini Born Tehran, Iran, 1967. Lives and works in Tehran education 1987–92 B.A., Painting, Tehran Art University practice 1989–present Freelance graphic designer••2003 Professor for Poster Design, Tehran University••1998–2001 Professor of Printmaking (1998), Graphic Design (1999), and Poster Design (2000–2001), Faculty of Art and Architecture, Azad University••1996–97 Professor of Graphic design & Visual Design, Fine Arts School, Tehran selected projects 2001 Poster for *Wisdom and Philosophy of Art*, Tehran Museum of Contemporary Art••2000 Book design, *A Tale of Dwarfs and Linker*, Nai Publications, Tehran••1999 Book design, Tehran University Press••1999 Mowlana poster, Marc Bloch University, Strasbourg••1993/1995 Posters for 11th & 13th Fajr International Film Festivals (FIFF), FIFF, Tehran selected bibliography 2002 "*Réveil Iranien*," *Étapes Graphiques* magazine 87, Paris••2001 *AutoBioGraphic*, Rouzaneh Publications, Tehran selected exhibitions 2002 Essen Poster Museum, Germany••2002 *Answer?* poster exhibition, Iranian Artists House, Tehran••2002 20th International Biennale of Graphic Design Brno••2002 Korea International Poster Competition, Seoul••2002 *Un cri persan*, Echirolles Visual Communication Center, Echirolles, France awards 1999 Special Award for Creativity, Iranian Graphic Designers Society, Tehran••1999 Poster Award, 6th Biennial of Iranian Graphic Designers, Tehran••1993/1996 Honorary Diploma for best film poster, FIFF, Tehran••1994 Crystal Simorq award for best film, FIFF, Tehran

memberships 2001 Alliance Graphique Internationale (AGI)••1997 Iranian Graphic Designers Society (IGDS)

Aficionado Born Buenos Aires, Argentina, 1977. Lives and works in London education 1997–2000 Graphic Design, Central Saint Martins College of Art and Design, London practice 2002–present Operating under the name Aficionado••2000–present Lecturer, Graphic Design, Central Saint Martins College of Art and Design, London••1998–2002 Partner, Praline, London••2000–2001 Designer, Jannuzzi Smith, London••2000 Intern, Omnific, London selected projects 2003–present *Graphic Magazine*, BIS Publishers, Amsterdam••2003 Civilian™, self-published T-shirt, London••2002 Interactive Surfaces, Harper Mackay Architects, London••2001 *Chat and Business*, by Ikara Colt, Fantastic Plastic Records, London••2001 *The Mobile Effect*, by Sadie Plant, Milk Projects / Motorola, London••2000 Visions de futur, Channel N-4, Barcelona selected bibliography 2002 "Campos' guide to etiquette & modern manners," *Dot dot dot* magazine, Amsterdam••2001–02 *Lab Magazine* 3 and 4, London••2001 *Transmission 002—Utopia*, :phunk, Singapore selected exhibitions 2003 *Graficas Ocultas*, FAD, Barcelona••2002 *Graphic Britain*, Magma Bookshop, London••2002 *The Book Corner*, British Council, London / Milan••1999 *Conversations*, Galeria Visions, Barcelona awards 2000 First Prize, Environmental Design, D&AD, United Kingdom memberships 2000–02 British Design & Art Direction (D&AD)

Kum Nam Baik Born Seoul, Korea, 1948. Lives and works in Seoul education 2000 Ph.D. course work, History of Korean Arts, Dong-Kuk University, Seoul••1992 M.F.A., Advertising & Public Relations, Chung-Ang University, Seoul••1981 M.F.A., Fine Arts, Kyung-Hee University, Seoul••1974 M.F.A., Art , Hong-Ik University, Seoul••1969 B.F.A., Art, Hong-Ik University, Seoul practice 1976–2003 Professor, College of Art, Sungkyunkwan University, Seoul••2002 Member of Design Committee, Metropolitan City of Seoul••2002 Chairman of Executive Committee, Korean International Poster Biennale••1998–2002 Chairman of Design Committee, Korean Organizing Committee for 2002 FIFA World Cup, Korea selected projects 2002 Posters for Gahoe Museum Opening••2002 Posters for Haein-Sa Museum Opening ••2001 Poster, Korean Contemporary Poster Exhibition••2001 Poster, Seoul International Fax Art Exhibition selected bibliography 2002 *Impress Graphic Design Magazine*, Seoul••2002 *Design Net* magazine, Seoul••2001 *Travel & Culture* magazine, Seoul selected exhibitions 2002 Korea International Poster Biennale, Seoul••2002 France International Poster Salon, Paris••2001 Chaumont International Poster Exhibition, Chaumont••2001 International Poster Biennale Warsaw, Poster Museum Wilanow, Warsaw awards 2002 Diploma of Excellence, 6th International Graphic Annual, Stockholm••2001 The Most Innovative Artist Award, 5th International Graphic Annual, Stockholm memberships 2002–03 Member of Special Committee, Visual Information Design Association of Korea, Seoul••2000–2003 Member of Advisory Committee, Korean Society for Experimentation in Contemporary Design, Seoul••1976–2003 Invited artist and member of Jury and Executive Committee, Korean National Design Exhibition

André Baldinger Born Zurich, Switzerland, 1963. Lives and works in Paris and Lausanne education 1994 Postgraduate studies, Visual Communication (specialization typography and type design), Atelier National de Recherche Typographique, Paris••1992 Diploma in Typography, Kunstgewerbeschule Zürich practice 2001–present Guest Professor, Atélier Nationale de Recherche Typographique, Nancy••1995–present Independent graphic designer••1995–present Professor, Faculty of Visual Communication, Graphic Design and Typography, University of Art and Design, Lausanne••1990–1992 Freelance designer for graphic-design agencies such as Eclat, GGK, Aebi and ASGS/BBDO••1988–1990 First coworker of design agency Eclat selected projects 2001 Conception of an interactive typeface for Integral Ruedi Bauer, Paris••1996 Conception and realization of visual identity for winter Olympic candidature of Sion 2006, Switzerland••1997 Design and realization of two stamps for the Swiss Post••1995 Book design, Editions de la Bibliothèque Nationale de France••1995 Redesign and extension of corporate typeface for the Centre Georges Pompidou (in assistance of H.J. Hunziker), Paris••2000 Lettering and mural, Librairie Pacifique, Geneva bibliography 2002 *Étapes Graphiques* 76, Paris••2001 *Type Directors Club Annual 2001*, Nippon Books, Tokyo••2001 *Swiss Typographic Monthly*, Zurich••1999 *1+2 color graphics*, P.I.E Books,Tokyo••1995 *Typographics*, Duncan Baird Publishers, London selected exhibitions 2002 *Toit du Monde*, Centre Culturel Suisse, Paris••2001 *Graphisme(s), 1997–2001*, Bibliothèque Nationale, Paris••2000 17th International Poster Biennale Warsaw, Poster Museum Wilanow••1996 Federal Design Competition, Museum Neuhaus, Biel, Switzerland awards 2001 Tokyo TDC Award (Type Directors Club)••1996 Winner of annual Swiss federal design competition••1993 Postgraduate student grant from French Ministry of Culture memberships 2002 Alliance Graphique Internationale (AGI)

Jop van Bennekom Born Scherpenzeel, Netherlands, 1970. Lives and works in Amsterdam education 1995–97, M.A. Design, Jan van Eyck Akademie, Maastricht••1990–94 Graphic Design, Hogeschool voor de kunsten, Arnhem practice 2001–present Editor/Designer, *BUTT* magazine, Amsterdam••2000–present Editor/Designer *Re-Magazine*, Amsterdam••2000–present Teacher, Graphic Design, Rietveld Academy, Amsterdam••1997–present Freelance graphic designer/art director••2000–2002 Art Director, fashion brand SO by Alexander van Slobbe, Amsterdam••1998–2000 Editor/Designer, *Forum* Magazine, Amsterdam••1998–99 Art Director, *Blvd. Magazine*, Amsterdam selected projects 2003 Exhibition catalogue, *Reality Machines—Mirroring The Everyday in Dutch Design*, NAi Publishers, Rotterdam••2001 Invitations for Droog Design, Amsterdam••2000 Invitations for fashion brand SO by Alexander van Slobbe, Amsterdam selected bibliography 2003 *Graphic Design for the 21st Century*, Taschen, London••2003 *Reality Machines—Mirroring the Everyday in Dutch Design*, exhibition catalogue, NAi Publishers, Rotterdam••2002 "Butt and Kutt, Who's got the crack?," *The Face*, April issue, London••2002 "Re-Magazine," *NRC Handelsblad* newspaper, April 15, Netherlands selected exhibitions 2003 *Magasin*, Marres Gallery, Maastricht••2003 *Reality Machines—Mirroring The Everyday in Dutch Design*, Netherlands Architecture Institute (NAi), Rotterdam••2002 *Commitment*, Las Palmas Gallery, Rotterdam••2001 *Play-Use*, Witte de With, Rotterdam

awards 2003 Charlotte Köhler Prize, Prince Bernhard Foundation, Netherlands••2001 Rotterdam Design Prize, Netherlands••2000 Mercur Award, Art Director of the Year, Netherlands

Andrew Blauvelt Born West Point, New York, USA, 1964. Lives and works in Minneapolis, Minnesota education 1986–88 M.F.A., Design, Cranbrook Academy of Art, Bloomfield Hills, Michigan••1982–86 B.F.A., Visual Communications, Herron School of Art, Indianapolis, Indiana practice 1998–present Design Director, Walker Art Center, Minneapolis, Minnesota••1997–98 Department Head, Associate Professor of Graphic Design, School of Design, North Carolina State University••1996–97 Director of Graduate Studies, Graphic Design, School of Design, North Carolina State University••1995–97 Visiting Lecturer, Design Department, Jan van Eyck Akademie, Maastricht••1991–96 Assistant Professor of Graphic Design, School of Design, North Carolina State University••1995 Designer in Residence, 2D Design Department, Cranbrook Academy of Art, Bloomfield Hills, Michigan••1989–91 Assistant Professor, Visual Communications, Herron School of Art, Indianapolis, Indiana selected projects 2002–05 Media Communications and Wayfinding Program (with Lisa Strausfeld of Pentagram, New York), Walker Art Center, Minneapolis••2001–05 Experience Design Planning (with Steve Dietz and Sarah Schultz), Walker Art Center, Minneapolis••2003 *Strangely Familiar: Design and Everyday Life*, Walker Art Center, Minneapolis••2003 *LOT—EK: Mobile Dwelling Unit*, Distributed Art Publishers, New York••2002 Student Recruitment and Membership Materials, American Institute of Graphic Arts, New York••2001 *The Indexical Archive, 100 Show of Excellence*, American Center for Design, Chicago selected bibliography 2002 *Metropolis Magazine*, January, New York••2000 *Eye* magazine, Spring issue, London••1996 *Typography Now 2*, Booth-Clibborn Editions, London••1994 *Emigre Magazine* 31, Sacramento, California selected exhibitions 2002 *Design Now: Graphics*, Design Museum, London••2001 *100 Show of Excellence*, American Center for Design, Chicago••1997 *Mixing Messages: Graphic Design in Contemporary Culture*, Cooper-Hewitt National Design Museum, Smithsonian Institution, New York••1990 *Cranbrook Design: The New Discourse*, Cranbrook Art Museum, Bloomfield Hills, Michigan; IBM Gallery, New York; Axis Gallery, Tokyo awards 2001 Nominee, Chrysler Award for Design Innovation, Daimler-Chrysler Inc., USA••2001 Nominee, National Design Award, Cooper-Hewitt National Design Museum, USA••2000 Design Distinction Award, *I.D. Magazine*, USA••1995 Young Educator Award, Graphic Design Education Association, USA memberships 1996 American Institute of Graphic Arts (AIGA)••1993 American Center for Design

Blue Source Alice Cowling, born London, United Kingdom, 1971; Simon Earith, born Manchester, United Kingdom, 1973; Andrew Flack, born Bury St. Edmunds, 1971; Seb Marling, born Hull, United Kingdom, 1969; Pete Richardson, born Whitehaven, United Kingdom, 1978; and Mark Tappin, born Exeter, United Kingdom, 1973. Live and work in London practice 1995 Established Blue Source education 1997–2000 (Hons), Graphic Arts, Liverpool School of Art, Liverpool••B.A. 1992–95 B.A. (Hons), Visual Communication Design, Middlesex University, London••1991–94 B.A. (Hons), Visual Communication Design, Middlesex University, London••1990–93 B.A.

(Hons), Fine Art, Bath Academy of Art, Bath selected projects 2002–03 Consultancy and Art Direction, Zakee Shariff Limited, London••2002–03 Brand consultancy including identity design, on-screen graphics, and marketing campaign for launch of music television channel The Amp, BSkyB, London••2002–03 Identity and typography design for Contemporary Art Gallery, Modern Art, London••2001–02 Music packaging and campaign art direction, Chemical Brothers, Virgin Records, London••2000–01 Design and art direction of print advertising campaign, Adidas, Amsterdam selected bibliography 2003 This End Up—Original Approaches To Packaging Design, London••2002 Gas Book 08—Blue Source, Tokyo••2002 Soon—Brands Of Tomorrow, London••2001 Blue Source Special Feature, IDEA magazine, Tokyo selected exhibitions 2001–03 Great Expectations: New British Design Stories, international touring exhibition••2002 Remix: Contemporary Art and Pop Music, Tate Liverpool••1999–2000 Ultravision, touring exhibition organized by the British Council••1996 Jam: Style, Music and Media, Barbican Art Gallery, London awards 2002 Best Design Team, Music Week: Creative and Design Awards, London••2002 Best Visual Effects and Graphic Design, BAFTA: Television Craft Awards, London••2000 Best Design Team, Music Week: Creative and Design Awards, London

Tom Bodkin
Born New York, USA, 1953. Lives and works in New York education 1973 School of Visual Arts, New York••1973 Columbia University, New York••1971–73 Brown University, Providence, Rhode Island practice 2000–present Assistant Managing Editor and Design Director, The New York Times••1987–2000 Design Director, The New York Times••1980–87 Section Art Director, The New York Times••1978–80 Art Director, Us Magazine••1977–78 Designer, CBS Broadcast Group••1974–77 Creative Director, Avant-Garde Media selected exhibitions 2004 New York Times Op-Ed Illustration, Society of Illustrators, New York••2003 Picturing the Times—Eastern European Illustrators at The New York Times, School of Visual Arts, New York••1999 New York Times Magazine, Art Directors Club, New York awards 1988 Design Leadership Award, American Institute of Graphic Arts, New York••2002 Best of Show, Society of News Design, USA••2002 Special Achievement Award for Design in the Public Interest, American Institute of Graphic Arts, New York memberships 1990 Society of Publication Design••1986 Society of News Design••1985 American Institute of Graphic Arts (AIGA)

Günter Karl Bose
Born Debstedt, Wesermünde, Germany, 1951. Lives and works in Berlin and Leipzig education 1970–76 German Studies, Art History, and Politics, University of Freiburg, Germany practice 2000–present lmn-studio, Berlin••1998–present Head of Typography Department, Institute for Book Design, Hochschule für Grafik und Buchkunst, Leipzig••1993–present Professor of Typography, Hochschule für Grafik und Buchkunst, Leipzig••1980–96 Publisher, Brinckmann & Bose, Berlin selected projects 1997–present Posters for Musica Viva, Bayerischer Rundfunk, Munich••1986–present Posters for Literaturhaus Berlin••2002 Posters for Kunststiftung Nordrhein-Westfalen, Düsseldorf••2001 Posters for the Deutsche Oper Berlin••1997–99 Posters for the Oper Leipzig selected bibliography 2002 "German Graphic

Design," IDEA magazine 292, Tokyo••2001 Design 271, Seoul••1998 Typography. Typographie. Typographie, Könemann, Cologne••1997 Lesemaschine. Buchgestaltung im 20. Jahrhundert, Stiftung Buchkunst, Frankfurt selected exhibitions 2003 Summit. The Best Posters at the End of the 20th Century, PAN Kunstforum, Emmerich, Germany••2002 Plakate aus Berlin, Deutsches Plakat Museum, Essen••1997 In Augenhöhe. Günter Karl Bose Graphik Design, Hochschule für Grafik und Buchkunst, Leipzig awards 1999 Bronze Medal, The Most Beautiful Books in the World, Stiftung Buchkunst, Germany••1990–present The 100 Best Posters, German Design Associations AGD/BDG memberships 2000 Alliance Graphique Internationale (AGI)

Mayo Bucher
Born Zurich, Switzerland, 1963. Lives and works in Zurich education 1981–86 Graphic Design, Hochschule für Kunst und Gestaltung Zürich practice 1990 Beginning of collaboration with artist/designer Seraina Feuerstein••1986–present Artist and graphic designer selected projects 2002 Exhibition and poetry performance, Mayo Bucher: OPEN SIGN in progress, Academy of Visual Arts, Leipzig••2002 Art and architecture project BUCH & SCHRIFT (with DGJ architects), Museum Deutsche Bücherei, Leipzig••2000 Facade-design concept for public building in Emmenbrücke, Switzerland••1998 CD design for Keith Jarrett at La Scala, ECM, Munich selected bibliography 2002 Mayo Bucher monograph OPEN SIGN, Lars Müller Publishers / ECM, Munich selected exhibitions 2002 Mayo Bucher: OPEN SIGN in progress, Academy of Visual Arts (HGB), Leipzig••2002 Le nouveau salon des cent, international touring exhibition••1999 ECM: Selected Signs, Gallery of the University of Brighton, UK awards 1994 Federal grant for applied arts, Switzerland••1991 Award of recognition, city and canton of Lucerne memberships 1995–2000 Executive Board, Schweizerischer Werkbund (SWB), Zurich••1998 Alliance Graphique Internationale (AGI)

Vladimir Chaika
Born Kapustin Yar, Astrakhan Region, Russia, 1955. Lives and works in Moscow education 1977–82 Stroganov Higher School of Arts and Crafts, Moscow••1968–72 Art School 1, Moscow practice 1982–present Freelance graphic designer selected projects 1988–present Personal project "HE-story"••2002 Poster for Moscow International Festival of Visual Anthropology••1997 Logo for World Youth Games, Moscow••1991 Logo for International Cultural Collaboration Art-Ark, Moscow selected bibliography 1995 Best Signs and Logo 1990–1995, Linia Graphic Publishers, Moscow••1993 Greatis magazine 3, Moscow••1992 New Russian Design, Rizzoli, New York selected exhibitions 2000 International Biennale of Graphic Design Brno, Czech Republic••2000 Golden Bee Moscow International Biennale of Graphic Design••2000 International Poster Festival, Chaumont, France••1998 Troika: Three Dimensions of Russian Graphic Design, DDD Gallery, Osaka••1997 Solo exhibition as part of IX Colorado International Invitational Poster Exhibition, Lincoln Centre, Fort Collins, USA selected awards 2000 Golden Bee Award, 5th Moscow International Biennale of Graphic Design••1999 Excellence Award, International Exhibition of Graphic Design Zgraf 8, Zagreb, Croatia••1998 Grand Prix, Best Sign national exhibition/competition, Moscow••1997 Second Prize, Football. Culture of the Twentieth

Century international poster exhibition/competition, Pantin, France member-ships 1999 Alliance Graphique Internationale (AGI)••1998 Honorary member, International Biennale of Graphic Design Brno, Czech Republic••1993 International Academy of Graphic Design, Moscow

COMA
Cornelia Blatter, born Aarau, Switzerland, 1960; Marcel Hermans, born Utrecht, Netherlands, 1961. Live and work in Amsterdam and New York education 1986–88 Painting, Yale University School of Art, New Haven, Connecticut (CB)••1986 (summer), Multimedia, Skowhegan School of Painting and Sculpture, Skowhegan, Maine (CB)••1985–90 Graphic Design, Rietveld Academie, School of Art and Design, Amsterdam (MH)••1984–86 Multimedia, School of the Museum of Fine Arts, Boston, Massachusetts (CB)••1980–84 Printing Techniques, Grafische MTS, Amsterdam (MH)••1976–81 Sculpture and Education, Hochschule für Gestaltung und Kunst, Zurich (CB) practice 2002 Guest Lecturers, Minneapolis College of Art and Design, Minneapolis, Minnesota••2000 Guest Lecturers, International Center of Photography, New York••1997 Guest Lecturer, Rhode Island College, Providence (CB)••1996–present Cofounders of COMA interdisciplinary art & design studio••1996 Lecturer, Hoge School voor de Kunsten, Utrecht (MH)••1995 Guest Lecturer, Merz Akademie, Stuttgart, Germany (CB)••1993–95 Guest Lecturer, Merz Akademie, Stuttgart, Germany (MH)••1990–95 Adjunct Lecturer, State University of New York, Purchase (CB)••1989–91 Visiting Assistant Professor, Pratt Institute, New York (CB)••1988–96 Practicing artist (CB)••1986–89 Head Designer, Studio Anthon Beeke, Amsterdam (MH) selected projects 2003 Art Direction, FRAME Magazine, Amsterdam••2003 Book design, Hella Jongerius, by Louise Schouwenburg, Phaidon Press, London and New York••2003 Exhibition design, John M. Johansen, STROOM, The Hague's center for visual arts••2002 Book design, Architectural Laboratories: Greg Lynn & Hani Rashid, NAi Publishers, Rotterdam••2002 Book design, The Hugo Boss Prize 2002, Solomon R. Guggenheim Museum, New York select-ed bibliography 2001 "Coma een open retour Zeeburg-Brooklyn," ITEMS, Amsterdam ••2000 "Topvorm-De Nuchtere Vorm van COMA," Het Parool, Amsterdam••2000 "Speed Reading," I.D. Magazine, New York••1998 Visible, Graphische Sammlung der Schweizerischen Landesbibliothek, Bundesamt für Kultur, Bern selected exhibitions 2002 Roadshow: Dutch Graphic Design, American Institute of Graphic Arts, New York••2001 Designprijs Rotterdam 2001, Museum Boijmans Van Beuningen, Rotterdam••2000 10 Letters from Furka Pass, Sandra Gering Gallery, New York••2001 The Best Dutch Book Design, Stedelijk Museum, Amsterdam awards 2002 AIGA 50 Books/50 Covers, American Institute of Graphic Arts, New York••2001 Nominated for Rotterdam Design Prize, Rotterdam ••2000 I.D. Magazine Design Review winner, New York••2001 The Best Dutch Book Designs of 2000, Stichting De Best Verzorgde Boeken, Amsterdam member-ships 1998 American Institute of Graphic Arts (AIGA)

Das Haus Rüegger + Albisetti
Judith Rüegger, born Solothurn, Switzerland, 1973; Anna Albisetti, born Bern, Switzerland, 1969. Live and work Bern and Zurich education 1991–95 Graphic design, Kantonale Schule für Gestaltung, Biel (JR+AA) practice 1998–present Self-employed graphic designers selected projects 2003 Glückwunsch poster,

Schlachthaus Theater Bern••2002 Poster series for Ja'salâm! festival, Pro Helvetia, Bern••2001–02 Poster series "aus 1 mach 3," Schlachthaus Theater Bern••2000–2001 Poster series "Gruppenbild," Schlachthaus Theater Bern••1998–99 Poster series "Unikate," Schlachthaus Theater Bern••1998–99 Poster series "Kürzest-Dialoge," Schlachthaus Theater Bern selected bibliography 2000 Benzin—Young Swiss Graphic Design, Lars Müller Publishers, Baden, Switzerland•• 1999 Trigger, Die Gestalten Verlag, Berlin

De Designpolitie
Richard van der Laken, born Amstelveen, Netherlands, 1970; Pepijn Zurburg, born Amsterdam, Netherlands, 1971; Alexander Clay, born Lørenskog, Norway, 1974; Karin van den Brandt, born Blerick, Netherlands, 1975; Roel Stavorinus, born Zwolle, Netherlands, 1971; Gaelle Rivet, born Laval, France, 1972. Live and work in Amsterdam education 1997–2000 Dance education, Arnhem school of the Arts, Arnhem (GR)••1996–97 Postgraduate studies, Graphic Design, Sandberg Institute, Amsterdam (RvdL+PZ)••1996–2000 Graphic Design, Arnhem school of the Arts, Arnhem (KvdB+AC)••1995–96 Communication Management, Utrecht University, Utrecht (RS)••1992–96 Commercial and Presentation Techniques, St. Lucas, Boxtel (KvdB)••1993–95 Graphic Design School, Oslo (AC)••1991–95 Design and Communication, Ichthus College, Rotterdam (RS)••1989–95 Graphic Design, Utrecht School of the Arts, Utrecht (RvdL+PZ) practice 2002–present Project Manager, De Designpolitie (RS)••2001–present Graphic Designer, De Designpolitie (KvdB)••2001–present Office Manager, De Designpolitie (GR)••2000–present Graphic Designer, De Designpolitie (AC)•• 1995–present Founder and Graphic Designer, De Designpolitie (RvdL+PZ)••1999–2002 Project Manager, Funcke designers (RS) ••1998–99 Communication Adviser, Informatiebeheergroep, Netherlands (RS) ••1998–99 Teacher, Graphic Design, Academy St. Joost, Breda (RvdL)••1997–98 Teacher, Graphic Design, Utrecht School of the Arts (RvdL)••1996–98 Marketing Coordinator, Wolters-Noordhoff publishers (RS)••1996–97 Teacher, Graphic Design, Arnhem school of the Arts (RvdL) selected projects 2002–present Illustrations for De Volkskrant newspaper, Amsterdam••2001 Social annual report, KPN Telecom, The Hague••2000 Corporate identity, Novib, Oxfam Netherlands, The Hague••1995–2000 Art direction, MillenniuM magazine, Amsterdam••1998 Annual report, Raad van Cultuur, The Hague••1997–98 Art direction, Blvd. Magazine, Amsterdam selected bibliography 2001 New Design: Amster-dam, Rockport, Gloucester, Massachusetts••2001 Apples & Oranges: Best Dutch Graphic Design, BIS Publishers, Amsterdam selected exhibitions 2000 18th International Biennale of Graphic Design Brno, Czech Republic••1999 Mooi maar Goed, Stedelijk Museum, Amsterdam••1998 Do Normal, San Francisco Museum of Modern Art awards 2003 Nominations, Dutch Art Directors Club, Netherlands ••1999 Selection, Rotterdam Design Prize, Rotterdam••1998 Dutch Art Directors Club Award, Netherlands••1997 Selection, Best Book Design, Netherlands mem-berships 1995–present Dutch Designers Association (BNO)••1998–2002 Art Directors Club Netherlands (ADCN)

Delaware
Masato Samata, born Gunma, Japan, 1959; Aya Honda, born Kanagawa, Japan, 1969; Morihiro Tajiri, born Kumamoto, Japan, 1970; Yoshiki Watanabe, born Tokyo, Japan, 1972. Live and work in Tokyo education Self-educated

practice 1993–present Graphic-design and music group Delaware **selected projects** 2003 Graphic design and music for Pitti Uomo Trade Fair, Florence••2001 Music for e-Kawasemi television commercial, Tokyo••1998 Audio-visual live show for Mac Expo '98, Japan••1996 Music and motion graphics for Iwata-ya television commercial, Fukuoka, Japan **selected bibliography** 2002 *The Face* magazine 68, London••2001 Fourth CD, *Artoon*••2001 *IDEA* magazine 285, Tokyo••1999 Third CD, *with the delaware*••1997 Second CD and CD-ROM, *Surfin' USSR*••1996 First CD, *Private CD* **selected exhibitions** 2002 *JaPan Graphics*, FAD Convent Dels Angeles, Barcelona••2002 *Motion Graphic Art*, Wild Cat Gallery, London••2001 *Mobile Gallery*, Japanese mobile phone web••2001 *Artoon at P.S. 1*, P.S. 1 Contemporary Art Center, New York

Chris Dixon
Born Regina, Saskatchewan, Canada, 1968. Lives and works in New York **education** 1993–96 Communication Design, Emily Carr Institute, Vancouver, Canada••1990–93 Psychology, University of Saskatchewan, Canada **practice** 2002–present Art Director, Studio Plural, New York••2002–03 Design faculty, New York University••2002–03 Design faculty, Parsons School of Design, New York••2000–2002 Editorial Designer, *New York Times Magazine*••1996–2000 Art Director, *Adbusters* magazine **selected projects** 2002 Book cover, *Women at The Intersection*, Rutgers University, New York••2002 In-house magazine *rd*, RD/Microsoft, Seattle••2002 *Financial Times* special anniversary issue, Financial Times, U.S. Edition, New York••2000 Poster to launch First Things First 2000 manifesto, The Media Foundation, Vancouver **selected bibliography** 2002 *Eye* magazine, London••2001 *Azure* magazine, Toronto••2001 *Digital Lab–Editorial Design*, Rotovision, London••2001 *Issues: New Magazine Design*, Ginko Press, California••1999 *Emigre Magazine* 49, Sacramento, California **selected exhibitions** 2001 *Young Guns New York*, Art Directors Club, New York••2000 Society of Publication Design Exhibit, Parsons School of Design, New York **awards** 2000 Gold medal, Magazine of the Year, National Magazine Awards, Canada••2000 Selected, 100 Show Award, American Center for Design, Chicago••2000 Gold Medal, Judges Choice Award, Graphex: Society of Graphic Designers of Canada••1999 Magazine of the Year finalist, Society of Publication Design, USA **memberships** 2002 Board member, American Institute of Graphic Arts (AIGA), New York

Daniel Eatock/Foundation 33
Born Manchester, United Kingdom, 1975. Lives and works in London **education** 1996–98 M.A., Graphic Design, Royal College of Art, London••1993–96 B.A., Communication Design, Ravensbourne College of Design and Communication, London **practice** 2001–present Lecturer, Graphic Design, University of Brighton••2000–present Cofounder and Graphic-Design Director, Foundation 33 (Foundation 33 is Sam Solhaug, Architectural-Design Director, Hanna Werning, Graphic Designer, Sara de Bondt, Graphic Designer)••1998–99 Graphic Design Intern, Walker Art Center, Minneapolis **selected projects** 2001–03 Self-commissioned Sun Light photographs/postcards••2002 *Big Brother* identity, Channel 4, London••2001 MOBO 96 sheet billboard, Channel 4, London••2002 The world's largest signed and numbered limited edition artwork, Channel 4, London••2000 Self-commissioned Untitled Beatles

poster **selected bibliography** 2003 *The New Handmade Graphics, Beyond Digital Design*, Rotovision, London••2002 *GB: Graphic Britain*, Laurence King Publishing, London••2002 *No Brief, Graphic Designers' Personal Projects*, Rotovision, London••2001 *Specials*, Booth-Clibborn Editions, London **selected exhibitions** 2002 *Infotecture*, Artist Space, New York••2001 *Design Now: London*, Design Museum, London••2001 *16.8/10.2/8.4*, Pentagram Gallery, London••1998 *Creative Review Creative Futures*, Kings Cross Gallery, London **awards** 2000 *I.D. Magazine* Award, Top Forty Designers Under Thirty••1998–1999 100 Show Award, American Center for Design, Chicago••1997 Energy Efficiency Award, first prize, Royal College of Art, London

Eboy
Kai Vermehr, born Caracas, Venezuela, 1964; Steffen Sauerteig, born Prenzlau, Germany, 1967; Peter Stemmler, born Berlin, Gemany, 1966; Svend Smital, born Berlin, Germany, 1967. Live and work in Berlin and New York **education** Kunsthochschule Berlin (PS)••Hochschule der Künste Berlin (SS+SS) **practice** 1995–present Freelance designers••1998 Founded eboy **selected projects** 2002 Book *eboy hello*, by eboy, Laurence King Publishing, London **selected bibliography** 2000 *72 dpi*, Die Gestalten Verlag, Berlin••2000 *The Face* magazine 36, London••1999 *Reload*, Laurence King Publishing, London••1999 *Trigger*, Die Gestalten Verlag, Berlin••1998 *IMS 100*, Auras, Tokyo **selected exhibitions** 2002 *eboy hello*, Magma Books, London••2002 *I love to meet you*, Palazzo Fortuny, Venice

Dave Eggers
Born Boston, Massachusetts, USA, 1970. Lives and works in San Francisco **education** 1988–92, Journalism/Painting, University of Illinois, Champaign-Urbana **practice** 2003–present Art Director, *The Believer* magazine, Brooklin, Maine••2002–present Founder/Teacher, 826 Valencia, San Francisco••1998–present Founder/Editor/Designer, *McSweeney's*, New York and San Francisco••1998 Editor at Large, *Esquire* magazine, New York••1993–1997 Founder/Designer, Gigantic Design, San Francisco••1994–1997 Founder/Editor/Designer, *Might* magazine, San Francisco **selected projects** 2002 Vinyl design, *The Only Blip Hop Record You Will Ever Need* vol. 1, Luka Bop, USA••2001 Book design, *The New Sins*, by David Byrne, McSweeney's Publishing, San Francisco••1998–present Design/editorial, *McSweeney's* literary journal, New York and San Francisco **selected bibliography** 2002 Editor, *The Best American Nonrequired Reading*, Houghton-Mifflin, Boston••2002 *You Shall Know Our Velocity*, by Dave Eggers, McSweeney's Books, San Francisco••2000 *A Heartbreaking Work of Staggering Genius*, by Dave Eggers, Simon & Schuster, New York••1998 Editor, *Shiny Adidas Tracksuits and the Death of Camp*, Penguin/Putnam, New York **selected exhibitions** 2003 National Design Triennial, Smithsonian Cooper-Hewitt National Design Museum, New York **awards** 2002 50 Books Award/365 Illustration Award, American Institute of Graphic Arts••2002 *Print* Design Regional Award, USA

Jonathan Ellery
Born Welwyn Garden City, United Kingdom, 1964. Lives and works in London **education** 1982–84 Falmouth College of Arts & Design••1986–89 Bournemouth and Poole College of Art & Design **practice**

1998–present Founding Partner, Browns, London••1989–98 Sampson Tyrrell, Addison, Design House, London **selected projects** 1999 Pure Football. Pure Hope. poster campaign, FIFA/UNICEF••2000 European Clichés poster campaign, Trebruk, United Kingdom••2001 Coney Island poster campaign, Trebruk, United Kingdom••2002 Crash Happy exhibition poster, Grant Scott, London **selected bibliography** 2003 *Browns: A Walk Through Books*, GCE Publishing, London••1999–2002 D&AD Annuals••2002 *No Brief: Graphic Designers Personal Projects*, RotoVision, London••2002 *Branding: From Brief to Finish Solution*, RotoVision, London••2002 *100 Graphics International*, Graphics International, London••2001 *Graphis Design Annual*, *Graphis* magazine, New York **awards** 2002 Best Annual Report, Investor Relations Awards, London••2002 Silver Nomination: Poster Campaign, D&AD, London••2002 Graphic Design: Posters, Crafts, and Corporate Identity, D&AD, London••2002 Merit Award, Art Directors Club, New York••2000 Best Business to Business Advertising Campaign, Marketing Week Advertising Excellence Awards, United Kingdom **memberships** 1995–present D&AD, London••1998–2000 The Typographic Circle, London

Experimental Jetset
Erwin Brinkers, born Rotterdam, Netherlands, 1973; Danny van den Dungen, born Rotterdam, Netherlands, 1971; Marieke Stolk, born Amsterdam, Netherlands, 1967. Live and work in Amsterdam **education** 1993–97 Graphic design, Gerrit Rietveld Academy, Amsterdam **practice** 1997–present Experimental Jetset•• 2000–present Teachers, Graphic Design, Gerrit Rietveld Academy••2001–03 Lectures/workshops at Fabrica, Italy, CCS Detroit Art Academy, University of Western Michigan, and GraficEurope, Barcelona **selected projects** 2002 Catalogue and exhibition design, *Display*, Stedelijk Museum, Amsterdam••2002 Christmas stamps "DecemberThoughts," Royal Dutch Mail (PTT/TPG), The Hague••2001 Guest-editing and graphic design, "Lost Formats Preservation Society," *Emigre Magazine* 57, Sacramento••2000 Catalogue for group exhibition *Elysian Fields*, Centre Georges Pompidou/Purple Institute, Paris••2000 Set of three plastic wristbands "Been There/Done That," Purple Institute, Paris••1999 Stamps "I Love Stamps/Stamps Love Me," Royal Dutch Mail (PTT/TPG), The Hague **selected exhibitions** 2002 Solo exhibition *Kelly 1:1*, Casco Gallery, Utrecht••1999 Installation *Modular Meaning*, group exhibition *AEX*, Stedelijk Museum, Amsterdam ••1999 *31 Flavours of Doom*, solo exhibition, De Gele Rijder, Arnhem••1998 Installation *Black Metal Machine*, group exhibition *SuperNova*, Bureau Amsterdam **selected bibliography** 2002 *What is Graphic Design?*, Rotovision, London••2002 *No Brief, Graphic Designers' Personal Projects*, RotoVision, London••2001 *IDEA* magazine 287, Tokyo••2000 *Eye* magazine 38, London

Sara Fanelli
Born Florence, Italy, 1969. Lives and works in London **education** 1993–95 M.A., Illustration, Royal College of Art, London••1990–93 B.A. (Hons), Graphic Design, Camberwell College of Arts, London••1989–90 Foundation Course Diploma, City and Guilds of London Art School, London **practice** 1993–present Independent graphic designer, writer, and illustrator **selected projects** 2002–03 Invitations for Ron Arad at the Salone del Mobile, Milan••2002 Design, writing, and illustrations, *First Flight*, Jonathan Cape, London••2001–02 Invitations for Alessi's London showroom and Issey Miyake's London

A-POC presentation••2001 Images for "Family and Events" brochure, Tate Modern and Tate Britain, London **selected exhibitions** 2001–03 *A Baker's Dozen*, touring exhibition••2002 *The Magic Pencil*, British Library, London••2000 *Peter Blake—About Collage*, Tate Liverpool••1995 *Hidden Treasures— An Adventure in Contemporary, Innovative, Children's Book Illustration*, Djangoli Art Gallery, Nottingham **selected bibliography** 2002 *The Graphics Book*, Mastercraft Series, D&AD, London••2002 *Originals—Designers Who Work Beyond the Brief*, RotoVision, London••2001 *Print* magazine, March/April issue, New York **awards** 2001/2003 Honorable Mention, Bologna Ragazzi, Italy••2000 National Art Library Illustration Award, Victoria & Albert Museum, London••2000 Silver Award, D&AD, London••1999 Kall-Kwik Award, Images 24, Association of Illustrators, London **memberships** 2001 Alliance Graphique Nationale (AGI)

Isidro Ferrer
Born Madrid, Spain, 1963. Lives and works in Huesca, Spain **education** 1986 Mime, Mouvement Théâtre, École Jacques Lecoq, Paris••1982–85 Drama, Escuela de Teatro, Zaragoza **practice** 1996 Establishment of own studio in Huesca••1995 Conceived storyboards for animation production company Tijuana Films, Valencia••1990–95 Part of the studio Camaleón, Zaragoza••1989 One-year internship in Peret's graphic-design studio, Barcelona **selected projects** 2000 Television advertisement for Volkswagen's New Beetle, Spain••1999 Cover designs for publishers Alfaguara y Santillana••1999 Designs for television station Canal Plus, Paris••1997 Illustrations for daily newspaper *El País*, Madrid **selected bibliography** 2002 *El sentido de lo dicho se consume en los silencios*, Mores Ediciones, Spain••2001 *Caprichos*, Bedeteca de Lisboa, Portugal••1999 *La voz ajena*, Diputación Provincial de Huesca, Spain••1999 *Exils*, AMOK editions, France••1994 *Te leo*, Ediciones Ambiguas, Spain **selected exhibitions** 2002 *Ojo por hoja*, Museo de Arquitectura, Universidad Nacional, Bogotá••2001 *La palabra dibujada*, Centro de Cultura Antiguo Instituto, Gijón, Spain••2001 *Impresiones*, Insula Galérie, Paris••2000 *Isidro Ferrer*, Armazém 7, Lisbon••2000 *Exils*, Les Index, Rouen, France••1995 Biennale Mladih, Mali Salon, Rijeka, Croatia **awards** 2002 National Design Prize, Spain••2001 Award, 12th International Poster Festival Chaumont, France••2000 PROMAX Gold Award for animation, Canada••1996 Gold Award for Illustration, Spain **memberships** 2000 Alliance Graphique Internationale (AGI)

Laurent Fétis
Born Orsay, France, 1970. Lives and works in Paris **education** 1994–99 Ecole Nationale Supérieure des Arts Décoratifs ••1991–93 Ecole d'Architecture de Versailles **practice** 1999–present Independent graphic designer••2000–present Guest Lecturer, Reims Superior Design School, France **selected projects** 2002 Poster for Beck's "Sea Change" tour, Geffen, USA••2002 CD packaging, *Rocker's Delight*, Quatermass, Belgium (With Elisabeth Arkhipoff)••2001 Book, *ABC+*, by Laurent Fétis, Die Gestalten Verlag, Germany••2001 "Anna Sui" insert for *Vogue Nippon* (with Elisabeth Arkhipoff) **selected bibliography** 2002 *ABC+*, by Laurent Fétis, Die Gestalten Verlag, Germany••2002 "Laurent Fetis," *IdN* 9, no. 1, Hong Kong••2001 *Specials*, Booth-Clibborn Editions, United Kingdom••2001 Centerfold in *Creative Review*, July issue, London **selected exhibitions** 2002 13, London

Underground, London●●2001 *Signes, The New Generation of Graphic Design*, Centre Georges Pompidou, Paris●●2001 *Idea about a Place*, Transmission Gallery, Glasgow●●2000 Solo exhibition, Gallery Kreo, Paris

Field Study
Roy Brooks, born Stanfield, North Carolina, USA, 1975; Matthew Peterson, born Cary, North Carolina, USA, 1975. Live and work in Chicago **education** 1994–98 Graphic Design, North Carolina State University School of Design, Raleigh, North Carolina (MP)●●1993–97 Graphic Design, North Carolina State University School of Design, Raleigh, North Carolina (RB) **practice** 2002–present Field Study●●2001–02 Freelance designer (MP)●●1999–2002 Senior Designer, Pentagram, New York (RB)●●1999–2000 Design Intern, Walker Art Center, Minneapolis, Minnesota (MP)●●1998–99 Graphic Designer, Whitney Museum of American Art, New York (RB)●●1998–99 Graphic Designer, x Design Group, Raleigh, North Carolina (MP) **selected projects** 2003 Corporate identity, Geotrack, Inc.●●2003 CD design, *Lullaby for Sue*, by Clogs, Brassland Records●●2003 Exhibition-catalogue design, *Speculative Chicago*, Gallery 400, University of Illinois at Chicago●●2002 Web-site design for Vincent Whitehurst **selected exhibitions** 2003 *GraficEurope*, Barcelona **memberships** 2003 American Institute of Graphic Arts (AIGA)

Lizzie Finn
Born London, United Kingdom, 1973. Lives and works in London **education** 1993–96 B.A. (Hons.), Graphic Design, Central Saint Martins College of Art and Design, London●●1992–93 Foundation in Art & Design, Central Saint Martins College of Art and Design, London **practice** 1998–present Freelance graphic designer●●2002–2003 Visiting Lecturer, Surrey Institute of Art & Design, Epsom ●●2001–2002 Visiting Lecturer, Camberwell College of Art & Design, London ●●1996–98 Junior Designer, Blue Source, London **selected projects** 1998–present Art direction, fabric repeat, embroidery, and T-shirt designs, SILAS, London●●2003 Album-sleeve image for *Songbird*, single by Oasis, Big Brother Recordings, London●●2002–03 Graphic design, "Eye Spy" fashion special (four issues), *Dazed & Confused* magazine, London●●2002–03 Fashion illustration (four issues), British *Vogue*, London●●2000 Promotional material, Hysteric Glamour UK, London●●2000 Album-sleeve design, *Things to make and do*, by Moloko, The Echo Label, London **selected bibliography** 2002 *GB: Graphic Britain*, Laurence King Publishing, London●●2001 *Specials*, Booth-Clibborn Editions, London●●2001 *Annual*, Vision On, London●●1998 *20th Century Type*, Laurence King Publishing, London **selected exhibitions** 2002 *I Love to Meet You*, Palazzo Fortuny, Venice●●2001 *Annual*, Dazed & Confused Gallery, London●● 2000 *Product 250 "t-shirts,"* Artomatic Gallery, London●●2000 Poster show, Gavin Brown's Enterprise, New York **awards** 2002 Creative Future for Illustration, Creative Review Awards, United Kingdom●●2001 Nominated for Best Designer, CAD Music Week Awards, United Kingdom

Amy Franceschini
Born Patterson, California, USA, 1970. Lives and works in San Francisco and Gent, Belgium **education** 2000–2002 Art, Stanford University, Palo Alto, California●●1988–92 Art, San Francisco State University, San Francisco **practice** 2002–present Visiting Faculty, Stanford University Art Department, Palo Alto, California●●1995–present Founder, Furturefarmers, San Francisco●●1994–present Interaction designer, illustrator, and artist **selected projects** 2002 Stanford University Art Department Web site●● 2002 Poster for *Communication What?* exhibition, Venice●●2002 Cell-phone graphics for MTV Japan **selected bibliography** 2002 *Harvest, Futurefarmers Anthology*, Futurefarmers/IdN Publication, San Francisco●●2002 *Pictoplasma*, Die Gestalten Verlag, Berlin●●2002 "Exlibris," *Page Magazine*, Berlin●●2002 "3d Characters," *Eye Magazine*, London●●2001 "Silicon Valley Issue," *National Geographic Magazine* **selected exhibitions** 2004 *Gaming Show*, Yerba Buena Center for the Arts, San Francisco●●2003 National Design Triennial, Cooper-Hewitt, NationalDesign Museum, Smithsonian Institution, New York●● 2002 *Vasi Communicanti*, Palazzo Fortuny, Venice **awards** 2002 Net Excellence Award, Arts Electronica, Austria●●2001 DNA Prize, Die Kulturinitiative von Videor Technical, Rödermark, Germany

Vince Frost
Born Brighton, United Kingdom, 1964. Lives and works in London **education** 1985–87 Graphic Design, West Sussex College of Design, Worthing **practice** 1994–present Frost Design, London●●1987–98 Design Assistant to Howard Brown, London●●1993–94 Associate Partner, Pentagram Design, London●●1989–93 Junior to Senior Designer, Pentagram Design, London **selected projects** 2003 Redesign of identity for Rüshlikon Center for Global Dialogue, Zurich●●2001–02 Art direction of Laurence King Publishing●●2000 Redesign launch of Laurence King Publishing●●2000 Album design, *Forever*, by the Spice Girls●●1998 Stamp design, Royal Mail, United Kingdom●●1998 Design of *Financial Times, The Business Magazine*, London●●1995 Redesign of the *Independent* magazine, London **selected bibliography** 2003 *Creative Review Annual*, United Kingdom●●2003 *Making and Breaking the Grid*, Rockport Publishers, Gloucester, Massachusetts●●2002 *Rewind: Fourty Years of Design and Advertising*, Phaidon Press, London and New York●●2001 *Graphis* magazine, New York **selected exhibitions** 2002 *Rewind*, Victoria & Albert Museum, London●●2002 Design Council traveling exhibition●●2002 Book exhibition, British Council, London **awards** 2003 Silver nominations, D&AD, London●●2003 Best Annual Report, Design Week Awards, London●●2003 Silver, Art Directors Club, New York **memberships** 2002 Alliance Graphique Internationale (AGI)●●2001 International Society of Typographic Designers (ISTD)●●1994 British Design & Art Direction (D&AD)

Tom Gauld
Born Aberdeen, Scotland, 1976. Lives and works in London **education** 1999–2001 M.A., Communication Art and Design, Royal College of Art, London●●1995–99 B.A., Illustration, Edinburgh College of Art, Edinburgh **practice** 2001–present Copublisher (with Simone Lia), Cabanon Press ●●2000–present Freelance illustrator **selected projects** 2003 Illustrations for members' brochure, Royal Society of Arts, London●●2002–03 Designed watches and prints, United Arrows, Tokyo●●2002–03 *Move to the City*, weekly comic strip, *Time Out*, London●●2002 *The Moving Finger*, series of Illustrations for the *Guardian*, London●●2001 Billboard design, Happiness in Brockley Project, London **selected bibliography** 2003 *Both* (with Simone Lia), Bloomsbury, London●●2002 *Second* (with Simone Lia), Cabanon Press, London●●2001

Guardians of the Kingdom, Cabanon Press, London●●2001 *First* (with Simone Lia), Cabanon Press, London selected exhibitions 2002 *Wedding or Funeral?*, District Gallery, Tokyo●●2001 *Between the Lines*, Pumphouse Gallery, London●●2000 *Folio Society Illustration Awards*, RCA, London●●2000 *The Instruction Manual*, Blue Room, London awards 2002 Pentagram Illustration Award●●2001 Deutsche Bank Pyramid Award

Juli Gudehus Born Hamburg, Germany, 1968. Lives and works in Berlin

education 1990–96 Visual Communication, University of Applied Arts, Düsseldorf●●1994 Omnific Studios, London●●1994 Internships, Alan Kitching, Pentagram, and Phaidon Press, London●●1987–90 Apprenticeship, Wienand, Cologne practice 1996–present Freelance graphic designer and visual consultant●●1999–2000 Lecturer, Graphic Design Department, University of Applied Arts, Düsseldorf●●1996–2000 Design studio with friends●●1996 Freelance work for Birnbach Design, Bonn selected projects 2000–present Design for various publications, exhibitions, and events of the German Parliament, Berlin●●1999 *Gestern war heute morgen*, project for newspaper *Die Zeit*, Zeit Verlag, Hamburg●●1998 *Mindestens haltbar bis*, calendar, Verlag Hermann Schmidt, Mainz, Germany●●1996 Showroom design, Bayer Corporation, Leverkusen, Germany●●1992 *Genesis*, by Juli Gudehus, Lars Müller Publishers, Baden, Switzerland selected bibliography 2003 *Type & Typography*, Laurence King Publishing, London●●1999 *Art Directors Club (ADC) Yearbook*, Verlag Hermann Schmidt, Germany●●1999 *Zoo Book*, Zoo, London●●1996 *Typoundso*, Verlag Hans-Rudolf Lutz, Zurich selected exhibitions 1999 *Type Directors Show*, traveling exhibition●●1999 *Wie Zeit vergeht*, Kölnisches Stadtmuseum, Cologne●●1996 *13 Forum Typografie*, Düsseldorf●●1993 *Mediale*, Museum für Kunst und Gewerbe, Hamburg awards 1999 Gold Award, Art Directors Club, Germany●●1999 Gold Award, Art Directors Club, Europe●●1999 Award for Typographic Excellence, Type Directors Club, New York

Yuri Gulitov Born Sevastopol, Crimea, Ukraine, 1964. Lives and works in Moscow education 1986–91 Graphic design, Art Industrial Institute, Kharkov, Ukraine●●1980–84 Art College, Samokish, Simpheropol, Ukraine practice 2002–present Art Director of design studio Rocolor, Moscow●●2001–present Professor, High Academic School of Graphic Design, Moscow College of Applied Arts●●1998–2001 Freelance graphic designer●●1996–98 Art Director, *Kommersant*, Moscow●●1993–95 Art Director, Oda, Sevastopol, Ukraine●●1991–93 Art Director, Zerkalo, Sevastopol, Ukraine selected projects 2002 *Ladies' Night* identity, packaging, and poster, Rocolor and Independent Theatrical Project, Moscow●●2002 Poster, Sergei Rachmaninov *Vespers*, St. Nikolai Church Choir of the State Tretyakov Gallery, Moscow●●2002 Poster, Christmas Concert mystery *Lestvica*, St. Nikolai Church Choir of the State Tretyakov Gallery, Moscow●●2002 Book design, *Sotheby's Russian Art on Auction 1990–2000*, Artlibris, Moscow●●2002 Series of booklets for French Cultural Center, Embassy of France, Moscow●●1999 Poster and invitation for all-Russian competition/exhibition *Design '99*, Society of Russian Designers, Moscow selected bibliography 2002 "Outside of Road Signs," *Design Illustrated*, Moscow●●2001 "Yuri Gulitov," *Novum World of Graphic Design* magazine, Munich●●2000 "No modern urgency of Yuri Gulitov," *Kak*, Moscow●●1999 "Yuri Gulitov," *Fusion 2002*

International, Tokyo selected exhibitions 2001 *Yuri Gulitov. Beach Pictures*, Gallerie Pinacotheke, Moscow●●2000 *Yuri Gulitov. Typeface*, Art Industrial Institute, Kharkov and Gallerie Dom, Moscow●●2000 6th International Poster Triennial, Toyama awards 2001 Association Typographique Internationale (ATypI) Award, Bukva:Raz!, Moscow●●2000 Golden Bee Award, poster category, Moscow International Biennale of Graphic Design●●1998 Silver Diploma , Best Calendar Design of Russia Exhibition, Moscow●●1996 Grand Prix, logo category, and Golden Bee Award, typeface category, Golden Bee Moscow International Biennale of Graphic Design memberships 1994 Society of Designers of Russia●●1992 Union of Ukrainian Artists

Julia Hasting Born Bremen, Germany, 1970. Lives and works in New York

education 1992–97 Graphic Design, Staatliche Hochschule für Gestaltung Karlsruhe, Germany●●1990–92 Visual Communications, Gesamthochschule Kassel, Germany practice 2000–present Art Director, Phaidon Press, New York●●2000–present Professor, Design Faculty, Cooper Union School of Art, New York●●1998 Designer, Phaidon Press, London●●1993–98 Freelance designer, Karlsruhe, Germany selected projects 1998–2003 Book design, *Cream*, *Magnum°*, *Breuer Houses*, *Acta Est*, *Annunciation, Descent, Crucifixion, Last Supper*, *10x10*, *Chaos*, *Fresh Cream*, Phaidon 55 photography series, *Robert Capa*, *The Sound I Saw*, *The Andy Warhol Catalogue Raisonné: Volume I*, *Blink.*, *Vitamin P*, *Gordon Matta-Clark*, *Red-Color News Soldier*, Phaidon Press, London and New York●●1997 Corporate identity, European Institute of Cinema, Karlsruhe (EIKK)●●1997 Corporate identity, Central Education Institute (ZFP) of television and radio stations ARD/ZDF, Cologne●●1995 Participant in official logo competition EXPO 2000 Hannover●●1994 Corporate identity and books *Camera Silens*, *Mienenspiele*, *buna 4*, Media Museum—Zentrum für Kunst und Medientechnologie (ZKM), Karlsruhe●●1993 Catalogue for the architects COOP Himmelb(l)au, Erich Schelling Architecture Foundation, Karlsruhe, Germany●●1993 Posters, invitations, and catalogue for exhibition *Bühnenbild heute, Bühnenbild der Zukunft*, Zentrum für Kunst und Technology (ZKM) and Cantz Verlag, Stuttgart selected bibliography 2003 *First Choice—Leading international designers select the very best of their work*, edited by Ken Cato, Images, Australia●●2003 D&AD Annual, London●●2003 *50 Books/50 Covers*, American Institute of Graphic Arts, New York●●2002–03 "Regional Design Annual," *Print* magazine, Cincinnati, Ohio●●2002 Type Directors Club Annual, New York●●1999–2001 "I.D. Annual Design Review", *I.D. Magazine*, New York●●1997 *form* magazine 158, Germany●●1997 *Rambow Studenten*, Cantz Verlag, Stuttgart selected exhibitions 2001 *AGI—Graphisme(s)*, Bibliothèque Nationale de France, Paris●●2000 19th International Biennale of Graphic Design Brno, Czech Republic●●1998 International Poster Triennial, Toyama, Japan●●1995 *The Nicest Books 1995*, Book Fair Frankfurt and Leipzig●●1994 *The 100 Best Posters*, Berlin●●1993 *The Best Posters 1990–1993*, 7th Triennale, German Poster Museum, Essen awards 2003 Gold Medal, Art Directors Club, New York●●2003 Silver Award Nomination, D&AD, London●●2002 First Prize, *Print* magazine's A–Z Competition, New York●●2000 25th Kodak Fotobuchpreis, Stuttgart●●1999 Certificate of Typographic Excellence, Type Directors Club, New York●●1993 Henri de Toulouse-Lautrec Gold Medal, 7th Triennale, German Poster Museum, Essen memberships 2003 International Jury, 21st International

Biennale of Graphic Design Brno, Czech Republic, 2004●●2001 American Institute of Graphic Arts (AIGA)●●2000 Alliance Graphique Internationale (AGI)●●2000 Art Directors Club, New York

Fons Hickmann
Born Hamm, Germany, 1966. Lives and works in Berlin and Vienna **education** 1988–93 Philosophy, Creative Writing, Photography, Art, and Design, Universities of Düsseldorf and Wuppertal, Germany **practice** 1999–present Design studio Fons Hickmann m23, Berlin●●1995–2002 Lecturer in Essen, Dortmund, London, and Beijing●●2001 Professor of Graphic Design, New Media, and Applied Football, University of Applied Art Vienna, Austria●●1993–96 Artist group "kairos," Düsseldorf **selected projects** 2001–02 Posters for classical concerts, Johanneskantorei, Düsseldorf●●1999–2002 Posters for the Labor für Soziale und Ästhetische Entwicklungen, Düsseldorf●●1996 Posters for silent film festival, Graz, Austria●●2002 Fons Goes China poster for lecture in Beijing●●2002 Posters for sailing regatta Kieler Woche 2002, Kiel, Germany●●2000 Poster series "Anonyme Idylle" for music concerts, B8, Düsseldorf **selected bibliography** 1996–2003 The Annual of the Type Directors Club, HBI, New York **selected exhibitions** 2000 Golden Bee International Biennale of Graphic Design, Moscow●●2001 Poster Biennial Ningbo, China●●2002 Heiligenkreuzer Hof, Vienna●●1998 International Stage Poster Triennial, Sofia **awards** 2002–2003 Excellence Award, Type Directors Club, New York●●1999–2003 100 Best Posters, Berlin●●2002 Joseph Binder Award for Multimedia Design, Design Austria●●2001 Excellence Award, Poster Biennial Ningbo, China●●2000 Golden Bee Award, Golden Bee International Biennale of Graphic Design, Moscow●●1997 Silver Cube, Art Directors Club, New York **memberships** 1999 Art Directors Club, Germany●●1996 Type Directors Club, New York

Kim Hiorthøy
Born Trondheim, Norway, 1973. Lives and works in Oslo **education** 1999–2001 Royal Academy of Fine Art, Copenhagen●●1991–96 Fine Art, Kunstakademiet i Trondheum, Trondheim, Norway●●1994–95 Film, School of Visual Arts, New York **selected projects** 2003 Book design, Money Will Ruin all Good Things, Rune Grammofon, Oslo●●2003 Album sleeve, Jaga Jazzist: The Stix, Ninja Tune, London●●2003 Jeg er nesten alltid redd, 7 films, The Photographers' Gallery, Oslo●●2002 Flowers, mural design, Thisisrealart Associates/Peter Smith, Tokyo **selected bibliography** 2003 Graphic Design in the 21st Century, Taschen, Cologne●●2001 Pen&Mouse, Laurence King Publishing, London●●2000 Tree Weekend, Die Gestalten Verlag, Berlin●●2000 Sampler2, Laurence King Publishing, London **selected exhibitions** 2003 Kim Hiorthøy: Jeg er nesten alltid redd, The Photographers' Gallery, Oslo●●2001 Generation X: Young Nordic Design, Scandinavian House, New York●●2000 Kim Hiorthøy: Tegninger for en hundrings, Tegner-forbundet, Oslo

Keiko Hirano
Born Himeji city, Hyogo Prefecture, Japan, 1959. Lives and works in Tokyo **education** self-educated **professional** 1986–present Independent Graphic Designer, founder of Hirano Studio **selected projects** 2002 Package design, Awai sake, Gekkeikan●●2001 Visual Identity, The National Museum of Modern Art, Tokyo●●2000 Art direction for brand image for qiora, Shiseido, Tokyo●●1999 Package design for Carita Le Visage, Cartita, France●●1998 Packaging and logotype design for Vocalise perfume, Shiseido, Tokyo●●1997 CD jacket design for Dogs, by Kenji Ozawa, Toshiba EMI, Tokyo **selected bibliography** 2003 Axis magazine 104, Tokyo●●2000 "Design X2000 pt.01," IDEA 280, revised edition, Tokyo **selected exhibitions** 2002 What is qiora's creation?, Hirano Studio, Tokyo●●1995 Today's Japan—Design, Harbor Front Center, Canada●●1994 Keiko Hirano Graphic Works, Matsuya Ginza Design Gallery, Tokyo●●1986 The Portrait of Light and Shadow, INAX Gallery, Tokyo **awards** 2001 Mainichi Design Award, Mainichi Newspapers Co., Japan●●1998 Gold Prize, 77th Annual Art Directors Award, Art Directors Club, New York●●1998 ADC Award ,Tokyo Art Directors Club, Japan●●1996 New Designer Award, Japan Graphic Designers Association **memberships** 2002 Japan Design Committee●●1999 Tokyo Art Directors Club●●1996 Japan Graphic Designers Association (JAGDA)

Hon Bing-wah
Born Guangzhou, China, 1949. Lives and works in Hong Kong **education** 1973 Graphic Design, Extramural Studies of the Chinese University of Hong Kong **practice** 2000–present Partner, H + S Design, Hong Kong●●2000–present Visiting Professor, University of Shanghai●●1998–present Museum Honorary Adviser, Leisure and Cultural Services Department, Hong Kong●●2002 Juror, China Star, Red-Cross International Poster Contest, China; Biennale in Design, Macau; and Taiwan Design Biennale●●1998–99 Chairman, Hong Kong Designers Association●●1988–90 Judging panel, Regional Flag and Emblem of the Hong Kong Special Administration Region **selected projects** 2002 Poster, information brochure, and gift-packaging design for the bidding of World Expo, 2010 Shanghai China, Expo 2010 Shanghai China Bidding Office●●1999 Book design, Image of Shanghai, Information Office of Shanghai Municipal People's Government, Shanghai●●1999 Corporate Identity design for Shanghai Public Transportation Card, Shanghai Public Traffic Card Co. Ltd., Shanghai●●1997 Environmental graphic and signage design for Riverside Point Singapore, Far East Organization, Singapore●●1997 Mascot design for the celebration of reunification of Hong Kong with China, Hong Kong Special Administrative Government, Hong Kong **selected bibliography** 2002 Package & Design, Guangzhou, China●●2000 Graphis Poster Annual, USA●●1998 Monthly Design, Korea●●1998 New Logo and Trademark Design, Japan **selected exhibitions** 2002 Art & Design Exhibition, Xintiandi Shanghai, China;●●2001 Hon Bing-wah Poster & Corporate Identity Design Exhibition, Shanghai International Convention Centre, Shanghai, China●●1997 Back to Nature, Artworks by Hon Bing-wah, Hong Kong●●1986 The Poster Works of Hon Bing-wah, Landmark Central, Hong Kong **awards** 2002 Gold Award, China Corporate Identity System Award, Beijing●●1998 Gold Award, Signage System Design, Hong Kong Designers Association, Hong Kong●●1997 Gold Medal of Publication Design, Creativity Annual, USA●●1992 Designer of the Year Award, Hong Kong Artist Guide, Hong Kong **memberships** 2001 Adviser, Hong Kong Designers Association ●●1998–2000 Chairman, Hong Kong Designers Association

Inkahoots
Robyn McDonald, born Melbourne, Australia, 1958; Jason Grant, born Blenheim, New Zealand, 1971; Ben Mangan, born Ballarat, Australia, 1976; Lucas Surtie, born Sydney, Australia, 1980; Joel Booÿ, born Brisbane, Australia, 1981. Live and

work in Brisbane education 2001 Graphic Design, Queensland College of Art, Brisbane (JB)••2001 Graphic Design, Queensland College of Art, Brisbane (LS)••1990–92 Graphic Design, Queensland College of Art, Brisbane (JG)••1989 Visual Arts, BCAE, Brisbane (JG)••1989 University of Ballarat, Ballarat (BM)••1980–87 Bachelor of Arts, Art History and Philosophy, Queensland University (RM)••1984–86 Diploma of Illustration, Queensland Art College (RM) practice 1990 Establishment of Inkahoots selected projects 2001 CD artwork, *Quietly Building an Empire*, by The Carousel, Australia••2001 Visual identity and promotional material, Ecodomo, Australia••2000 Visual identity and promotional material, Foresters ANA Friendly Society, Australia••1997 Logo for independent bookstore Avid Reader, Australia selected bibliography 2003 *Graphic Design for the 21st Century*, Taschen, Cologne••2002 *Eye* magazine 46, London

Karlssonwilker
Hjalti Karlsson, born Reykjavik, Iceland, 1967; Jan Wilker, born Marl, Germany, 1972. Live and work in New York education 1996–2001 Communication Design, State Academy of Fine Arts, Stuttgart (JW)••1989–92 Graphic Design, Parsons School of Design, New York (HK)••1984–88 Design, Menntaskolinn I Reykjavik, Iceland (HK) practice 2000–present karlssonwilker Inc., New York••1996–2000 Sagmeister Inc., New York (HK) selected projects 2002 Book design, *Curious Boym*, by Studio Boym & Partners, Princeton Architectural Press, New York••2002 CD packaging, *Highly Evolved*, by the Vines, Capitol Records, New York••2001 Poster and CD packaging, *Live 2001*, by Kraan, Kraan and Bassball Records, Germany••2001 "Doglamp" design, Worldstudio Foundation, New York selected bibliography 2003 *tellmewhy –the first 24 months of karlssonwilker inc.*, Princeton Architectural Press, New York••2003 *ID Magazine*, USA••2002 *Coast to Coast—Contemporary American Graphic Design*, Die Gestalten Verlag, Berlin••2002 *55 Degrees North*, Laurence King Publishing, London selected exhibitions 2003 *designIS*, Berlin••2002 *Soundblast*, American Institute of Graphic Arts, Los Angeles••2001 *Young Guns 3*, Art Directors Club, New York

Siobhan Keaney
Born London, United Kingdom, 1959. Lives and works in London education 1978–82 B.A. (Hons.), Graphic Design, London College of Printing, London practice 1985–present Independent designer and consultant••2002–present Year Tutor, School of Arts & Communication, University of Brighton••2000–present External Assessor, B.A. (Hons.) Art & Design Communication course, Bath Spa University College••1999–present External Assessor, B.A. (Hons.) Art & Design Communication course, Leeds Metropolitan University ••1998–2001 External Assessor, M.A. Communication Design course, Manchester Metropolitan University ••1995–98 Visiting Lecturer, Royal College of Art, London••1995–98 External Assessor, B.A. (Hons.) Graphic Design course, Central St. Martin's, London selected projects 2002 Yearpack 2002, The Royal Mail, London ••2000 Film promoting the United Kingdom, Foreign & Commonwealth Office, London••1990–97 Identity program, The Mill, London••1997, 1991, 1989, 1988 Apicorp Annual Reports, Apicorp, London••1995 "Science Fiction" special edition stamps, first-day cover and presentation pack, The Royal Mail, London selected bibliography 2002 *Rewind: 40 Years of Design and Advertising*, Phaidon Press, London and New

York••1998 *Design Without Boundaries: Visual Communication in the Nineties*, Booth-Clibborn Editions, London••1993 *International Women in Design*, USA selected exhibitions 2002–2003 *Rewind: 40 Years of Design & Advertising from the D&AD Awards*, Victoria & Albert Museum, London••1996–98 *Work from London*, international traveling exhibition••1995 *Siobhan Keaney*, Hochschule fur Gestaltung Offenbach, Germany••1994 *British Design*, Maison du Livre et de l'Image et du Son, Villeurbanne, France awards 1990 Silver Award, Most Outstanding Annual Report, D&AD, London••1990 Silver Award, Most Outstanding Brochure, D&AD, London••1987 Gold Award, Most Outstanding Brochure, United Kingdom memberships 1997–2002 Alliance Graphique Internationale (AGI)

Kerr/Noble
Frith Kerr, born Surrey, United Kingdom, 1973; Amelia Noble, born London, United Kingdom, 1973. Live and work in London education 1995–97 Royal College of Art, London (FK+AN)••1992–95 Camberwell College of Arts, London (FK)••1992–95 Central Saint Martins College of Art and Design, London (AN) practice 1997–present Kerr/Noble (FK+AN)••1997–present Visiting Lecturer, Camberwell College of Arts, London (FK)••1997–present Visiting Lecturer, Central Saint Martins College of Art and Design, London (AN) selected projects 2003 Modified Pop, typeface created for *No More Rules—Graphic Design & Postmodernism*, by Rick Poynor, Laurence King Publishing, London••2003 Identity and publicity material for *user_mode*, Central Saint Martins College of Art and Design and Tate Modern, London••2002 Printed material and exhibition graphics, *Gio Ponti—A World*, Design Museum, London••2002 *Lost But Not Forgotten*, self-published magazine, London••2002 *Accommodating Change: Innovation in Housing*, Architecture Foundation, London••1999 Fold-out souvenir for Channel Four riverboat trip, London selected bibliography 2003 "Art & Craft—Awards," *Graphics International* 103, London••2002 "Freed from Technology's Spell," *IDEA* 295. Tokyo••2002 "The Top Brass," The Sunday *Independent*, London••2001 *Specials*, Booth-Clibborn Editions, London selected exhibitions 2003 *The Arts Foundation's 10th Anniversary Exhibition*, Pentagram Gallery••2002 *The Book Corner*, British Council, Milan and London••2002 *Creative Futures 2002*, Creative Review, London awards 2003 Arts Foundation Award for Graphic Design••2002 Creative Futures Award for Editorial Design, Creative Review••2002 Best of Show, Design Week Awards••1997 Chris Garnham Award, Royal College of Art, London

Rene Knip
Born Hoorn, Netherlands, 1963. Lives and works in Amsterdam education 1985–90 Graphic and Type Design, Saint Joost Academy of Fine Arts, Breda••1984–85 Painting, Royal Academy, The Hague practice 1996–present Atelier Rene Knip, Amsterdam••1992–95 Assistant to Anthon Beeke, Studio Anthon Beeke, Amsterdam; part-time designer, Studio Lidewij Edelkoort, Paris selected projects 2003 Calender, Calff & Meischke, Amsterdam ••2002 Self-commissioned Firebasket (with Edgar Knip), Amsterdam••2001 *Dutch Design 2000–2001*, BNO and BIS Publishers, Amsterdam••1999 Laundry Sans typeface, (used for exhibition *Mooi Maar Goed*), Amsterdam••1999 Housenumber design, Merkx+Girod Architects, Amsterdam selected bibliography 2003 *Fontshop* magazine, April, Belgium••2002 "Rene Knip, Unconventional Spatial Typography," *Designer's Workshop* magazine 121, Tokyo••2001 *Apples + Oranges—Best*

Dutch Graphic Design, BIS Publishers, Amsterdam● ● 2001 "Rene Knip, Ideas that can't wait," *Graphis* magazine 333, New York● ● 1999 *Items* magazine 1, Amsterdam **memberships** 2001 Association of Dutch Designers (BNO)

Elisabeth Kopf
Born Vorarlberg, Austria, 1963. Lives and works in Vienna **education** 1996–present Personal studies in graphic design and visual concepts● ● 1989–present Personal studies in photography● ● 1981–84 Psychology, History, and Philosophy, University of Vienna **practice** 1996–present Freelance graphic designer and photographer● ● 1992–96 Assistant in a graphic-design studio● ● 1989–91 Freelance photographer, Hong Kong **selected projects** 2002 Self-commisioned Air Cigarettes Project, Vienna and Beijing● ● 2002 Baustelle First Aid Project, Lesson 9: The Recovery Position● ● 2000 Little Theatre project, *Peter Herbert & Aktionstheater Ensemble 2000*, Aziza Music, New York and Vienna● ● 1999–present Scratch Gallery, Peter Herbert & David Tronzo: *Segmente*, Aziza Music and Peter Herbert, New York● ● 1997 Little Orchestra project, Vienna Art Orchestra, Vienna **selected bibliography** 2003 *This End Up: Original Approaches to Packaging Design*, RotoVision, London● ● 2002 *Lighter* magazine, Beijing● ● 2002 *PAGE*, Hamburg● ● 2001 *Print: European Design Annual 2001*, New York **selected exhibitions** 2002 *Hans Koller Music Awards Exhibition*, Vienna● ● 2000–2001 Joseph Binder Awards touring exhibition, Austria, Switzerland, Germany● ● 1999 Limites—Festival for Contemporary Music and Art, VHS Stöbergasse, Vienna● ● 1997 Vienna Art Orchestra Anniversary World Tour, Brucknerhaus, Linz and Vienna **awards** 2001 Gustav Klimt Award, Cultural Department of the City of Vienna and GEWISTA, Austria● ● 2000 Joseph Binder Award, Design Austria● ● 2000 79th Annual Award, Art Directors Club, New York● ● 2000 Certificate of Excellence, European Design Annual 5, USA and United Kingdom **memberships** 2001 Design Austria

Ji Lee
Born Seoul, Korea, 1971. Lives and works in New York **education** 1995 B.F.A., Communication Design, Parsons School of Design, New York **practice** 1999–present Art Director, Saatchi & Saatchi, New York● ● 2001–02 Instructor, Graphic Design, Parsons School of Design, New York● ● 1996–97 Graphic Designer, Tsang Seymour Design, New York● ● 1995–96 Graphic Designer, Frankfurt Balkind, New York **selected projects** 2003 3-D Chess Board, New York● ● 2002 Speech-bubbles sticker project, New York● ● 2002 Abstractor, New York● ● 2002 Nonnumeric Calendar, New York● ● 1997 Universe Revolved, a 3-D alphabet, New York **selected bibliography** 1997 *New York Times Magazine*, special issue on technology, New York● ● 1996 *Dimensional Typography*, by J. Abbott Miller, Princeton Architectural Press, New York **awards** 1998 Finalist, Innovation in Communication Award, Saatchi & Saatchi, USA

Ken-Tsai Lee
Born Taipei, Taiwan, 1968. Lives and works in Taipei **education** 1999–2001 Graduate Degree, Design, National Taiwan Normal University, Taipei● ● 1988–91 Department of Applied Art, Shih Chien University, Taipei **practice** 2001–02 Lecturer for Visual Communication, Mingchi Institute of Technology, Taipei● ● 1996–present Ken-Tsai Lee Design Studio, Taipei **selected projects** 1996–2002 Visual design, poster, and advertising for Chinese

Society of Preventive Medicine—Living with Hope Organization, Taipei● ● 1997–99 Poster design for Soho Cosmetic Accessories Co., Taipei● ● 1998 Visual design, poster, and advertising, Fonso Enterprise Co., Taipei● ● 1997 Cover Design for Japan Design Foundation booklet, Osaka **selected bibliography** 2003 *Communication Arts* magazine, USA● ● 2002 *Graphis Poster 2002*, USA● ● 2002 *P.I.E Book*, Japan● ● 2002 *International Graphis Design Annual*, Germany **selected exhibitions** 2003 Colorado International Invitational Poster Exhibition, Colorado, USA● ● 2002 Howon University Invitational International Design Exhibition, Seoul, Korea● ● 2001 *Das AvantgardePlakat aus China*, Hochschule der Künste, Berlin● ● 2001 *Chinese Graphic Design towards the International Sphere*, Lubalin Study Center of Design and Typography, Cooper Union School of Art, New York **awards** 2001–02 Two-time winner, Red Dot Award, Red Dot Communication Design Competition, Germany● ● 2000 Two Gold Awards, Hong Kong Designers Association● ● 1999 Best of Printed Design Award, *IdN Magazine*, Hong Kong● ● 1999 Taiwan National Design Award

Anette Lenz
Born Esslingen am Neckar, Germany, 1964. Lives and works in Paris **education** 1984–88 Communication Design, Fachhochschule München **practice** 1993–present Independent Designer, Atelier Anette Lenz, Paris● ● 1991–93 Founding Member, Nous Travaillons Ensemble, Paris● ● 1990 Grapus, Paris● ● 1988–89 AWG, Munich **selected projects** 2002 Season poster and brochure, Théâtre d'Angoulême, France● ● 2001 Poster series, "The Concerts of Radio France," Paris● ● 2000 Poster series, Théâtre de Rungis, Paris **selected bibliography** 2002 *Etapes Graphiques* 89, Paris● ● 2002 "European Design Annual," *Print* magazine, New York● ● 2000 *Le 20ème siècle s'affiche*, Éditions Larousse, Paris● ● 1996 "Young Graphic Creation in France," *Signes* 15/16, Paris **selected exhibitions** 2002 International Biennale of Graphic Design Brno, Czech Republic● ● 2001 Graphic-design exhibition, Bibliothèque Nationale de France, Paris● ● 2001 *La Fête de la Musique*, Centre Georges Pompidou, Paris● ● 1996 *Approche*, international traveling exhibition of 10 young graphic-design studios in France **awards** 2002 Gold Medal for Corporate Identity, International Biennale of Graphic Design Brno, Czech Republic **memberships** 1999 Alliance Graphique Internationale (AGI)● ● 1996 Verband der Grafik Designer, Berlin

Apex Lin
Born Pintung, Taiwan, 1957. Lives and works in Taipei, Macao, and Singapore **education** 1981–84 Master of Fine Arts, National Taiwan Normal University, Taipei● ● 1976–80 Bachelor of Fine Arts, National Taiwan Normal University, Taipei **practice** 1996–present Managing Director, Graphic Design Association, Taipei● ● 1986–present Professor, Graduate School of Fine Arts, National Taiwan Normal University, Taipei● ● 2002–04 President, Taiwan Poster Design Association, Taipei● ● 1988–2004 Consultant, Macao Designers Association, Macau● ● 2001–03 Treasurer, International Council of Graphic Design Association (ICOGRADA), Brussels● ● 1989–2002 Consultant, Apex Design Consultant Corporation, Taipei● ● 1990–96 Founder and President, Taiwan Image Poster Design Association, Taipei **selected projects** 2002 Curator of international touring exhibition *Discover Asia International Touring Exhibition*, Taipei and Kaoshiung, Taiwan; Singapore; Kuala Lumpur, Malaysia● ● 2001 Curator, *The Trio of Asia Poster Exhibition* (Japan, Korea, Taiwan), Taipei● ● 2000 Curator, *Say Good-Bye to the 20th Century*

design exhibition, Taipei and Beijing••1997 Corporate identity, Chunghwa Telcom Corporation & Taiwan Stock Exchange Corporation, Taipei••1996 Corporate identity, Vantone Corporation & Greatwall Oil Corporation, Beijing••1989 Corporate identity, Taiwan Sugar Corporation, Taipei selected exhibitions 2000 *Apex Lin in Macau*, Macao UNESCO Center••1997 *Taiwan Image Poster Design*, Taiwan Cultural Center, New York and Paris••1997 *The Design World of Apex Lin*, China Fine Art Academy, HangZhou; Beijing Design Museum, Beijing••1995 *The Design World of Apex Lin*, NTNU Gallery, Taipei awards 2002 ICOGRADA Achievement Award, Taiwan memberships 2002–present Jury Member, 2008 Beijing Olympic Design Competition Committee••1999 ICOGRADA••1990 Taiwan Poster Design Association ••1989 Graphic Design Association, Taiwan

Andrey Logvin Born Ipatovo, Russia, 1964. Lives and works in Moscow
education 1984–87 Graphic Design, Moscow 1905 Art School••1981–82 Graphic Design, Moscow 1905 Art School practice 1997 Established virtual design group LOGVINDESIGN••1992–97 Freelance graphic designer••1989–92 Art Director, IMA-Press publishers, Moscow••1987 Graphic Designer, Studio of the Russian Artists Union, Moscow selected projects 2002 Packaging for Hennessy GQ Reserve, Condé Nast, Moscow••2001 Poster for international project "10 Graphic Designers for Human Rights," French Ministry of Education, Paris••1999 Advertising campaign, Bosch kitchen systems, Moscow••1987 Poster for Moscow Marathon of Peace, Russian Ministry of Sport, Moscow selected bibliography 2001 *The Russian Poster. 100 Masterpieces from 100 Years*, Kontakt-Kultyra, Moscow ••2000 *Graphistes Autour Du Monde*, Les Éditions Textuel, Paris••1998 "Pin-up Boy," *I.D. Magazine* 40, New York••1994 *Who's Who In Graphic Design*, Benteli-Werd Verlag AG, Zurich selected exhibitions 2002 *Logvin, Peret, Pluta, Tartakover*, Warsaw••2001 *5 Grafist*, MSU Tophane i Amire Cultural Center Art Gallery, Istanbul••2000 *Graphistes Autour Du Monde*, Échirolles, France••1998 *Troyka. Kitajeva, Logvin, Chaika*, DDD Gallery, Osaka awards 2001 Russian State Prize for Art••1996 Gold Medal, 15th Warsaw Poster Biennale••1994 Critics Award, 16th International Biennale of Graphic Design Brno, Czech Republic••1992 Grand-Prix, First Golden Bee International Biennale of Graphic Design, Moscow memberships 2002 Russian Academy of Graphic Design••1999 Alliance Graphique Internationale (AGI)

Victor Hugo Marreiros Born Macao, China, 1960. Lives and work in Macao education 1986 Painting and Printmaking, Escola Superior de Belas Artes do Porto, Porto, Portugal practice 1990–present Head of the Graphic Department, Macao Cultural Institute; Art Director, *Revista da Cultura*••1998 Founded Victor Hugo Design••1990 Founded MARR Design••1984–88 Art Director, Macao Television, Teledifusão de Macau (TDM) selected projects 2002 Poster series for fourth Chinese Drama Festival in Macao, Macao Cultural Institute ••2001 Poster for XII Macao Arts Festival, Macao Cultural Institute••2001 Poster for Portuguese Movies Fortnight in Macao, Instituto Português do Oriente, Macao••1998 Artistic Director, *Presença de Macau na Expo 98*, World Expo 98, Lisbon selected exhibitions 2002 *Discover Asia* international poster exhibition, Taipei••2001 *Chinese Graphic Design Towards the International Sphere*, Lubalin Study

Center of Design and Typography, Cooper Union School of Art, New York••2001 *Das AvantgardePlakat Aus China*, Hochschule der Künste, Berlin••1999 *Victor Hugo Marreiros—Design*, Casa Garden Gallery, Orient Foundation, Macao••1999 *Victor Hugo Marreiros & Ung Vai Meng*, DDD Gallery, Osaka••1998 International Art Fair of Guangzhou, Guangzhou, China awards 2002 Two Bronze and Thirteen Excellence Awards, HKDA Design Show, Hong Kong••2001 Distinction Award, Prémio Bienal de Design de Macau 00/01, Macao••2000 Nominated, International Designers Network Design Awards, Hong Kong ••1999 Medal of Professional Merit, Government of Macao memberships 1986 Design Association of Macao••1986 Founding Member, Círculo dos Amigos da Cultura (CAC) de Macau

Malte Martin Born Berlin, Germany, 1958. Lives and works in Paris
education 1978–86 Graphic Design and History of Art, Akademie für Bildende Kunst, Stuttgart••1980–81 Graphics and Painting, Ecole Supérieure des Beaux Arts, Paris practice 1995–2000 Professor of Graphic Design and Image Concepts, ECV (École de Communication Visuelle)••1996–present Cofounder, Agrafmobile••1996 Establishment of Malte Martin, Atelier Graphique ••1989–1996 Freelance graphic designer selected projects 2002 Typographic installation *Galerue*, Agrafmobile, Paris ••2002 Installation and performance, *Théâtre des Questions*, Agrafmobile, Chaumont, France••2002 Corporate identity, Festival d'Avignon, France••2002 Program, Fondation Royaumont, Paris••2001 Installations and performances *Instants Mobiles*, Agrafmobile, Chaumont, France••1999 Program, 2E2M Orchestra, Paris selected bibliography 2003 "Malte Martin," *Design and Designers*, Éditions Pyramid, Paris••2000 *New Design Paris*, Rockport Publishers, Gloucester, Massachusetts ••1998 *Cent Affiches Francaises*, SNG, Paris••1995 *Signes*, Paris selected exhibitions 2000–2002 Visual Installations, Festival of Graphic Arts, Chaumont, France••2000 Bibliothèque François Mitterrand, Paris••1998 Galerie Vivienne, Paris memberships 2003 Alliance Française des Designers (AFD)••2000 Association Typographique Internationale (ATypI), France••1995 Syndicat National des Graphistes (SNG), France

Kei Matsushita Born Yokohama, Japan, 1961. Lives and works in Tokyo
education 1987 M.A., Visual Design, Tokyo University of Fine Arts and Music, Tokyo••1985 General Design, Tokyo University of Fine Arts and Music, Tokyo••1981–85 Fine Arts General Design Course, Tokyo National University of Fine Arts and Music (GEI-DAI—Tokyo Geijutsu Daigaku) practice 1999–present Part-time Lecturer, General Design Course, Tokyo National University of Fine Arts and Music••1995–98 Part-time Lecturer, Department of Arts and Design, Faculty of Humanities and Culture, Tokai University••1990 Founded Kei Matsushita Design Office selected projects 2000 Brochure for Japan Team at Venice Biennale, 30x100 Committee, Tokyo••2000 AIBO, Poster for development of AIBO entertainment robot, Sony Creative Products, Tokyo••1999 Signage and logo plan for Japan Pavilion, Hannover International EXPO, Japan External Trade Organization, Tokyo••1997–99 Poster Designs, 100x30 congress and exhibitions, Japan Institute of Architects, Tokyo••Poster for exhibition of 30 Residential Areas by 100 Architects in their Thirties, Japan Institute of Architects, Tokyo••1998 CD booklet design *Islands & Continents*

600MHz, by Ken Ishii, Sony Music Entertainment (Japan), Tokyo••1997 Demand on Demand, posters and leaflets for sales promotion, PCM TAKEO, Tokyo••Poster series "Nipponjin" (for *Close-up on Japan* exhibition), Tokyo selected bibliography 2002 *Sendendaigi*, Tokyo••1999 *Illustration*, Genko-Sha Publishing Co., Tokyo••1999 *Graphic Wave: Mamoru Suzuki, Kei Matsushita, Hiroshi Yonemura*, TransArt, Tokyo••1998 *i Magazine*, Amana Inc., Tokyo selected exhibitions 2002 *The Doraemon*, Suntory Museum, Osaka••2002 *DI+VISION*, Ginza Matsuya Design Gallery, Tokyo••1999 *Graphic Wave*, Ginza Graphic Gallery, Tokyo••1995 *Close-up of Japan*, Museo de Arte de São Paulo, São Paulo, Brazil awards 1997 Tokyo ADC Prize, Tokyo Art Directors Club, Tokyo••1997 JAGDA New Designer Award, Japan Graphic Designers Association, Tokyo••1991 Tokyo TDC Bronze Prize, Tokyo Type Directors Club, Japan••1986 Mainichi Design Awards First Advertisement Prize, Mainichi Shinbun-Sha, Japan memberships 1996 Japan Graphic Designers Association (JAGDA)

Chaz Maviyane-Davies
Born Harare, Zimbabwe, 1952. Lives and works in Boston education 1990–91 Advanced Diploma, Filmmaking, Central Saint Martins College of Art and Design, London••1980–81 M.A., Central School of Art & Design, London••1976–80 B.A., Middlesex University, London practice 2001–present Associate Professor, Massachusetts College of Art, Boston••1983–2000 Principal, The Maviyane-Project, Harare selected projects 2002 Poster, Circle of Hell, American Institute of Graphic Design, USA••2001 Homage to Lautrec, Nouveau salon des Cent, France••1996 Rights Article 4 poster, Zimbabwe••1998 Disease poster, Aujourd' hui pour demain, Switzerland ••1996 Rights Article 21 poster, Zimbabwe••1996 Rights Article 19 poster, Zimbabwe ••1996 Rights Article 15 poster, Zimbabwe selected bibliography 1998 "ID Forty," *I.D. Magazine*••1996 *Who's Who in Graphic Design*, Benteli-Werd Verlag, Switzerland, 2nd edition••1996 *First Choice: Leading International Designers*, Craftsman House, Australia, 2nd edition••1993 *Graphic Agitation*, Phaidon Press, London and New York selected exhibitions 2002 *Human Rights Human Lives: The Graphic Design of Chaz Maviyane-Davies*, Massachusetts College of Art, Boston••2001 Toulouse Lautrec, *Nouveau Salon des Cents* traveling exhibition••1999 *Dignity: The World of Chaz Maviyane-Davies*, Dai Nippon Gallery, Osaka, Japan••1997 "Rights," series of 13 posters, more than 25 countries worldwide awards 2003 "Yet with a Steady Beat" Award, Museum of Fine Arts, Boston••1993 Poster Award Ekoplagat, Gbel'any, Slovakia••1993 Best Director, Southern African Film Festival, Harare, Zimbabwe••1984 Bronze Medal, 11th International Biennale of Graphic Design Brno, Czech Republic memberships 2003 American Institute of Graphic Design (AIGA)••1985 Graphics Association of Zimbabwe

Ung Vai Meng
Born Macao, China, 1958. Lives and works in Macao education 1999–2002 Master studies, Theory of Chinese Painting, Academy of Fine Art of Guangzhou, Guangzhou, China••1991–92 Fine Art, ArCo, Lisbon, Portugal practice 1999–present Director, Macao Museum of Art••1985–98 Designer, Instituto Cultural de Macau selected projects 2001 Green Beijing, Great Olympics poster, Beijing Organizing Committee for the Games of the XXIX

Olympiad, Beijing••1999 The Macanese poster, Leal Senado de Macau••1998 Orquestra Chinesa de Macao poster, Instituto Cultural de Macau••1998 Poster design for XII Macao Internacional Music Festival, Instituto Cultural de Macau selected bibliography 2002 *Discover Asia International Poster Exhibition*, International Council of Graphic Design Associations (ICOGRADA) and Taiwan Poster Design Association••2002 *Korea International Poster Exhibition*, CDAK Communication Design Association of Korea, Seoul••1999 *China Design Yearbook 1998–99*, Jiu Zhou Books Publishing House, Beijing••1996 *HKDA Design 96 Show*, Hong Kong Designers Association, Hong Kong selected exhibitions 1998 *Traços sobre Macau*, World Trade Center, Macao••1998 *Tales of two cities*, Gallery of First Institute of Art & Design, Hong Kong••1993 *Works by Ung Vai Meng*, Zen Gallery, Oporto, Portugal••1992 *Landscapes of Body*, Macanese Mission in Lisbon awards 1997 Best of Visual Images, IdN Design Awards, Hong Kong••1996 Judge's Award, HKDA Design 96 Show, Hong Kong••1995 Distinction Award in the 1st Macao Design Contest, Macao••1989 1st prize for mural design, Central Library of Macau memberships 1987 Founding Member, Circulo dos Amigos de Cultura (CAC) de Macao

Saed Meshki
Born Gonabad, Iran, 1964. Lives and works in Tehran education 1988–93 Graphics, Faculty of Arts, Tehran University, Tehran••1986–88 Art, Teacher Training Faculty, Tehran practice 1989–present Freelance graphic designer selected projects 2002 Art director and graphic designer, 4th International Theatre Festival of Iranzamin, Ahvaz••2002 Design for the Constantinople, Constantinople music group, Montreal••2001 Art director and graphic designer, 3rd Abadan Film Festival, Abadan••2000 Organizer, *A Remarkable Event* exhibition, Tehran••1999 Art Director and Graphic Designer, EYE collection, Mahriz Publications, Tehran selected bibliography 2003 *World Graphic Design*, Merrill Publishing, London••2002 *Étapes Graphiques*, Paris selected exhibitions 2003 *Boof-e-Koor Iranian Typography*, Seyhoon Gallery, Tehran••2002 *Un cri persan*, Échirolles, France••2002 *Solidarity*, Galerie Bratri Capku, Prague••2002 *First stone*, Iranian Artist's house, Tehran awards 1997 Silver Medal for Book Cover Design, 6th Biennial of Iranian Graphic Designers, Tehran••1997 Creativity and Innovation Award, 6th Biennial of Iranian Graphic designers, Tehran••2002 Gold Medal for Book Cover Design, 7th Biennial of Iranian Graphic designers, Tehran memberships 2002 Alliance Graphique Internationale (AGI)••1997 Iranian Graphic Designers Society (IGDS)

Mooren + van der Velden
Maureen Mooren, born Dordrecht, Netherlands, 1969; Daniel van der Velden, born Rotterdam, Netherlands, 1971. Live and work in Amsterdam education 1996–98 Postgraduate Design, Jan van Eyck Academy, Maastricht (DvdV)••1990–96 Graphic Design, Rotterdam Academy of Arts (MM)••1992–96 Graphic Design, Rotterdam Academy of Arts (DvdV) practice 1998–present Freelance graphic designers••2001–present Guest Lecturers, Arnhem Academy of Arts••2000–present Guest Lecturers, Willem de Kooning Academy, Rotterdam••2001 Guest Lecturers, Gerrit Rietveld Academy, Amsterdam••2001 Guest Lecturers, Maryland Institute School of Arts, Baltimore selected projects 2001–04 *Archis* magazine, Artimo Foundation, Amsterdam••1999–2003 Invitations, ROOM art space, Rotterdam••2001 Informational beer cups in cooperation

with Fanclub, Lowlands Festival, Amsterdam••2001 Intersubjective novel *Oscillations*, La Lettre Volée, Brussels••1998 Invitations, Marres art space, Maastricht selected bibliography 2003 *Democratic Design: The Lectures*, Casco Projects, Utrecht••2003 *Reality Machines*, NAi Publishers, Rotterdam••2002 "File under Archis," *Eye* magazine 45, London selected exhibitions 2003 *Reality Machines*, Netherlands Architecture Institute, Rotterdam••2003 *Rotterdam Design Prize 2003*, Museum Boijmans van Beuningen, Rotterdam••2000 International Biennale of Graphic Design Brno, Czech Republic••1999 *Mode(s) d' Emploi*, Foundation for Visual Arts, Design and Architecture, Amsterdam awards 2003 Honorable Mention, Rotterdam Design Prize

Peter Moser
Born Lucerne, Switzerland, 1962. Lives and works in Lucerne education 1978–83 Graphic Design, Schule für Gestaltung, Lucerne practice 1995–present Partner, Velvet Creative Office, Lucerne••1984–95 Personal studios in Zurich and Lucerne selected projects 2002 *Sedel 1981–2001*, Velvet-Edition, Lucerne••2002 Poster series for Viper Basel International Festival for Film Video and New Media••2001 Poster for exhibition *Happy—Das Versprechen der Werbung*, Museum für Kommunikation, Bern••2001 Book design, *Suggestions*, Architekturgalerie Luzern••1997 Poster for exhibition *Frankensteins Kinder—Film und Medizin*, Museum für Gestaltung Zurich••1989 Poster series for Viper Lucerne International Festival for Film Video and New Media awards 2002 Most Beautiful Swiss Books, Federal Office for Culture, Switzerland••2002 100 Best Posters Award, Berlin••2001 Bronze Poster Award, Art Directors Club, Switzerland••1999 Poster of the Year, APG and Eidgenössisches Departement des Innern, Switzerland memberships 2001 Alliance Graphique Internationale (AGI)

Melanie Mues
Born Bielefeld, Germany, 1970. Lives and works in London education 1991–95 Communication Design, Academy of Art, Bremen practice 2001–present Freelance designer, London••1997–2001 Designer, Frost Design, London••1996–97 Designer, Meta Design, London••1995–96 Freelance designer, Berlin selected projects 2003 Poster design for resource room, Tate Modern, London••2003 Exhibition design, *Eva Hesse*, Tate Modern, London••2003 Poster design for *Butterfly* installation by Richard Wilson, The Wapping Project, London••2003 Installation for the Classic Design Awards, Victoria & Albert Museum, London••2002 Exhibition design, *Eija-Liisa Ahtila*, Tate Modern, London••2002 *Sanctuary*, by Steve McCurry, Phaidon Press, London and New York••2001 Invitation, Omni Colour, London

Müller + Hess
Beat Müller, born Basel, Switzerland, 1965; Wendelin Hess, born Basel, Switzerland, 1968. Live and work in Basel and Zurich education 1986–92 Graphic Design, Schule für Gestaltung, Basel (WH)••1986–91 Graphic Design, Schule für Gestaltung, Basel (BM) practice 1995–present Müller + Hess••1994–present Various teaching jobs in design schools, Basel, Lucerne, Zurich••1993 Started Hoch drei design studio selected projects 2001 Art Directors Club Switzerland Yearbook 2001 (with Ludovic Balland), ADC, Switzerland••1999 Poster and invitations for exhibition *Richard Paul Lohse—*

Konstruktive Gebrauchsgrafik, Museum für Gestaltung Zürich••1999–2002 Redesign and art direction of *Das Magazin*, Tamedia AG, Zurich••1997 Poster and program for music festival Neue Musik Rümlingen, Switzerland selected bibliography 2000 *Swiss Graphic Design*, Die Gestalten Verlag, Berlin••2000 *Benzin: Young Swiss Graphic Design*, Lars Müller Publishers, Baden, Switzerland••1999 "Dismantling the Basel Principle," *Eye* magazine 32, London selected exhibitions 2002 *Design Now*, Design Museum, London awards 1998 Jan Tschichold Award, Switzerland

Hideki Nakajima
Born Saitama, Japan, 1961. Lives and works in Tokyo education No specific education for graphic design practice 1999–present Member of creative unit Code••1995–present Director, Nakajima Design••1992–95 Art director, Rockin' on, Tokyo••1988–91 Senior Designer, Masami Shimizu Design Office, Tokyo selected projects 1992–present Art direction, *CUT* magazine, Rockin' on, Tokyo••1996–present Art direction and design for Ryuichi Sakamoto's CDs and LPs, Warner Music Japan and For Life Records, Tokyo••2002 Cover design, *Argentine Hag*, by Banana Yoshimoto, Rockin' on, Tokyo••1999 Promotional posters for Tag Heuer, Switzerland••1999 "Sampled Life" art box for Ryuichi Sakamoto's opera *LIFE*, Code, Tokyo selected bibliography 2002 *IDEA* magazine 295, Tokyo••2001 "Artist, Designer and Director Hideki Nakajima," *Scan #13*, Rikuyosha Publishing, Tokyo••1999 *Revival*, Rockin' on, Tokyo selected exhibitions 2002 *Code exhibition: new village*, Tokyo, Osaka, and Kyoto••2001 *AGI—Graphisme(s)*, Bibliothèque Nationale de France, Paris••2001 *032c / The searching stays with you*, vonRot and The Pineal Eye, Berlin and London••2000 *Graphic wave 5* , Ginza Graphic Gallery, Tokyo awards 2001 Chicago Athenaeum's Good Design Award••2000 Best Design Award, 19th International Biennale of Graphic Design Brno, Czech Republic••1995–2000 Five Gold and seven Silver Awards, Art Directors Club, New York••1999 Tokyo Art Directors Club Award memberships 2002 Art Directors Club, Tokyo••2002 Type Directors Club, Tokyo••1998 Alliance Graphique Internationale (AGI)••1997 Art Directors Club, New York

Dylan Nelson
Born Albany, Oregon, USA, 1977. Lives and works in Portland education 2000–2002 M.F.A., Graphic Design, Cranbrook Academy of Art, Bloomfield Hills, Michigan••1995–99 B.F.A., Graphic Design, Oregon State University, Corvallis, Oregon practice 1997–present Co-Owner/Creative Director, Spare Parts, Portland, Oregon••2002–present Art direction/motion design, Nike, Beaverton, Oregon••2000–2002 Designer, Cranbrook Academy of Art/Museum, Bloomfield Hills, Michigan••1999–2000 Designer, Wieden + Kennedy, Portland, Oregon selected projects 2003 Print campaign, Nike Cycling Patch Kit, TREK, Wisconsin••2002 Broadcast campaign Yellow, Nike, Beaverton, Oregon••2002 Book design, Cranbrook Academy of Art catalogue, Cranbrook Academy of Art, Bloomfield Hills, Michigan••2002 *Zine Scene* identity, Cranbrook Art Museum, Bloomfield Hills, Michigan••2002 Self-promotional mixed-media installation *Don't Stop Living in the Red* ••2001 Self-promotional poster, Albany, OR 97321 selected bibliography 2003 Art Directors Club Yearbook, New York••2003 Nederlandse Designselectie Yearbook, Netherlands••2003 "Design Competition

Winner," *CMYK* Magazine●●2002 "New Talent Design," *Graphis* magazine

selected exhibitions 2002 *Walk on Water*, Basil Hallward Art Gallery, Portland, Oregon●●2002 *Zine Scene*, Cranbrook Art Museum, Bloomfield Hills, Michigan●●2001 *GM Design Exhibition*, General Motors, Detroit, Michigan●●2001 *Exhibit of Evidence*, Center for Creative Studies, Detroit, Michigan **awards** 2003 Typography of Distinction Winner, New York Type Directors Club●●2003 Design Competition Winner, *CMYK* Magazine●●2002 Featured Talent, Blood Bank●●1998 AIGA Harvest Award, Portland, Oregon

Yves Netzhammer
Born Schaffhausen, Switzerland, 1970. Lives and works in Zurich **education** 1990–95 Graphic Design, Hochschule für Gestaltung und Kunst, Zurich●●1986–90 Studies in architectural drawing, Schaffhausen **professional** 1995–present Independent artist and graphic designer **selected projects** 2003 Exhibition project including film, installation, book, poster, and invitation, Helmhaus Zürich●●2002 Theater production, *Die Stelle im Park*, Theater Neumarkt, Zurich●●2001 "Chocolate" stamp design for Swiss Post (with Ralph Schraivogel)●●2000 Exhibition works and catalogue with CD-ROM, "Statements"●●1999 Concept and imagery, *Das Magazin no. 47*, Tamedia AG, Zurich **selected bibliography** 2003 *Die überraschende Verschiebung der Sollbruchstelle eines in optimalen Verhältnissen aufgewachsenen Astes*, by Yves Netzhammer, Verlag für Moderne Kunst, Nuremberg●●1999/2003 *Wenn man etwas gegen seine Eigenschaften benützt, muss man dafür einen anderen Namen finden*, by Yves Netzhammer, Verlag für Moderne Kunst, Nuremberg●●2000 *Grosse Spiegel werden verloren: Informationen von Abwesenheit, damit Anwesenheit entstehen kann*, Statements IV catalogue and CD-ROM●●1997 *Was sich erzählen lässt, wird verbessert werden*, by Yves Netzhammer, Verlag Ricco Bilger, Zurich **selected exhibitions** 2003 *Die überraschende Verschiebung der Sollbruchstelle eines in optimalen Verhältnissen aufgewachsenen Astes*, solo exhibition, Helmhaus Zürich●●2001 *Body As Bite*, Neues Kunstmuseum, Lucerne●●2000 *Statements*, solo exhibition, Kunst-Werke Berlin●●1999 Manor-Kunstpreis solo exhibition, Museum zu Allerheiligen, Schaffhausen **awards** 2002 One-year "Atelier" grant from City of Zurich to work in New York●●2001 Most Beautiful Swiss Books Award, Federal Office for Culture, Switzerland●●2000 Most Beautiful Swiss Posters Award, Federal Office for Culture, Switzerland●●1998 Most Beautiful Swiss Books Award, Federal Office for Culture, Switzerland

Christoph Niemann
Born Waiblingen, Germany, 1970. Lives and works in New York **education** 1991–97 Graphic Design, State Academy of Fine Arts, Stuttgart, Germany **practice** 1999–present Teacher, Conceptual Design, School of Visual Arts, New York●●1995–present Freelance designer/illustrator for magazines, newspapers, and corporate clients **selected projects** 2003 F-Stop Catalogue for Font-Shop Berlin (art director Stefan Sagmeister)●●2001 Cover, *American Illustration Annual XX* (art director Robert Priest) **selected bibliography** 2002 *D&AD Graphics Book*, RotoVision, London●●1999 *Fresh Dialogue 1*, with Nicholas Blechman and Paul Sahre, Princeton Architectural Press, New York●●1998 *The Good Portrait*, Maro Verlag, Germany **selected exhibitions** 2003 National Design Triennal, Cooper-Hewitt, National Design

Museum, Smithsonian Institution, New York●●2002–03 Young Guns I & II, Art Directors Club, New York **awards** 2001 American Illustration Award●●2000 ADC Award, Art Directors Club, New York●●1998 Student Talent Award, Art Directors Club, Germany **memberships** 1999 Alliance Graphique Internationale (AGI) ●●1997 American Institute of Graphic Arts (AIGA)

Nagi Noda
Born Tokyo, Japan, 1973. Lives and works in Tokyo **education** 1991–95 Graphic, Product and Interior Design, Women's College of Fine Arts, Tokyo **practice** 2003–present Founder, Uchu Country, Tokyo●●1997–2003 Designer, Sun-AD, Tokyo●●1995–97 Designer, I & S Onuki Design, Tokyo **selected projects** 2002 Poster and TV commercials for Japanese fashion brand Theatre PRODUCTS', Theatre PRODUCTS', Tokyo●●2002 Poster and music video for Yuki, Epic Records, Japan●●2001 Book covers, *It's Good Because It's Love*, by Shungiku Uchida, Koudansha, Tokyo●●2001–02 Posters and TV campaign for department store Laforet, Laforet Harajuku, Tokyo●●2001 Poster campaign for Nike women's swimwear, Nike, Japan **selected bibliography** 2002 *New Blood*, rikuyou-sha, Japan **selected exhibitions** 2003 *Graphic Wave 2003*, Ginza Graphic Gallery, Tokyo **awards** 2002–03 TDC Prize, Tokyo Type Directors Club●●2002 Silver Award, Art Directors Club, New York●●2001 ADC Prize, Tokyo Art Directors Club●●1999 Gold Prize, Tokyo Type Directors Club **memberships** 2001 Tokyo Type Directors Club●●2001 Japan Graphic Designers Association (JAGDA)

Norm
Dimitri Bruni, born Biel, Switzerland, 1970; Manuel Krebs, born Bern, Switzerland, 1970. Live and work in Zurich **education** 1991–96 Graphic Design, Kantonale Schule für Gestaltung, Biel (DB+MK) **practice** 2000–present Professors of Graphic Design, École Cantonale d'Art de Lausanne●●1999–present Norm **selected projects** 2002 *Norm: The Things*, Norm, Zurich●●2001 Typeface Simple, Lineto, Zurich and Berlin●●2000 *Norm: Introduction*, Norm, Zurich●●1999 Typeface Normetica, Lineto, Zurich and Berlin **selected bibliography** 2002 *Super–Welcome to Graphic Wonderland*, Zurich●●2001 *Restart: New Systems in Graphic Design*, Thames & Hudson, London●●2000 *Swiss Graphic Design*, Die Gestalten, Berlin●●2000 *Benzin: Young Swiss Graphic Design*, Lars Müller Publishers, Baden, Switzerland **selected exhibitions** 2002 *Postscript*, Künstlerhaus Wien, Vienna●●2002 *We love to meet you*, Palazzo Fortuny, Venice●●2002 *Swiss Design Awards*, Museum für Gestaltung, Zurich●●2001 *Swiss Design Awards*, Museum Bellerive, Zurich **awards** 2003 Jan Tschichold Prize, Switzerland●●2002 Swiss Design Award, Switzerland●●2001 Swiss Design Award, Switzerland●●1999 Swiss Design Award, Switzerland

Nowakteufelknyrim
Stefan Nowak, born Hoexter, Germany, 1964; Philipp Teufel, born Altshausen, Germany, 1958; Petra Knyrim, born Wermelskirchen, Germany, 1967. Live and work in Düsseldorf **education** 1989–92 Visual Communication, University of Applied Arts, Düsseldorf (PK+SN)●●1986–89 Communication Design, University of Applied Arts, Darmstadt, Germany (PK+SN)●●1980–85 Visual Communication, Hochschule für Gestaltung, Schwäbisch Gmünd, Germany (PT) **practice** 1995–present Partner, Nowakteufelknyrim (PT) ●●1992–present

Founding Partners, Nowakteufelknyrim (PK+SN)●●1994–present Professor of Communication Design, University of Applied Arts, Düsseldorf (PT)●●1995–2001 Lecturer, University of Applied Arts, Düsseldorf (SN)●●1993–95 Lecturer, University of Applied Arts, Dortmund (SN)●●1985–94 Concept Design, Illner & Teufel, Frankfurt (PT) selected projects 2003 Corporate and exhibition design, Museum Römerkastell, Monheim, Germany●●2002 Orientation System for Pedestrians, Düsseldorf, Germany ●●2001 Pilon, Orientation System for Dresden●●2000 Corporate design, *Continental Shift—A Voyage Between Cultures* exhibition, Bonnefanten Museum Maastricht, Belgium●●2000 Communication design, *Totale* exhibition, Museum für Neue Kunst Freiburg, Germany ●●1996–99 Corporate and exhibition design, Geldmuseum Frankfurt, German Federal Bank selected bibliography 2003 *Sushi* magazine, HfG Offenbach, Germany●●2001 *Museografie und Ausstellungsdesign*, avedition, Ludwigsburg, Germany●●1999 *Einszueins—Positionen zum ausstellen*, Nowakteufelknyrim, Düsseldorf●●1997 *Design Ausstellen—Austellungsdesign*, Lars Müller Publishers, Baden, Switzerland selected exhibitions 2002 International Poster Biennale, Seoul●●2001 International Design Exhibition, Osaka●●2000 German Award for Communication Design exhibition, Essen awards 2001 Grand Prize, Prime Ministers Prize, International Design Competition, Osaka●●2001 Society of Typographic Design Award, London●●2002 Joseph Binder Award, Silver, Vienna●●2000 German Award for Communication Design, Design Zentrum, Essen memberships 2002 Art Directors Club (ADC), Germany (PK+SN+PT)●●2000 2id, Founding Member, Institute for Interdisciplinary Design, Leipzig (PT)

Fabio Ongarato
Born Melbourne, Australia, 1971. Lives and works in Melbourne education 1987–91 Visual Communication, Royal Melbourne Institute of Technology, Melbourne practice 1992–present Creative Director, Fabio Ongarato Design selected projects 2002 Identity, Australian Centre for Contemporary Art, Melbourne●●2001 Event and catalogue design, *Lineage— The Architecture of Daniel Libeskind*, Jewish Museum, Melbourne●●2000–2001 Event identity, Melbourne Festival Australia●●1997 Winter fashion campaign featuring artist Bill Henson, Scanlan & Theodore, Melbourne●●2002 Editorial design, *BIG* magazine, New York●●2001 Summer fashion campaign, Karen Walker, Auckland, New Zealand selected bibliography 2003 *I.D. Magazine*, New York●●2003 "Melbourne Drawing on Culture," *Composite* Magazine, Tokyo●●2002 Australian Special Issue, *Eye* magazine, London●●2001 *Graphics International*, London awards 2002 Distinction, Australian Graphic Design Association (AGDA)●●2001 Major Award, International Society of Typographic Designers (ISTD), London●●2000 Judge's Prize, Australian Graphic Design Association (AGDA)●●1999 Silver Award Nomination, Design & Art Direction (D&AD), London memberships 2000 International Society of Typographic Designers (ISTD), London●●1999 Design Institute of Australia (DIA)●●1998 Design & Art Directors (D&AD), London●●1997 Australian Graphic Design Association (AGDA)

Tania Prill
Born Hamburg, Germany, 1969. Lives and works in Zurich education 1990–96 Visual Communication, University of Fine Arts, Bremen, Germany●●1993–95 Visual Communication, University of Art and Design, Zurich practice 2001–present Lecturer, Lucerne School of Arts of Design,

Lucerne●●2001 Cooperation with Alberto Vieceli, Zurich●●2000 Lecturer, School for Art and Media Design, Zurich●●1996–2000 Lecturer, School for New Media, Karlsruhe, Germany●●1998 Founding of the GmbH für visuelle Gestaltung, Zurich●●1997 Professional Designer, Zintzmeyer & Lux, Zurich, and running own studio, Zurich selected projects 2003 Book Design, *Inchoate: An Experiment in Architectural Education*, ETH, Zurich, and ACTAR, Barcelona●●2002 Posters for *Stand der Dinge: Neustes Wohnen in Zürich* (with Alberto Vieceli), Federal Building Department of Zurich●●1999 Book project, *Die Schweizer Autobahn*, Museum für Gestaltung, Zurich●●1998 *Werkschau Hans-Rudolf Lutz*, exhibition of the work of the Swiss typographer, author, publisher, and teacher Hans-Rudolf Lutz, Emmenbrücke, Lucerne selected bibliography 2001 *KAK* magazine, January issue, Moscow●●2001 "Swiss Design Now," *KAK* magazine, February issue, Moscow ●●2000 *Benzin: Young Swiss Graphic Design*, Lars Müller Publishers, Baden●●1996 *Typoundso*,Verlag Hans-Rudolf Lutz, Zurich selected exhibitions 2003 *Die schönsten Schweizer Bücher*, Museum für Gestaltung, Zurich ●●2001 2nd International Poster Exhibition, Ningbo, China●●2000 19th International Biennale of Graphic Design Brno, Czech Republic awards 2003 Most Beautiful Swiss Books (with Alberto Vieceli), Federal Office for Culture, Switzerland

QWER
Iris Utikal, born Kassel, Germany, 1966; Michael Gais, born Hagen, Germany, 1965. Live and work in Cologne education 1986–92 Graphic Design, University of Applied Arts, Düsseldorf (IU+MG) practice 2002–present Professors of Typography and Book Design, Cologne International School of Design (IU +MG)●●1994–present Founding Partners, QWER, since 1995 in Cologne●●1991–94 Assistance in the Arbeitsgemeinschaft Loesch, Düsseldorf (IU+MG)●●1988–90 Internships in London, Helsinki, and Turku (MG)●●1985–90 Internships in London, New York, Paris, Zurich, Madrid, and Tokyo (IU) selected projects 1997–present Graphic design, Zanders Feinpapiere, Bergisch Gladbach, Germany●●2001 Corporate Design, Kommunalverband Ruhrgebiet, Essen●●2001 Corporate and communication design, Kulturregion Hannover●●2001 Corporate and communication design, Niedersächsische Sparkassenstiftung, Hannover●● 1994–2000 Corporate identity and Web design, World EXPO 2000 Hannover●●2000 Corporate and communication design, Wilhelm Lehmbruck Museum, Duisburg selected exhibitions 2000 *Corporate Design der Stadt Frankfurt am Main*, Frankfurt●●1998 *Brecht 100 Plakate*, Berlin●●1996 German Award for Communication Design exhibition, Essen●●1994 Triennial of the German Poster Museum, Essen●●1994 International Poster Festival Chaumont, France●●1994 14th International Poster Biennial, Warsaw, Poland selected bibliography 2003 *QWER*, Floating Design, Beijing●●1998 *Typographie Wann Wer Wie*, Könemann, Cologne●●1997 *Corporate Identity und Corporate Design*, avedition, Ludwigsburg●●1997 *form* magazine, January, Germany awards 2002 Second Prize, Kalenderschau, Stuttgart●●2001 Art Directors Club Award, Berlin●●2001 100 Best Posters Award, German Design Associations, Berlin●●2001 Merit Award, Art Directors Club, New York●●1999 Winner, Pro Carton CMA Carton Award Competition, Belgium

Reala
Laurent Benner, born Langenthal, Switzerland, 1975; Samuel Nyholm born Lund, Sweden, 1973; Jonas Wlliamson, born Umeå, Sweden, 1973. Live and work in

London (LB) and Stockholm (SN+JW) education 1998–2000 M.A., Royal College of Art, London (LB)••1995–99 M.F.A., Konstfack University College of Art, Stockholm (SN+JW)••1995–98 B.A. (Hons.), Central Saint Martins College of Art and Design, London (LB)••1998 Central Saint Martins College of Art and Design, London (SN)••1997 Parsons School of Design, New York (JW) practice 1998–present Founders and Principals, Reala••1996–present Freelance graphic design, illustration, animation••2002 Professors, Beijing Institute of Art and Design••2002 Professors, Brighton University••2000–2002 Professors, Konstfack University, College of Arts, Craft and Design, Stockholm••2001 Professors, École Cantonale d'Art de Lausanne (ECAL)••2000 Professors, Beckman's School of Design, Stockholm selected projects 2003 Design Concept, "Perfect Performance," Performance Festival, Stockholm••1998–2003 Graphic Design, Lydmar Hotel, Stockholm••2002 Music Video, Garbage, Harry Nash, London••2001–02 Research project and motion graphics, Konstfack, Stockholm••2001–02 Graphic concept and motion graphics, Swedish National Television selected bibliography 2003 Super-Welcome to Graphic Wonderland, Zurich••2003 Reala DVD, GAS, Tokyo••2000 01+81, Tokyo••2000 Benzin:Young Swiss Graphic Design, Lars Müller Publishers, Baden selected exhibitions 2003 From Sweden with Love, Museum für Gestaltung, Zurich••2002 I Love To Meet You, Palazzo Fortuny, Venice••2001 Stealing Eyeballs, K-Haus, Vienna awards 2000 Winner of the Swiss Federal Design Competition••2000 Company of the Year, Konstfack••1999 Ung Svensk Form, Sweden

Casey Reas
Born Troy, Ohio, USA, 1972. Lives and works in Ivrea, Italy education 1999–2001 Media Arts and Sciences, Aesthetics + Computation Group, MIT Media Laboratory, Cambridge, Massachusetts••1991–96 Graphic Design, School of Design, Architecture, Art, and Planning, University of Cincinnati practice 2001–03 Associate Professor, Interaction Design Institute, Ivrea, Italy••1999–2001 Research Assistant, Aesthetics + Computation Group, MIT Media Laboratory, Cambridge, Massachusetts••1997–99 Design Director/Designer, I/O 360° Digital Design, New York selected projects 2003 Processing, Interaction Design Institute Ivrea, Italy••2002 HairyRed, GroupC, Troy, Ohio••2002 Tissue, GroupC, Troy, Ohio••2001 Path, GroupC, Troy, Ohio••2001 RPM, IAMAS, Ogaki, Japan••2000 Dakadaka, Ars Electronica Center, Linz, Austria selected bibliography 2003 Ubersee #2, Die Gestalten Verlag, Berlin••2002 The Graphics Book, D&AD, London••2002 "Behavioral Kinetic Sculpture," The Art of Programming, Sonic Acts Press, Amsterdam••2002 "New Visual Artists Review: 20 Under 30," Print magazine, New York selected exhibitions 2002 Casey Reas/Golan Levin, Bitforms Gallery, New York••2001 Animations, P.S. 1 Contemporary Art Center, New York••2001 Interaction '01, Dialog with Expanded Images, IAMAS, Ogaki, Japan••2001 Workspheres, Museum of Modern Art, New York awards 2001 Silver Medal, 80th Annual Art Directors Club Awards, New York••2000 Honorable Mention, Tokyo Type Directors Club••1999 Communication Graphics 20 Award, American Institute of Graphic Arts, New York••1998 Web 100 Show, American Center for Design, Chicago

David Richmond
Born Manchester, United Kingdom, 1964. Lives and works in London education 1983–86 Graphic Design, London School of Printing practice 2000–present R Design, London (with Iain Dobson, Steve Sheffield, Helen Brewer, Beverly Cook, Lindsey Webb, Janey Barrett)••1991–92 David Richmond Associates, London••1990–91 Michael Abramson, New York••1986–90 Smith & Milton, London selected projects 2001 Branding, packaging, and advertising, The Food Doctor, London••2003 Packaging, Selfridges, London••2000 Identity and packaging, Mea Cosmetics, London••1996 Packaging, Inventory Olive Oil, London••2003 Identity, Sara Bruce Food Consultant, London••2001 Identity, Martin Pritchard Dentist, London selected bibliography 1996 British Packaging 1996, BC Editions, London••1990 Power Packaging 1990, USA memberships 1998 D&AD••1998 Design Business Association

Sanja Rocco
Born Zagreb, Croatia, 1955. Lives and works in Zagreb education 2003 Marketing, Faculty of Economics, University of Zagreb••1982 M.A., Architecture, Faculty of Architecture, University of Zagreb practice 2000–present Art Director and Manager, Rocco & Partner••1990–2000 Freelance designer working in team with T. Bratelj at Castelvenere design studio••1984–90 Designer, Zagreb Publishing House••1983–84 Graffiti design studio selected projects 2002–03 Visual identity, Rocco & Partner Music Production Label, Zagreb••1996–2003 Visual identity and promotion, Sobota Art Gallery, Zagreb••1998–2000 Package redesign project, Pik Vrbovec meat industry, Vrbovec••1998–99 Visual identity, Radio Drama International Festival, Croatian Radio and Television, Zagreb••1991–96 Visual identity and promotion, Croatian Union for the Blind, Zagreb selected bibliography 2000 European Design Annual, RotoVision, London••2000 Print magazine 54, no. 2, New York••1999 78th Art Directors Club Annual, New York••1996 BIO 15, Biennial of Industrial Design catalogue, Ljubljana selected exhibitions 2000 19th International Biennale of Graphic Design Brno, Czech Republic••1998 ZGRAF 8, Zagreb••1996 BIO 15, Ljubljana••1995 UNESCO, Paris••1995 Golden Bee Biennale of Graphic Design, Moscow awards 1999 Merit Award, 78th Art Directors Club Annual Design Competition, New York••1996 Golden Award, Third Crane European Letterhead Competition, London and Amsterdam••1996 Silver Bell, 3rd Festo Croatian Advertising Festival, Croatia••1992 1st Prize, Visual Identity Competition, Croatian National and University Library, Croatia memberships 2001 Friends of ICOGRADA••1991 ICOGRADA••1984 Croatian Association of Applied Arts Artists (ULUPUH)

Gabriela Rodriguez
Born Mexico City, 1956. Lives and works in Mexico City education 1981–83 Fine Art, San Carlos Academy, Mexico City••1976–81 Graphic Design, National School of Fine Arts, Mexico City practice 2001–present Working in collaboration with Ken Cato on various design projects••1993–present Principal, own studio, Mexico City••1983–present Freelance graphic designer, Mexico City••1981–83 Director of Graphic Design Department, National Institute of Education for Adults, Mexico City selected projects 2002 Channel Eleven Identities, Canal Once, Mexico City••2002 "Greece: Women, Eroticism & Poetry," Agipinu Restaurant, Mexico City••2001 Monterrey Airport ceiling design, Grupo Aeroportuario Centro Norte, Monterrey••1996 Homage to Breton, Embassy of France/CONACULTA/UNAM, Mexico City••1993 Spanish Textbooks, Public Education Ministry, Mexico City••1986 Values of Democracy posters, Federal Electoral

Institute, Mexico City selected bibliography 2003 *Eye* magazine, London••2003 *Package & Design*, Beijing••2002 *A! Diseño*, Mexico City••2000 *Étapes Graphiques*, Paris selected exhibitions 2003 *Mexican Design*, Milan Biennale••2001 *Homage to Toulouse-Lautrec*, international touring exhibition••2000 *Traces of Light*, Museo Santa Domingo, Oaxaca••1997 *10 Mexican Graphic Designers*, DNP Duo Dojima, Osaka and Ginza Graphic Gallery, Tokyo awards 2003 Creative Consulting, DVA Platinum Total Package Design, Los Angeles••1998 Gold Award, Political Graphics, Fifth International Biennial of the Poster in Mexico, Mexico City••1996 Silver Award, Cultural Graphics, Fourth International Biennial of the Poster in Mexico, Mexico City••1992 and 1993 Textbook Design, Public Education Ministry, Mexico City memberships 1998 Alliance Graphique Internationale (AGI)

Joe Sacco
Born Kirkop, Malta, 1960. Based in New York education 1978–81 B.A., Journalism, University of Oregon, Eugene practice 1981–present Independent cartoonist/journalist••2000 Lecturer, School of Visual Arts, New York••1986 Editor, *The Comics Journal*, Los Angeles••1985–86 Coeditor and copublisher, Portland Permanent Press selected bibliography 2002 *Eye* magazine 44, London••2000 *Safe Area Gorazde*, by Joe Sacco, Fantagraphics Books, Seattle••1998 *Details* magazine, September issue, New York••1993–96 *Palestine*, by Joe Sacco, Fantagraphics Books, Seattle selected exhibitions 2001 *Joe Sacco a Ravenna*, Museo d'Arte della Citta, Ravenna, Italy••2000 State University of New York, Buffalo awards 2002 VPRO Grand Prix, Haarlem, Netherlands••2001 Will Eisner Award for Best Original Graphic Novel, USA••2001 Guggenheim Fellowship

Ahn Sang-Soo
Born Chungju, Korea, 1952. Lives and works in Seoul education 2001 Hon. Doctor of Design, Kingston University, London••1995 Ph.D., Hanyang University, Seoul••1981 M.F.A., Graphic Design, Hongik University, Seoul••1977 M.A., Graphic Design, Hongik University, Seoul practice 1991–present Graphic Designer and Professor, Hongik University, Seoul••1985–91 President, Ahn Graphics••1981–85 Art Director, *Madang Magazine* selected projects 1985–present Design for magazine *Bogoseo/Bogoseo*••1995–present Poster designs for the Jooksan International Art Festival••1995–present Ahn Graphics Calendar Design••2001 Seoul TypoJanchi Symbol Design••2000 ICOGRADA Millennium Congress, *Oullim* symbol design••1999 Ssamzie Art Book Project selected bibliography 2002 *Graphis* 327, New York••2002 *Baseline* magazine, United Kingdom••1999 *Hangul Design*, Ahn Graphics, Seoul selected exhibitions 1990 *Front DMZ Cultural Arts Movement Exhibition*, Seoul City Museum••2001 *Hangul Exhibition*, GGG Gallery, Tokyo; Osaka DDD Gallery, Japan••2002 Solo exhibition, Rodin Gallery, Seoul••2002 *Works*, Rhode Island School of Design, Providence awards 1999 Grand Prix, Zgraf, Croatia memberships 1999 Alliance Graphique Internationale (AGI)••1990 Visual Designers' Association of Korea (VIDAK)

Yasuhiro Sawada
Born Tokyo, Japan, 1961. Lives and works in Tokyo education 1981–85 Graphic Design, Tokyo University of Fine Arts and Music, Tokyo practice 1994–present Assistant Professor, Department of Graphic Design, Tama Art University••1989–present Sawada Yasuhiro Design Studio••1985–89 Art Director, Creative Department, Suntory, Japan selected projects 1998–2000 Posters for architectural consultancy, Kosaka Giken, Tokyo••1994 Poster for hundredth birthday of Sharaku, Mainichi Newspapers, Tokyo••1991 Poster for Amnesty International event, Tokyo••1989 Catalogue, Y's for men, Yohji Yamamoto, Tokyo selected exhibitions 1997 *4 From Tokyo*, New York Art Directors Club Gallery, New York••1997 *100 Japan Plakat 20 Tevezotol*, Decsi Galerie, Budapest••1995 *Close-up of Japan*, São Paolo Art Museum••1999 *Graphic Message for Ecology*, Ginza Graphic Gallery, Tokyo••1996 International Poster Triennial, Toyama••1991 Solo exhibition *P2*, Ginza Graphic Gallery, Tokyo awards 1994 Bronze Prize, International Poster Triennial, Toyama••1993 New Designer Award, Japan Graphic Designers Association, Tokyo••1991 Silver Prize, Tokyo Type Directors Club selected bibliography 2002 *Graphic Wave 7*, Ginza Graphic Gallery, Tokyo••1999 *Sawada Yasuhiro, No Graphic Design*, Kohoku Art Publishers, Tokyo memberships 2001 Alliance Graphique Internationale (AGI)••1992 Japan Graphic Designers Association••1992 Tokyo Type Directors Club

Claudia Schmauder
Born Zurich, Switzerland, 1967. Lives and works in Zurich education 1992–97 Visual Communication, Schule für Gestaltung, Zurich practice 1998–present Freelance graphic designer••1998–99 Research Projects, Schule für Gestaltung, Zurich selected projects 2001 Illustrations for in-flight magazine, *Swissair Gazette*, Swissair••1996–2001 Posters and book designs, Johann Jacobs Museum, Zurich••2000 Cover illustration, Trucks calendar 2001, Daimler-Benz (Mercedes)••1999 Research project for Blister Packaging, Schule für Gestaltung, Zurich selected bibliography 1998 "Claudia Schmauder," *IDEA* magazine 271, Tokyo selected exhibitions 2002 Poster exhibition, *Swiss Posters: Collection of the National Museum*, Poznan, Poland••1999 *Type Directors Exhibition*, New York••1998 18th International Biennale of Graphic Design Brno, Czech Republic awards 2000 Tokyo Type Directors Club Award••1999 Diploma for Typographic Excellence, Type Directors Club, New York••1998 18th International Biennale of Graphic Design Brno, Czech Republic••1996 Swiss Posters of the Year

Nico Schweizer
Born Zurich, Switzerland, 1969. Lives and works in New York education 1992–94 School of Visual Arts, New York••1990–92 Art Center College of Design, Montreux, Switzerland practice 2003–present Art Director, *I.D. Magazine*, New York••2000–present Professor, Typography and Design, Cooper Union School of Design, New York••1997–98 Collaborated with J. Abbott Miller, Design/Writing/Research, New York••1997 Collaborated with Cornel Windlin, Switzerland••1994 Collaborated with Jonathan Hoefler, The Hoefler Type Foundry, New York selected projects 2003 Book design, *Room 606—The SAS House and the Work of Arne Jacobsen*, by Michael Sheridan, Phaidon Press, London and New York••2002 Record cover, *Kamaal/The Abstract*, by Q-Tip, Arista Records, USA••2002 Typeface, LeCorbusier Bold, Mediadub.com, New York••2001 Record cover, *Young Lawyers*, by French Kicks, Startime Records, USA••2000 Book cover, *Goldfinger*, by Ian Fleming, Flagstick Publications, USA selected bibliography 2001 *Young Guns 3*, Art Directors Club, New York selected exhibitions 2002

Chen Shaohua

Born Zhejiang, China, 1954. Lives and works in Shenzhen and Beijing **education** 1982 Graduated from Tingshua University, Academy of Art and Design, Beijing••1978 Graduated from Central Academy of Craftwork and Art, Beijing••1975 Graduated from Central Academy of Arts & Design, Xi'an, China **practice** 2001 Established Beijing Chen Shaohua Design••1992 Established Shenzhen Chen Shaohua Design••1988 Engaged in advertising and design in Shenzhen••1982–88 Professor, Xi'an Academy of Art, Xi'an, China **selected projects** 2002 Logo, Beijing Foreign Studies University, Beijing••2002 Logo, China Development Bank••2001 Logo, Beijing 2008 Olympic Games Bid Committee ••2001 Logo, Asian Development Bank 35th annual meeting, Shanghai••1995 Stamp design for Fourth United Nations World Conference on Women, Stamp Printing Bureau, China **selected exhibitions** 1998 16th International Poster Biennale, Warsaw••1998 *L'affiche Chinoise* exhibition and lecture, Centre Georges Pompidou, Paris••1997 Included in the *Asia-Pacific Poster Exhibition*, Hong Kong••1997 5th Best Advertising Exhibition of China **awards** 1998 Chairman's Prize, 18th International Graphic Design Biennale Brno, Czech Republic••1996 Judge's Award and silver prize for poster design, *Graphic Design in China* exhibition••1992 Silver Prize, Poster Design, *Graphic Design in China* exhibition••1984 Gold Prize, 6th Exhibition of Fine Art of China••1984 Gold Rooster Award, Fine Art Direction of Chinese film **memberships** 1999 Alliance Graphic International (AGI)••1984 China Association of Artists

So Man-yee

Born Hong Kong, 1953. Lives and works in Hong Kong **education** 1973 Graphic Design, First Institute of Art and Design, Hong Kong••1972 Western Painting, Hong Kong Ninghoi Arts School, Hong Kong **practice** 2000–present Partner, H + S Design, Hong Kong••2000–present Visiting Professor, University of Shanghai••2000–present Adviser, Shanghai Hong Kong Culture Exchange Association••1996–present Chairperson, Hong Kong Female Contemporary Art Association••1994–present Board of Directors, Hong Kong Chingying Institute of Visual Arts **selected projects** 2002 Gift-pack design, Expo 2010 Shanghai China Bidding Office, Shanghai••2000 Calendar design 2002, Tai Tak Takeo Fine Paper, Hong Kong••2002 Product and packaging design, H + S Gallery, Shanghai••1999 Book design, *Image of Shanghai*, Information Office, Shanghai Municipal People's Government, Shanghai••1999 Poster design, Macau Return to China, Macao Designers Association, Macao••1998 Book Design, *Colours of Macau*, Society of Worldwide Ethnic Chinese Photographers, China **selected bibliography** 2002, 1999, 1998 *Package & Design*, Guangzhou, China ••1998 *Monthly Design*, Korea••1981 *Graphic Design*, Japan••1981 *Asian Designers*, Taiwan **selected exhibitions** 2002 *Art & Design Exhibition*, Xintiandi, Shanghai••1998 *Century Woman Art Exhibition*, Beijing••1996 *Hong Kong Artist Series*, Hong Kong Museum of Art••1981 *Design Now Hong Kong*, Japan **awards** 2002 Gold Award, Packaging Design, China Star, China ••1998–2002 Award of Distinction, Creativity Annual, USA••1998 Publication Gold Award, Hong Kong Designers Association Show••1982 Professional Gold Award, Conqueror Corporate

Leonardo Sonnoli

Born Trieste, Italy, 1962. Lives and works in Rimini and Trieste **education** 1982–87 Graphic Design, High Institute for Applied Arts (ISIA), Urbino **practice** 2002–present Cofounder and Partner, CODEsign ••1989–2002 Creative Director, Dolcini Associati **selected projects** 2003 Venice Biennale, International Art Exposition••2000–2003 Posters for University of Architecture in Venice (IUAV)••2000–2003 Corporate identity, Province of Rimini••2002 Calendar 2003, Scheufelen Paper Company, Stuttgart••1996–2002 Corporate posters for cultural events, Don Gaudiano Foundation, Pesaro••1998–99 Corporate posters for cultural events, City of Pesaro **selected bibliography** 2002 *Up Against the Wall*, Mies, Switzerland••2002 *New AGI Members*, China••2002 *Images du Monde, Monde des Images*, Chaumont, France ••2000 *Type Graphics*, Rockport Publishers, Gloucester, Massachusetts••2000 *4:3-50 Years of Italian and German Design*, Bonn **selected exhibitions** 2002 *AGI Poster Exhibition*, California College of Arts and Crafts, San Francisco••2002 *Images du Monde, Monde des Images*, Chaumont Poster Festival, France••2001 *Graphisme(s)*, Bibliothèque Nationale de France, Paris••2001 *Leonardo Sonnoli and the City of Pesaro*, Chaumont, France **awards** 2002 Merit Award, Art Directors Club, New York••2001 Honorable Mention, XIX Compasso d'Oro, Italy•• 2000 Silver Medal, 6th International Poster Triennal, Toyama, Japan••1998 Golden Bee poster award, Golden Bee Internationale Biennale of Graphic Design, Moscow **memberships** 2000 Alliance Graphique Internationale (AGI)

Jennifer Sterling

Born Miami, USA, 1964. Lives and works in San Francisco **practice** 1997–present Professor, Typography and Graphic Design, California College of Arts and Crafts, San Francisco••1995–present Principal, Sterling Design, San Francisco **selected projects** 2003 Book design, Sterling Design Monograph, Ginko Press, California••2001 Yahoo! Interactive Instant Messenger Design, San Francisco••2000 Branding design for a coalition under the direction of Hillary Clinton and Madeline Albright, New York••2000 Poster design, San Francisco Museum of Modern Art **selected exhibitions** 2001 Solo exhibition, San Francisco Museum of Modern Art••2001 National Design Triennial, Cooper-Hewitt, National Design Museum, Smithsonian Institution, New York••Part of the permanent collections of the Library of Congress, Cooper-Hewitt, National Design Museum, Museum für Kunst und Gewerbe Hamburg, San Francisco Museum of Modern Art, and Bibliothèque Nationale de France **awards** 2002 Communication Arts award for book design, American Institute of Graphic Arts (AIGA)••2000 *ID* Design Review Award for interactive video••1999 and 2000 Walter Landor Award for Design, San Francisco••1999, 2000 Best of Show, San Francisco Advertising Association •• 1999, 2000 Marget Larson Award, San Francisco Advertising Association••1998 *Graphis* Magazine, voted one of the top 12 gobal design firms **memberships** 2000 Alliance Graphique Internationale (AGI)••2000 Architecture and Design Accessions Board, San Francisco Museum of Modern Art••2000 Who's Who in America••1995 Type Directors Club••1995 American Center for Design••1993 American Institute of Graphic Arts (AIGA)

Swip Stolk

Born Zaandam, Netherlands, 1944. Lives and works in Zaandam **education** self-educated **practice** 1965–present Freelance graphic designer••2003 Designer, Visionair, 2D-3D, Netherlands••1996–2000 Art Director/Designer, Rembrandt House museum, Amsterdam••1980–87 Professor, Graphic Design, Illustration, and Miixed Media, Gerrit Rietveld Academy, Amsterdam••1977–79 Art director, VARA Television, Netherlands••1974–79 Professor, Graphic Design, Aki (Academy of Art and Industry), Enschede, Netherlands **selected projects** 2003 Corporate identity, *D Magazine*, Berlin••2002 Code—Uncode project, ID Laser, Netherlands••2001 Shop design for shoe designer Jan Jansen, Amsterdam••2001 Corporate Indentity, *Chiq* magazine, Amsterdam••1987–2000 Corporate Indentity, New Groninger Museum, Groningen (with Allesandro Mendini, Philppe Starck and Coop Himmelb(l)au) **selected bibliography** 2003 "A –Z," by Swip Stolk and Valerio Spada, *Stile* magazine no. 4, Italy••2002 "Radically Swip Stolk," *Graphis* magazine 340, New York••2000 *Swip Stolk—Master Forever*, by Han Steenbruggen and Frans Haks, Groninger Museum, Netherlands••2000 "Swift Swift Swip," *Dutch* magazine, Netherlands **selected exhibitions** 2001 Solo exhibition *106 Poster Designs*, Groninger Museum, Netherlands••2000 *Rembrandt Series*, Gallery Flatland, Utrecht and Paris••2000 Swip Stolk retrospective exhibition, Groninger Museum, Netherlands **awards** 1998–2003 Best Dutch Book Design Award, BNO, Netherlands••1990 H.N.Werkman Award, City of Amsterdam••1969 Frans Duwaer prize for Typography, City of Amsterdam••1968–1974 Several awards from the Art Directors Club, Netherlands **memberships** 2001 Alliance Graphique Internationale (AGI)••1996 Dutch Designers Association (BNO)

Remo Stoller

Born Thun, Switzerland, 1977. Lives and works in Bern **education** 1993–98 Graphic Design, Schule für Gestaltung, Bern **practice** 1998–present Independent graphic designer **selected bibliography** 2001 *Benzin, Young Swiss Graphic Design*, Lars Müller Publishers, Baden, Switzerland••2000 *Swiss Graphic Design*, Die Gestalten Verlag, Berlin **awards** 1998 SGV Förderpreis, Design Network, Switzerland **memberships** 2000 Rainbow, Switzerland

Kosta Stratigos

Born Ann Arbor, Michigan, USA, 1974. Lives and works in Metro-Detroit **education** 2002 M.F.A., 2D Design, Cranbrook Academy of Art, Bloomfield Hills, Michigan••1997 B.A., Film and Video Studies, University of Michigan, Ann Arbor, Michigan **practice** 2001–present Principal, MEDIA-LUXE••2002–03 Adjunct Faculty, School of Art and Design, University of Michigan, Ann Arbor, Michigan••2001–02 Instructor, Digital Media and Animation, College for Creative Studies, Detroit••1999–2000 Production Artist, Organic, Inc., Bloomfield Hills, Michigan••1998–99 Traffic Coordinator, Ross Roy Communications, Inc., Bloomfield Hills, Michigan••1992–98 Worked in a record store **selected projects** 2002 Miss Thunder National, Rock and Roll Music and Packaging, Bloomfield Hills, Michigan••2002 Dirty Whore Megastore, Zine, Bloomfield Hills, Michigan••2001 Insomniac's Handbook, Narrative Cycle, Illustrations and Binding, Bloomfield Hills, Michigan••2000 Composite event flyer, Detroit Bitter, Detroit, Michigan **selected bibliography** 2002 Insomniac's Handbook, Cranbrook Academy of

Art Catalogue••2002 Fairy Tale, Cranbrook Academy of Art Catalogue **selected exhibitions** 2003 *Zine Scene*, Orange County Art Museum, Costa Mesa, California••2002 Cranbrook Academy of Art Student Degree Show, Bloomfield Hills, Michigan••2002 Cranbrook Academy of Art Student Video Show, Cranbrook Art Museum, Bloomfield Hills, Michigan••1999 New York International Film and Video Festival, New York••1997 University of Michigan Student Film Show, Ann Arbor, Michigan

Yuri Surkov

Born Moscow, Russia, 1961. Lives and works in Moscow **education** 1986–90 Graphic Design, 1905 Art School, Moscow **practice** 1992–present Freelance graphic designer **selected projects** 2000 Coexistence poster for international invitational poster action, Museum on the Seam, Jerusalem••2000 Poster for Golden Bee 5, Moscow International Biennale of Graphic Design••2000 Water for human kind poster for international poster action, Association pour une Banque d'Images, Paris••1998 Brecht 100 poster for International Invitational Poster Action, Berliner Ensemble, Verband der Grafik-Designer (VGD), Berlin **selected bibliography** 2000 "Yuri Surkov," *Design Exchange*, China Youth Press, China••1999 "Born a Survivor," *Graphis* 320, New York••1999 *Fusion 2002 International*, Fusion Art Institute, Tokyo••1996, 1994 *Graphis Poster*, Zurich and New York **selected exhibitions** 1995–2002 International poster biennials and triennials in Chaumont, Helsinki, Mons, Moscow, Toyama, and Warsaw••2000, 1998, 1996 Ogaki International Invitational Poster Exhibition, Japan••1999, 1997 Colorado International Invitational Poster Exhibition, Colorado State University Gallery, Fort Collins••1998 International poster exhibition on the occasion of Bertolt Brecht's hundredth birthday, Deutsches Plakat Museum, Essen, Germany **awards** 2002 Bronze Medal, 18th International Poster Biennale, Warsaw••2000, 1997 Gold Medals, "Fourth Block" International Ecological Graphics and Poster Triennale, Kharkiv, Ukraine••1998, 1996, 1994 Golden Bee Awards, Golden Bee International Biennale of Graphic Design, Moscow••1995 Encouraging Diploma, *ZGRAF 7*, International Exhibition of Graphic Design in Zagreb **memberships** 2000 Alliance Graphique Internationale (AGI)••1999 Academy of Graphic Design, Moscow••1993 Society of Russian Designers

Thonik

Nikki Gonnissen, born Amsterdam, Netherlands, 1967; Thomas Widdershoven, born Maastricht, Netherlands, 1960. Live and work in Amsterdam **education** 1993 B.A., Art School, Utrecht (NG)••1993 B.A., Rietveld Academy for Fine Arts, Amsterdam (TW)••1988 M. Phil., University of Amsterdam (TW) **practice** 2001–present Professors, Rietveld Academy for Fine Arts, Amsterdam••1993–present Founding Partners, Gonnissen and Widdershoven; since 2000 Thonik••2000 Professor, Eindhoven Design Academy (TW)••1995–2000 Professor, Arnhem Art School (TW) **selected projects** 2003 Visual communication, *2003 van Gogh Year*, Van Gogh Museum, Amsterdam••2002 Identity program, City of Amsterdam, in collaboration with Eden, Amsterdam••2002 Book design, *Less and More*, 010 publishers, Rotterdam••2000 Visual communication, *Over the Edges*, S.M.A.K., Ghent, Belgium••1996 Identity program and communication, Centraal Museum, Utrecht••1996 Literary-magazine covers, *Tirade*, van Oorschot, Amsterdam **selected bibliography** 2003 *Type at Work: The Use* of Type in Editorial Design, Index Books••2001 Thonik®, New Dutch Graphic Design, BIS Publishers, Amsterdam••2001 Apples & Oranges 01: Best Dutch Graphic Design, BIS Publishers, Amsterdam••2001 HD: Holland Design New Graphics, exhibition catalogue, ACTAR, Barcelona selected exhibitions 2003 Super Woman, Hong Kong Heritage Museum••2003 Reality Machines, Netherlands Architecture Institute, Rotterdam••2001 010101—Art in Technological Times, San Francisco Museum of Modern Art••1999 Mooi maar Goed: Graphic Design in the Netherlands 1987–1998, Stedelijk Museum, Amsterdam awards 2003 Nederlandse Huisstijlprijs (Dutch Corporate Identity Award 2003), Grafische Cultuurstichting, Netherlands••2001, 1999, 1997, 1996, 1995, 1994, 1993, De Best Verzorgde Boeken (The Best Book Designs), Stedelijk Museum, Amsterdam••1997 Gold Award for Graphic Design, Art Directors Club Europe, London••1998 Graphics Best of Category, I.D Magazine, New York Annual Design Review memberships 1993 Dutch Designers Association (BNO)••1993 Art Directors Club Netherlands

TRUE
Born Los Angeles, USA, 1968. Lives and works in Brooklyn, New York education 1992–96 Design, Cooper Union School of Art, New York••1991–92 Art and Psychology, Sarah Lawrence College, Bronxville, New York practice 1997–present Principal, HGX DESIGN, Brooklyn, New York••2002 Artist in Residence, El-Hajj Malik el-Shabazz School, Brooklyn, New York••2000–2001 Design Teacher, Parsons School of Design, New York selected projects 2002 "Japanese Internment Camps 1942, INS Detention Centers 2002—What's the Difference?," Guerrilla Art, New York••1998–2002 Editorial illustrations, Source magazine, New York••2001 "Oodles of Doodles for Your Noodle," American Institute of Graphic Arts (AIGA) / Art with Heart, Seattle••1996 GOD & us (an illustrated book of theosophy), self-published, New York••1994 "Life Instructions," Guerrilla Art, New York••1993 "Crosswalks," Guerrilla Art, Los Angeles, New York selected bibliography 2001 How magazine••2001 Eye magazine 41, London••2000 "I.D. 40," I.D. Magazine, New York••1999 Metropolis Magazine selected exhibitions 2002 Visions, Museum of Contemporary African Diasporian Art (MoCADA), New York awards 1992 Full-tuition scholarship, Cooper Union School of Art, New York memberships 2000 Graphic Artists Guild

2x4
Michael Rock, born Rhode Island, USA, 1959; Susan Sellers, born Pennsylvania, USA, 1967; Georgie Stout, born New York, USA, 1967. Live and work in New York education 1998 B.F.A., Graphic Design, Rhode Island School of Design, Providence (GS)••1994 M.A., American Studies, Yale University, Connecticut (SS)••1989 B.F.A., Graphic Design, Rhode Island School of Design, Providence (SS)••1984 M.F.A., Graphic Design, Rhode Island School of Design, Providence (MR)••1981 B.A., Literature, Union College, New York (MR) practice 1997–2003 Lecturer in Design, Yale University, Connecticut (SS)••1991–2003 Professor of Art, Yale University, Connecticut (MR)••1995–99 Visiting Fellow, Jan Van Eyck Academy, Maastricht, Netherlands (MR)••1995 Establishment of 2x4 (MR+SS+GS)••1989–94 Bethany Johns Design (GS)••1986–91 Adjunct Professor for Graphic Design, Rhode Island School of Design, Providence (MR) selected projects 2003 Environmental design, Dia Center/Beacon, Beacon, New York••2002–03 Graphic and environmental design, Nasher Sculpture Center (with Renzo Piano Building Workshop), Dallas, Texas

••2001–03 Wallpaper and short films (with OMA/Rem Koolhaas), Prada Epicenter store, New York••2001–03 Graphic and environmental design, Mori Art Museum, Tokyo••2001–03 Graphic and environmental design, IIT Campus Center (with OMA/Rem Koolhaas), Chicago ••2001 Graphic and environmental design, Guggenheim Las Vegas, Nevada selected bibliography 2002 "Designer as Author," Looking Closer Four: Critical Writings on Graphic Design, Allworth Press and AIGA, New York••2000 "Saving Jelly," Emigre magazine 54, Sacramento, California••1999 "Forest of Signs," I.D. Magazine, September/October, New York••1998 "Museum of the Ordinary," Eye magazine 28, London••1996 "Mixed Messages," I.D. Magazine, September/October, New York selected exhibitions 2003 Design Triennial, Cooper Hewitt National Design Museum, Smithsonian Institution, New York••2002 Artist Space, New York City awards 2000 Rome Prize, American Academy in Rome (MR)

Tycoon Graphics
Yuichi Miyashi, born Tokyo, Japan, 1964; Naoyuki Suzuki, born Niigata prefecture, Japan, 1964. Live and work in Tokyo education 1983–87 Graphic Design, Tokyo Institute of Art and Design (NS) practice 1991–present Art Directors/Graphic Designers, Tycoon Graphics, Tokyo ••1987–90 Graphic Designer for Contemporary Production (NS)••1985–90 Graphic Designer, Diamond Heads Inc. (YM) selected projects 2002–present Lucky Strike, British American Tobacco Japan, Tokyo••2002–present TyGun project, TyGun/Tycoon Graphics, Tokyo••2002 Atehaca project, Toshiba Corporation, Tokyo••2002 Versus Exhibition 02, Parco Museum, Tokyo••2002 CD packaging, Gokujo Hybrid, by Bird, Sony Music Associated Records, Tokyo••2001-02 Motion Element, Motion Element, Tokyo selected bibliography 1999 A&D scan Tycoon Graphics, Rikuyosha, Tokyo••1995 G-Men, Little more, Tokyo selected exhibitions 2002 Versus Exhibition 02, Parco Museum, Tokyo 2002 The Doraemon, Suntory Museum, Osaka awards 1999 Gold Award for Graphic Design and Silver Award for Advertising, Art Directors Club, New York ••2000 79th Merit Award for Graphic Design, 78th Art Directors Club Awards, New York memberships Graphickers (MY+NS)

Rick Valicenti
Born Pittsburgh, Pennsylvania, USA, 1951. Lives and works in Barrington, Illinois education 1976 M.F.A., Photography, University of Iowa ••1973 B.F.A., Painting and Drawing, Bowling Green State University practice 1981–present Self-employed, Thirst (3st.com and thirstype.com) selected projects 2003 Apex sans Font Family, Thirstype.com, USA, in collaboration with Chester••2002 Oxford, The Holly Hunt Collection, Gilbert Paper, USA••2001 Infinity Font Family, Thirstype.com, USA, in collaboration with Chester••1999–2000 Herman Miller Neocon Experience, Chicago, in collaboration with Joyce Mast••1992 Manhattan Gentle Luv, Osaka••1990 ESSE introduction, Gilbert Paper, USA selected bibliography 2002 Emigre magazine, Sacramento, California••2000 Graphic Radicals/Radical Graphics, by Laurel Harper, Katherine McCoy, Chronicle Books, San Francisco••1999 Typography Now: The Next Wave, by Rick Poyner, Booth-Clibborn Editions, London••1992 Eye magazine, London selected exhibitions 2001 First Seoul Typography Biennale, Seoul••1997 Solo exhibition, Canon Digital Gallery, Tokyo••1992 solo exhibitions, GGG and DDD Galleries, Osaka and

Tokyo••Selected Thirst works have also been included in the permanent collection of the Cooper-Hewitt National Design Museum, Smithsonian Institution awards 2001 Silver Medal, Art Directors Club New York••1995 *ID Magazine*, 40 top designers (first listing)••ACD 100, American Center for Design••Two-time nomination for Chrysler Design Awards memberships 1998 Alliance Graphique Internationale (AGI)••1981–83 President, Society of Typographic Arts (later known as the American Center for Design)••1985 Board Member, Chicago chapter, American Institute of Graphic Arts (AIGA)

Alberto Vieceli
Born Zurich, Switzerland, 1965. Lives and works in Zurich education 1988–92 Graphic Design, School of Design, Zurich practice 2001–present, Cooperation with graphic designer Tania Prill, Zurich••1996 Founded own graphic design studio, Zurich••1995–96 Graphic Designer, Lars Müller Publishers, Baden, Switzerland••1992–94 Graphic Designer, Polly Bertram & Jul Keyser, Zurich selected projects 2003 Book design, *Inchoate, An experiment in architectural education*, ETH, Zurich and ACTAR, Barcelona (with Tania Prill)••2002 Posters for *Stand der Dinge: Neustes Wohnen in Zürich*, Federal Building Department of Zurich, Zurich (with Tania Prill) selected bibliography 2003 *Graphic Design for the 21st Century*, Taschen, Cologne••2001 *Swissmade*, Verlag Hochparterre, Zurich••2000 *Benzin: Young Swiss Graphic Design*, Lars Müller Publishers, Baden, Switzerland selected exhibitions 2001 *Swissmade, An Exhibition of Contemporary Swiss Design*, Museum of Applied Arts, Cologne••1997 Swiss Design Competition Show (Eidgenössischer Wettbewerb für Gestaltung), organised by the Swiss Arts Office, Basel awards 2003 Most Beautiful Swiss Books, Federal Office for Culture, Switzerland (with Tania Prill)••2003 Swiss Poster Award, APG, Switzerland (with Tania Prill)••2000 Most Beautiful Swiss Books, Federal Office for Culture, Switzerland••1997–98 Most Beautiful Swiss Books, Federal Office for Culture, Switzerland

Garth Walker
Born Pretoria, South Africa, 1957. Lives and works in Durban, South Africa education 1976–78 Diploma, Graphic Design, Technikon Natal, Durban practice 1995–present Founder and Director, Orange Juice Design, Durban••1995–present Graphic Design mentor for Durban Institute for Technology, Vaal Triangle Technikon, Imagination Lab Durban, Vega School of Design selected projects 1995–present Publisher of *i-jusi*, Orange Juice Design's experimental studio magazine, Durban••2003 Typeface and signage design, New Constitutional Court of South Africa, Johannesburg Development Agency, Johannesburg••2002-03 Ideas That Matter project, SAPPI Paper, Johannesburg••1998–2003 Unilever SA Pension Fund Annual Reports, Unilever South Africa, Durban••2002 Aids Management Standard identity, Liberty Life Limited, Cape Town selected bibliography *Design Week*, January, London••2001 *Issues—New Magazine Design*, Gingko Press, London••2000 *Étapes Graphiques* magazine, November, Paris••1999 *Creative Review*, September, London••1997 *Emigre Magazine 43*, Sacramento, California selected exhibitions 2003 *No Boundaries: Visions of Design Today*, Palacio de Sastago, Zaragoza, Spain••2002 *Vive le Graphisme!*, Galerie Anatome, Paris••2000 *Graphistes Autour du Monde*, Echirolles, France••2001 *TypoJanchi 2001*, Seoul Arts Centre, Seoul••1998 *Forum*

Typografie, Potsdam, Germany awards 2001 Grand Prix, Loeries, South Africa••1998, 2002 D&AD Annual, D&AD, London••1998 Silver Award, Art Directors Club, New York memberships 2002 Alliance Graphique Internationale (AGI)••2000 THINK (South African Design Council)••1998 British Design & Art Directors Club (D&AD)••1992 Type Directors Club, New York

Chris Ware
Born Omaha, Nebraska, 1967. Lives and works in Chicago education 1991–93 Printmaking, School of the Art Institute of Chicago••1991 B.F.A., Painting, University of Texas at Austin••1989 Skowhegan School of Painting and Sculpture, Skowhegan, Maine selected projects 1993–present *The ACME Novelty Library*, Fantagraphics Books, Seattle••1986-present Weekly or daily newspaper cartoon strip••2003 *Quimby the Mouse*, by Chris Ware, Fantagraphics Books, Seattle••2003 *The Acme Novelty Datebook*, Oog and Blik, Amsterdam••2000 *Jimmy Corrigan, The Smartest Kid on Earth*, by Chris Ware, Pantheon Books, New York selected bibliography 2001 "The Book You Have to Read," *Entertainment Weekly*, 23 February, New York••2000 "After Wham! Pow! Shazam!," *New York Times Book Review*, 26 November, New York••2000 "Right Way, Corrigan," *Time* magazine, 11 September, New York••1999 "Wie Musik auf Papier," *Der Spiegel*, October, Hamburg selected exhibitions 2002 *American Comics*, Centre Angoulême de la Bande Dessinée, Angoulême, France••2002 Whitney Biennial, Whitney Museum of American Art, New York••2001 *Summer Reading: The Recreation of Language in 20th Century Art*, Frances Lehman Loeb Art Center, Vassar College, Poughkeepsie, New York••2000 National Design Triennial, Cooper-Hewitt, National Design Museum, Smithsonian Institution, New York selected awards Best Book of the Year (L'Alph d'Art), Angoulême, France••2001 Guardian First Book Award, London••2000 American Book Award, USA memberships 1998 American Banjo Fraternity

Martin Woodtli
Born Bern, Switzerland, 1971. Lives and works in Zurich education 1996–98 Visual Communication, Academy of Art and Design, Zurich••1990–95 Graphic Design, School of Design, Bern practice 2002–present Teacher, Academy of Art and Design, Lucerne, Switzerland••1999–present Head of individual studio in Zurich••2002–03 Guest Professor, Staatlichen Akademie der Bildenden Künste, Stuttgart, Germany••2002 Workshop, School of Design, Biel, Switzerland••1998–99 Worked for Stefan Sagmeister, New York selected projects 2003 Poster for Jazzfestival Schaffhausen, Schaffhausen••2003 Poster for the Internationales Video and Film Festival VideoEx, VideoEx, Zurich••2001 Book design *Woodtli*, Die Gestalten Verlag, Berlin••2000 Poster for art event "onthespot," Bern••1999 Corporate design for contemporary-art space Stadtgalerie, Stadtgalerie Bern••1995 Corporate design for contemporary-art space Kiosk, Kunstkanal Bern selected bibliography 2001 *Woodtli*, Die Gestalten Verlag, Berlin••2001 *IDEA 285*, Tokyo••2000 *Benzin: Young Swiss Graphic Design*, Lars Müller Publishers, Baden, Switzerland••2000 "The I.D. Forty," *I.D. Magazine*, New York selected exhibitions 2002 *Postscript*, Künstlerhaus Wien, Vienna awards 2002 Most Beautiful Swiss Books and Book of the Jury, Federal Office for Culture, Switzerland••1999 Swiss Federal Design Prize, Swiss Federal Department, Section Art and Design, Switzerland memberships 2000 Alliance Graphique Internationale (AGI)

Michael Worthington Born St. Ives, United Kingdom, 1966. Lives and works in Los Angeles education 1993–95 M.F.A., Graphic Design, California Institute of the Arts, Los Angeles••1988–91 B.A. (Hons.), Graphic Design, Central Saint Martins College of Art and Design, London practice 1998–present Codirector, Graphic Design Program, California Institute of the Arts, Los Angeles••1995–present Design Faculty, California Institute of the Arts, Los Angeles••1991–present Practicing graphic designer selected projects 2003 "From B.J. With Love," essay on medalist Robert Brownjohn, AIGA 365 Annual, USA••2001 "Personal Modernism," *Restart: New Systems in Graphic Design*, Thames and Hudson, London••2001 "Right On!," essay, *Eye* magazine 41, London ••2000 Book design (with Lorraine Wild), *In Between Places*, Henry Art Gallery, Seattle, Washington••1999 Book design, *Bas Jan Ader*, University of California, Irvine ••1999 "Seduced by Stillness," essay, *Eye* magazine 33, London••1999 Catalogue design (with Geoff McFetridge), CalArts Bulletin, CalArts, Los Angeles selected bibliography 2002 *East coast/West coast*, Textuel, France••1999 "Designers in LA," *Eye* magazine 31, London••1998 *New Design: Los Angeles*, Rockport Press, USA selected exhibitions 2003 *Remix*, CENAR, San Salvador, El Salvador••2002 *Californian Dream, Graphic Designers in California*, Echirolles, France••2002 City of Los Angeles (COLA) fellowship show, Japanese American National Museum awards 2001–2002 Individual Artist Fellowship, City of Los Angeles (COLA) memberships 1996 American Institute of Graphic Design

Wang Xu Born Chaozhou, Guangdong, China, 1955. Lives and works in Guangzhou and Beijing education 1997 Graduated from Design Department of Guangzhou Fine Arts College, Guangzhou practice 1995–present Founder and Creative Director, Wang Xu & Associates, Beijing••1986–95 Graphic designer, Hong Kong••1980–86 Graphic designer, Guangzhou selected projects 2002–present Designer and Editor, *Lighter Magazine*, Exchange Publishing, China••2000 Book design and promotional posters, *Artistic Conception Writing*, China Youth Press, China••1986–2000 Designer, editor, and publisher, *Design Exchange* magazine, China••2000 Poster for Second International Ink Painting Biennial of Shenzhen, China selected bibliography 2002 *New AGI Members*, China••1998 *Graphis* 316, New York awards 1996–2003 Two Silver Medals, one Distinctive Award, and eight Merit Awards, Art Directors Club, New York ••1998 and 2000 Golden Bee Awards, 4th and 5th International Biennale of Graphic Design, Moscow••1996 Icograda Excellence Award, 17th International Biennale of Graphic Design Brno, Czech Republic memberships 2000 Alliance Graphique Internationale (AGI)••1996 Art Directors Club, New York

Catherine Zask Born Paris, France, 1961. Lives and works in Paris, France education 1979–84 École Supérieure d'Arts Graphiques (ESAG), Paris practice 1986–present Freelance graphic designer selected projects 1997–present Visual identity and visual communications, L'Hippodrome de Douai••1993–present Visual identity and visual communications, Société Civile des Auteurs Multimedia (SCAM), Paris••2001 Visual identity, École d'Architecture Paris Malaquais, Paris••1994 Creation of "Alfabetempo Roma"••1998 Book design, *Les Cahiers de la Recherche Architecturale*, Paris••1998 Visual identity, École d'Architecture de Marne-la-Vallée selected bibliography 2002 "2 + 3D," *Polish Design Quarterly*, Krakow••2001 *TypoJanchi*, Seoul Typography Biennale, Seoul Art Center Desin Gallery, Seoul••1999 *New Design: Paris*, Rockport Publishers, Gloucester, Massachusetts••1996 HOW, *International Design Annual*, Cincinnati, USA selected exhibitions 2002 First Korea International Poster Biennale, Seoul••2002 20th International Biennale of Graphic Design, Brno••2002 Festival d'Affiches de Chaumont, Chaumont, France••2001 *TypoJanchi*, Seoul Typography Biennale, Seoul awards 2002 Grand Prix, 20th International Biennale of Graphic Design Brno, Czech Republic••1993–94 Grant from the Villa Medici, Académie de France, Rome••1988 Typography Excellence Award, Type Directors Club, New York memberships 1997 Alliance Graphique Internationale (AGI)

032c Joerg Koch, born Wuppertal, Germany, 1974; Petra Langhammer, born Seoul, Korea, 1967; Sandra von Mayer-Myrtenhain, born Vienna, Austria, 1966. Live and work in Berlin and New York education 1997 History and North American Studies, Freie Universiät Berlin and Technische Universität Berlin (JK) practice 2000–present Cofounder and Creative Director, 032c, Berlin (JK)•• 2000–present Co-founder and Project Manager, 032c, Berlin (SvM)••2000–present Art Director, 032c Magazine (PL) selected projects 2003 *032c*, issue 5, "Shanghai Desire," 032c workshop, Berlin••2002 *032c*, issue 4, "Embrace Instability," 032c workshop, Berlin••2000–2001 *032c*, issues 1–3, "Professionalism," "Destruction," "What's Next?" (with Vladimir Llovet Casademont), 032c workshop, Berlin selected exhibitions 2003 Group exhibition *Magasins*, Contemporary Art Center Marres, Maastricht••2003 *032c/Berlin Flair*, GAS, Tokyo••2001 *Destroy the Good Taste*, Colette, Paris••2001 *The Searching Stays With You*, The Pineal Eye, London selected bibliography 2002 "Red is the Colour," *I.D Magazine* 225, London••2001 *Vogue*, April issue, Paris••2001 "Better Read than Dead," *V Magazine* 11, New York••2001 "*Wir finde ich das? 032c*," *Die Zeit* 22, Hamburg ••2001 "*Berlin la constructiviste*," *Le Monde*, 20 September, Paris awards 2003 Bronze Award, Art Director Clubs, Germany••2003 Visual Lead Award for Innovative Design of the Year, Germany

Viola Zimmermann Born Biel, Switzerland, 1962. Lives and works in Zurich education 1997–1998 MA, Communication Design, Central Saint Martins School of Art and Design, London••1978–1983 Graphic Design, School of Art and Design, Biel, Switzerland practice 2001–present Assistant professor for Graphic Design, Bern, Switzerland••1993–present, Self-employed graphic designer with own studio••1983-93 Art director of numerous companies, Bern and Zurich selected projects 2002–2003 Skateboard design, Airflow Skateboards, Switzerland••2002–03 Book design, *Outlet*, School for Design, Art and Conservation (HGKK), Bern••2002 Corporate design, Restaurant Zurlinden, Zurich••2002 Campaign for short story and poetry competition "*abgefahren*", VBZ, Zurich••2000 Design for card game Chuko, Inka Druck, Zurich••1997 Identity for a Drum'n'Bass club SNOT, Zurich selected bibliography 2002 *HELVETICA – Homage to a Typeface*, Lars Müller Publishers, Baden, Switzerland••2001 "Swiss Survey," *Wallpaper* magazine, May issue, London••1999 *Benzin, Young Swiss*

Graphic Design, Lars Müller Publishers, Baden, Switzerland selected exhibitions 2003 *Swiss Design—Traditionally Progressive*, New York ●●1999 *FRED*, Migros Museum, Zurich●●Viper Palace, Lucerne●●1998 *Follow The Signs*, Museum für Gestaltung, Zurich awards 1998 ADC Award, Art Directors Club, Switzerland●●1992–94 ADC Award, Art Directors Club, Switzerland

Graphic Design, Lars Müller Publishers, Baden, Switzerland selected exhibitions 2003 *Swiss Design—Traditionally Progressive*, New York ●●1999 *FRED*, Migros Museum, Zurich●●Viper Palace, Lucerne●●1998 *Follow The Signs*, Museum für Gestaltung, Zurich awards 1998 ADC Award, Art Directors Club, Switzerland●●1992–94 ADC Award, Art Directors Club, Switzerland index